_14_
ver
_$54.00_

 create™

Annual Editions:
Child Growth and Development,
Twenty-First Edition

Ellen N. Junn
Chris J. Boyatzis

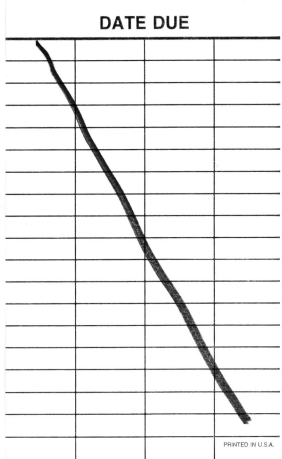

DATE DUE

PRINTED IN U.S.A.

http://create.mheducation.com

ISBN-10: 1259182673   ISBN-13: 9781259182679

Contents

Preface

We are delighted to welcome you to this edition of *Annual Editions: Child Growth and Development.* The amazing sequence of events of prenatal development that lead to the birth of a baby is an awe-inspiring process. Perhaps more intriguing is the question of what the future may hold for this newly arrived baby. For instance, will this child become a doctor, a lawyer, an artist, a beggar, or a thief? Although philosophers and prominent thinkers such as Charles Darwin and Sigmund Freud have long speculated about the importance of infancy on subsequent development, not until the 1960s did the scientific study of infants and young children flourish.

Since then, research and theory in infancy and childhood have exploded, resulting in a wealth of new knowledge about child development. Past accounts of infants and young children as passive, homogeneous organisms have been replaced with investigations aimed at studying infants and young children at a microlevel—as active individuals with many inborn competencies who are capable of shaping their own environment—as well as at a macrolevel—by considering the larger context surrounding the child. In short, children are not "blank slates," and development does not take place in a vacuum; children arrive with many skills and grow up in a complex web of social, historical, political, economic, and cultural spheres.

As was the case for previous editions, we hope to achieve at least four major goals with this volume. First, we hope to present you with the latest research and thinking to help you better appreciate the complex interactions that characterize human development in infancy and childhood. Second, in light of the feedback we received on previous editions, we have placed greater emphasis on important contemporary issues and challenges, exploring topics such as understanding development in the context of current societal and cultural influences. Third, attention is given to articles that also discuss effective, practical applications. Finally, we hope that this anthology will serve as a catalyst to help students become more effective future professionals and parents.

To achieve these objectives, we carefully selected articles from a variety of sources, including scholarly research journals and texts as well as semiprofessional journals and popular publications. Every selection was scrutinized for readability, interest level, relevance, and currency. In addition, we listened to the valuable input and advice from members of our Academic Advisory board,

consisting of faculty from a range of institutions of higher education, including community and liberal arts colleges as well as research and teaching universities. We are most grateful to the board as well as to the excellent editorial staff of McGraw-Hill Education.

Annual Editions: Child Growth and Development is organized into five major units: (1) Conception to Birth; (2) Cognition, Language, and Learning; (3) Social and Emotional Development; (4) Parenting and Family Issues; and (5) Cultural and Societal Issues.

In addition, we provide an overall topic guide, as well as student learning outcomes, critical thinking questions, and relevant Internet References for each article so that instructors will have a variety of important resources and options available for students.

Instructors for large lecture courses may wish to adopt this anthology as a supplement to a basic text, while instructors for smaller sections might also find the readings effective for promoting student presentations or for stimulating discussions and applications. Whatever format is utilized, it is our hope that the instructor and the students will find the readings interesting, illuminating, and provocative.

As the title indicates, *Annual Editions: Child Growth and Development* is by definition a volume that undergoes continual review and revision. Thus, we welcome and encourage your comments and suggestions for future editions of this volume.

Editors

Ellen N. Junn is provost and vice president for academic affairs and professor of psychology at California State University, Dominguez Hills. She received her BS with distinction in psychology and with high honors from the University of Michigan and her MA and PhD in cognitive and developmental psychology from Princeton University. Dr. Junn's areas of research include college teaching effectiveness, educational equity, faculty development, and public policy as it affects children and families. She served as a Past President for the California Association for the Education of Young Children and as a Governing Board member of the National Association for the Education of Young Children.

Chris J. Boyatzis is professor of psychology at Bucknell University and Director of the Bucknell in Denmark program. He received a BA with distinction in psychology from Boston University and his MA and PhD in developmental psychology from Brandeis University. His primary interests are religious and spiritual development and cultural influences on child development. He is president of Div. 36, Psychology of Religion, of the American Psychological Association, and is Associate Editor of the APA journal, *Psychology of Religion and Spirituality* as well as serving on the editorial board of four other journals.

Academic Advisory Board

Members of the Academic Advisory Board are instrumental in the final selection of articles for each edition of ANNUAL EDITIONS. Their review of articles for content, level, and appropriateness provides critical direction to the editors and staff. We think that you will find their careful consideration well reflected in this volume.

Correlation Guide

The *Annual Editions* series provides students with convenient, inexpensive access to current carefully selected articles from the public press. **Annual Editions: Child Growth and Development, 21/e** an easy-to-use reader that presents articles on important topics such as *fertility technology, prenatal development, brain development,* and many more. For more information on *Annual Editions* and other *McGraw-Hill Create*™ titles and collections, visit www.mcgrawhillcreate.com.

This convenient guide matches the articles in **Annual Editions: Child Growth and Development, 21/e** with **A Child's World: Infancy Through Adolescence, 13/e** by Martorell/Papalia/Feldman.

A Child's World: Infancy Through Adolescence, 13/e	**Annual Editions: Child Growth and Development, 21/e**
Chapter 1: Studying A Child's World	
Chapter 2: A Child's World: How We Discover It	
Chapter 3: Forming a New Life: Conception, Heredity, and Environment	Genes in Context: Gene–Environment Interplay and the Origins of Individual Differences in Behavior
Chapter 4: Pregnancy and Prenatal Development	
Chapter 5: Birth and the Newborn Baby	Daddy Track: The Case for Paternity Leave
Chapter 6: Physical Development and Health During the First Three Years	
Chapter 7: Cognitive Development during the First Three Years	Contributions of Neuroscience to Our Understanding of Cognitive Development Do Babies Learn from Baby Media? Infant Intelligentsia: Can Babies Learn to Read? And Should They? New Advances in Understanding Sensitive Periods in Brain Development The Other-Race Effect Develops during Infancy: Evidence of Perceptual Narrowing
Chapter 8: Psychosocial Development during the First Three Years	Evidence of Infants' Internal Working Models of Attachment The Conscious Infant The Power of Talking to Your Baby The Moral Life of Babies
Chapter 9: Physical Development and Health in Early Childhood	Recess—It's Indispensable!
Chapter 10: Cognitive Development in Early Childhood	1 in 68 Children Now Has a Diagnosis of Autism Spectrum Disorder. Why? The Touch-Screen Generation ADHD among Preschoolers
Chapter 11: Psychosocial Development in Early Childhood	Certain Television Fare Can Help Ease Aggression in Young Children, Study Finds Is Your Child Gay? Kindergartners Explore Spirituality Same Place, Different Experiences: Bringing Individual Differences to Research in Child Care Social Awareness + Emotional Skills = Successful Kids The Role of Neurobiological Deficits in Childhood Antisocial Behavior The Case Against Spanking: Physical Discipline Is Slowly Declining as Some Studies Reveal Lasting Harms for Children The Human Child's Nature Orientation The Role of Parental Control in Children's Development in Western and East Asian Countries
Chapter 12: Physical Development and Health in Middle Childhood	Caring for Chronically Ill Kids
Chapter 13: Cognitive Development in Middle Childhood	9 Ways to Support Your Child's Creativity Why Can Some Kids Handle Pressure While Others Fall Apart?

Topic Guide

This topic guide suggests how the selections in this book relate to the subjects covered in your course.

All the articles that relate to each topic are listed below the bold-faced term.

Aggression
Certain Television Fare Can Help Ease Aggression in Young Children, Study Finds
Don't! The Secret of Self-Control
Parent Training Can Improve Kids' Behavior
Raising a Moral Child
The Role of Neurobiological Deficits in Childhood Antisocial Behavior

Antisocial behavior
Parent Training Can Improve Kids' Behavior
Parental Divorce and Children's Adjustment
Raising a Moral Child
The Problem with Rich Kids
The Role of Neurobiological Deficits in Childhood Antisocial Behavior

Attachment
Daddy Track: The Case for Paternity Leave
Evidence of Infants' Internal Working Models of Attachment
The Power of Talking to Your Baby

Autism
1 in 68 Children Now Has a Diagnosis of Autism Spectrum Disorder. Why?

Birth and birth defects
Daddy Track: The Case for Paternity Leave
Genes in Context: Gene–Environment Interplay and the Origins of Individual Differences in Behavior

Brain development
Contributions of Neuroscience to Our Understanding of Cognitive Development
Infant Intelligentsia: Can Babies Learn to Read? And Should They?
The Conscious Infant
The Power of Talking to Your Baby
The Role of Neurobiological Deficits in Childhood Antisocial Behavior

Cognitive development
9 Ways to Support Your Child's Creativity
Contributions of Neuroscience to Our Understanding of Cognitive Development
Do Babies Learn from Baby Media?
Evidence of Infants' Internal Working Models of Attachment
Infant Intelligentsia: Can Babies Learn to Read? And Should They?
New Advances in Understanding Sensitive Periods in Brain Development
The Conscious Infant
The Moral Life of Babies
The Other-Race Effect Develops during Infancy: Evidence of Perceptual Narrowing
The Power of Talking to Your Baby
Why Parents Need to Let Their Children Fail

Cross-cultural issues
Daddy Track: The Case for Paternity Leave
Sibling Experiences in Diverse Family Contexts
The Other-Race Effect Develops during Infancy: Evidence of Perceptual Narrowing
The Role of Parental Control in Children's Development in Western and East Asian Countries

Culture
Certain Television Fare Can Help Ease Aggression in Young Children, Study Finds
Daddy Track: The Case for Paternity Leave
Parent Training Can Improve Kids' Behavior
Parental Divorce and Children's Adjustment
Same Place, Different Experiences: Bringing Individual Differences to Research in Child Care
The Human Child's Nature Orientation
The Problem with Rich Kids
The Role of Parental Control in Children's Development in Western and East Asian Countries
The Touch-Screen Generation

Development
Evidence of Infants' Internal Working Models of Attachment
New Advances in Understanding Sensitive Periods in Brain Development
Same Place, Different Experiences: Bringing Individual Differences to Research in Child Care
Sibling Experiences in Diverse Family Contexts
The Conscious Infant
The Power of Talking to Your Baby

Developmental disabilities
1 in 68 Children Now Has a Diagnosis of Autism Spectrum Disorder. Why?
ADHD among Preschoolers
The Role of Neurobiological Deficits in Childhood Antisocial Behavior

Discipline
Parent Training Can Improve Kids' Behavior
Raising a Moral Child
The Case Against Spanking: Physical Discipline Is Slowly Declining as Some Studies Reveal Lasting Harms for Children
The Role of Parental Control in Children's Development in Western and East Asian Countries

Education/School
ADHD among Preschoolers
Do Babies Learn from Baby Media?
Same Place, Different Experiences: Bringing Individual Differences to Research in Child Care
The Role of Neurobiological Deficits in Childhood Antisocial Behavior
The Touch-Screen Generation
Why Parents Need to Let Their Children Fail

Unit 1

UNIT

Prepared by: Chris J. Boyatzis, *Bucknell University*

Conception to Birth

Former carefree and more conventional sentiments of starting a family was exemplified by the old nursery rhyme, *"First comes love. Then comes marriage. Then comes baby in a baby carriage."*

However, this old adage belies the much more complex family realities facing pregnant couples and young women today. Moreover, the new and exciting science regarding the critically important role that a healthy prenatal environment may play in ensuring optimal development after birth and into childhood and beyond continues to expand and fascinate the public.

For example, new research shows the powerful influence of our genes over environment and vice versa. However, the differential effects of genes and environment vary depending on specific domains—such as brain development, temperament or personality development, resiliency, and other areas.

The articles in this unit highlight the compelling and enduring effects of the prenatal environment in shaping and supporting the genetic foundations for a given infant, and underscore the critical importance of optimal prenatal development.

Article

Prepared by: Chris J. Boyatzis, *Bucknell University*

Genes in Context

Gene–Environment Interplay and the Origins of Individual Differences in Behavior

FRANCES A. CHAMPAGNE AND RAHIA MASHOODH

Learning Outcomes

After reading this article, you will be able to:

- Describe how genes are "turned on" or off due to environmental factors.

- Evaluate the validity of the old-fashioned dichotomy of "nature versus nurture."

- Explain how traits can be passed from one generation to the next.

Historically, the question of the origins of individual differences in personality, aptitudes, and even physical features has led to debates over nature *versus* nurture. However, it is becoming increasingly clear that creating a division between genes and environment limits our understanding of the complex biological processes through which individual differences are achieved. The reality that the interaction between genes and environment is a critical feature of development is emerging as a central theme in laboratory studies and longitudinal analyses in human populations. However, appreciating the existence of this interaction is simply the first step in broadening our theoretical approach to the study of behavior. To move forward, we must ask "What do genes do?" and "How do genes and environments interact?" Recent studies combining molecular biology with the study of behavior may provide insight into these issues and perhaps even call into question our current understanding of mechanisms involved in the transmission of traits across generations. Here we will highlight these new findings and illustrate the importance of putting genes in context.

Laboratory and Longitudinal Approaches to Gene–Environment Interactions

Though recent advances in our ability to detect genetic variations have led to rapid progress in the study of gene-by-environment ($G \times E$) effects, clues that $G \times E$ was critical in considering the origins of behavior have been available for a long time. In 1958, Cooper and Zubek published a report in which rats selectively bred to be either "maze-dull" or "maze-bright" were reared after weaning in either "enriched" environments containing increased sensory stimuli or "impoverished" environments containing limited sensory stimuli (Cooper & Zubek, 1958). In the rats reared under standard conditions, stable and heritable group differences in cognitive ability were observed in adulthood. However, maze-dull animals reared in an enriched environment showed a significant improvement in learning ability, and maze-bright animals reared under impoverished conditions showed a significant decline in performance. This study provides evidence that, even when considering a genetically derived characteristic, our prediction of behavior must incorporate knowledge of the environmental context of development.

A more recent example of $G \times E$ comes from the Dunedin longitudinal study (Caspi et al., 2003), which explored the roles of variation in a gene that alters serotonin levels and exposure to stressful life events across a 20-year period in determining risk of depression. Levels of serotonin within neural circuits are altered by the number of serotonin transporter proteins, and in humans, there are genetic variations that lead to either high or low levels of the serotonin transporter. The serotonin system has been implicated in variations in mood, and this system is the target of most pharmacological interventions in the treatment of depression. Among individuals within the Dunedin study, risk of depression was predicted by the interaction of serotonin transporter genotype and the number of stressful life events experienced. Thus, no differences in risk of depression emerged as a function of genotype when the number of stressful life events was low. However, when an individual had experienced a high frequency of stressful events, genotype effects were observed, with individuals possessing the low-serotonin-transporter-level gene variant being at greater risk of depression. Though certain genetic variations can lead to risk or resilience to psychological disorder (see Kim-Cohen & Gold, 2009, this issue), this "potential" may not be observed unless variation in the environment is considered.

Contextual Determinants of Gene Function

Empirical findings from G × E studies raise an important question: "If the effects of genetic variation can vary depending on characteristics of the environment, then what are environments doing to genes to alter their impact?" To address this question, we must first address the following question: "What do genes do?" Historically, *gene* was a term used to describe a unit of heritable material. Since the discovery of DNA, the study of genetics has come to mean the study of DNA, with *gene* defined as a particular sequence of DNA. Due to the complex nature of DNA, it is perhaps easier to employ an analogy that conveys the basic notions of gene function. Think of an individual's DNA as books in a library that have been ordered and arranged very precisely by a meticulous librarian. These books contain a wealth of knowledge and the potential to inspire whoever should choose to read them. Asking what DNA does is like asking what a book in this library does. Books sit on a shelf waiting to be read. Once read, the information in those books can have limitless consequences. Likewise, DNA sits in our cells and waits to be read by an enzyme called RNA polymerase, leading to the production of messenger RNA (mRNA)—a process referred to as *transcription* (Figure 1a). The mRNA transcript is a copy of the DNA sequence that can further be "translated" into protein. The reading, or *expression,* of DNA can, like the books in our library, have limitless consequences. However, without the active process that triggers such expression, this potential may never be realized. Importantly, it is the environment around the DNA that contains those critical factors that make it possible to read the DNA (Figure 1b; also see Cole, 2009, for extended discussion of the regulation of gene expression).

The control of gene expression is ultimately determined by how accessible the sequence of DNA is to factors within the

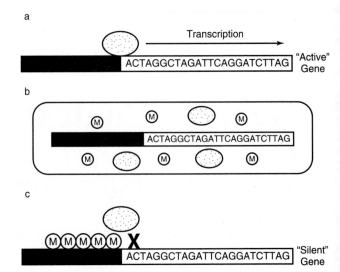

Figure 1 Illustration of the epigenetic control of gene expression and the environmental context of DNA. As shown in panel (a), genes consist of a sequence of DNA consisting of "C," "T," "A," and "G" nucleotides preceded by a promotor region of DNA (the black bar). The promoter region responds to factors that control the likelihood of transcription (reading of the DNA). In order for transcription to occur, enzymes that "read" the DNA (the gray oval) must bind to the promotor region of the gene. When this occurs, the gene is "active" and can alter the function of the cell. The environmental context of the gene, shown in panel (b), includes factors that increase gene activity (i.e., enzymes that read the DNA, shown as gray ovals) and factors that decrease gene activity (i.e., methyl groups, illustrated as circles labeled "M"); these factors will determine the likelihood that a gene will be expressed. When a methyl chemical group attaches to the promotor region, as shown in panel (c), the enzymes that transcribe DNA are blocked and the gene becomes "silent"; this is referred to as DNA methylation.

cell that are involved in transcription. Influences that determine the expression of DNA without altering the sequence of DNA are referred to as epigenetic, meaning "in addition to genetic." One particular epigenetic mechanism that may have consequences for long-term changes in gene activity is DNA methylation (Figure 1c). DNA can become modified through the addition of a methyl chemical group to particular sites within the gene sequence. DNA methylation typically reduces the accessibility of DNA and can lead to "silencing" of the gene (Razin, 1998). In the library analogy, one can think of multiple factors that will influence the likelihood a book will or will not be read. Even books containing very valuable information may sit undisturbed and unread, gradually collecting dust. This may be particularly true if the book is hard to get to. It may be located on a shelf that is particularly difficult to reach or blocked by some piece of furniture. DNA methylation reduces the likelihood of transcription much in the same way that shifting furniture in a library can reduce the likelihood that a book will be read. The gene is there, but sits unread, collecting dust.

Environmental Influences on Gene Activity

A recent breakthrough in our understanding of gene–environment interplay comes from studies exploring the epigenetic processes that are altered by an individual's experiences during development. Based primarily on studies in rodents, these paradigms address the question raised by G × E research: "What are environments doing to genes to alter their impact?" In rodents, variations in maternal care lead to individual differences in the expression of genes that alter the stress response. Low levels of glucocorticoid receptors (*GR*) within the hippocampus, a brain region critical for learning and memory, result in a prolonged response to stress. Analysis of DNA methylation within the regulatory region of the *GR* gene indicates that low levels of maternal care are associated with elevated levels of DNA methylation, which epigenetically silence this gene (Weaver et al., 2004). Moreover, the epigenetic status of the *GR* gene can be targeted pharmacologically in adulthood. Treatment with a drug that promotes increases in accessibility of DNA results in decreased *GR* methylation and a dramatic shift in the phenotype of adult offspring who received low levels of maternal care (Weaver et al., 2004). Conversely, when adult offspring who experienced high levels of care are treated with a drug that increases the availability of methyl groups within the brain, they become indistinguishable from offspring who received low levels of maternal care (Weaver et al., 2005). These dynamic alterations in DNA methylation in adulthood have also been observed in studies of learning and memory (Miller & Sweatt, 2007). The experience of learning is associated with rapid changes in methylation of genes within the hippocampus, and if DNA methylation is inhibited, there will be impairment in memory for the experience. These studies illustrate the role of epigenetic mechanisms in shaping the activity of the genome in response to environmental cues and demonstrate the plasticity that is possible through shifts in DNA methylation.

The prenatal period is characterized by rapid changes in brain development and is thus a sensitive time during which the quality of the environment can exert sustained effects on functioning. In rodents, exposure to chronic variable stress during the first trimester is associated with increased methylation of the regulatory region of the *GR* gene (Mueller & Bale, 2008). This effect could potentially be mediated by (a) stress-induced decreases in postnatal maternal behavior (Champagne & Meaney, 2006), (b) alterations to gene expression in the placenta (Mueller & Bale, 2008) that may restrict access of the fetus to maternal resources, or (c) a direct influence of maternal stress hormone on fetal gene expression. Modification to the fetal "epigenome" can also be achieved through variations in maternal diet during pregnancy. A striking example of this phenomenon comes from work with a mouse model in which a mutation of the *Agouti* gene leads to alterations in coat color and metabolism. The severity of the effects of this mutation depends on the level of DNA methylation of the *Agouti* gene; high levels of DNA methylation will epigenetically silence this mutation and induce a "pseudoagouti" mouse that is comparable in phenotype to a mouse without the mutation. When pregnant female mice with the *Agouti* mutation are placed on a diet that is rich in methyl groups, the methylation status of this gene is altered such that offspring develop a pseudoagouti phenotype (Dolinoy, 2008). Thus, experience-dependent change in the epigenetic status of genes is not limited to the postnatal period.

Implications of Gene–Environment Interplay for Psychological Functioning

The molecular processes described in laboratory studies may also be critical in understanding the origins of individual differences in humans. Analyses of DNA methylation in cells extracted from fetal cord blood suggest that antenatal maternal depression and anxiety during the third trimester can lead to increased levels of DNA methylation of the GR gene promotor region, having consequences for the stress response of infants at 3 years of age (Oberlander et al., 2008). These effects emerge even in the absence of depression-induced decreases in postnatal mother–infant interactions. The stability of DNA methylation also permits analysis of the epigenetic status of genes in postmortem brain tissue, which can be correlated to life experiences and psychological functioning. In a recent study, DNA methylation of ribosomal genes in hippocampal tissue of suicide victims with a history of abuse and neglect was compared to that of controls. Elevated levels of methylation were detected in ribosomal RNA genes among suicide victims (McGowan et al., 2008), and this effect was found to be specific to the hippocampus. Ribosomes are critical for the production of proteins and thus serve as a critical link between the expression of genes and the level of protein created.

Studies of monozygotic (MZ) twins also provide important insights into epigenetic effects in humans. Comparison of the gene expression of 3-year-old and 50-year-old MZ twins indicates a higher level of discordance in patterns of gene expression among older twins that is associated with increasing differences in DNA methylation in older compared to younger twins (Fraga et al., 2005). Though it is unknown whether concordance in young twins is due to germ line (the cells that transmit genetic material across generations) or prenatal factors and whether the emerging discordance is random or driven by specific environmental events, there is evidence that epigenetic variation in MZ twins may account for differential risk of mental illness. Analysis of methylation patterns within the catechol-O-methyltransferase *(COMT)* gene in tissue samples from 5-year-old MZ twins indicates varying degrees of discordance, with some MZ twin pairs showing a high degree of discordance and others being very similar in epigenetic status (Mill et al., 2006). *COMT* is an enzyme involved in the inactivation of neurotransmitters such as dopamine and norepinephrine, and disruptions in these neurotransmitter systems have been implicated in many forms of psychopathology. The divergence in methylation of the *COMT* gene within these twin pairs may predict differential risk of neurodevelopmental disorder in later life. Incorporating epigenetic analysis into twin studies represents a novel approach to the study of the origins of individual differences.

Transmission of Traits Across Generations: Rethinking Inheritance

In addition to shaping developmental trajectories within an individual's life span, DNA methylation may also have implications for the transmission of traits from one generation to the next. There are two distinct pathways through which this transmission can occur: (a) the behavioral transmission of traits through experience-dependent changes in the methylation of genes and (b) environmental effects that change DNA methylation in germ cells and are thus transmitted through the germ line of subsequent generations. An example of the first pathway comes from studies of the transmission of maternal care across generations. Variations in maternal care in rodents have been demonstrated to alter the epigenetic status of hypothalamic estrogen receptors of female offspring (Champagne et al., 2006). These receptors are critical in regulating maternal behavior and coordinate the sensitivity of females to hormonal cues. Experience of low levels of maternal care in infancy is associated with increased estrogen receptor promotor methylation, decreased receptor expression, and subsequent decreases in the adult maternal behavior of these offspring. Thus, there is a behavioral transmission of individual differences in maternal care across generations. Interestingly, the quality of environmental conditions experienced by these females at later periods in development can alter this transgenerational inheritance. Prolonged social isolation from peers and prenatal stress can lead to reductions in maternal care that are passed on to subsequent generations

(Champagne & Meaney, 2006, 2007). These studies, which are conducted in rodents that have limited genetic variability, suggest that similarities in traits between parental and offspring generations involve far more than the inheritance of genes.

Though epigenetic characteristics of DNA are dynamic in response to environmental cues, these modifications are also stable and heritable. Thus, both genetic and epigenetic factors are transmitted down cell lineages with consequences for the activity of genes within these lineages. However, when considering the question of inheritance at the level of an individual, we must know whether epigenetic patterns within the germ line are correlated to those patterns found within the developing organism. In rodents, prenatal exposure to endocrine disruptors leads to abnormal methylation patterns in sperm cells that are observed several generations beyond the point of initial exposure (Anway, Cupp, Uzumcu, & Skinner, 2005). This germ-line epigenetic inheritance of environmentally induced effects provides further support for the notion that the transmission of traits across generations is not limited in scope to the inheritance of DNA.

Conclusion

Just as a library is more than a collection of books, the genome is more than just DNA. The challenge for the field of epigenetics is to determine the origins of the "uniqueness" of each individual's library by exploring the relationship between genetic and epigenetic variation. Though there are many basic questions to be addressed regarding the pathways whereby specific experiences target particular genes, this field of research certainly has promise in uncovering the nature of experience-dependent changes in development both within and across generations. Advances in tools available to study these effects in humans will be critically important in further exploring the role of epigenetics within the broad field of psychological science.

Recommended Readings

Champagne, F.A. (2008). Epigenetic mechanisms and the transgenerational effects of maternal care. *Frontiers of Neuroendocrinology, 29,* 386–397. Provides a thorough review of the potential role of epigenetic factors in mediating the effects of maternal care within and across generations.

Jirtle, R.L., & Skinner, M.K. (2007). Environmental epigenomics and disease susceptibility. *Nature Reviews Genetics, 8,* 253–262. A review of our current understanding of environmentally induced epigenetic changes and the influence of these processes on individual risk of disease.

Maher, B. (2008). Personal genomes: The case of the missing heritability. *Nature, 456,* 18–21. An interesting commentary on the relationship between heritability estimates and the biological processes that determine the relationship between genes and behavior.

Meaney, M.J. (2001). Maternal care, gene expression, and the transmission of individual differences in stress reactivity across generations. *Annual Review of Neuroscience, 24,* 1161–1192. A review of the profound influence of maternal care on gene expression and behavior of offspring.

References

Anway, M.D., Cupp, A.S., Uzumcu, M., & Skinner, M.K. (2005). Epigenetic transgenerational actions of endocrine disruptors and male fertility. *Science, 308,* 1466–1469.

Caspi, A., Sugden, K., Moffitt, T.E., Taylor, A., Craig, I.W., Harrington, H., et al. (2003). Influence of life stress on depression: Moderation by a polymorphism in the 5-HTT gene. *Science, 301,* 386–389.

Champagne, F.A., & Meaney, M.J. (2006). Stress during gestation alters postpartum maternal care and the development of the offspring in a rodent model. *Biological Psychiatry, 59,* 1227–1235.

Champagne, F.A., & Meaney, M.J. (2007). Transgenerational effects of social environment on variations in maternal care and behavioral response to novelty. *Behavioral Neuroscience, 121,* 1353–1363.

Champagne, F.A., Weaver, I.C., Diorio, J., Dymov, S., Szyf, M., & Meaney, M.J. (2006). Maternal care associated with methylation of the estrogen receptor-alpha1b promoter and estrogen receptor alpha expression in the medial preoptic area of female offspring. *Endocrinology, 147,* 2909–2915.

Cole, S.W. (2009). Social regulation of human gene expression. *Current Directions in Psychological Science, 18,* 132–137.

Cooper, R.M., & Zubek, J.P. (1958). Effects of enriched and restricted early environments on the learning ability of bright and dull rats. *Canadian Journal of Psychology, 12,* 159–164.

Dolinoy, D.C. (2008). The Agouti mouse model: An epigenetic biosensor for nutritional and environmental alterations on the fetal epigenome. *Nutrition Reviews, 66*(Suppl 1), S7–S11.

Fraga, M.F., Ballestar, E., Paz, M.F., Ropero, S., Setien, F., Ballestar, M.L., et al. (2005). Epigenetic differences arise during the lifetime of monozygotic twins. *Proceedings of the National Academy of Sciences USA, 102,* 10604–10609.

Kim-Cohen, J., & Gold, A.L. (2009). Measured gene–environment interactions and mechanisms promoting resilient development. *Current Directions in Psychological Science, 18,* 138–142.

McGowan, P.O., Sasaki, A., Huang, T.C., Unterberger, A., Suderman, M., Ernst, C., et al. (2008). Promoter-wide hypermethylation of the ribosomal RNA gene promoter in the suicide brain. *PLoS ONE, 3,* e2085.

Mill, J., Dempster, E., Caspi, A., Williams, B., Moffitt, T., & Craig, I. (2006). Evidence for monozygotic twin (MZ) discordance in methylation level at two CpG sites in the promoter region of the catechol-O-methyltransferase (COMT) gene. *American Journal of Medical Genetics B: Neuropsychiatric Genetics, 141,* B421–B425.

Miller, C.A., & Sweatt, J.D. (2007). Covalent modification of DNA regulates memory formation. *Neuron, 53,* 857–869.

Mueller, B.R., & Bale, T.L. (2008). Sex-specific programming of offspring emotionality after stress early in pregnancy. *Journal of Neuroscience, 28,* 9055–9065.

Oberlander, T.F., Weinberg, J., Papsdorf, M., Grunau, R., Misri, S., & Devlin, A.M. (2008). Prenatal exposure to maternal depression, neonatal methylation of human glucocorticoid receptor gene (NR3C1) and infant cortisol stress responses. *Epigenetics, 3,* 97–106.

Razin, A. (1998). CpG methylation, chromatin structure and gene silencing-a three-way connection. *EMBO Journal, 17,* 4905–4908.

Weaver, I.C., Cervoni, N., Champagne, F.A., D'Alessio, A.C., Sharma, S., Seckl, J.R., et al. (2004). Epigenetic programming by maternal behavior. *Nature Neuroscience, 7,* 847–854.

Weaver, I.C., Champagne, F.A., Brown, S.E., Dymov, S., Sharma, S., Meaney, M.J., et al. (2005). Reversal of maternal programming of stress responses in adult offspring through methyl supplementation: Altering epigenetic marking later in life. *Journal of Neuroscience, 25,* 11045–11054.

Critical Thinking

1. What are some environmental factors, from maternal diet, stress, or exposure to toxins, that can influence genetic processes in the fetus?

2. What is DNA methylation, and how does it illustrate the interplay of genes and environment?

3. How is the field of epigenetics a new way of thinking beyond the simple nature vs. nurture debate?

Create Central

www.mhhe.com/createcentral

Internet References

American Academy of Pediatrics
http://www.aap.org/en-us/Pages/Default.aspx

American Board of Genetic Counseling
http://www.abgc.net/Resources_Links/resources.asp

American Society of Human Genetics
http://www.ashg.org/pages/about_otherorg.shtml

From *Current Directions in Psychological Science,* June, 2009, pp. 127–131. Copyright © 2009 by the Association for Psychological Science. Reprinted by permission of Sage Publications via Rightslink.

Unit 2

UNIT

Prepared by: Chris J. Boyatzis, *Bucknell University*

Cognition, Language, and Learning

We have come a long way from the days when the characterization of the minds of infants and young children included phrases like "tabula rasa" and "booming, buzzing confusion."

Today, infants and young children are no longer viewed by researchers as blank slates, passively waiting to be filled up with knowledge. Current experts in child development and cognitive science are calling for a reformulation of assumptions about children's cognitive abilities, as well as calling for reforms in the ways we teach children in our schools.

Researchers today continue to discover the complex interplay between brain maturational development and external or environmental experience in scaffolding and supporting the emergence of abilities such as language acquisition, perceptual and cognitive advances, and early learning.

Hence, the articles in this unit highlight some of the new knowledge of the impressive and foundational cognitive abilities of infants and young children and how these abilities may be influenced by parents, teachers, and schooling.

Indeed, today, perhaps more than ever in the last few decades, public and parents' thirst for not only knowing about these foundational cognitive skills, but more importantly, how they can as parents, teachers, and educators further promote and nurture these cognitive skills has increased dramatically.

We hope that readers will enjoy the variety of articles, research, approaches, and real-life applications in thinking about how to optimize the development of young children.

Infant Intelligentsia: Can Babies Learn to Read? And Should They? by Janet Hopson

19

Article

Prepared by: Chris J. Boyatzis, *Bucknell University*

Infant Intelligentsia: Can Babies Learn to Read? And Should They?

JANET HOPSON

Learning Outcomes

After reading this article, you will be able to:

- Comprehend various language acquisition processes.

- Understand the role of spoken language in the acquisition of written language.

- Analyze the reasoning behind why some children become early readers and why some do not.

The Video Clip on Larry Sanger's website shows the cofounder of Wikipedia looking both scholarly and paternal with his owlish glasses, thinning pate, open book, and lapful of chubby-cheeked 3-year-old. Sanger's son is gazing hard at the book pages and pronouncing words with the charming *r*-lessness of a toddler: "Congwess shall make no waw wespecting an establishment of wewigion or pwohibiting the fwee exewcise theweof or abwidging the fweedom of speech or of the pwess . . ." It's not clear whether the boy is working toward a doctorate, like his dad's, or training to be our future pwesident. But it is stunningly obvious that the boy is sight-reading the First Amendment to the U.S. Constitution at an age when most tots can't tell an *a* from a *b*. When an influential philanthropist viewed the video, says Sanger, "he was gobsmacked."

True, the Sanger child inherited both the genes and home-schooling attention of a high-tech icon. But YouTube now overflows with videos of tiny tykes reading words off of book pages, flash cards, and computer screens. And these images have stirred a Battle of the Experts flinging epithets like "witch hunt" and "snake oil." Are the munchkin-voiced 2- and 3-year-olds actually reading those multisyllabic words? Or have they merely associated sights of certain words with their sounds? Is a baby's brain even capable of decoding words and extracting meaning? And if it can, should we program it this way, this early? Or should we channel its effervescing language ability in other directions?

Any curious web surfer can track the recent baby-reading brouhaha. Here is a PhD who blogs for *Psychology Today* describing trademarked videos and games by Your Baby Can Read! and wondering, "Is there a 'baby can read' witch hunt?" LeapFrog, Baby Einstein, and BrillKids make similar products and could elicit similar questions. There is the *Today* show investigating Your Baby Can Read! And citing numerous critics. Here is news of a consumer group filing a complaint with the Federal Trade Commission alleging "deceptive marketing." There is a blog called NeuroLogica labeling the whole business "gimmicky schemes promising easy answers," and headlining it "Your Baby Can Read—Not!" Here, a medical doctor warning that pushing children to write, read, or spell in preschool or kindergarten "might create learning disabilities." There, a self-published author whose children read at age 2½ warning that "late reading" (age 6) might lead to dyslexia. And finally, here is Larry Sanger himself, with the help of the "gobsmacked" philanthropist, starting a website called Reading Bear to help other parents use his favorite techniques—gratis.

For more than a century, kids have encountered letters in kindergarten and reading in first grade, although many pre-schools now teach "preliteracy skills." Complete reading lessons in the playpen, however, probably grew out of the 1990s enrichment movement. Journalist Susan Gregory Thomas traces the drive to buy a smarter baby to a 1994 Carnegie Corporation report on the importance of nurturing and stimulation for babies from birth to 3. In 1997, a media blitz brought similar themes from that year's White House Conference on Early

Childhood Development and Learning into virtually every home. Within months, stores were selling Baby Einstein videos, Mozart Effect CDs, and baby enrichment products bearing the logos of several well-known toy companies. To paraphrase Noam Chomsky, writes Thomas in her book *Buy, Buy Baby,* "Our American consumer economy takes our concerns, commodifies them, and sells them back to us."

New millennial baby-reading videos and books are logical extensions of that process, and so are the parental motivations for buying them. "Some parents worry that their child comes from an impoverished language background," says Tufts University Center for Reading and Language Research director Maryanne Wolf, "and they want to give their children everything they can." Wolf sees less idealism, however, in the parents who are "worried about their child not getting into the right preschools" and eventually, "into an Ivy League college." The photogenic professor appeared on the *Today* show, criticizing the pricey Your Baby Can Read! videos and flash cards and their repetitious presentations of written words, illustrations, and pronunciations. "To force a 3-year-old or infant" to watch and repeat these things, she says, is akin to the "paired associative learning" B.F. Skinner used with his laboratory pigeons. The result is "memorization, but it's not reading with comprehension."

Every early-reading product this writer reviewed warns parents to stop the instant a youngster seems bored or resistant, to use the lessons sparingly, and to make them fun. Every parent contacted swears their child loved the baby-reading materials. Children are "getting a lot of exposure to words and letters," Wolf says, "and that is one good thing. But forcing this child—whether they say they are, or not—is, in my book, coercion," and it risks "turning a child off [to reading] and making them feel like a failure."

Larry Sanger read storybooks to his first son (now 6) for an hour or more at a sitting, starting in infancy. He also used alphabet books, homemade flash cards, and the Your Baby Can Read! videos. "He really liked [it], he just ate it up," Sanger declares. "By 25 months he could read brand-new words he had never seen." When asked about pressuring kids to learn, Sanger replies, "From what I can gather and what people say about how they use such programs online, very few do that."

"But I have yet to encounter a single reading expert," he continues, "or psychologist specializing in development and language who says, 'Well, I have interviewed early readers and based on my observations of them, I conclude the following.' The fact is they haven't even dealt with the phenomenon. They are still in the stage of denying that it even exists." Young children, he says, "may not be able to read and understand a long story, that's true. That's more advanced. But are they beginning readers? Absolutely. What really is the point in denying that?"

One major federal report on early reading does confirm this dearth of data. In 2008, the National Institute for Literacy published a report called "Developing Early Literacy" by a stellar panel of reading and child-development experts. Led by Timothy Shanahan, director of the University of Illinois at Chicago Center for Literacy, the academics sifted through more than 8,000 scientific research articles on newborns through 5-year-olds. They eventually picked out 500 studies that reliably documented the skills, abilities, programs, environments, and personal traits that determine whether young kids will go on to read, write, and spell well in school. Of those 500, just a handful considered kids under age 4.

Tim Shanahan is a charismatic reading guru who writes a popular, authoritative blog on literacy issues in addition to his internationally recognized scholarship. Shanahan estimates that only two or three of the studies his panel reviewed looked at 1-, 2-, or 3-year-olds, and even those looked only at the prereading skills that underlie reading, not reading itself. Chief among them is "phonemic awareness"—mastering the "code" or the association between letters and their sounds individually and in words. In the reading world, "decoding" means sounding out the letters in words, and then reassembling them into a pronounceable whole.

"To learn to read in our language," Shanahan says, "you need to be able to hear the sounds in a word like pig—*puh-ih-ga*"—not just say the letters—*pee-I-gee.* If you tested "whomever you thought were the smartest 3-year-olds in the world, you would find very few with phonemic awareness. It's not an IQ thing," he adds. "They can't hear it; they are not programmed to perceive it." Existing studies do seem to show, however, that you can begin teaching "the code" to kids under 4 and "it does make a difference in their reading achievement." Shanahan also acknowledges that the majority of deaf readers, a fair number of Baby Boom adults, and nearly all of the Boomers' now-elderly parents learned to read without phonics lessons or learning the "code."

Most intriguing are the children who take an intuitive leap to reading after no instruction at all. In his book, *Native Reading,* self-published author Timothy D. Kailing describes how his children learned to read simply by watching him point to every word he was reading aloud from hundreds of children's books. Likewise, psychiatrist Darold A. Treffert of the University of Wisconsin School of Medicine and Public Health reports a form of "hyperlexia," or precocious reading, in his own daughter. She would watch her mother's lips closely during storybook sessions. Then one day, he writes, "she read the book to her mother instead of the other way around." By age 3, she was reading at a sixth-grade level with "full comprehension ability," he reported to the Wisconsin Medical Society. His report also describes savantlike forms of hyperlexia in children with autism spectrum disorder.

Shanahan finds neither pathology nor mystery in most cases of early reading. Some precocious kids "figure things out themselves," he says, but quite often the parents were working on letters and sounds in their daily storybook reading. And sometimes, he adds, "an older sister had been 'playing school,' and teaching Junior what she learned down at the local school." If, as Louis Pasteur famously stated, "Chance favors only the prepared mind," then perhaps the family inadvertently stacked the mental kindling that ignited with an intuitive spark.

At least one language expert is probing that ignition process itself and trying to jump-start it through technology. Dominic Massaro, an emeritus professor of psychology (with whom this author collaborated briefly last year) from the University of California, Santa Cruz, is a wiry long-distance bike rider with a reputation for being both "brilliant" and "a maverick." He co-veloped a model for how the brain makes simultaneous sense out of separate inputs such as the sound of a person's voice and the sight of his or her lips moving. Most of his colleagues who study language perception look at either speech or writing. For 40 years, however, Massaro has researched how *both* modes operate and interact.

One practical offshoot was a smooth-pated, mocha-colored avatar called Baldi. Massaro and coworkers programmed this on-screen representation of a head to be a patient and affably neutral tutor that can help autistic and hearing-impaired children learn to speak and read. While studying children's language acquisition, he concluded that "babies are statistical learners," meaning they integrate multiple cues such as "expressions, gestures, and the language they hear, to bootstrap the meaning of what people are saying to them." These cues include subtle rules such as "which pairs of letters go together and occur in certain positions, but not others." For example, "th" is common, but "gx" isn't. "You don't have to teach a child the phonemes of their spoken language," he says, "and you don't need to create fun word games to tell a child 'dinner is ready.' They are motivated by communication itself and by a desire to understand their world."

Massaro is convinced that because spoken and written language share many innate rules, a young child should be able to pick up reading "naturally and without intentional instruction" as long as he or she is immersed in an environment that presents written and spoken words simultaneously. Massaro has applied for a patent on new technology that could, for example, instantaneously translate a caregiver's words ("Here's your toy bear!") into written words on the screen of his or her "digital T-shirt." The words could simultaneously appear on a screen embedded in the stuffed teddy she is handing the child. Other technology Massaro envisions could perceive, interpret, and label the child's familiar surroundings ("Your bedroom"); actions ("Throwing the ball"); experiences ("It's raining outside today"); and words ("Want juice!").

From infancy, Massaro says, "the child would process in parallel fashion both written and spoken information, like two horses on a track. Neither horse would win, though, and there is no finish line. Both would simply gallop toward an understanding based on a synergy between the two sources."

Tim Shanahan finds this "a really fascinating idea. And if someone can pull it off, Dom would be one of those people. But I think it's pretty far away from anything like a reality at this point."

Massaro himself is much more optimistic about developmental timetables, both for his products and for their young users. He points to the well-documented period in a child's early neurological development when internal programming and external experience allow attention, listening, talking, and understanding to skyrocket. Through high-tech devices, Massaro would like to add reading to that list, even though most language researchers believe literacy requires deliberate training while spoken language gets an automatic free pass.

Some who market reading programs for babies, however, exploit the specific intervals within that time of rapid learning—so-called "critical periods."

Neurologists have known since the 1960s that intervals exist for every baby's brain during which light patterns, sounds, and other inputs stimulate the pruning, shaping, and hooking up of specific permanent neural circuits. For example, researchers in the 1990s confirmed that children deprived of spoken or signed language during a critical period, from birth to age 6, or so can have lasting deficits in grammar, pronunciation, vocabulary, and understanding words. The ads for some baby-reading products infer that children who first encounter reading after this critical period for spoken language may be doomed to mediocrity or even dyslexia.

A 2009 study on Colombian guerrilla fighters disproved this claim. Spanish and British neurologists using fMRI scanners imaged changes in the brains of almost two dozen adult fighters who had quit the movement, emerged from the jungle as illiterate adults, and only then took up reading. Not only did they learn to read at a sixth-grade level or higher, but their brains accumulated gray and white matter in the same spots as their compatriots who had learned to read during childhood.

French cognitive scientist Stanislas Dehaene and others have been methodically scanning kids and grown-ups to see where the ability to read resides in the brain. Dehaene nicknamed a region in the left hemisphere's visual cortex "the brain's letterbox." In a fluent reader, this small area recognizes strings of letters, then rapidly signals to nearly a dozen other left-brain areas. The result is the lightning-fast decoding of letter and word sounds and the retrieval of word meanings from a potentially vast mental dictionary. Readers need phonics to sound out unfamiliar words, and they also need vocabulary and general world knowledge to comprehend text. Recent research by Karin James at Indiana University also shows that a learner's "letterbox" works most actively while printing letters, not just recognizing ABC's or touching them on an iPad. This, James explains, is because the child must imagine each letter mentally before creating it on paper.

Although the critical-period claim is probably wrong, the purveyors of early-reading products do make another assertion with scientific footing: early readers generally go on to become better readers and higher academic achievers.

Education professors Anne Cunningham of the University of California, Berkeley and Keith Stanovich of the University of Toronto tested reading in a large group of first-graders, then again when the students were high school juniors. They found that kids who could already read well in first grade also scored the highest on several measures in 11th grade. This was more than just smart kids staying smart, they concluded: A fast start to reading unlocks an upward spiral of skills, achievement, positive attitudes, and willing practice. Conversely, a slow start tends to touch off difficulty, discouragement, dislike, and avoidance.

The early reader's steady ascent can explode into a towering geyser of literacy because, Cunningham explains, reading is largely self-taught and begets its own mastery. Only through reading—not listening to talk—can a youngster expand his or her mental lexicon enough to allow truly fluid reading, with its rapid line-by-line scanning and its effortless absorption of meaning. Cunningham and Stanovich cite earlier statistics showing that a fifth grader in the lowest percentiles for time spent reading typically devotes less than a minute per day to independent reading and encounters 21,000 written words in a year. A classmate at the 50th percentile will spend an average of about five minutes per day reading independently and encounter 282,000 written words. A fifth-grader at the 98th percentile will spend more than an hour a day and input almost 4.4 million words that reinforce the mental dictionary. "Those who read a lot will enhance their verbal intelligence," write Cunningham and Stanovich, "that is, reading will make them smarter." And, they add, this goes for good readers and struggling readers alike.

Spoken Language multiplies the same bootstrapping effect. Researchers Betty Hart and Todd Risley have written about an "early catastrophe" of generational word poverty set in motion by socioeconomic factors such as poor educational opportunity. In the first three years of life, a child of welfare parents hears 974 different words in daily conversation (9.6 million total), the working-class child 1,498 (19.5 million total), and the child with professional parents 2,176 (33.6 million overall).

No surprise, then, that middle-class kids come to school with far bigger tinder piles of preliteracy skills than lower-class kids. Reading expert Marilyn Jager Adams calculates that parents who read actively to their children daily and play simple alphabet and phonics games provide 3,000 to 4,000 hours of

prereading exposure compared with tens, hundreds, or none. A first-grade teacher with 20 students and 90 minutes to devote to each day's reading lesson could never equalize the "piles" kids bring from word-rich and word-poor homes.

Dominic Massaro's theories and proposed high-tech gadgets could someday help level that playing field. If spoken and written language can horse-race from the same starting gate on the same learning track, then early literacy needn't rely as much on parental vocabulary, motivation, or time on task. The reading-acquisition devices Massaro envisions such as digital T-shirts and electronic teddy bears would no doubt start out as the pricey domain of high-earning parents. But Massaro hopes the prices would fall so that public day care and preschools could bring such devices—and early-reading acquisition—to a wider group. Observes Tim Shanahan: "I wouldn't bet my children's education on it quite yet." But any approach that would make reading acquisition "easier and more universal in the future— I'm all for that."

In the meantime, virtually every traditional reading expert and baby-reading advocate consulted had similar advice: get children reading-ready by reading out loud to them every day from infancy onward in a lively way. The experts also say that to help children learn the alphabet, letter sounds, rhyming, and simple printing, parents can use home-designed or commercially available programs. Most children exposed to this kind of developmental smorgasbord can enter kindergarten already reading or primed to readily pick up the traditional skills.

Tufts professor Maryanne Wolf tells parents to "use the Grandmother Principle. Do what makes sense! Get into conversations with children while you are reading to them. Just have a natural desire to speak, read, and talk to your children—that's the best set of things you can ever do." For those who choose to try to teach their babies to read, experts underscore that extra admonition: don't pressure! A child who feels pushed into early reading and senses parental impatience or disapproval could become discouraged. Far worse than reading at a later age would be missing out altogether on the wonder and fountain of learning that reading brings.

Critical Thinking

1. Are children truly learning to read? Describe the theories of what may be taking place instead.

2. What does it mean to have "phonemic awareness"? How does it play a role in the process of learning to read?

3. What are the pros and cons of children becoming early readers? What are other variables that impact whether a child will become an early reader?

Infant Intelligentsia: Can Babies Learn to Read? And Should They? by Janet Hopson

23

Create Central

www.mhhe.com/createcentral

Internet References

Baby Center.com
http://www.babycenter.com/404_what-is-phonemic-awareness-and-why-is-it-important-to-my-chi_69637.bc

Kid Source Online
http://www.kidsource.com/kidsource/content2/disability.phonological.html

Reading Rockets.org Phonemic Awareness in Young Children
http://www.readingrockets.org/article/408

Zero to Three
http://www.zerotothree.org/early-care-education/early-language-literacy/why-begin-with-infants.html

Hopson, Janet, "Infant Intelligentsia: Can Babies Learn to Read? And Should They?" Republished with permission of Miller-McCune Center for Research, Media and Public Policy, from *Pacific Standard*, September/October 2012; permission conveyed through Copyright Clearance Center, Inc.

Article   Prepared by: Chris J. Boyatzis, *Bucknell University*

The Other-Race Effect Develops during Infancy
Evidence of Perceptual Narrowing

Experience plays a crucial role in the development of face processing. In the study reported here, we investigated how faces observed within the visual environment affect the development of the face-processing system during the 1st year of life. We assessed 3-, 6-, and 9-month-old Caucasian infants' ability to discriminate faces within their own racial group and within three other-race groups (African, Middle Eastern, and Chinese). The 3-month-old infants demonstrated recognition in all conditions, the 6-month-old infants were able to recognize Caucasian and Chinese faces only, and the 9-month-old infants' recognition was restricted to own-race faces. The pattern of preferences indicates that the other-race effect is emerging by 6 months of age and is present at 9 months of age. The findings suggest that facial input from the infant's visual environment is crucial for shaping the face-processing system early in infancy, resulting in differential recognition accuracy for faces of different races in adulthood.

David J. Kelly et al.

Learning Outcomes

After reading this article, you will be able to:

- Describe how a habituation procedure tested infants' other-race effect.

- Describe what "perceptual narrowing" is and how it develops.

Human adults are experts at recognizing faces of conspecifics and appear to perform this task effortlessly. Despite this impressive ability, however, adults are more susceptible to recognition errors when a target face is from an unfamiliar racial group, rather than their own racial group. This phenomenon is known as the *other-race effect* (ORE; see Meissner & Brigham, 2001, for a review). Although the ORE has been widely reported, the exact mechanisms that underlie reduced recognition accuracy for other-race faces, and precisely when this effect emerges during development, remain unclear.

The ORE can be explained in terms of a modifiable face representation. The concept of a multidimensional *face-space* architecture, first proposed by Valentine (1991), has received much empirical support. According to the norm-based coding model, individual face exemplars are represented as vectors within face-space according to their deviation from a prototypical average. The prototype held by each person represents the average of all faces that person has ever encoded and is therefore unique. Although it is unclear which dimensions are most salient and used for recognition, it is likely that dimensions vary between individuals and possibly within each person over time. The prototype (and therefore the entire face-space) continually adapts and is updated as more faces are observed within the environment. Consequently, individuating face-space dimensions of a person living in China are expected to be optimal for recognition of other Chinese persons, but not, for example, for recognition of African individuals.

Other authors have hypothesized that the dimensions of the face prototype present at birth are broad and develop according to the type of facial input received (Nelson, 2001). According to this account, predominant exposure to faces from a single racial category tunes face-space dimensions toward that category. Such tuning might be manifested at a behavioral level in differential responding to own- versus other-race faces, for example, in spontaneous visual preference and a recognition advantage for own-race faces.

Recent findings regarding spontaneous preference have confirmed the impact of differential face input on the tuning of the face prototype during early infancy. It has been demonstrated that selectivity based on ethnic facial differences emerges very early in life, with 3-month-old infants preferring to look at faces from their own group, as opposed to faces from other ethnic groups (Bar-Haim, Ziv, Lamy, & Hodes, 2006; Kelly et al., 2005, 2007). We (Kelly et al., 2005) have shown that this preference is not present at birth, which strongly suggests that own-group preferences result from differential exposure to faces from one's particular ethnic group. In addition, Bar-Haim et al. (2006) tested a population of Ethiopian infants who had been raised in an absorption center while their families awaited housing in Israel. These infants were frequently exposed to both Ethiopian and Israeli adults and subsequently demonstrated no preference for either African or Caucasian faces when presented simultaneously.

Collectively, these results provide strong evidence that faces observed in the visual environment have a highly influential role in eliciting face preferences during infancy. Additional evidence supporting this conclusion comes from a study concerning gender preference (Quinn, Yahr, Kuhn, Slater, & Pascalis, 2002), which showed that 3- to 4-month-old infants raised primarily by a female caregiver demonstrate a visual preference for female over male faces, whereas infants raised primarily by a male caregiver prefer to look at male rather than female faces.

Although the literature on differential face recognition contains discrepancies regarding the onset of the ORE, evidence points toward an early inception. Some of the initial investigations reported onset at 8 (Feinman & Entwhistle, 1976) and 6 (Chance, Turner, & Goldstein, 1982) years of age. More recent studies have found the ORE to be present in 5-year-olds (Pezdek, Blandon-Gitlin, & Moore, 2003) and 3-year-olds (Sangrigoli & de Schonen, 2004a). In addition, Sangrigoli and de Schonen (2004b) showed that 3-month-old Caucasian infants were able to recognize an own-race face, but not an Asian face, as measured by the visual paired-comparison (VPC) task. However, the effect disappeared if infants were habituated to three, as opposed to one, other-race face exemplars. Thus, although the ORE may be present at 3 months of age, it is weak enough to be eliminated after only a few instances of exposure within an experimental session.

Additional lines of evidence indicate that the face representation undergoes change throughout development. At 6 months of age, infants are able to individuate human and monkey faces, and although the ability to individuate human faces

is maintained in later development, the ability to individuate monkey faces is absent in 9-month-old infants and in adults (Pascalis, de Haan, & Nelson, 2002). Although the face-processing system appears to adapt toward own-species faces, it still retains flexibility for within-species categories of faces (i.e., other-race faces). Korean adults adopted by French families during childhood (ages 3–9 years) demonstrated a recognition deficit for Korean faces relative to their ability to recognize European faces (Sangrigoli, Pallier, Argenti, Ventureyra, & de Schonen, 2005). Their pattern of performance was comparable to that of the native French people who were tested in the same study.

The purpose of the study reported here was to clarify the developmental origins of the ORE during the first months of life. Using the VPC task, we assessed the ability of 3-, 6-, and 9-month-old Caucasian infants to discriminate within own-race (Caucasian) faces and within three categories of other-race faces (African, Middle Eastern, and Chinese). This task measures relative interest in the members of pairs of stimuli, each consisting of a novel stimulus and a familiar stimulus observed during a prior habituation period. Recognition of the familiar stimulus is inferred from the participant's tendency to fixate on the novel stimulus. Previous studies have found that 3-month-old infants can perform this task even when they are exposed to different views of faces (e.g., full view vs. 3/4 profile) during the habituation period and the recognition test (Pascalis, de Haan, Nelson, & de Schonen, 1998). We also varied face views between familiarization and testing, a procedure that is preferable to using identical pictures in the habituation and testing phases because it ensures that face recognition—as opposed to picture recognition (i.e., image matching)—is tested. Our selection of which age groups to test was based on previous research demonstrating that the ORE is found in infancy (3-month-olds; Sangrigoli & de Schonen, 2004b) and that the face-processing system appears to undergo a period of tuning between 6 and 9 months of age (Pascalis et al., 2002).

Method
Participants

In total, 192 Caucasian infants were included in the final analysis. There were 64 subjects in each of three age groups: 3-month-olds (age range = 86–102 days; 33 females, 31 males), 6-month-olds (age range = 178–196 days; 31 females, 33 males), and 9-month-olds (age range = 268–289 days; 30 females, 34 males). All participants were healthy, full-term infants. Within each age group, the infants were assigned in equal numbers (n = 16) to the four testing conditions (Caucasian, African, Middle Eastern, and Chinese). The infants were recruited from the maternity wing of the Royal Hallamshire Hospital, Sheffield, United Kingdom. In each age group, we tested additional infants who were excluded from the final analysis. Twenty-two 3-month-old infants were excluded because of failure to habituate ($n = 4$), side bias during testing (>95% looking time to one side; $n = 15$), or fussiness ($n = 3$); sixteen 6-month-old infants were excluded because of failure to habituate ($n = 7$), side bias during testing ($n = 3$), parental interference ($n = 2$), or fussiness ($n = 4$); and eleven 9-month-old infants were excluded because of a failure to habituate ($n = 3$) or fussiness ($n = 8$).

Stimuli

The stimuli were 24 color images of male and female adult faces (age range = 23–27 years) from four different ethnic groups (African, Asian, Middle Eastern, and Caucasian). All faces had dark hair and dark eyes so that the infants would be unable to demonstrate recognition on the basis of these features. The images were photos of students. The Africans were members of the African and Caribbean Society at the University of Sheffield; the Asians were Han Chinese students from Zhejiang Sci-Tech University, Hangzhou, China; the Middle Easterners were members of the Pakistan Society at the University of Sheffield; and the Caucasians were psychology students at the University of Sheffield.

For each ethnic group, we tested male and female faces in separate conditions. The images for each combination of ethnic group and gender consisted of a habituation face and two test faces, a novel face and the familiar face in a new orientation. The two faces in the test phase were always in the same orientation, and this orientation differed from the orientation of the face seen during habituation. In one orientation condition, infants were habituated to full-view faces and saw test faces in 3/4-profile views; in the other orientation condition, the views were reversed. Equal numbers of infants were assigned to the two orientation conditions.

All photos were taken with a Canon S50 digital camera and subsequently cropped using Adobe Photoshop to remove the neck and background details. All individual pictures were then mounted on a uniform dark-gray background, and the stimuli were resized to the same dimensions to ensure uniformity. Sixteen independent observers rated a pool of 32 faces for attractiveness and distinctiveness, using a scale from 1 to 10, and the final set of 24 faces was selected so as to match gender, attractiveness, and distinctiveness within each face pair.

Procedure

All infants were tested in a quiet room at the department of psychology at the University of Sheffield. They were seated on their mother's lap, approximately 60 cm from a screen onto which the images were projected. Each infant was randomly assigned to one of the four ethnic-group conditions (African, Asian, Middle Eastern, or Caucasian). Within each of these four conditions, infants were tested with either male or female faces; testing was counterbalanced appropriately, with half the infants assigned to the male-faces condition and half the infants assigned to the female-faces condition. Equal numbers of infants were tested in the male and female conditions. Before the session started, all mothers were instructed to fixate centrally above the screen and to remain as quiet as possible during testing.

Habituation Phase

Each infant was first presented with a single face projected onto a screen measuring 45 cm × 30 cm. The face measured 18 cm × 18 cm (14° visual angle). The experimenter observed the infant's eye movements on a control monitor from a black-and-white closed-circuit television camera (specialized for low-light conditions) that was positioned above the screen. Time was recorded and displayed on the control monitor using a Horita (Mission Viejo, CA) II TG-50 time coder; video was recorded at 25 frames per second.

The experimenter recorded the infant's attention to the face by holding down the "z" key on a keyboard whenever the infant fixated on the image. When the infant looked away from the image, the experimenter released the key. If the infant's attention was averted for more than 2 s, the image disappeared from the screen. The experimenter then presented the image again and repeated the procedure. The habituation phase ended when the infant's looking time on a presentation was equal to or less than 50% of the average looking time from the infant's first two presentations. Thus, our measure of looking time was the sum of looking time across all presentations until the habituation criterion was reached.

Test Phase

The test phase consisted of two trials. First, two face images (novel and familiar), each measuring 18 cm × 18 cm (14° visual angle), were presented on the screen. The images were separated by a 9-cm gap and appeared in the bottom left and bottom right corners of the screen. When the infant first looked at the images, the experimenter pressed a key to begin a 5-s countdown. At the end of the 5 s, the images disappeared from the screen. The faces then appeared with their left/right position on the screen reversed. As soon as the infant looked at the images, another 5-s countdown was initiated. Eye movements were recorded throughout, and the film was digitized for frame-by-frame analysis by two independent observers who used specialized computer software to code looking time to each of the two faces. The observers were blind to both gender and ethnic-group condition and to the screen positions of the faces being viewed by the infants. The average level of interobserver agreement was high (Pearson $r = .93$). Recognition was inferred from a preference for the novel face stimulus across the two 5-s test trials.

Results
Habituation Trials

A preliminary analysis revealed no significant gender differences for stimuli or participants, so data were collapsed across stimulus gender and participant's gender in subsequent analyses. Habituation time (total looking time across trials) was analyzed in a 3 (age: 3, 6, or 9 months) × 4 (face ethnicity: African, Middle Eastern, Chinese, or Caucasian) × 2 (face orientation: full face or 3/4 profile) between-subjects analysis of variance (ANOVA). The ANOVA yielded only a significant effect of age, $F(2, 189) = 73.193$, $p < .0001$, $\eta^2 = .535$. Post hoc Tukey's honestly significant difference (HSD) tests revealed that the habituation times of 6- and 9-month-old infants did not differ significantly, but both 6-month-old ($M = 42.67$ s) and 9-month-old ($M = 38.88$ s) infants habituated significantly more quickly ($p < .0001$) than 3-month-old infants ($M = 70.74$ s). There were no main effects of face ethnicity or face orientation, nor were there any interactions.

Test Trials

Again, a preliminary analysis yielded no significant gender differences for stimuli or participants, so data were collapsed across stimulus gender and participant's gender in subsequent analyses. Percentage of time spent looking at the novel stimulus, combined from both trials of the test phase, was analyzed in a 3 (age: 3, 6, or 9 months) × 4 (face ethnicity: African, Middle Eastern, Chinese, or Caucasian) × 2 (face orientation: full face or 3/4 view) between-subjects ANOVA. The ANOVA yielded a significant effect of age, $F(2, 189) = 5.133$, $p < .007$, $\eta^2 = .058$. Post hoc Tukey's HSD tests revealed that 3-month-olds ($M = 60.15\%$) showed significantly greater preference for the novel face ($p < .003$) than did 9-month-olds ($M = 53.19\%$). There were no main effects of face ethnicity or face orientation.

To investigate novelty preferences within each age group, we conducted one-way between-groups ANOVAs on the percentage of time spent looking at the novel stimuli in the four face-ethnicity conditions. A significant effect of face ethnicity was found for 9-month-old infants, $F(3, 60) = 3.105$, $p < .033$, $\eta^2 = .134$, but not for 3- or 6-month-old infants. These results suggest that novelty preferences differed between face-ethnicity conditions only within the group of 9-month-old infants.

To further investigate novelty preferences within each age group, we conducted a series of two-tailed t tests to determine whether the time spent looking at novel stimuli differed from the chance level of 50% (see Table 1). The results showed that

3-month-old infants demonstrated significant novelty preferences in all four face-ethnicity conditions, 6-month-old infants demonstrated significant novelty preferences in two of the four conditions (Chinese and Caucasian), and 9-month-old infants demonstrated a novelty preference for Caucasian faces only.

Discussion

The aim of the current study was to investigate the onset of the ORE during the first months of life, following up on previous findings that 3-month-olds already show a preference for own-race faces (Bar-Haim et al., 2006; Kelly et al., 2005, 2007). The results reported here do not provide evidence for the ORE (as measured by differential recognition capabilities for own- and other-race faces) in 3-month-old infants, but they do indicate that the ORE emerges at age 6 months and is fully present at age 9 months.

Our results are consistent with the notion of general perceptual narrowing during infancy (e.g., Nelson, 2001). Our findings are also consistent with those of Pascalis et al. (2002), further demonstrating that the face-processing system undergoes a period of refinement within the 1st year of life. Collectively, these findings lend weight to the concept of a tuning period between 6 and 9 months of age. However, differences between the present study and the work by Pascalis et al. should be noted. For example, there is the obvious difference that Pascalis et al. found between-species effects, and our study focused on within-species effects. It should not be assumed that identical mechanisms necessarily underlie the reductions in recognition accuracy observed in the two cases. In addition, once the ability to discriminate between nonhuman primate faces has diminished, it apparently cannot be recovered easily (Dufour, Coleman, Campbell, Petit, & Pascalis, 2004; Pascalis et al., 2002), whereas the ORE is evidently modifiable through exposure to other-race populations (Sangrigoli et al., 2005) or simple training with other-race faces (Elliott, Wills, & Goldstein, 1973; Goldstein & Chance, 1985; Lavrakas, Buri, & Mayzner, 1976). Furthermore, event-related potential (ERP) studies have shown that in 6-month-olds, the putative infant N170 (a face-selective ERP component elicited in occipital regions) is sensitive to inversion for both human and monkey faces, whereas the N170 recorded in adults is sensitive to inversion only for human faces (de Haan, Pascalis, & Johnson, 2002). An adult-like N170 response is not observed in subjects until they are 12 months of age (Halit, de Haan, & Johnson, 2003). The ERP response for other-race faces has not yet been investigated during infancy, but studies with adults have revealed no differences in the N170 response to own- and other-race faces (Caldara et al., 2003; Caldara, Rossion, Bovet, & Hauert, 2004).

Our findings differ from those reported by Sangrigoli and de Schonen (2004b) in the only other study to have investigated

Table 1   Results of the Novelty-Preference Test, by Age Group and Face Ethnicity

Age and Face Ethnicity	Mean Time Looking at the Novel Face (%)	$t(15)$	p	p_{rep}
3 months				
African	60.88 (16.52)	2.635	.019*	.942
Middle Eastern	57.31 (11.37)	2.572	.021*	.937
Chinese	58.72 (14.07)	2.479	.026*	.929
Caucasian	63.71 (13.47)	4.072	.001*	.988
6 months				
African	55.35 (11.40)	1.880	> .05	.840
Middle Eastern	56.70 (12.89)	2.079	> .05	.871
Chinese	56.42 (7.79)	3.295	.005*	.965
Caucasian	58.27 (8.88)	3.725	.002*	.979
9 months				
African	51.33 (10.53)	0.505	> .05	.414
Middle Eastern	53.51 (8.47)	1.658	> .05	.799
Chinese	48.23 (13.31)	0.530	> .05	.642
Caucasian	59.70 (11.16)	3.476	.003*	.971

Note. Standard deviations are given in parentheses. Asterisks highlight conditions in which the infants viewed novel faces significantly more often than predicted by chance.

the emergence of the ORE during infancy. In their initial experiment, Sangrigoli and de Schonen found that 3-month-old infants discriminated own-race faces, but not other-race faces, as measured by the VPC task. However, numerous methodological differences between our study and theirs (e.g., color stimuli in our study vs. gray-scale stimuli in theirs) could have contributed to these contrasting results. Furthermore, Sangrigoli and de Schonen were able to eliminate the ORE with only a few trials of exposure to multiple exemplars, which suggests that even if the ORE is already present in 3-month-olds, it is weak and reversible. Between Sangrigoli and de Schonen's work and our own, there are now three VPC experiments (one here, two in Sangrigoli & de Schonen)[1] that have been conducted with 3-month-old infants, yet only one has yielded evidence for the ORE. The weight of the evidence thus suggests that a strong and sustainable ORE may not be present at 3 months of age, but rather develops later.

One might ask whether the ORE arises from differences in the variability of faces from different ethnic groups. However, the available evidence indicates that no category of faces has greater homogeneity than any other (Goldstein, 1979a, 1979b). Moreover, the data suggest that the ORE does not exclusively reflect a deficit for non-Caucasian faces: Individuals from many ethnic groups demonstrate poorer recognition of other-race than own-race faces (Meissner & Brigham, 2001). Evidently, a full account of the ORE will involve factors other than heterogeneity.

We have argued elsewhere (Kelly et al., 2007) that the ORE may develop through the following processes: First, predominant exposure to faces from one's own racial group induces familiarity with and a visual preference for such faces. Second, a preference for faces within one's racial group produces greater visual attention to such faces, even when faces from other racial groups are present in the visual environment. Third, superior recognition abilities develop for faces within one's racial group but not for faces from groups that are infrequently encountered. Although supporting evidence for the first two processes has been obtained previously (Bar-Haim et al., 2006; Kelly et al., 2005, 2007), the data reported here provide the first direct evidence for the third. According to our account, the ORE can be explained by a modifiable face prototype (Valentine, 1991). If each person's face prototype is an average of all faces that person has encoded during his or her lifetime, then one may assume that it will resemble the race of the faces most commonly encountered. Furthermore, one would expect that individuating dimensions will be optimized for recognition of own-race faces but not other-race faces.

An alternative to the single-prototype account is that people may possess multiple face-spaces that represent different face categories (e.g., gender, race) separately within a global space. In this contrasting scheme, rather than individuating dimensions being unsuitable for recognition of other-race faces, a face-space for other-race faces (e.g., Chinese faces) either does not exist or is insufficiently formed because of a general lack of exposure to those face categories. In both accounts, recognition capabilities improve through exposure to other-race faces. In the case of the single-prototype account, individuating dimensions acquire properties of newly encountered other-race faces that facilitate recognition. Alternatively, in the multiple-face-spaces account, a relevant space for other-race faces develops through similar exposure.

In summary, this is the first study to investigate the emergence of the ORE during infancy by comparing three different age groups' ability to recognize faces from their own race and a range of other races. The data reported here support the idea that very young infants have a broad face-processing system that is capable of processing faces from different ethnic groups. Between 3 and 9 months of age, this system gradually becomes more sensitive to faces from an infant's own ethnic group as a consequence of greater exposure to such faces than to faces from other racial groups. This shift in sensitivity is reflected in the emergence of a deficit in recognition accuracy for faces from unfamiliar groups. Future research should address whether the pattern of results we obtained with Caucasian infants is universal or whether the ORE emerges at different ages in other populations.

Notes

1. But note that in a recent study using morphed stimuli, Hayden, Bhatt, Joseph, and Tanaka (2007) demonstrated that 3.5-month-old infants showed greater sensitivity to structural changes in own-race faces than in other-race faces.

References

Bar-Haim, Y., Ziv, T., Lamy, D., & Hodes, R.M. (2006). Nature and nurture in own-race face processing. *Psychological Science, 17,* 159–163.

Caldara, R., Rossion, B., Bovet, P., & Hauert, C.A. (2004). Event-related potentials and time course of the 'other-race' face classification advantage. *Cognitive Neuroscience and Neuropsychology, 15,* 905–910.

Caldara, R., Thut, G., Servoir, P., Michel, C.M., Bovet, P., & Renault, B. (2003). Faces versus non-face object perception and the 'other-race' effect: A spatio-temporal event-related potential study. *Clinical Neurophysiology, 114,* 515–528.

Chance, J.E., Turner, A.L., & Goldstein, A.G. (1982). Development of differential recognition for own- and other-race faces. *Journal of Psychology, 112,* 29–37.

de Haan, M., Pascalis, O., & Johnson, M.H. (2002). Specialization of neural mechanisms underlying face recognition in human infants. *Journal of Cognitive Neuroscience, 14,* 199–209.

Dufour, V., Coleman, M., Campbell, R., Petit, O., & Pascalis, O. (2004). On the species-specificity of face recognition in human adults. *Current Psychology of Cognition, 22,* 315–333.

Elliott, E.S., Wills, E.J., & Goldstein, A.G. (1973). The effects of discrimination training on the recognition of White and Oriental faces. *Bulletin of the Psychonomic Society, 2,* 71–73.

Feinman, S., & Entwhistle, D.R. (1976). Children's ability to recognize other children's faces. *Child Development, 47,* 506–510.

Goldstein, A.G. (1979a). Race-related variation of facial features: Anthropometric data I. *Bulletin of the Psychonomic Society, 13,* 187–190.

Goldstein, A.G. (1979b). Facial feature variation: Anthropometric data II. *Bulletin of the Psychonomic Society, 13,* 191–193.

Goldstein, A.G., & Chance, J.E. (1985). Effects of training on Japanese face recognition: Reduction of the other-race effect. *Bulletin of the Psychonomic Society, 23,* 211–214.

Halit, H., de Haan, M., & Johnson, M.H. (2003). Cortical specialisation for face processing: Face-sensitive event-related potential components in 3- and 12-month-old infants. *NeuroImage, 19,* 1180–1193.

Hayden, A., Bhatt, R.S., Joseph, J.E., & Tanaka, J.W. (2007). The other-race effect in infancy: Evidence using a morphing technique. *Infancy, 12,* 95–104.

Kelly, D.J., Ge, L., Liu, S., Quinn, P.C., Slater, A.M., Lee, K., et al. (2007). Cross-race preferences for same-race faces extend beyond the African versus Caucasian contrast in 3-month-old infants. *Infancy, 11,* 87–95.

Kelly, D.J., Quinn, P.C., Slater, A.M., Lee, K., Gibson, A., Smith, M., et al. (2005). Three-month-olds, but not newborns, prefer own-race faces. *Developmental Science, 8,* F31–F36.

Lavrakas, P.J., Buri, J.R., & Mayzner, M.S. (1976). A perspective on the recognition of other-race faces. *Perception & Psychophysics, 20,* 475–481.

Meissner, C.A., & Brigham, J.C. (2001). Thirty years of investigating the own-race bias in memory for faces: A meta-analytic review. *Psychology, Public Policy, and Law, 7,* 3–35.

Nelson, C.A. (2001). The development and neural bases of face recognition. *Infant and Child Development, 10,* 3–18.

Pascalis, O., de Haan, M., & Nelson, C.A. (2002). Is face processing species-specific during the first year of life? *Science, 296,* 1321–1323.

Pascalis, O., de Haan, M., Nelson, C.A., & de Schonen, S. (1998). Long-term recognition assessed by visual paired comparison in 3- and 6-month-old infants. *Journal of Experimental Psychology: Learning, Memory, and Cognition, 24,* 249–260.

Pezdek, K., Blandon-Gitlin, I., & Moore, C. (2003). Children's face recognition memory: More evidence for the cross-race effect. *Journal of Applied Psychology, 88,* 760–763.

Quinn, P.C., Yahr, J., Kuhn, A., Slater, A.M., & Pascalis, O. (2002). Representation of the gender of human faces by infants: A preference for female. *Perception, 31,* 1109–1121.

Sangrigoli, S., & de Schonen, S. (2004a). Effect of visual experience on face processing: A developmental study of inversion and non-native effects. *Developmental Science, 7,* 74–87.

Sangrigoli, S., & de Schonen, S. (2004b). Recognition of own-race and other-race faces by three-month-old infants. *Journal of Child Psychology and Psychiatry and Allied Disciplines, 45,* 1219–1227.

Sangrigoli, S., Pallier, C., Argenti, A.M., Ventureyra, V.A.G., & de Schonen, S. (2005). Reversibility of the other-race effect in face recognition during childhood. *Psychological Science, 16,* 440–444.

Valentine, T. (1991). A unified account of the effects of distinctiveness, inversion, and race in face recognition. *The Quarterly Journal of Experimental Psychology, 43A,* 161–204.

Critical Thinking

1. In face recognition and preferences for faces of different races, what role does biological or natural factors play and what role does experience and nurture play?

2. In infants' ability to perceive faces of different races, what is perceptual narrowing and when does it occur?

Create Central

www.mhhe.com/createcentral

Internet References

ScienceDaily.com
http://www.sciencedaily.com/releases/2012/05/120502132949.htm

UTDallas, School of Behavioral and Brain Sciences
http://bbs.utdallas.edu/ilp/pdf/discrimination.pdf

DAVID J. KELLY: University of Sheffield, Sheffield, United Kingdom; **PAUL C. QUINN:** University of Delaware; **ALAN M. SLATER:** University of Exeter, Exeter, United Kingdom; **KANG LEE:** University of Toronto, Toronto, Ontario, Canada; **LIEZHONG GE:** Zeijiang Sci-Tech University, Hangzhou, People's Republic of China; and **OLIVER PASCALIS:** University of Sheffield, Sheffield, United Kingdom.

From *Psychological Science*, December 2007, pp. 1084–1089. Copyright © 2007 by the Association for Psychological Science. Reprinted by permission of Sage Publications via Rightslink.

Article   Prepared by: Chris J. Boyatzis, *Bucknell University*

New Advances in Understanding Sensitive Periods in Brain Development

MICHAEL S. C. THOMAS AND MARK H. JOHNSON

Learning Outcomes

After reading this article, you will be able to:

• Describe how "plasticity" is an important feature of the brain.

• Explain the sensitive period in second language acquisition.

• Contrast different mechanisms that influence different sensitive periods.

The idea that there are "critical" or sensitive periods in neural, cognitive, and behavioral development has a long history. It first became widely known with the phenomenon of *filial imprinting* as famously described by Konrad Lorenz: After a relatively brief exposure to a particular stimulus early in life, many birds and mammals form a strong and exclusive attachment to that stimulus. According to Lorenz, a critical period in development has several features, including the following: Learning or plasticity is confined to a short and sharply defined period of the life cycle, and this learning is subsequently irreversible in the face of later experience. Following the paradigmatic example of filial imprinting in birds, more recent studies on cats, dogs, and monkeys, as well as investigations of bird song and human language development, have confirmed that critical periods are major phenomena in brain and behavioral development (see Michel & Tyler, 2005, for review). However, it rapidly became evident that, even in the prototypical case of imprinting, critical periods were not as sharply timed and irreversible as first thought. For example, the critical period for imprinting in domestic chicks was shown to be extendable in time in the absence of appropriate stimulation, and the learning is reversible under certain circumstances (for review, see Bolhuis, 1991). These and other modifications of

Lorenz's original views have led most current researchers to adopt the alternative term *sensitive periods* to describe these widespread developmental phenomena.

A fundamental debate that continues to the present is whether specific mechanisms underlie sensitive periods or whether such periods are a natural consequence of functional brain development. Support for the latter view has come from a recent perspective on developing brain functions. Relating evidence on the neuroanatomical development of the brain to the remarkable changes in motor, perceptual, and cognitive abilities during the first decade or so of a human life presents a formidable challenge. A recent theory, termed *interactive specialization*, holds that postnatal functional brain development, at least within the cerebral cortex, involves a process of increasing specialization, or fine-tuning, of response properties (Johnson, 2001, 2005). According to this view, during postnatal development, the response properties of cortical regions change as they interact and compete with each other to acquire their roles in new computational abilities. That is, some cortical regions begin with poorly defined functions and consequently are partially activated in a wide range of different contexts and tasks. During development, activity-dependent interactions between regions sharpen up their functions, such that a region's activity becomes restricted to a narrower set of stimuli or task demands. For example, a region originally activated by a wide variety of visual objects may come to confine its response to upright human faces. The termination of sensitive periods is then a natural consequence of the mechanisms by which cortical regions become increasingly specialized and finely tuned. Once regions have become specialized for their adult functions, these commitments are difficult to reverse. If this view is correct, sensitive periods in human cognitive development are intrinsic to the process that produces the functional structure of the adult brain.

In order to better understand how sensitive periods relate to the broader picture of vertebrate functional brain development, researchers have addressed a number of specific questions. In any given species are there multiple sensitive periods or just a few (e.g., one per sensory modality)? If there are multiple sensitive periods, do they share common underlying mechanisms? What are the processes that underlie the end of sensitive periods and the corresponding reduction in plasticity?

Varieties of Sensitive Period

Recent work indicates that there are multiple sensitive periods in the sensory systems that have been studied. For example, within the auditory domain in humans, there are different sensitive periods for different facets of speech processing and other sensitive periods, having different timing, related to basic aspects of music perception. Similarly, in nonhuman-primate visual systems there are, at a minimum, different sensitive periods related to amblyopia (a condition found in early childhood in which one eye develops good vision but the other does not), visual acuity, motion perception, and face processing (see Johnson, 2005, for review).

How these different and varied sensitive periods relate to each other is still poorly understood. But high-level skills like human language involve the integration of many lower-level systems, and plasticity in language acquisition is therefore likely to be the combinatorial result of the relative plasticity of underlying auditory, phonological, semantic, syntactic, and motor systems, along with the developmental interactions among these components. The literature currently available suggests that plasticity tends to reduce in low-level sensory systems before it reduces in high-level cognitive systems (Huttenlocher, 2002).

While it is now agreed that there are multiple sensitive periods even within one sensory modality in a given species, there is still considerable debate as to whether these different sensitive periods reflect common underlying mechanisms or whether different mechanisms and principles operate in each case.

Mechanisms Underlying Sensitive Periods

A major feature of sensitive periods is that plasticity appears to be markedly reduced at the end of the period. There are three general classes of explanation for this: (a) termination of plasticity due to maturation, (b) self-termination of learning, and (c) stabilization of constraints on plasticity (without a reduction in the underlying level of plasticity).

According to the first view, endogenous changes in the neurochemistry of the brain region in question could increase the rate of pruning of synapses, resulting in the "fossilization" of existing patterns of functional connectivity. Thus, the termination of sensitive periods would be due to endogenous factors, would have a fixed time course, and could be specific to individual regions of the cortex. Empirical evidence on neurochemical changes associated with plasticity (such as expression of glutamatergic and GABA receptors in the human visual cortex) indicate that the periods of neurochemical change can occur around the age of functional sensitive periods. However, this does not rule out the possibility that these neurochemical changes are a consequence of the differences in functional activity due to termination of plasticity for some other reason, rather than its primary cause (Murphy, Betson, Boley, & Jones, 2005).

The second class of mechanism implies that sensitive periods involve self-terminating learning processes. By this, we mean that the process of learning itself could produce change that reduce the system's plasticity. These types of mechanism are most consistent with the view of sensitive periods as a natural consequence of typical functional brain development. An important way to describe and understand self-terminating learning comes from the use of computer-simulated neural networks (Thomas & Johnson, 2006). These models demonstrate mechanistically how processes of learning can lead to neurobiological changes that reduce plasticity, rather than plasticity changing according to a purely maturational timetable. Such computer models have revealed that, even where a reduction in plasticity emerges with increasing experience, a range of different specific mechanisms may be responsible for this reduction (see Thomas & Johnson, 2006). For example, it may be that the neural system's computational resources, which are critical for future learning, have been claimed or used up by existing learning, so that any new learning must compete to capture these resources. Unless earlier-learned abilities are neglected or lost, new learning may always be limited by this competition. Another mechanism discovered through modeling is called entrenchment. In this case, prior experience places the system into a state that is nonoptimal for learning the new skill. It takes time to reconfigure the system for the new task and learning correspondingly takes longer than it would have done had the system been in an uncommitted state. A third mechanism is assimilation, whereby initial learning reduces the system's ability to detect changes in the environment that might trigger further learning.

Evidence from humans relevant to self-terminating sensitive periods is reported by Lewis and Maurer (2005), who have studied the outcome of cases of human infants born with dense bilateral cataracts in both eyes. Such dense bilateral cataracts restrict these infants to near blindness, but fortunately the condition can be rectified with surgery. Despite variation in the age of treatment from 1 to 9 months, infants were found to have the visual acuity of a newborn immediately following surgery to remove the cataracts. However, after only 1 hour of patterned vision, acuity had improved to the level of a typical 6-week-old; and after a further month of visual experience, the gap to age-matched controls was very considerably reduced. These findings correspond well with experiments showing that rearing animals in the dark appears to delay the end of the normal sensitive period. Thus, in at least some cases, plasticity seems to wait for the appropriate type of sensory stimulation. This is consistent with the idea that changes in plasticity can be driven by the learning processes associated with typical development.

Returning to the paradigmatic example of filial imprinting in birds, O'Reilly and Johnson (1994) constructed a computer model of the neural network known to support imprinting in the relevant region of the chick brain. This computer model successfully simulated a range of phenomena associated with imprinting behavior in the chick. Importantly, in both the model and the chick, the extent to which an imprinted preference for one object can be "reversed" by exposure to a second object depends on a combination of the length of exposure to the first object and the length of exposure to the second object (for review, see Bolhuis, 1991). In other words, in the model, the sensitive period was dependent on the respective levels of learning and was self-terminating. Additionally, like the chick, the network generalized from a training object to one that shared some of its features such as color or shape. By gradually changing the features of the object to which the chick was exposed, the chick's preference could be shifted even after the "sensitive period" had supposedly closed. The simulation work demonstrated the sufficiency of simple learning mechanisms to explain the observed behavioral data (McClelland, 2005).

The third class of explanation for the end of sensitive periods is that it represents the onset of stability in constraining factors rather than a reduction in the underlying plasticity. For example, while an infant is growing, the distance between her eyes increases, thereby creating instability in the information to visual cortical areas. However, once the inter-eye distance is fixed in development, the visual input becomes stable. Thus, brain plasticity may be "hidden" until it is revealed by some perturbation to another constraining factor that disrupts vision.

This mechanism offers an attractive explanation of the surprising degree of plasticity sometimes observed in adults, for instance after even brief visual deprivation. Sathian (2005) reported activity in the visual cortex during tactile perception in sighted human adults after brief visual deprivation—activity similar to that observed in those who have suffered long-term visual deprivation. While this line of research initially appears consistent with life-long plasticity, it is important to note that this tactile-induced visual-cortex activity is much greater if vision is lost early in life or was never present. Thus, although there appears to be residual connectivity between sensory systems that can be uncovered by blocking vision in sighted

people, there is also a sensitive period during which these connections can be more drastically altered.

Sensitive Periods in Second Language Acquisition

Given the variety of mechanisms that may underlie sensitive periods, it would be interesting to know how such periods affect the acquisition of higher cognitive abilities in humans. Recent research on learning a second language illustrates one attempt to answer this question. If you want to master a second language, how important is the age at which you start to learn it? If you start to learn a second language as an adult, does your brain process it in a different way from how it processes your first language?

It is often claimed that unless individuals acquire a second language (L2) before mid-childhood (or perhaps before puberty), then they will never reach native-like levels of proficiency in the second language in pronunciation or grammatical knowledge. This claim is supported by deprivation studies showing that the acquisition of a first language (L1) is itself less successful when begun after a certain age. Further, functional brain-imaging studies initially indicated that in L2 acquisition, different areas of the cortex were activated by the L2 than by the L1; only in individuals who had acquired two languages simultaneously were common areas activated (e.g., Kim, Relkin, Lee, & Hirsch, 1997).

However, subsequent research has painted a more complex picture. First, claims for sensitive periods have tended to rely on assessing final level of attainment rather than speed of learning. This is because there is evidence that adults can learn a second language more quickly than children can, even if their final level of attainment is not as high. Indeed adults and children appear to learn a new language in different ways. Children are relatively insensitive to feedback and extract regularities from exposure to large amounts of input, whereas adults adopt explicit strategies and remain responsive to feedback (see, e.g., Hudson Kam & Newport, 2005).

Second, even when the final level of L2 attainment is considered, it has proved hard to find an age after which prospective attainment levels off. That is, there is no strong evidence for a point at which a sensitive period completely closes (see, e.g., Birdsong, 2006). Instead, L2 attainment shows a linear decline with age: The later you start, the lower your final level is likely to be (Birdsong, 2006).

Third, recent functional imaging research has indicated that at least three factors are important in determining the relative brain-activation patterns produced by L1 and L2 during comprehension and production. These are the age of acquisition, the level of usage/exposure to each language, and the level of proficiency attained in L2. Overall, three broad themes have emerged (Abutalebi, Cappa, & Perani, 2005; Stowe & Sabourin, 2005): (a) The same network of left-hemisphere brain regions is involved in processing both languages; (b) a weak L2 is associated with more widespread neural activity compared to L1 in production (perhaps because the L2 is more effortful to produce) but less activation in comprehension (perhaps because the L2 is less well understood); and (c) the level of proficiency in L2 is more important than age of acquisition in determining whether L1 and L2 activate common or separate areas. In brief, the better you are at your L2, the more similar the activated regions become to those activated by your L1. This finding fits with the idea that certain brain areas have become optimized for processing language (perhaps during the acquisition of L1) and that, in order to become very good at L2, you have to engage these brain areas. The idea that later plasticity is tempered by the processing structures created by earlier learning fits with the interactive-specialization explanation for the closing of sensitive periods.

Finally, in line with the idea that language requires integration across multiple subskills, increasing evidence indicates that sensitive periods differ across the components of language (Neville, 2006; Wartenburger et al., 2003; Werker & Tees, 2005). Plasticity may show greater or earlier reductions for phonology and morphosyntax than it does for lexical-semantics, in which there may indeed be no age-related change at all. In other words, for the late language learner, new vocabulary is easier to acquire than new sounds or new grammar.

Conclusion

It is important to understand the mechanisms underlying sensitive periods for practical reasons. Age-of-acquisition effects may shape educational policy and the time at which children are exposed to different skills. The reversibility of effects of deprivation on development has important implications for interventions for children with congenital sensory impairments or children exposed to impoverished physical and social environments. And there are clinical implications for understanding the mechanisms that drive recovery from brain damage at different ages.

Exciting vistas for the future include the possibility of using genetic and brain-imaging data to identify the best developmental times for training new skills in individual children, and the possibility that a deeper understanding of the neuro-computational principles that underlie self-terminating plasticity will allow the design of more efficient training procedures (McClelland 2005).

Recommended Readings

Birdsong, D. (2006). (See References). Discusses recent research on sensitive periods and second-language acquisition.

Huttenlocher, P.R. (2002). (See References). An overview of neural plasticity.

Johnson, M.H. (2005). *Developmental cognitive neuroscience* (2nd ed.). Oxford, UK: Blackwell. An introduction to the relationship between brain development and cognitive development.

Knusden, E.I. (2004). Sensitive periods in the development of brain and behavior. *Journal of Cognitive Neuroscience, 16,* 1412–1425. A discussion of mechanisms of plasticity and sensitive periods at the level of neural circuits.

References

Abutalebi, J., Cappa, S.F., & Perani, D. (2005). What can functional neuroimaging tell us about the bilingual brain? In J.F. Kroll & A.M.B. de Groot (Eds.), *Handbook of bilingualism* (pp. 497–515). Oxford, UK: Oxford University Press.

Birdsong, D. (2006). Age and second language acquisition and processing: A selective overview. *Language Learning, 56,* 9–49.

Bolhuis, J.J. (1991). Mechanisms of avian imprinting: A review. *Biological Reviews, 66,* 303–345.

Hudson Kam, C.L., & Newport, E.L. (2005). Regularizing unpredictable variation: The roles of adult and child learners in language formation and change. *Language Learning and Development, 1,* 151–195.

Huttenlocher, P.R. (2002). *Neural plasticity: The effects of the environment on the development of the cerebral cortex.* Cambridge, MA: Harvard University Press.

Huttenlocher, P.R., & Dabholkar, A.S. (1997). Regional differences in synaptogenesis in human cerebral cortex. *Journal of Comparative Neurology, 387,* 167–187.

Johnson, M.H. (2001). Functional brain development in humans. *Nature Reviews Neuroscience, 2,* 475–483.

Johnson, M.H. (2005). Sensitive periods in functional brain development: Problems and prospects. *Developmental Psychobiology, 46,* 287–292.

Kim, K.H.S., Relkin, N.R., Lee, K.M., & Hirsch, J. (1997). Distinct cortical areas associated with native and second languages. *Nature, 388,* 171–174.

Lewis, T.L., & Maurer, D. (2005). Multiple sensitive periods in human visual development: Evidence from visually deprived children. *Developmental Psychobiology, 46,* 163–183.

McClelland, J.L. (2005). How far can you go with Hebbian learning and when does it lead you astray? In Y. Munakata & M.H. Johnson (Eds.), *Attention and Performance XXI: Processes of change in brain and cognitive development* (pp. 33–59). Oxford, UK: Oxford University Press.

Michel, G.F., & Tyler, A.N. (2005). Critical period: A history of the transition from questions of when, to what, to how. *Developmental Psychobiology, 46,* 156–162.

Murphy, K.M., Betson, B.R., Boley, P.M., & Jones, D.G. (2005). Balance between excitatory and inhibitory plasticity mechanisms. *Developmental Psychobiology, 46,* 209–221.

Neville, H.J. (2006). Different profiles of plasticity within human cognition. In Y. Munakata & M.H. Johnson (Eds.), *Attention and Performance XXI: Processes of change in brain and cognitive development* (pp. 287–314). Oxford, UK: Oxford University Press.

O'Reilly, R., & Johnson, M.H. (1994). Object recognition and sensitive periods: A computational analysis of visual imprinting. *Neural Computation, 6,* 357–390.

Sathian, K. (2005). Visual cortical activity during tactile perception in the sighted and the visually deprived. *Developmental Psychobiology, 46,* 279–286.

Stowe, L.A., & Sabourin, L. (2005). Imaging the processing of a second language: Effects of maturation and proficiency on the neural processes involved. *International Review of Applied Linguistics in Language Teaching, 43,* 329–353.

Thomas, M.S.C., & Johnson, M.H. (2006). The computational modelling of sensitive periods. *Developmental Psychobiology, 48,* 337– 344.

Wartenburger, I., Heekeren, H.R., Abutalebi, J., Cappa, S.F., Villringer, A., & Perani, D. (2003). Early setting of grammatical processing in the bilingual brain. *Neuron, 37,* 159–170.

Werker, J.F., & Tees, R.C. (2005). Speech perception as a window for understanding plasticity and commitment in language systems of the brain. *Developmental Psychobiology, 46,* 233–251.

Critical Thinking

1. Compare and contrast the concepts of imprinting, sensitive periods, and plasticity. Discuss and make reference to past and current research that supports, refutes, or expands our scientific understanding of these concepts.

2. The article describes three mechanisms (maturation, self-termination of learning, and stabilization of constraints on plasticity) underlying sensitive periods. Elucidate and explain these three possible mechanisms and provide examples for each type.

3. Suppose you are a person who acquires multiple languages with high fluency as an adult. However, your close friend does not share this skill. Based on this article, how would you explain this differential ability to your friend? Are there interventions you could recommend that might improve your friend's second language acquisition skill? Why or why not?

4. Recently, researchers have shown the importance of supporting early interactions and experiences during infancy and preschool to support brain development. Explain how this information has or has not changed your perceptions and interactions with babies as a result. If you were a parent of an infant or toddler, explain in more detail what you would do to optimize their early development?

5. Based on this article, what implications does this research have for policy recommendations concerning interventions with children born with visual impairments? Are similar policy recommendations needed for second language learning in the public schools?

Create Central

www.mhhe.com/createcentral

Internet References

Better Brains for Babies
http://bbbgeorgia.org/brainExpSensitive.php

MentalHelp.net
http://www.mentalhelp.net/poc/view_doc.php?type=doc&id=7923&cn=28

Zero to Three.org
http://main.zerotothree.org/site/PageServer?pagename=ter_key_brainFAQ

From *Current Directions in Psychological Science,* January, 2008, pp. 1–5. Copyright © 2008 by the Association for Psychological Science. Reprinted by permission of Sage Publications via Rightslink.

Article   Prepared by: Chris J. Boyatzis, *Bucknell University*

Contributions of Neuroscience to Our Understanding of Cognitive Development

ADELE DIAMOND AND DIMA AMSO

Learning Outcomes

After reading this article, you will be able to:

- Explain how the prefrontal dopamine system plays a role in cognitive deficits in PKU.

- Describe how nurturing touch is important for various domains of development early in life.

- Evaluate evidence for the claim that nurturing touch promotes cognitive and emotional development.

N euroscience research has made its greatest contributions to the study of cognitive development by illuminating mechanisms (providing a "how") that underlie behavioral observations made earlier by psychologists. It has also made important contributions to our understanding of cognitive development by demonstrating that the brain is far more plastic at all ages than previously thought—and thus that the speed and extent by which experience and behavior can shape the brain is greater than almost anyone imagined. In other words, rather than showing that biology is destiny, neuroscience research has been at the forefront of demonstrating the powerful role of experience throughout life. Besides the surprising evidence of the remarkable extent of experience-induced plasticity, rarely has neuroscience given us previously unknown insights into cognitive development, but neuroscience does offer promise of being able to detect some problems before they are behaviorally observable.

Providing Mechanisms That Can Account for Behavioral Results Reported by Psychologists

Here we describe two examples of behavioral findings by psychologists that were largely ignored or extremely controversial until underlying biological mechanisms capable of accounting for them were provided by neuroscience research. One such example concerns cognitive deficits documented in children treated early and continuously for phenylketonuria (PKU). The second example involves neonatal imitation observed by psychologists and mirror neurons discovered by neuroscientists.

Prefrontal Dopamine System and PKU Cognitive Deficits

Since at least the mid-1980s, psychologists were reporting cognitive deficits in children with PKU that resembled those associated with frontal cortex dysfunction (e.g., Pennington, VanDoornick, McCabe, & McCabe, 1985). Those reports did not impact medical care, however. Doctors were skeptical. No one could imagine a mechanism capable of producing what psychologists claimed to be observing.

PKU is a disorder in the gene that codes for phenylalanine hydroxylase, an enzyme essential for the conversion of phenylalanine (Phe) to tyrosine (Tyr). In those with PKU, that enzyme is absent or inactive. Without treatment, Phe levels skyrocket, resulting in gross brain damage and mental retardation. Phe is an amino acid and a component of all dietary protein. PKU treatment consists primarily of reducing dietary intake of protein to keep Phe levels down, but that has to be balanced against the need for protein. For years, children with PKU were considered adequately treated if their blood Phe levels were below 600 micromoles per liter (μmol/L; normal levels in the general public being 60–120 μmol/L). Such children did not have mental retardation and showed no gross brain damage, although no one disputed that their blood Phe levels were somewhat elevated and their blood Tyr levels were somewhat reduced (Tyr levels were not grossly reduced because even though the hydroxylation of Phe into Tyr was largely inoperative, Tyr is also available in protein). Since Phe and Tyr compete to cross into the brain, a modest increase in the ratio of Phe to Tyr in the bloodstream results in a modest decrease in how much Tyr can reach the brain. Note that this is a global effect—the entire brain receives somewhat too little Tyr. How was it possible to make sense of psychologists' claims that the resulting cognitive deficits were not global but limited to the cognitive functions dependent on prefrontal cortex?

Neuroscience provided a mechanism by which psychologists' findings made sense. Research in neuropharmacology had shown that the dopamine system in prefrontal cortex has unusual properties not shared by the dopamine systems in other brain regions such as the striatum. The dopamine neurons that project to prefrontal cortex have higher rates of firing and dopamine turnover. This makes prefrontal cortex sensitive to modest reductions in Tyr (the precursor of dopamine) that are too small to affect the rest of the brain (Tam, Elsworth, Bradberry, & Roth, 1990). Those unusual properties of the prefrontal dopamine system provide a mechanism by which children treated for PKU could show selective deficits limited to prefrontal cortex. The moderate imbalance in the bloodstream between Phe and Tyr causes a reduction in the amount of Tyr reaching the brain that is large enough to impair the functioning of the prefrontal dopamine system but not large enough to affect the rest of the brain. Diamond and colleagues provided evidence for this mechanism in animal models of PKU and longitudinal study of children (Diamond, 2001). That work, presenting a mechanistic explanation and providing convincing evidence to support it, resulted in a change in the medical guidelines for the treatment of PKU (blood Phe levels should be kept between 120 and 360 μmol/L) that has improved children's lives (e.g., Stemerdink et al., 2000). Also, by shedding light on the role of dopamine in the prefrontal cortex early in development, such work offers insights on the development of cognitive control (executive function) abilities that are relevant to all children.

Mirror Neurons and Neonate Imitation

In 1977, Meltzoff and Moore created a sensation by reporting that human infants just 12 to 21 days old imitated facial expressions they observed adults making. That was followed by a second demonstration of such imitation in infants as young as 42 minutes (Meltzoff & Moore, 1983). For years, those reports met strong resistance. Such imitation was thought to be far too sophisticated an accomplishment for a neonate. After all, infants can feel but not see their own mouth and tongue movements, and they can see but not feel the mouth and tongue movements of others. To equate their own motor movements with the perception of those same movements by others would seem to involve high-level cross-modal matching.

The discovery of mirror neurons by Rizzolatti and his colleagues, Fadiga, Fogassi, and Gallese (for review, see Rizzolatti & Craighero, 2004) provided a mechanism that could conceivably underlie newborns' ability to show such imitation rather automatically. Mirror neurons fire when an individual executes an action or when an individual observes someone else executing that action. The cross-modal association occurs at the neuronal, single-cell level. It has since been demonstrated that 3-day-old rhesus monkeys also imitate the facial movements of adult humans (Ferrari et al., 2006) and that the close link between perception and action is not limited to vision; hearing a sound associated with an action activates mirror neurons associated with that action just as does the sight of that action (Kohler et al., 2002).

While the preceding examples are of neuroscience elucidating possible neurobiological bases for observed psychological phenomena, we move on to describe phenomena—concerning plasticity and environmental influences—that neuroscientists have brought to the attention of developmentalists.

Powerful Effects of Early Experience on Brain, Body, Mind, Behavior, and Gene Expression

Ironically, one of the most important findings to emerge from neurobiology is that biology is not destiny. Neuroscience research has shown that experience plays a far larger role in shaping the mind, brain, and even gene expression than was ever imagined. This insight is particularly important in advancing theory in cognitive development, where debates have raged about the importance of nature versus nurture.

Examples of striking experience-induced plasticity abound—for example, the groundbreaking work of Greenough, Merzenich, Maurer, Neville, Pascual-Leone, Taub, Sur, and Kral. Here we highlight work by Schanberg and Meaney, in part because that work emphasizes a sensory system that has received far less attention by psychologists than have vision and audition: the sense of touch.

Nurturing Touch and Its Importance for Growth

Two independent, elegant lines of work have demonstrated the powerful effects of touch. Schanberg and colleagues have shown that the licking behavior of rat mothers is essential for the growth of rat pups. If rat pups are deprived of this touch for even just 1 hour, DNA synthesis is reduced, growth-hormone secretion is inhibited, and bodily organs lose their capacity to respond to exogenously administered growth hormone (Butler, Suskind, & Schanberg, 1978; Kuhn, Butler, & Schanberg, 1978). Schanberg and colleagues have identified molecular mechanisms through which deprivation of the very specific kind of touch rat mothers administer to their pups produces these effects (e.g., Schanberg, Ingledue, Lee, Hannun, & Bartolome, 2003).

Nurturing Touch and Its Importance for Reducing Stress Reactivity and Cognitive Development

Meaney and colleagues have demonstrated that rat moms who more frequently lick and groom their pups produce offspring who, throughout their lives, explore more, are less fearful, show milder reactions to stress, perform better cognitively as adults, and preserve their cognitive skills better into old age (Liu, Diorio, Day, Francis, & Meaney, 2000). It is the mother's behavior that produces these effects rather than a particular genetic profile that produces both a particular mothering style and particular offspring characteristics. Pups of high-licking-and-grooming moms raised by low-licking-and-grooming moms do not show these characteristics, and pups of low-touch moms raised by high-touch moms do show this constellation of attributes (Francis, Diorio, Liu, & Meaney, 1999).

Furthermore, rats tend to raise their offspring the way they themselves were raised, so these effects are transmitted inter-generationally, not through the genome but through behavior. Biological offspring of low-touch moms who are cross-fostered to high-touch moms lick and groom their offspring a lot; in this way, the diminished stress response and cognitive enhancement is passed down through the generations (Francis et al., 1999).

Meaney and colleagues have elegantly demonstrated that maternal behavior produces these behavioral consequences through several mechanisms that alter gene expression. Not all genes in an individual are expressed—many are never expressed. Experience can affect which genes are turned on and off, in which cells, and when. For example, methylation (attaching a methyl group to a gene's promoter) stably silences a gene; demethylation reverses that process, typically leading to the gene being expressed. High licking by rat mothers causes demethylation (i.e., activation) of the glucocorticoid receptor gene, hence lowering circulating glucocorticoid (stress hormone) levels as receptors for the stress hormone remove it from circulation.

Nurturing Touch and Human Cognitive and Emotional Development

Unlike newborn rats, human newborns can see, hear, and smell, as well as feel touch. Yet despite the additional sensory information available to them, touch is still crucial. Human infants who receive little touching grow more slowly, release less growth hormone, and are less responsive to growth hormone that is exogenously administered (Frasier & Rallison, 1972). Throughout life, they show larger reactions to stress, are more prone to depression, and are vulnerable to deficits in cognitive functions commonly seen in depression or during stress (Lupien, King, Meaney, McEwen, 2000).

Touch plays a powerful role for human infants in promoting optimal development and in counteracting stressors. Massaging babies lowers their cortisol levels and helps them gain weight (Field et al., 2004). The improved weight gain from neonatal massage has been replicated cross-culturally, and cognitive benefits are evident even a year later. It is not that infants sleep or eat more; rather, stimulating their body through massage increases vagal (parasympathetic nervous system) activity, which prompts release of food-absorption hormones. Such improved vagal tone also indicates better ability to modulate arousal and to attend to subtle environmental cues important for cognitive development. Passive bodily contact also has substantial stress-reducing, calming, and analgesic effects for infants and adults (e.g., Gray, Watt, & Blass, 2000). Thus, besides "simple touch" being able to calm our jitters and lift our spirits, the right kind of touch regularly enough early in life can improve cognitive development, brain development, bodily health throughout life, and gene expression.

Future Directions

Neuroscience may be able to make extremely important contributions to child development by building on repeated demonstrations that differences in neural activity patterns precede and predict differences in cognitive performance. Often, when the brain is not functioning properly, people can compensate so their performance does not suffer until the neural system becomes too dysfunctional or until performance demands become too great. Thus, an underlying problem may exist but not show up behaviorally until, for example, the academic demands of more advanced schooling exceed a child's ability to compensate.

So far, differences in neural activity patterns have been demonstrated to precede and predict differences in cognitive performance only in adults. For example, Bookheimer and colleagues tested older adults (ranging in age from 47 to 82 years) with a genetic predisposition for Alzheimer's disease, selected because they performed fully comparably to controls across diverse cognitive tasks. Nevertheless, functional neuroimaging revealed that the brains of several of the genetically predisposed individuals already showed predicted differences. Two years later, those individuals showed the cognitive impairments predicted by their earlier neural activity patterns (Bookheimer et al., 2000). Similarly, adults in the early stages of other disorders may show no behavioral evidence of a cognitive deficit while neuroimaging shows their brains are compensating or working harder to achieve that behavioral equivalence. As the disease progresses, the compensation is no longer sufficient and the cognitive deficit becomes evident (e.g., Audoin et al., 2006).

What this suggests is that functional neuroimaging in developing children may perhaps be able to detect evidence of learning disorders—such as attentional, sensory-processing, language, or math deficits—before there is behavioral evidence of a problem. Already, research is being undertaken to see if infants' neural responses to auditory stimuli might be predictive of later linguistic problems (e.g., Benasich et al., 2006). The earlier a problem can be detected, the better the hope of correcting it or of putting environmental compensations in place.

Recommended Readings

Diamond, A. (2001). (See References). Summarizes studies with young children and animals showing the role of maturation of prefrontal cortex in the early emergence of executive function abilities and the importance of dopamine for this.

Grossman, A.W., Churchill, J.D., Bates, K.E., Kleim, J.A., & Greenough, W.T. (2002). A brain adaptation view of plasticity: Is synaptic plasticity an overly limited concept? *Progress in Brain Research, 138,* 91–108. Argues that synaptic, even neuronal, plasticity is but a small fraction of the range of brain changes that occur in response to experience, and that there are multiple forms of brain plasticity governed by mechanisms that are at least partially independent, including non-neuronal changes.

Meaney, M.J. (2001). Maternal care, gene expression, and the transmission of individual differences in stress reactivity across generations. *Annual Review of Neuroscience, 24,* 1161–1192. Provides an overview of research demonstrating that naturally occurring variations in maternal care modify the expression of genes affecting offspring's cognitive development as well as their ability to cope with stress throughout life, and that these changes are passed down intergenerationally (epigenetic inheritance).

Meltzoff, A.N., & Decety, J. (2003). What imitation tells us about social cognition: A rapprochement between developmental psychology and cognitive neuroscience. *Philosophical Transactions of the Royal Society of London – B: Biological Sciences, 358,* 491–500. Reviews the psychological evidence concerning imitation in human neonates and the neurophysiological evidence of a common coding at the single cell level (in mirror neurons) between perceived and generated actions.

Neville, H.J., & Bavelier, D. (2002). Human brain plasticity: Evidence from sensory deprivation and altered language experience. *Progress in Brain Research, 138,* 177–188. Summarizes research, using behavioral measures and neuroimaging, on individuals with altered visual, auditory, and/or language experience, showing ways in which brain development can, and cannot, be modified by environmental input, and how that varies by the timing of the altered input and by specific subfunctions within language or vision.

References

Audoin, B., Au Duong, M.V., Malikova, I., Confort-Gouny, S., Ibarrola, D., Cozzone, P.J., et al. (2006). Functional magnetic resonance imaging and cognition at the very early stage of MS. *Journal of the Neurological Sciences, 245,* 87–91.

Benasich, A.A., Choudhury, N., Friedman, J.T., Realpe Bonilla, T., Chojnowska, C., & Gou, Z. (2006). Infants as a prelinguistic model for language learning impairments: Predicting from event-related potentials to behavior. *Neuropsychologia, 44,* 396–441.

Bookheimer, S.Y., Strojwas, M.H., Cohen, M.S., Saunders, A.M., Pericak-Vance, M.A., Mazziota, J.C., et al. (2000). Patterns of brain activation in people at risk for Alzheimer's disease. *New England Journal of Medicine, 343,* 450–456.

Butler, S.R., Suskind, M.R., & Schanberg, S.M. (1978). Maternal behavior as a regulator of polyamine biosynthesis in brain and heart of the developing rat pup. *Science, 199,* 445–447.

Diamond, A. (2001). A model system for studying the role of dopamine in prefrontal cortex during early development in humans. In C. Nelson & M. Luciana (eds.), *Handbook of developmental cognitive neuroscience* (pp. 433–472). Cambridge, MA: MIT Press.

Field, T., Hernandez-Reif, M., Diego, M., Feijo, L., Vera, Y., & Gil, K. (2004). Massage therapy by parents improves early growth and development. *Infant Behavior & Development, 27,* 435–442.

Ferrari, P.F., Visalberghi, E., Paukner, A., Fogassi, L., Ruggiero, A., & Suomi, S. (2006). Neonatal imitation in rhesus macaques. *PLoS Biology, 4,* 1501–1508.

Francis, D., Diorio, J., Liu, D., & Meaney, M.J. (1999). Nongenomic transmission across generations of maternal behavior and stress responses in the rat. *Science, 286,* 1155–1158.

Frasier, S.D., & Rallison, M.L. (1972). Growth retardation and emotional deprivation: Relative resistance to treatment with human growth hormone. *Journal of Pediatrics, 80,* 603–609.

Gray, L., Watt, L., & Blass, E.M. (2000). Skin-to-skin contact is analgesic in healthy newborns. *Pediatrics, 105,* 1–6.

Kohler, E., Keysers, C., Umiltà, M.A., Fogassi, L., Gallese, V., & Rizzolatti, G. (2002). Hearing sounds, understanding actions: Action representation in mirror neurons. *Science, 297,* 846–848.

Kuhn, C.M., Butler, S.R., & Schanberg, S.M. (1978). Selective depression of serum growth hormone during maternal deprivation in rat pups. *Science, 201,* 1034–1036.

Liu, D., Diorio, J., Day, J.C., Francis, D.D., & Meaney, M.J. (2000). Maternal care, hippocampal synaptogenesis and cognitive development in rats. *Nature Neuroscience, 3,* 799–806.

Lupien, S.J., King, S., Meaney, M.J., & McEwen, B.S. (2000). Child's stress hormone levels correlate with mother's socioeconomic status and depressive state. *Biological Psychiatry, 48,* 976–980.

Meltzoff, A.N., & Moore, M.K. (1977). Imitation of facial and manual gestures by human neonates. *Science, 198,* 75–78.

Meltzoff, A.N., & Moore, M.K. (1983). Newborn infants imitate adult facial gestures. *Child Development, 54,* 702–709.

Pennington, B.F., VanDoornick, W.J., McCabe, L.L., & McCabe, E.R.B. (1985). Neuropsychological deficits in early treated phenylketonuric children. *American Journal of Mental Deficiency, 89,* 467–474.

Rizzolatti, G., & Craighero, L. (2004). The mirror-neuron system. *Annual Review of Neuroscience, 27,* 169–192.

Schanberg, S.M., Ingledue, V.F., Lee, J.Y., Hannun, Y.A., & Bartolome, J.V. (2003). PKC mediates maternal touch regulation of growth-related gene expression in infant rats. *Neuropsychopharmacology, 28,* 1026–1030.

Stemerdink, B.A., Kalverboer, A.F., van der Meere, J.J., van der Molen, M.W., Huisman, J., de Jong, L.W., et al. (2000). Behaviour and school achievement in patients with early and continuously treated phenylketonuria. *Journal of Inherited Metabolic Disorders, 23,* 548–562.

Tam, S.Y., Elsworth, J.D., Bradberry, C.W., & Roth, R.H. (1990). Mesocortical dopamine neurons: High basal firing frequency predicts tyrosine dependence of dopamine synthesis. *Journal of Neural Transmission, 81,* 97–110.

Critical Thinking

1. How does neuroscience help us understand mechanism or "the how" of cognitive development?

2. What evidence is there that nurturing touch affects babies in positive ways, and what are some biological processes that are triggered by such nurturing touch?

3. How do mirror neurons help explain how very young infants are able to imitate facial expressions?

Create Central

www.mhhe.com/createcentral

Internet References

The Science of Early Brain Development
http://developingchild.harvard.edu/resources/briefs/inbrief_series inbrief_the_science_of_ecd

Development Cognitive Neuroscience.com
http://www.devcogneuro.com

Contributions of Neuroscience to Our Understanding of Cognitive Development
http://www.ncbi.nlm.nih.gov/pmc/articles/PMC2366939

Article   Prepared by: Chris J. Boyatzis, *Bucknell University*

The Conscious Infant

A new study finds a possible brain signature of consciousness in infants as young as five months.

CHRISTOF KOCH

Learning Outcomes

After reading this article, you will be able to:

- Describe how psychologists measure consciousness in infants.
- Contrast infant consciousness with that of older children.

How do you know that your cute five-month-old infant is truly aware, that she is fully sentient, capable of having a phenomenal conscious experience of her mother's face or voice? Let me hasten to add that the question here is not whether or not normal, healthy babies can selectively identify their mom's face or voice; of course, they can turn their head and fixate with their eyes onto the face and eyes of their mother even very soon after birth. The question I am after is whether such visuomotor or audiomotor behavior goes along with the kind of subjective experiences you or I have when we look at our mother or hear her voice. It is a legitimate question for two reasons.

For one, babies can't speak. They can't tell us whether or not they are seeing faces or hearing voices. It is a different matter once they mature enough to be able to talk to us about their inner experiences. So we have to trust our intuitions, which are deeply colored by our biases about when life starts, when consciousness begins, and who is or is not conscious. The second reason the question is valid is that 150 years of psychology experimentation has shown time and again that adults are perfectly capable of carrying out a range of complex tasks unconsciously.

For instance, subjects can distinguish between a face that looks angry or one that has a neutral expression even if those faces are rendered "invisible" by flashing them only very briefly onto a screen and by adding distracting images just before and just after the picture to effectively mask or erase the picture from the mind's eye. People can also unconsciously detect gender, do simple adding problems when "invisible" numbers are flashed onto the screen, or distinguish between depictions of inappropriate and appropriate actions (for example, discerning between an invisible image of an athlete batting a ball with a baseball bat and an image that has been doctored to show the player swatting at the ball using a flower bouquet). Perhaps babies' behaviors also rely on unconscious, rather than on conscious, processes?

So it becomes critical to find ways to distinguish conscious from unconscious processing in preverbal infants. What is a psychologist to do? One answer is to measure the brain's electrical activity using a common tool we call the electroencephalogram (EEG).

Using such tools, a group in Paris led by cognitive neuroscientist Stanislas Dehaene of the Collège de France has argued for several years that a hallmark of conscious visual perception is a particular type of electric wave, called P300, that occurs whenever an adult subject is attending to a consciously perceived picture or a sound. These signals start roughly around 300 milliseconds after the onset of the image or sound, can be long-lasting, are depolarizing (positive) relative to a reference electrode, and are particularly prominent above the frontal lobe. Most important, they are not present when, for instance, the image is flashed on the screen but is not consciously seen because it is masked. Looking at an image produces a host of faster electrical responses, which are thought to relate to the processing of the image that occurs prior to conscious recognition. Assuming that the P300 slow wave is one of the brain signatures of conscious perception, can they be found in young children?

Thinking Like Adults?

How can you tell whether infants are consciously aware? One way is to see if their brains respond as adult brains do to visible and "invisible" pictures. In an experiment, EEG recordings were made from 80 five- to 15-month-old infants as they looked at photographs flashed briefly (for 17 to 300 milliseconds), either of faces or of random patterns (as a control). These face/random images were preceded and followed by other random patterns. If the face photo is present for longer than 50 milliseconds, adults—who can tell us about their experiences—can report that they briefly saw a face. The EEG recordings of one-year-old children resembled those of the adults consciously seeing something, although they were only a half or a third as fast.

Recording Brain Waves in Infants

Psychologist Sid Kouider of the Laboratory of Cognitive and Psycholinguistic Sciences at the Ecole Normale Supérieure in Paris, together with Dehaene and other French and Danish researchers, undertook the difficult task of measuring brain waves in 80 infants. Difficult because, unlike undergraduate research subjects, very young children (just like puppies) wiggle around, don't pay attention for long and can't easily be instructed. Their head covered by an EEG cap, the infants sat on the lap of their parents, who were blindfolded so that they would not influence their children's responses. They had to look at streams of images, some that contained photographs of a smiling young woman and some that were only random patterns. What varied across experiments was the duration for which the face was exposed, from barely a glimpse—unlikely to be seen at all—to a sizable fraction of a second that, at least in older children, is invariably associated with the conscious sight of a smiling young woman.

The scientists then subtracted the EEG signals taken in response to a face sequence from those of a pattern-only sequence to extract the unique signature associated with the face stimulus and tracked how this electric signal evolved over time. Segregating these signals according to the age of the infant into groups of five, 12 and 15 months old, and expressed in terms of statistical significance, yields the results explained in the box.

All the kids showed the expected early response that develops in brain regions located at the back of the head, above the visual cortex. This response is proportional to the visual contrast and other image parameters, reflecting neuronal processing of the actual stimulus, whether or not the stimulus was actually consciously perceived. Subsequently, a sustained depolarization (relative to a reference electrode) develops over the front of the brain, in particular in infants 12 months or older. This component of the signal has a more all-or-none character, reflecting the all-or-none character of conscious experience. The data reveal that one-year-old children, at least, do have a brain signature similar to that associated with conscious perception in adults. The electrical signal is perhaps a third of the speed it is in an adult, reflecting the delayed myelination (myelin is the covering of the axon that speeds up transmission of long-distance electrical communication) and immaturity of the young brain.

Of course, the extent to which they truly do have a subjective experience of a smiling face is difficult to ascertain for now. Clever scientists in the future will likely develop some fancy technique to read out the content of these young minds.

The evidence for an even further delayed slow potential is less compelling in very young infants. This finding raises the general question of when does conscious sensation begin? In the infant's first year of life, at birth, in its last trimester in the womb or even earlier? Research on animal and human fetuses suggests that the baby in the womb is partially sedated, even though it can move around, as mothers can certainly attest to [see "When Does Consciousness Arise?" *Consciousness Redux*; *Scientific American Mind*, September/ October 2009].

Indeed, it may well be that the fetus feels as much as we do when we are in a deep, dreamless sleep. It may be that the dramatic events attending birth, including drawing its first breath, are the triggers for its first conscious experience of life. This, too, we shall know one day.

Critical Thinking

1. When does consciousness begin in life?
2. What would you imagine consciousness is like in young infants? What is their mental world like?
3. Why are physiological and neurological measures important in the study of early consciousness?

Create Central

www.mhhe.com/createcentral

Internet References

Healthy Child Healthy World
http://healthychild.org/?gclid=CjgKEAjw2pSdBRCc5Or_
vuWw7TgSJAA5txZgfxTdj5xF4izhqVp0TNnXgHbvYdd4LGpz7Rrt6l_
kXPD_BwE

States of Consciousness in Newborns
http://www.healthychildren.org/English/ages-stages/baby/Pages/States-of-
Consciousness-in-Newborns.aspx

The Riddle of Consciousness

http://www.newyorker.com/online/blogs/elements/2013/05/the-riddle-of-consciousness.html

When Does Consciousness Arise in Human Babies?

http://www.scientificamerican.com/article/when-does-consciousness-arise/

CHRISTOF KOCH is chief scientific officer at the Allen institute for Brain Science in Seattle. He serves on *Scientific American Mind's* board of advisers.

Article   Prepared by: Ellen Junn, *California State University, Dominguez Hills*

Do Babies Learn from Baby Media?

JUDY S. DELOACHE ET AL.

Learning Outcomes

After reading this article, you will be able to:

- Explain the research design used to determine whether baby videos affect development.

- Advise new parents on whether baby videos are worth the money and hope invested in them.

One of the most remarkable marketing phenomena of recent history was ignited by the 1997 release of the first Baby Einstein video (The Baby Einstein Co., Littleton, CO), which was followed by a host of other videos and DVDs designed and marketed specifically for infants and very young children. American parents alone spend hundreds of millions of dollars yearly on these products, with the Baby Einstein series leading in popularity and sales worldwide.

Most companies that market these DVDs feature quotes from parents touting the virtues of the company's products. In these testimonials on websites and in advertisements, parents frequently mention the remarkable degree of attention that children pay to the DVDs (as well as the fact that their children's absorption in the DVDs enables them to get household chores done and even take the occasional shower). Prominently featured are parent testimonials that their children learn a great deal from watching infant DVDs. Our own experience with parents of young children has led us to suspect that a substantial proportion believe that infants benefit from commercial media products, and recent research indicates that 40 percent of mothers of young children believe that their children learn from television (Rideout, 2007).

But how well do infants actually learn from visual media? Because development typically proceeds at a very rapid pace in the first years of life, parents may misattribute ordinary developmental progress to their children's media exposure. For example, on one commercial website, a parent reported that her 18-month-old child had very few words until she

started watching one of the company's videos, at which point her vocabulary "suddenly blossomed." However, a very well-documented phenomenon in early language development is the "word spurt," a rapid increase in the acquisition of new words during the second year of life (e.g., Benedict, 1979; Goldfield & Reznick, 1990). It would be easy for parents to misattribute their children's sudden linguistic advances to recent video experience.

Although several empirical studies have examined the relation between early television viewing and a variety of outcome measures, most have been large-scale surveys yielding correlational data (e.g., Rideout, Vandewater, & Wartella, 2003; Schmidt, Rich, Rifas-Shiman, Oken, & Taveras, 2009; Zimmerman, Christakis, & Meltzoff, 2007). Only a relatively small number of laboratory studies have examined specific aspects of young children's interaction with visual media (see Anderson & Pemipek, 2005; DeLoache & Chiong, 2009).

Further, only a few of those studies have specifically focused on infants' *learning* from video. In one such study (Kuhl, Tsao, & Liu, 2003), 9-month-olds from English-speaking families watched several presentations, either live or video, of an adult speaking Mandarin. A month later, the researchers tested whether this exposure had prolonged the infants' sensitivity to the Mandarin speech sounds. Only children whose Mandarin exposure had occurred in live interactions showed any impact of that experience.

Laboratory studies of infants' imitation of simple actions presented on video have established that 12- to 30-month-olds are able to reproduce a modest number of observed actions (e.g., Barr & Hayne, 1999; Hayne, Herbert, & Simcock, 2003; McCall, Parke, & Kavanaugh, 1977). Imitation is substantially better, however, when children experience the same demonstrations live.

Young children's word learning from commercial television has also been examined. A large-scale parent survey reported a negative correlation between vocabulary size and television exposure: For every hour of baby media that infants between 8 and 16 months of age watched on their own, they were reported to know 6 to 8 fewer words (Zimmerman et al., 2007). Krcmar, Grela, and Lin (2007) obtained similar results in a laboratory study, in which children under 22 months of age learned few object names presented on a clip from a Tele-tubbies television episode.

In a recent experimental investigation of early learning from video, Robb, Richert, and Wartella (2009) assessed word learning from home viewing of a commercial DVD designed to teach words to young children. According to parent reports, the 12- to 15-month-old participants learned relatively few of the words featured on the DVD: Children who had substantial exposure to it performed no better than did those with none. These results are intriguing, but the fact that the primary data were parent reports is of some concern.

Accordingly, we conducted an experiment using objective testing to directly examine the extent to which infants learn from a very popular commercial infant DVD promoted to foster word learning. Six aspects of the study were designed to ensure a highly valid assessment of the potential for early learning from video: (a) The entire experiment was conducted in the children's own homes. (b) The conditions mimicked everyday situations in which young children view videos. (c) A best-selling video was used. (d) The children received extensive exposure to the video. (e) They were tested for their understanding of the specific words featured on the video. (f) The tester was blind to the condition to which each child had been randomly assigned.

Method

Participants

Participants were 72 infants between 12 and 18 months of age ($M = 14.7$ months). They were recruited from a large metropolitan area and a small city. The sample was predominantly White and middle-class. None of the infants had had any exposure to the target DVD. Eighteen children (including approximately equal numbers of girls and boys) were randomly assigned to each of four conditions.

Materials

A best-selling commercial DVD designed and marketed for infants from "12 months of age and up" was used in the research. The 39-min DVD depicts a variety of scenes of a house and yard. A voice labels common household objects, each of which is named three times, with several minutes intervening between the repetitions of a given label. In addition, during the first and last labeling of a given object, a person is shown producing a manual sign for the object.

Conditions

In the three experimental conditions, the experimenter made three home visits to each family. During the first visit, the experimenter gave detailed oral and written instructions to the parents. The experimental conditions included two video conditions: video with interaction and video with no interaction. In both of these conditions, parents gave their children substantial experience with the DVD in their own homes over 4 weeks. To ensure that they followed the instructions, we asked them to complete a daily log of their child's experience with the video. Parents in the parent-teaching (non-video) condition estimated how often they had attempted to teach their children the target words. On the second and third home visits in all three of these conditions, the experimenter checked to make sure the parents had been following the protocol.

In the *video-with-interaction condition,* the child and a parent watched the DVD together at least five times a week over a 4-week period, for a total of 10 or more hours of viewing time in 20 or more viewing episodes. (Some advertisements for baby videos recommend that parents watch with their children.) Parents were instructed to interact with their child in whatever way seemed natural to them while viewing the video. This condition mimicked the common everyday experience of young children and parents watching television together.

In the *video-with-no-interaction* condition, the children watched the video alone, but had the same total amount of exposure to it as did the children in the video-with-interaction condition. (The parents were almost always in the room with their infants, but were not watching television with them.) This condition mimicked another common situation, in which young children watch television on their own while their parents are nearby but engaged in other activities.

In the *parent-teaching* condition, the children were not exposed to the video at all. Instead, the parents were given a list of the 25 words featured on the video and were instructed simply to "try to teach your child as many of these words as you can in whatever way seems natural to you."

The fourth condition, in which there was no intervention, was the control condition. It provided a baseline of normal vocabulary growth against which performance in the three intervention groups could be compared.

Testing

During the initial home visit, each child was tested for knowledge of 13 of the 25 words featured on the video in order to establish an individualized set of target words for that child. (As Table S1 in the Supplemental Material available online shows, children in the target age range perform around or below chance when tested for their knowledge of the majority of these words.) On each of 13 trials, the child was shown a pair of replica objects—a target representing an object featured in the video (e.g., clock, table, tree) and a distractor that did not appear in the video (e.g., fan, plate, fence). The experimenter named the target and asked the child to point to the appropriate object (e.g., "Can you show me the table?").

The names of the objects that a child failed to identify became that child's individualized set of target words. The number of target words ranged from 5 to 12; the mean number (6.4–6.9) did not differ across the four groups.

On the final visit, the child's knowledge of his or her target words was tested to determine how much word learning had taken place over the 4 weeks. The testing was conducted in the same way as in the initial visit, except that two trials were given for each of the child's target words, with the words presented in one order for the first set of trials and in the reverse order for the second. To be credited with knowing a word, the child had to choose the correct object on both trials; this criterion minimized the likelihood that children would be counted as knowing a word after simply guessing correctly. Parents in the video conditions completed a brief questionnaire concerning their and their child's experience with the video.

Results

Figure 1 shows the percentage of their target words that the children got correct on the posttest. Only the performance of the parent-teaching group was above chance ($p < .05$). The result of primary importance is clear: Children who had extensive exposure to a popular infant video over a full month, either with a parent or alone, did not learn any more new words than did children with no exposure to the video at all.

The absence of learning from experience with the video was not due to lack of attention to it. Representative comments from the logs of parents whose children were in the video groups include the following: "She was practically glued to the screen today"; "She was very quiet today—stared intently at the screen and ignored me when I asked her to talk"; "She loves the blasted thing. It's crack for babies!"

As Figure 1 shows, performance was highest in the parent-teaching group—those children who had no exposure to the video, but whose parents had attempted to teach them new words during everyday interactions. Preliminary examination of the individual scores indicated that the data were not normally distributed, so a median test was performed on the proportion of target words that the children in the four conditions identified on the posttest. There was a significant overall difference among the groups, $\chi^2 (3, N = 72) = 10.03$, $p < .05$. Post hoc tests indicated that the performance of the parent-teaching group was significantly better than that of all three of the other groups—video-with-interaction group: $\chi^2 (1, N = 36) = 4.0$, $p < .05$; video-with-no-interaction group: $\chi^2 (1, N = 36) = 11.11$, $p = .001$; and control group: $\chi^2 (1, N = 36) = 4.0$, $p < .05$. Neither of the video conditions differed from the control condition. Thus, significantly more learning occurred in the context of everyday parent–child interactions than in front of television screens.

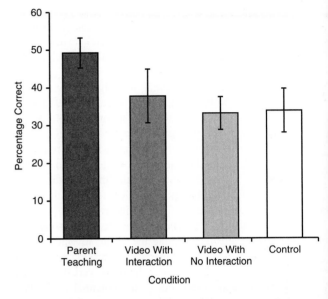

Figure 1 Children's mean performance on the posttest as a function of group. Each child was tested on an individualized set of target words. Error bars represent standard errors of the mean.

Finally, the parents' assessment of how much their children had learned from the DVD was unrelated to the children's performance on the posttest: Children whose parents thought that they had learned a substantial amount from their experience with the DVD performed no better than did children of less sanguine parents. There was, however, a significant correlation ($r = .64$, $p < .01$) between parents' own liking for the DVD and their estimate of how much their children had learned: The more a parent liked the DVD, the more he or she believed the child had learned from it.

Discussion

The results of this study provide a clear answer to our original question: Infants between 12 and 18 months of age learned very little from a highly popular media product promoted for this age group. Even with the substantial amount of exposure that they had to the video, the infants learned only a few of the words featured on it. Because great care was taken to ensure that the video-viewing conditions were as natural as possible, the results should be generalizable to young children's everyday experience.

These results are consistent with a body of theory and research that has established that very young children often fail to use information communicated to them via symbolic media, including pictures, models, and video (e.g., DeLoache, 2004; Troseth, Pierroutsakos, & DeLoache, 2004). For example,

2-year-olds who watch a live video of an adult hiding a desirable toy in the room next-door fail to find the toy when encouraged to search for it immediately afterward (Troseth, 2003a, 2003b; Troseth & DeLoache, 1998). This and related results indicate that infants and very young children have difficulty understanding the relation between what they see on a screen and the real world.

An additional finding from this experiment is directly relevant to the possibility that parents may misattribute normal developmental progress to their infants' video exposure. Parents who had a favorable attitude toward the DVD thought that their children had learned more from it than did parents who were less positively disposed to the DVD. There was, in fact, no difference in how many words were learned by the children of these two groups of parents. This result suggests that much of the enthusiasm expressed in parent testimonials about baby video products is misplaced.

In summary, the research reported here supports two important conclusions. First, parents whose infants have experience with baby videos tend to misattribute normal developmental change to that experience, thereby overestimating the impact of the videos on their children's development. Second, the degree to which babies actually learn from baby videos is negligible.

References

Anderson, D.R., & Pempek, T.A. (2005). Television and very young children. *American Behavioral Scientist, 48,* 505–522.

Barr, R., & Hayne, H. (1999). Developmental changes in imitation from television during infancy. *Child Development, 70,* 1067–1081.

Benedict, H. (1979). Early lexical development: Comprehension and production. *Journal of Child Language, 6,* 183–200.

DeLoache, J.S. (2004). Becoming symbol-minded. *Trends in Cognitive Sciences, 8,* 66–70.

DeLoache, J.S., & Chiong, C. (2009). Babies and baby media. *American Behavioral Scientist, 52,* 1115–1135.

Goldfield, B.A., & Reznick, J.S. (1990). Early lexical acquisition: Rate, content, and the vocabulary spurt. *Journal of Child Language, 17,* 171–184.

Hayne, H., Herbert, J., & Simcock, G. (2003). Imitation from television by 24- and 30-month-olds. *Developmental Science, 6,* 254–261.

Krcmar, M., Grela, B., & Lin, K. (2007). Can toddlers learn vocabulary from television? An experimental approach. *Media Psychology, 10,* 41–63.

Kuhl, P.K., Tsao, F.M., & Liu, H.M. (2003). Foreign-language experience in infancy: Effects of short-term exposure and social interaction on phonetic learning. *Proceedings of the National Academy of Sciences USA, 100,* 9096–9101.

McCall, R.B., Parke, R.D., & Kavanaugh, R.D. (1977). Imitation of live and televised models by children one to three years of age. *Monographs of the Society for Research in Child Development, 42*(5, Serial No. 173).

Rideout, V. (2007). *Parents, children, and media.* Menlo Park, CA: Henry J. Kaiser Family Foundation.

Rideout, V.J., Vandewater, E.A., & Wartella, E.A. (2003). *Zero to six: Electronic media in the lives of infants, toddlers and preschoolers.* Menlo Park, CA: Henry J. Kaiser Family Foundation.

Robb, M., Richert, R., & Wartella, E. (2009). Just a talking book? Word learning from watching baby videos. *British Journal of Developmental Psychology, 27,* 27–45.

Schmidt, M.E., Rich, M., Rifas-Shiman, S.L., Oken, E., & Taveras, E.M. (2009). Television viewing in infancy and child cognition at 3 years of age in a US cohort. *Pediatrics, 123,* 370–375.

Troseth, G.L. (2003a). Getting a clear picture: Young children's understanding of a televised image. *Developmental Science, 6,* 247–253.

Troseth, G.L. (2003b). TV guide: 2-year-olds learn to use video as a source of information. *Developmental Psychology, 39,* 140–150.

Troseth, G.L., & DeLoache, J.S. (1998). The medium can obscure the message: Young children's understanding of video. *Child Development, 69,* 950–965.

Troseth, G.L., Pierroutsakos, S.L., & DeLoache, J.S. (2004). From the innocent to the intelligent eye: The early development of pictorial competence. In R.V. Kail (Ed.), *Advances in child development and behavior* (Vol. 32, pp. 1–35). New York, NY: Academic Press.

Zimmerman, F.J., Christakis, D.A., & Meltzoff, A. (2007). Television and DVD/video viewing in children younger than 2 years. *Archives of Pediatric & Adolescent Medicine, 69,* 473–479.

Critical Thinking

1. Why might parents be so inclined to buy educational videos for their babies? Are some parents more likely to buy them than others? What findings from the research in the article suggest that parents are likely to believe the videos work, even when they don't?

2. Describe some strengths of the experimental design in this study. How did the researchers determine that children's vocabulary didn't improve due to any type of video? How did the researchers create the "parent teaching" condition?

3. Does this article prove to you that educational baby videos are not beneficial for all aspects of infant development, or just some? What are some other infant outcomes that could be studied to learn if educational videos have an effect on behaviors other than vocabulary?

Create Central

www.mhhe.com/createcentral

Internet References

Valley PBS Educational Videos for Kids

http://www.valleypbs.org/kids/index.php?gclid=CjwKEAjwiumdBRDZy vKvqb_6mkUSJABDyYOza1D4vBUGqMPIkJkm 0VVubSY02fQ6ZZGPR1hwa2nBZxoC3JTw_wcB

WatchLearnKnow.org

http://www.watchknowlearn.org/

YouTube Educational Videos for Kids

https://www.youtube.com/show/kidseducationalvideos

Supplemental Material—Additional supporting information may be found at http://pss.sagepub.com/content/by/supplemental-data

Article   Prepared by: Chris J. Boyatzis, *Bucknell University*

The Power of Talking to Your Baby

TINA ROSENBERG

Learning Outcomes

After reading this article, you will be able to:

- Describe the important study by Hart and Risley on the role of parents' conversation in child language development.

- Explain the training program Providence Talks and its goals.

By the time a poor child is 1 year old, she has most likely already fallen behind middle-class children in her ability to talk, understand and learn. The gap between poor children and wealthier ones widens each year, and by high school it has become a chasm. American attempts to close this gap in schools have largely failed, and a consensus is starting to build that these attempts must start long before school—before preschool, perhaps even before birth.

There is no consensus, however, about what form these attempts should take, because there is no consensus about the problem itself. What is it about poverty that limits a child's ability to learn? Researchers have answered the question in different ways: Is it exposure to lead? Character issues like a lack of self-control or failure to think of future consequences? The effects of high levels of stress hormones? The lack of a culture of reading?

A poor child is likely to hear millions fewer words at home than a child from a professional family. And the disparity matters.

Another idea, however, is creeping into the policy debate: that the key to early learning is talking—specifically, a child's exposure to language spoken by parents and caretakers from birth to age 3, the more the better. It turns out, evidence is showing, that the much-ridiculed stream of parent-to-child baby talk—*Feel Teddy's nose! It's so soft! Cars make noise— look, there's a yellow one! Baby feels hungry? Now Mommy is opening the refrigerator!*—is very, very important. (So put those smartphones away!)

The idea has been successfully put into practice a few times on a small scale, but it is about to get its first large-scale test, in Providence, R.I., which last month won the $5 million grand prize in Bloomberg Philanthropies' Mayors Challenge, beating 300 other cities for best new idea. In Providence, only one in three children enter school ready for kindergarten reading. The city already has a network of successful programs in which nurses, mentors, therapists and social workers regularly visit pregnant women, new parents and children in their homes, providing medical attention and advice, therapy, counseling and other services. Now Providence will train these home visitors to add a new service: creating family conversation.

The Providence Talks program will be based on research by Betty Hart and Todd R. Risley at the University of Kansas, who in 1995 published a book, *Meaningful Differences in the Everyday Experience of Young American Children.* Hart and Risley were studying how parents of different socioeconomic backgrounds talked to their babies. Every month, the researchers visited the 42 families in the study and recorded an hour of parent–child interaction. They were looking for things like how much parents praised their children, what they talked about, whether the conversational tone was positive or negative. Then they waited till the children were 9, and examined how they were doing in school. In the meantime, they transcribed and analyzed every word on the tapes—a process that took six years. "It wasn't until we'd collected our data that we realized that the important variable was how much talking the parents were doing," Risley told an interviewer later.

All parents gave their children directives like "Put away your toy!" or "Don't eat that!" But interaction was more likely to stop there for parents on welfare, while as a family's income and educational levels rose, those interactions were more likely to be just the beginning.

The disparity was staggering. Children whose families were on welfare heard about 600 words per hour. Working-class children heard 1,200 words per hour, and children from professional families heard 2,100 words. By age 3, a poor child would have heard 30 million fewer words in his or her home environment than a child from a professional family. And the disparity mattered: the greater the number of words children heard from their parents or caregivers before they were 3, the higher their IQ and the better they did in school. TV talk not only didn't help, it was detrimental.

Hart and Risley later wrote that children's level of language development starts to level off when it matches that of their parents—so a language deficit is passed down through generations. They found that parents talk much more to girls than to boys (perhaps because girls are more sociable, or because it is Mom who does most of the care, and parents talk more to children of their gender). This might explain why young, poor boys have particular trouble in school. And they argued that the disparities in word usage correlated so closely with academic success that kids born to families on welfare do worse than professional-class children *entirely* because their parents talk to them less. In other words, if everyone talked to their young children the same amount, there would be no racial or socio-economic gap at all. (Some other researchers say that while word count is extremely important, it can't be the only factor.)

While we do know that richer, more educated parents talk much more to their children than poorer and less educated ones, we don't know exactly why. A persuasive answer comes from Meredith Rowe, now an assistant professor at the University of Maryland. She found that poor women were simply unaware that it was important to talk more to their babies—no one had told them about this piece of child development research. Poorer mothers tend to depend on friends and relatives for parenting advice, who may not be up on the latest data. Middle-class mothers, on the other hand, get at least some of their parenting information from books, the Internet and pediatricians. Talking to baby has become part of middle-class culture; it seems like instinct, but it's not.

If you haven't heard of Hart and Risley's work, you are not alone—and you may be wondering why. These findings should have created a policy whirlwind: Here was a revolutionary way to reduce inequities in school achievement that seemed *actually possible*. How hard could it be to persuade poor parents to talk to their children more?

Very hard, it turned out—because there was no practical way to measure how much parents talk. Each hour of recording took many hours to transcribe and classify: to count the words uttered near a child and attribute them to a parent, the main child, a sibling, someone else or a TV. The cost was prohibitive.

"The only thing researchers could do was to ask the parent if they were talking a lot," said Jill Gilkerson, the language research director of the Lena Research Foundation, which develops technology for the study and treatment of language delay. "But you need an objective evaluation. Asking anyone to observe their own behavior with no reference point is completely useless." Without measurement, parents who did try new things couldn't know whether they were helpful. Hart and Risley's research languished.

What has revived it is the technology and measurement practices developed by Lena, which stands for Language Environment Analysis. A child wears clothing with a special pocket for a voice recorder that can unobtrusively record 16 continuous hours—plenty of time for the family to forget it's there and converse normally. The analysis is done by speech-recognition software, which can count and source words uttered, count conversational turns (one party says something and the other responds) and weed out background noise and TV. For privacy, the recorder can encrypt the actual speech and delete the speech after it is counted. And a family can hit the "erase" button whenever it wants.

Lena's system came out five years ago and is now being used in about 200 universities and research hospitals—with deaf children, autistic children and children developing normally. The first studies are only now being published.

The studies most relevant to Providence Talks come from two researchers. Gilkerson gave the recorder to 120 families, who used it and viewed the reports once a week for 10 weeks. Of those families, 27 started out below the baseline. Even with no coaching at all, over the 10 weeks their daily word average rose from about 8,000 to about 13,000—an increase of 55 percent. (The paper was presented at a conference, but not yet published.)

More recently, Dana Suskind, a pediatric cochlear implant surgeon at the University of Chicago who founded the school's Thirty Million Words project, did a study with 17 nannies in Chicago. Each attended a workshop on the importance of talk, strategies for increasing it, and how to use the Lena recorder. Then they used it once a week for six weeks. Suskind found that the nannies increased the number of words they used by 32 percent and the number of conversational turns by 25 percent.

Suskind has also done a randomized controlled trial with low-income mothers on Chicago's South Side—not yet published, but with good results: she said that parents asked if they could keep getting reports on their number of words even after the study finished.

All these studies were small, short-term and limited in scope. "One thing is to say we can change adult language behavior," Suskind said. "Another thing is to show that it is sustainable, and that it impacts child outcomes."

Providence has the money to be more ambitious. The city plans to begin enrolling families in January 2014, and hopes to eventually reach about 2,000 new families each year, said Mayor Angel Taveras. It will most likely work with proven home-visitation programs like the Nurse-Family Partnership. The visitors will show poor families with very young children how to use the recorders and ask them to record one 16-hour day each month.

Every month they will return to share information about the results and specific strategies for talking more: how do you tell your baby about your day? What's the best way to read to your toddler? They will also talk about community resources, like read-aloud day at the library. And they will work with the family to set goals for next month. The city also hopes to recruit some of the mothers and fathers as peer educators.

Taveras, who was raised by a single mother, an immigrant from the Dominican Republic, chose the program because of the role Head Start played in his own life. At Harvard, he found that his roommate and several friends were also Head Start babies. "It did and still does have a big impact," he said. "The research on the gap that exists is pretty startling in some ways. But this is something we can address with different strategies. We have an opportunity to level the playing field."

Critical Thinking

1. What are some differences based on social class in how parents talk with their children?
2. Based on the information in this article, what advice would you give family members or friends who have an infant or toddler?

3. What are some different outcomes that researchers could measure to determine if programs such as Providence Talks are effective?

Create Central

www.mhhe.com/createcentral

Internet References

Kids Health
http://kidshealth.org/parent/growth/communication/not_talk.html

Public Broadcasting Network: Speak Parentese, Not Baby Talk
http://www.pbs.org/parents/child-development/baby-and-toddler/baby-talk-speaking-parentese

Talking Point
http://www.talkingpoint.org.uk

The Hanen Centre
http://www.hanen.org/Helpful-Info/Parent-Tips.aspx

TINA ROSENBERG won a Pulitzer Prize for her book The Haunted Land: Facing Europe's Ghosts after Communism. She is a former editorial writer for The Times and the author, most recently, of Join the Club: How Peer Pressure Can Transform the World and the World War II spy story e-book *D for Deception.*

Article   Prepared by: Ellen Junn, *California State University, Dominguez Hills*

9 Ways to Support Your Child's Creativity

Margarita Tartakovsky

Learning Outcomes

After reading this article, you will be able to:

- Analyze why it is sometimes good for children to be "bored" and become acquainted with the power that comes in giving children "free time."

- Understand how subtle supports from parents can assist in fostering children's creativity.

- Identify multiple benefits in enhanced cognitive and social-emotional development by increasing children's opportunities for creativity.

- Learn simple methods for parents to use in supporting their children's creativity.

Kids are natural innovators with powerful imaginations. And creativity offers a bounty of intellectual, emotional, and even health benefits.

One study found that kids' imaginations helped them cope better with pain. Creativity also helps kids be more confident, develop social skills, and learn better. Below, three experts share how parents can encourage their kids' creativity.

1. **Designate a space for creating.** Carving out a space where your child can be creative is important, said Pam Allyn, executive director of Lit World and Lit Life and the author of many books, including *Your Child's Writing Life: How to Inspire Confidence, Creativity, and Skill at Every Age.*

   But this doesn't mean having a fancy playroom. It could be a tiny corner with a sack of LEGOs or a box of your old clothes for playing dress-up, she said. Allyn

has seen creativity flourish in the most cramped spaces, including the slums of Kenya. The key is for your child to feel like they have power over their space, she said.

2. **Keep it simple.** Just like you don't need to create an elaborate play area, you don't need the latest and greatest toys either. Child educational psychologist Charlotte Reznick, PhD, suggested keeping simple games and activities. For instance, she plays LEGOs with her child clients. But instead of following instructions, the kids let the wheels of their imagination spin and build what they want.

3. **Allow for "free time."** It's also important to give your child unstructured time, Allyn said. Spend a few hours at home without activities scheduled, so your child can just putter around and play, she said.

4. **Help your kids activate their senses.** Expose your kids to the world so they can use all of their senses, according to Reznick, who's also an associate clinical professor of psychology at UCLA and author of *The Power of Your Child's Imagination: How to Transform Stress and Anxiety into Joy and Success.*

   Again, this doesn't mean costly or complicated trips. Take them to the library, museum, and outdoors, she said. Ask them to imagine what traveling to faraway places, such as the African safari, might be like, Reznick said. What animals would they encounter? What would the safari look like? What would it smell like? What noises would the animals make?

5. **Discuss creativity.** Ask your kids when they come up with their best ideas or have their most creative moments, Allyn said. If it's in the car while getting to soccer practice, honor that by keeping a notebook, iPad, or even a tape recorder handy, she said.

6. **Cultivate creative critical thinking.** As your kids get older, ask them how they approach certain problems and how they might do things differently, Reznick said. Have your kids brainstorm their ideas on paper or use mind-mapping, she said.

7. **Avoid managing.** "Children have an amazing innate ability to be creative when they play freely on their own, and unfortunately, the act of overparenting dampens or even wipes out that innate ability," according to Mike Lanza of Playborhood.com and author of the upcoming book *Playborhood: Turn Your Neighborhood into a Place for Play.* So it's important to figure out how to facilitate your child's creativity without managing it, he said.

   Lanza and his wife don't hover over their three boys as they play, and they also don't enroll them in many activities. Recently, Lanza's oldest son invented an intricate game of marbles with its own complex rules. (As Lanza said, he doesn't really understand it.) He's even adjusted the rules so that his younger brother can win once in a while and the game continues.

   Kids learn a lot by playing on their own. Lanza cited Jean Piaget's *The Moral Judgment of the Child,* where he discusses "how children develop moral sensibilities and reasoning through playing marbles on their own."

   He also mentioned Alison Gopnik's *The Philosophical Baby,* which describes how babies' brains work. Gopnik asserts that babies are born experimental scientists that take in scrolls of information by trying things on their own and tweaking as they go. Being more hands-off helps kids figure out how to problem-solve and create in their own unique ways.

8. **Help kids pursue their passions.** Pay attention to your child's interests and make these materials and activities available to them. Lanza's oldest son is especially interested in geology, so Lanza buys him books on the topic along with rock samples.

9. **Take the time for your own creativity.** Since kids learn from watching their parents, be creative, too, Reznick said. Join your child when they're drawing or building or coloring. One little girl wanted her parents to help her build an art jungle in the living room, she said. At first mom was hesitant. But this provided a great opportunity for the family to bond, and everyone had a fun time.

Critical Thinking

1. The article mentions that a key to creativity is allowing children to feel like they have power over their space. How do you think empowerment leads to creativity?

2. The ninth suggestion is that parent's take the time to foster their own creative sides. Should parents use the advice from this article to practice what they are preaching?

Create Central

www.mhhe.com/createcentral

Internet References

Brainy-Child.com
   http://www.brainy-child.com/article/child-creativity.shtml
Center for Childhood Creativity.org
   http://www.centerforchildhoodcreativity.org/research/
Psychology Today.com
   http://www.psychologytoday.com/blog/freedom-learn/201209/children-s-freedom-has-declined-so-has-their-creativity

MARGARITA TARTAKOVSKY, MS, is an Associate Editor at Psych Central and blogs regularly about eating and self-image issues on her own blog, Weightless.

Article Prepared by: Chris J. Boyatzis, *Bucknell University*

Recess—It's Indispensable!

Learning Outcomes

After reading this article, you will be able to:

- Design an argument for the importance of recess in children's development.
- Describe statistical evidence on trends in the decline of recess periods at American schools.

The demise of recess in many elementary schools—and of outdoor play in general—is an issue of great concern to many members of the Play, Policy, and Practice Interest Forum. If there is any doubt that this is a problem, pick up publications as diverse as *Sports Illustrated, Pediatrics,* the *New York Times,* or your local newspaper to read about it.

Most of us remember recess as an important part of the school day. It was a time to be outdoors; to organize our own games; to play on the swings, slides, and other playground equipment; or just to hang out with friends.

In contrast, children today are likely to have 10 to 15 minutes of outdoor playtime during the school day, if they are lucky. No wonder there is an upswing in childhood obesity and an increase in childhood heart disease and type 2 diabetes. No wonder teachers are concerned about a generation of children who can't entertain themselves, have social difficulties, and are fidgety and off task in class.

Cutting Back on Recess

In the late 1980s, some school systems began cutting back on recess to allow more instructional time. The trend accelerated with the passage of No Child Left Behind in 2001 and was particularly widespread in urban schools with high numbers of children from marginalized populations (Jarrett 2003; Roth et al. 2003; NCES 2006).

The arguments against recess involved both academics and safety issues. Some administrators believed their school's test

How Many Children Have Recess?

How many children are deprived of recess every day? Although we don't know exactly, statistics reveal a troubling trend.

A 2005 National Center for Education Statistics (NCES 2006) survey found that

- 7 percent of first-graders and 8 percent of third-graders never had recess; and
- 14 percent of first-graders and 15 percent of third-graders had only 1 to15 minutes of recess a day.

According to official figures provided by school systems, since the enactment of No Child Left Behind,

- 20 percent of the school systems have decreased time for recess, averaging cuts of 50 minutes per week (Center on Education Policy 2008).

scores would improve if children spent more time on school work. Some feared lawsuits from playground injuries.

A number of school systems have a recess policy; others allow the principals or teachers to determine whether the children go out to play. Officially having recess and *actually* having recess are two different issues. A recent study in *Pediatrics* (Barros, Silver, & Stein 2009), using a national data set of 11,000 children, found that 30 percent of third graders had fewer than 15 minutes of recess a day. Recess time is often cut because of academic pressures or as punishment.

Recess's Many Benefits

To make recommendations for policy changes, we, as members of the Play, Policy, and Practice Interest Forum, spent the past decade investigating what research says about the need

> **We found no research to support administrators' assumptions that test scores required by No Child Left Behind could be improved by keeping children in the classroom all day.**

for recess. On the one hand, we found no research to support administrators' assumptions that test scores required by No Child Left Behind could be improved by keeping children in the classroom all day. On the other hand, there is considerable research to suggest that recess has many benefits for children in the cognitive, social-emotional, and physical domains. Jarrett (2002) gives a summary of many of the research studies that found the following cognitive, social-emotional, and physical benefits of recess:

Cognitive

- Children are less fidgety and more on-task when they have recess, and children with ADHD (attention deficit/hyperactivity syndrome) are among those who benefit most.

The Demographics of Recess

A nationwide study on how first through fifth grade children spend their time at school found that on a randomly selected day, 21 percent of children did not have any recess (Roth et al. 2003). The study noted demographic disparities:

- 39 percent of African American students versus 15 percent of White students did not have recess;
- 44 percent of children living below the poverty line versus 17 percent of those above the poverty line were deprived of recess; and
- 25 percent of the children scoring below the mean on a standardized test versus 15 percent of those above the mean did not have recess.

An NCES survey (2006) also found disparities, with rural schools and affluent schools more likely to have recess. A 2003 survey of Georgia school systems (unpublished data collected by Jarrett and colleagues) found the same patterns but with 25 percent of kindergartners having no recess.

- Research on memory and attention shows that recall is improved when learning is spaced out rather than concentrated. Recess provides breaks during which the brain can "regroup."
- Brain research shows a relationship between physical activity and the development of brain connections.
- A school system that devoted a third of the day to nonacademic activities (art, music, physical activity) improved attitudes and fitness and slightly increased test scores, in spite of spending less time on academics.

Social-Emotional

- On the playground, children exercise leadership, teach games to one another, take turns, and learn to resolve conflicts.
- In a free choice situation, children learn negotiation skills in order to keep the play going.
- On supervised playgrounds, particularly where children are taught games and conflict resolution skills, there is little fighting (see "Reconstructing Recess: One Principal's Story").
- Intervention programs during recess can successfully improve social skills.

Physical

- Recess before rather than after lunch leads to healthier eating.
- Children who are active during the day are more active after school, whereas children who are sedentary during the day tend to remain sedentary after school (couch potato syndrome).

Children's activity levels are generally higher during recess than during physical education (PE). PE is not seen by the PE teachers or the children as a substitute for recess. Recess and PE serve different purposes. Research also suggests benefits for teachers, even when the teacher is required to supervise on the playground. Recess can help with classroom management:

- Teachers rated children's behavior as better in classes where children had at least 15 minutes of recess (Barros, Silver, & Stein 2009).
- Teachers get to know the children better when supervising them on the playground. This knowledge can be useful in developing curriculum and in preventing bullying.
- Time on the playground is a change of pace for the teacher as well as for the children.

Reconstructing Recess: One Principal's Story

At Watsontown Elementary in central Pennsylvania, a small K-4 school where I am principal, the staff and I noticed conflicts, exclusion, and safety concerns on the playground during recess. We felt strongly that we needed to turn recess around.

We talked extensively and agreed that recess should be respectful, have safe play, include child choice, and encourage all children to participate. We also discussed the teachers' role at recess. We committed to simple, consistent rules—respect for self, others, the play environment, and the play equipment. Teachers brainstormed games that encourage responsibility, cooperation, and communication and made a list of the games to facilitate child choice.

We decided that before recess, children would choose from the list of cooperative games or old standbys—jump rope, hopscotch, four square. Children could also choose not to participate and instead play on their own. Teachers would review the rules and acceptable behaviors for the games before going to the playground ("What does it look like to tag someone?").

With the start of the new school year, we designated the second day Game Day for the staff to demonstrate the games, modeling the behaviors we wanted the children to use and allowing them to practice the skills in a safe environment. In a reflective writing activity at the end of Game Day, most children and teachers wrote about prosocial skills—inclusion, fair play, and teamwork.

Throughout the school year, teachers reinforced the concepts learned on Game Day. They helped children problem solve issues like what to do when teams had unequal skill levels and what happens if a child wants to jump rope but all the jump ropes are in use. Game Day didn't magically eliminate all of the playground concerns, but we now heard students supporting each other during recess.

Interested in reconstructing recess in your school? Here are some thoughts for teachers and administrators:

- Schedule recess every day for primary and elementary level children. Breaks from academics are important, and children need opportunities to practice positive social interactions.
- Agree on basic rules that apply throughout the school building and the day.
- Build a repertoire of games that encourage cooperation and responsibility and avoid conflicts.
- Teach the games using modeling and practice. Reinforce children's prosocial skills throughout the school year.
- Provide enough materials and equipment for several groups of children to play the same game. Help students make choices about which games to play.
- Provide teacher supervision during recess, and encourage the children during play.

—Susan Welteroth (swelteroth@wrsd.org)

Children's Right to Play

We believe that recess is a right, not a privilege. Article 31 of the U.N. Convention on the Rights of the Child (www.unicef.org/crc) recognizes

> The right of the child to rest and leisure, to engage in play and recreational activities appropriate to the age of the child and to participate freely in cultural life and the arts.

We believe that recess, with its fun, movement, and opportunities to socialize through play, is a basic need and that policies against recess, whether made at the school system, school, or teacher level, discriminate against children. Depriving a child of recess as punishment is similar to depriving a child of lunch. It is not only unfair, it is also unhelpful. Just as hungry children cannot concentrate well, children deprived of breaks cannot concentrate well either. Sometimes the most disruptive children need recess the most.

Stand up for Recess!

What can you do? Here are some steps you can take:

- Find out whether the schools in your community have recess, and if so, for how many minutes a day. Do *all* the children get recess?
- Check school playgrounds for safety. The National Program for Playground Safety (NPPS) has helpful online resources (www.playgroundsafety.org). Examine the needs for supervision. Generally, teachers supervise recess; but in some cases, other supervisors are hired.

Critical Thinking

1. What's happening to recess in public schools today? Is it as common or less than it used to be, and why?

2. In what ways is recess good for children? What domains of development does it seem to benefit?

Create Central

www.mhhe.com/createcentral

Internet References

American Academy of Pediatrics
http://pediatrics.aappublications.org/content/131/1/183.full.pdf+html

Early Childhood News.com
http://www.earlychildhoodnews.com/earlychildhood/article_view.aspx?ArticleID=39

USDA Agricultural Research Service
http://www.ars.usda.gov/News/docs.htm?docid=23287

Article Prepared by: Chris J. Boyatzis, *Bucknell University*

Social Awareness + Emotional Skills = Successful Kids

New funding and congressional support are poised to bring the best social and emotional learning research into more classrooms nationwide.

TORI DEANGELIS

Learning Outcomes

After reading this article, you will be able to:

- Explain why social and emotional learning is an important quality for children to possess.

- Describe some school-based programs to enhance childrnen's social and emotional learning.

The sad truth is that most U.S. schools don't foster good mental health or strong connections with friends and nurturing adults. Data show that only 29 percent of sixth- through 12th-grade students report that their schools provide caring, encouraging environments. Another 30 percent of high school students say they engage in high-risk behaviors, such as substance use, sex, violence and even suicide attempts.

For decades, a dedicated group of prevention experts—many of them psychologists—has been trying to improve those statistics through an approach called social and emotional learning, or SEL. They believe that if schools teach youngsters to work well with others, regulate their emotions and constructively solve problems, students will be better equipped to deal with life's challenges, including academic ones.

"It's about creating an environment where a child can learn—because if a child isn't emotionally prepared to learn, he or she is not going to learn," says SEL researcher and program developer Marc Brackett, PhD, head of the Emotional Intelligence Unit at Yale University's Edward Zigler Center in Child Development and Social Policy.

Critics charge that SEL programs are too broad-based and that social and emotional learning shouldn't necessarily fall on teachers' shoulders. Instead, families should oversee their children's social, emotional and character development, they contend. Yet studies show the programs improve mental health and behavior, boost children's social competence, and create more positive school climates. Students who participated in SEL programs gained an average of 11 percentage points more on achievement tests than youngsters who didn't take part in the programs, according to a meta-analysis of 213 studies of SEL programs, in press at Child Development, by prevention experts Joseph A. Durlak, PhD, of Loyola University Chicago; Roger P. Weissberg, PhD, of the University of Illinois at Chicago; and colleagues.

"That's pretty remarkable given how difficult it is to alter achievement test scores," says Mark Greenberg, PhD, director of the Prevention Research Center at Pennsylvania State University and creator of one of the longest-running and most rigorously studied SEL programs, PATHS (Promoting Alternative Thinking Strategies).

Some studies also show major gains long after an SEL program has ended. In the Seattle Social Development Project— a longitudinal study of 808 elementary school children who received a comprehensive SEL intervention in the first through sixth grade starting in 1981—participants reported significantly lower lifetime rates of violence and heavy alcohol use at age 18 than no-intervention controls. In addition, intervention-group students were more likely to complete high school than controls—91 percent compared with 81 percent—and to have lower rates of major depression, post-traumatic stress disorder, anxiety and social phobia at ages 24 and 27. (See the *Archives of Pediatrics and Adolescent Medicine,* Vol. 153, No. 3; Vol. 156, No. 5; and Vol. 159, No. 1).

In a related vein, Greenberg and others are starting to show that the programs affect executive functioning, an ability some researchers think may be even more important than IQ.

"The ability to maintain attention, to shift your set and plan ahead—these are obviously important learning skills that our programs are significantly improving upon," Greenberg says.

Other researchers are starting to examine other untapped areas the programs may be affecting, including health, parenting and even the behavior of children whose parents underwent the original interventions. Researchers are also applying SEL programs abroad, with military families and with special-education populations.

The Tenets of Social and Emotional Learning

Researchers have been studying a version of SEL since the 1970s, but it was first popularized in "Emotional Intelligence," the 1995 best-seller by psychologist Daniel Goleman, PhD. He argued that emotional intelligence can be taught and that schools should teach it systematically.

While SEL programs vary somewhat in design and target different ages, they all work to develop core competencies: self-awareness, social awareness, self-management, relationship skills and responsible decision-making. Instead of focusing on a single negative behavior—such as drug use, sexual risk-taking or aggression, for instance—SEL researchers take a broad-brush approach to tackling these problems. They believe all of these behaviors share common roots: a lack of social and emotional competence, often exacerbated by factors such as family disruption, violent neighborhoods and genetic and biological dispositions. Schools and families can counter these risks, SEL proponents say, by facilitating students' emotional and social skills and providing environments that both nurture and challenge children.

A look at the PATHS program shows how these programs work. Like many SEL programs, it uses easy-to-understand, teacher-led lessons and activities that help students learn to recognize feelings in themselves and others, manage their thoughts and emotions more effectively and solve interpersonal problems. One activity, for instance, has youngsters construct posters resembling a three-color traffic signal. Each signal light represents a different aspect of constructive problem-solving: Red is "stop and calm down," yellow is "go slow and think," and green is "go ahead, try my plan." Children apply this guide to real-life problems, then evaluate how their solutions worked.

Active strategies like this are embedded in a comprehensive program that teachers share in 131 sequential lessons over a seven-year period, from kindergarten to sixth grade. Children don't just get didactic information but have many chances to practice these skills both in and out of the classroom, Greenberg explains.

"Comprehensive SEL programs create many opportunities for children to practice these skills in the challenging situations they face every day in the classroom and on the playground," he says. "They also build caring, safe school climates that involve everyone in the school."

An interesting synergy results when these programs are offered, Greenberg adds. When children are taught these skills, they learn how to foster their own well-being and become more resilient. That, in turn, builds a more positive classroom climate that better engages children in learning. And as they become more absorbed in learning, children are more likely to do better in school.

"Building emotional awareness, self-control and relationship skills are master skills," Greenberg says. "When we nurture them, children do better in all areas of their daily lives, including school."

The programs, however, are far from perfect, critics and proponents say. While a 2005 review shows that about 59 percent of schools use some kind of SEL programming, the quality varies widely, says Weissberg. In fact, the Collaborative for Academic, Social and Emotional Learning, or CASEL—a non-profit organization founded by Goleman in 1994 dedicated to advancing the science and evidence base of SEL and promoting the quality of SEL programs—places only 22 of the nation's several hundred SEL programs (including Greenberg's and Hawkins') on its list of exemplary programs for being well-designed and evidence-based, among other criteria. Researchers also continue to debate whether universal or more targeted curricula are better, since SEL programs tend to have the greatest impact on troubled kids.

Meanwhile, educators are feeling an enormous pressure to have kids do well on standardized testing, even in tight economic times, says Weissberg. "So there are several barriers that make it a challenge to implement SEL programs with high quality and fidelity," he says.

SEL Goes National

That said, more money is pouring into the field, thanks to the positive research findings on social and emotional learning. The NoVo Foundation, a philanthropy headed by Peter and Jennifer Buffett (Peter is investor Warren Buffett's son), has offered $10 million in grants: $3.4 million in research funds and $6.3 million in development funds for CASEL.

Potentially more far-reaching is the Academic, Social, and Emotional Learning Act (H.R. 4223), announced at a CASEL forum in Washington, D.C., in December. The bill, introduced by Rep. Dale Kildee (D-Mich.) and co-sponsored by Rep. Tim Ryan (D-Ohio) and Rep. Judy Biggert (R-Ill.), would authorize the U.S. Department of Education to establish a national SEL training center and provide grants to support evidence-based SEL programs, as well as evaluate their success.

"I don't think I could have imagined that our field would have come this far," says Weissberg, CASEL's president.

In an effort to make the best SEL programming available nationwide, CASEL leaders plan to collaborate with evidence-based SEL providers, work with model school districts, share research to inform federal legislation and state policy and think realistically about how to implement these programs on a broad scale, says Weissberg. If the legislation passes, it should enhance these efforts, he adds.

The December CASEL forum underscored the field's growing clout and psychologists' central role in it, adds APA Chief Executive Officer Norman Anderson, PhD, who attended the meeting. There, psychologists and other SEL researchers and practitioners rubbed elbows with legislators, philanthropists, national media and even some Hollywood celebrities, including Goldie Hawn, who heads her own SEL-related organization.

"This group of experts is doing an outstanding job of moving the SEL model forward and making a real difference in the lives of our children," says Anderson. He is particularly pleased that research is starting to show a link between developing children's resilience and academic performance, he says.

"These efforts represent another bridge between the worlds of psychology and education," Anderson adds. "It's all very exciting."

Critical Thinking

1. Assume you have a close friend who is having problems with a child who is acting out consistently in class with teachers and peers. Describe how you would review, critique and present the data regarding SEL (Social and Emotional Leaning) programs to your friend.

2. Speculate as to whether SEL may differ in its effectiveness rates, depending on factors such as sex of participant, ethnicity, family history and demographics.

Create Central

www.mhhe.com/createcentral

Internet References

Collaborative for Academic, Social, and Emotional Learning (CASEL)

http://www.casel.org

Edutopia.org

http://www.edutopia.org/blog/sel-for-elementary-school-randy-taran

National School Climate Center

http://www.schoolclimate.org/guidelines/teachingandlearning.php

Tori DeAngelis is a writer in Syracuse, N.Y.

Article

Prepared by: Chris J. Boyatzis, *Bucknell University*

Kindergartners Explore Spirituality

The fun thing about studying different beliefs is that . . . they are different.

BEN MARDELL AND MONA M. ABO-ZENA

Learning Outcomes

After reading this article, you will be able to:

- Explain why it may be valuable to have kindergartens open to discussing spirituality with children.

- Describe the project used by this school to foster children's discussion about spirituality.

- Evaluate what worked well and what may have been improved in this school's project.

Max: You know who made flowers? God. Who made clouds? God. That's what my mom told me.

Emily: Just because your mom says he's real doesn't mean he is real.

Robert: Who made the first person on earth?

Max: God.

Emily: Gorillas. People evolved from gorillas and started to lose their hair to be more like people.

Max: God made the first person on Earth. The first people are Adam and Eve. I'm sure God is the one. Gorillas can't talk. They do nothing.

Emily: That's not true.

Max: It is true. Gorillas are not a person that has magic.

These kindergartners are sitting around the snack table, talking. Conversations like this are not uncommon in early childhood classrooms. Young children are actively working to make sense of the world, including what it means when people disagree about deeply held beliefs (many of which originate at home and reflect religious and spiritual values). Early childhood is a time when understandings of differences are formed (Derman-Sparks & Edwards 2010). Guided explorations about differences in beliefs are important because they help children develop healthy attitudes about spiritual plurality, and they cultivate meaningful home–school relations with diverse families.

This article is for early childhood teachers, administrators, and families interested in helping young children develop positive views about diverse spiritual beliefs and the people who embrace them. The article is based on a project in which Max, Emily, Robert, and their 15 classmates studied their own and others' understanding of creation, heaven, and the divine at the Eliot-Pearson Children's School, a lab school at Tufts University in Medford, Massachusetts. The Children's School is an inclusion model early childhood center serving 3-year-olds through second-graders. (At the time of the project, Ben was the kindergarten room's lead teacher. Mona, then a doctoral student in child development, consulted on the project.)

The article is organized around five questions readers may have about the project:

- Why was this project undertaken?
- What did the project involve?
- What did the parents say?
- What did the teachers learn?
- What did the children learn?

Our answers explain why we explored this unusual—and we suspect in many places, taboo—topic, and why we believe teachers should recognize and support children's learning about spirituality, beliefs, and religion.

Why Was This Project Undertaken?

The children's expressed interest led us to a study of beliefs. We were reluctant to undertake this project, unsure about opening up such a potentially controversial subject. This experience has led us to believe that in order to raise citizens who can navigate and contribute to our religiously diverse world, early childhood educators must create safe spaces for children to explore spirituality and differing beliefs (Baumgartner & Buchanan 2010).

In their play and conversations, the kindergartners demonstrated a strong interest in spiritual matters (for example, the conversation between Max, Emily, and Robert). While we noted this interest from the start of the year, we initially made no effort to integrate it into the curriculum. Midway through the year, several children asked directly to study God. The success of the ensuing God Study Group (four children who met for six weeks to pursue this interest) convinced us that it was possible to study beliefs with kindergartners.

It is not just our kindergarten students who are interested in spiritual matters. Many young children are particularly curious about beliefs, making frequent reference to topics with religious and spiritual implications (Coles 1990). Because early childhood is the genesis of knowledge about and dispositions toward differences, it is a good time for guided explorations of different beliefs that can help children develop healthy attitudes toward others and themselves.

> **Many young children are particularly curious about beliefs, making frequent reference to topics with religious and spiritual implications.**

Curricula on religion are supported from multiple perspectives. From an academic perspective, religion is a central component of social studies. From an interfaith perspective, leaders from faith traditions have collaborated to find common ground to guide religiously inclusive school policies, practices, and curricula (Haynes, Thomas, & Ferguson 2007). From the social justice perspective, religion and religious pluralism are essential elements of an anti-bias approach. Hence the wisdom of the NAEYC Early Childhood Program Standards and Accreditation Criteria that call for the acknowledgment and discussion of different beliefs in early childhood settings (NAEYC 2007, criteria 1.A.02, 2.L.03, 7.A.02).

The National Council for the Social Studies explains, "Knowledge about religions is not only characteristic of an educated person, but is also absolutely necessary for understanding and living in a world of diversity" (Haynes, Thomas, & Ferguson 2007, 44). While the study of specific world religions generally occurs in middle and high school, developing the disposition of tolerance is a task for early childhood education. This is particularly important in the United States, the world's most religiously diverse nation (Eck 2002). To help our youngest citizens appreciate and understand one another, we should provide safe places for them to explore spiritual beliefs and differences.

What Did the Project Involve?

During the final two months of the school year, our kindergarten curriculum focuses on one topic that all the children explore together (to view one such capstone project, see "An Example of a Developmentally Appropriate Kindergarten Study" on the CD-ROM that accompanies the third edition of *Developmentally Appropriate Practice* [Copple & Bredekamp 2009]). To guide this project, we use the tool of documentation to listen carefully to children's interests, ideas, and level of engagement to fashion developmentally appropriate activities (Katz & Chard 1989; Mardell 1999; Project Zero & Reggio Children 2000). Children generate questions, solve problems, and create collective products, participating in the "whole game of learning" (Perkins 2009).

The Beliefs Project began with children drawing pictures of their theories and questions (for example, Robert asked, "Why can you not see God? 'Cause God made something, but he doesn't have hands. It's just clear. So who made the first people on the earth? God?"). The children and teachers then discussed these theories and questions among ourselves, interviewed members of the school community and local experts (including a priest, imam, rabbi, and an atheist philosopher) about their beliefs, listened to and then discussed music with spiritual significance, and transformed the dramatic play area into some children's vision of heaven. The children shared what they had learned with their families and school community by each contributing a piece to a class puzzle and describing the piece in a short video.

> **To help our youngest citizens appreciate and understand one another, we should provide safe places for them to explore spiritual beliefs and differences.**

To provide a detailed picture of our teaching practices, we focus on how the children turned the dramatic play area into heaven. The impetus to transform dramatic play had several sources. Play is a core resource for young children's learning (Carlsson-Paige 2008), and for the first few weeks of the Beliefs Project, we had been wondering how to access play to support the children's explorations. At the same time, looking over video and observation notes, we realized that two children with language delays had been having difficulty participating in conversations. These two children were wonderful and committed players, so dramatic play seemed an obvious way to help them engage in the inquiry. And all the children were interested in heaven. In their conversations, questions, and drawings, heaven appeared again and again.

So we invited the children to create their vision of heaven. The process took a week and involved intentionally choreographing individual, small group, and whole class activities. To begin, six children (including the two with language delays) chose to draw their ideas of heaven during exploration time. After a review of the diverse ideas about heaven that the class had encountered, the children drew and chatted for 40 minutes. This in-depth experience helped the children with language difficulties articulate their ideas. As one explained, "I'm making it beautiful. My friend told me how heaven looks."

Children then shared their ideas with their classmates:

Larissa: This is the stairs to get up, and here's a little slide, and you can lie down. And the curtains aren't finished.

Caroline: I think a heart would be the center of heaven.

Emily: I think heaven is a planet like Earth, but you can only go when you are dead. Some people think God is perfect, but if God is perfect, why are there wars? I think there is a good god and a bad god and they fight. And sometimes one wins and sometimes the other wins. I think heaven is nice because you should have what you want when you die. To get into heaven you climb in and slide down, like a playground. Stairs are narrow and hard to get up, so you have to be dead to go. If you're dead, you can slide up.

The next day another group convened. The teacher shared the drawings and comments from the previous day to launch plans for dramatic play. The children built on the playground idea, deciding to add swings. Perhaps because of an association with hearts, it was suggested that there be a lot of red. The group captured their ideas in a collective drawing, which they shared with the whole group to get feedback. The reaction was generally positive, and additional ideas were provided (for example, the need for clouds).

Work days followed. While children could come and go as they chose, the high level of engagement with the project was clear when four children asked to stay inside during recess to work on the dramatic play area. After three intensive days of construction, heaven was opened for play. It was a very popular destination.

After three intensive days of construction, heaven was opened for play. It was a very popular destination.

What Did the Families Say?

The parents were critical allies during the Beliefs Project. They encouraged us to pursue this inquiry, shared conversations they were having with their children, and made pivotal suggestions about the project. This is not surprising. Spiritual questions—religious and nonreligious—occupy a significant part of many adults' thoughts. Families embraced the opportunity to engage in something so important to their children's education. Of course, smooth sailing through such an emotionally charged topic was not guaranteed. The positive outcome we enjoyed was the result of efforts to respect and include all the families' beliefs, and the overall culture of the school.

The teaching team invited families to participate in the project even before its inception. As we considered undertaking this inquiry, we sent out information about our intentions and invited feedback. While generally supportive, parents asked to be kept informed and expressed the desire that certain points of view be represented. During the project we issued weekly newsletters and kept a binder that charted daily activities. Parents were invited to join us in our conversations with a local priest, rabbi, imam, and philosopher, and we held several meetings to discuss the directions of the project.

At one of these meetings, a family raised a concern that the curriculum's name (originally the God Project) was not inclusive; although all families have a belief system, not all of these include a belief in God or a higher being. We acknowledged this concern, and brought it to the children. They unanimously concluded that it would be important to rename the project (to the Beliefs Project) so that no one would feel left out.

Family involvement in the project reflected the level of parent involvement in the school generally and the positive regard for diversity. As one mother reflected, "Eliot-Pearson already has a whole culture of being able to talk about differences. . . . It was very comfortable for children, for parents, [and] for teachers to move into this kind of conversation, to push the frontier a little further. Because we were already so comfortable talking about [differences]."

Of course, it is conceivable that in other contexts families may be opposed to such a project. In such a situation, we recommend working to understand the nature of the opposition, explaining the goals of the project (to further a tolerance of different beliefs, not to teach specific beliefs), and explaining the importance of children participating in such experiences.

At a reunion of the families one year after the project was completed, parents indicated that they could not have imagined such public conversations about religious differences, because they had been raised at a time when such discussions were taboo. They were delighted their children were freed from this restriction. They marveled at young children's ability to engage in deep conversations about religion and beliefs. And they appreciated the potential long-term impact of the project.

What Did the Teachers Learn?

We learned that young children can engage in authentic and civil discussions about beliefs. These kindergartners were curious about their classmates' beliefs. They listened attentively to the views of members of our extended community. They enjoyed trying to make sense of questions that have perplexed humanity from the beginning of time. And we learned that allowing for such conversations in the classroom can help build connections between home and school.

We now believe that early childhood educators need to be proactive and intentional in incorporating issues of religious diversity into classrooms. Here, our foremost advice is to listen. We suspect that conversations that touch on religious and spiritual matters occur in classrooms with more frequency than many adults think. Teachers can model interest and tolerance, provide information about the images and practices that children encounter (for example, the Madonna statue in the yard across from the school playground or why Younnis is going to be absent from school for Eid), and help clarify misconceptions about others' beliefs.

Teachers can model interest and tolerance, provide information about the images and practices that children encounter, and help clarify misconceptions about others' beliefs.

Just as teachers include experiences about cultural and racial diversity in formal curricula, teachers should consider bringing differences in beliefs into classroom conversations. The objective is to support children's explorations of their own questions and learn about the perspectives of others. Listening will alert teachers to the specific interests of their students.

We acknowledge that some teachers may face greater opposition, receive less support, and feel less comfortable in discussing beliefs with young children. Not everyone will feel prepared in undertaking curriculum units on beliefs.

Nevertheless, we believe that these conversations should occur in all early childhood settings. As with other anti-bias topics, tolerance about differences in beliefs is an essential disposition for all children. Teachers should encourage children to ask questions about, discuss, and explore different beliefs whether they attend public or private, secular or religious schools. Parents, teachers, and administrators should discuss a range of developmentally appropriate ways to support open and curious attitudes toward different beliefs and the people who hold them.

As with other anti-bias topics, tolerance about differences in beliefs is an essential disposition for all children.

What Did the Children Learn?

When children are deeply engaged in a topic, they learn in many directions at once (Project Zero & Reggio Children 2000). Participation in the Beliefs Project promoted the children's problem-solving and critical-thinking abilities. It provided authentic experiences in using books and technology to gain information, in discussing and presenting ideas in a group, and in using drawing and writing to express ideas. In Massachusetts, these are among the language arts curriculum standards for kindergarten (Massachusetts Department of Education 2001).

To conclude the project, we helped the children create a video. Each child contributed a drawing of a puzzle piece with a verbal explanation of their thinking about beliefs. Some children discussed heaven while others focused on the big bang. Regardless of the topic, each child demonstrated a high level of commitment to producing quality work. The children drew several drafts, using peer feedback to improve their drawings, and embraced the challenge of explaining their beliefs. For example, one of the children who had difficulty with expressive language explained, "I believe in heaven and God lives in my heart. He acts for all of the children, and all of our prayers. And all the animals and all the earth. We have to go to God." Interestingly, despite this striking amount of verbal output, the child expressed dissatisfaction, saying she had not explained all she wanted to. I comforted her, noting that beliefs are something that people think and learn about for their entire lives.

The children also learned tolerance. At the conclusion of the project, we asked the children what they had learned. Larissa answered, "There are many different beliefs in this school and even more beliefs in the world." Caroline expressed her enjoyment of the study, explaining, "All of the ideas together, it looked nice for Dramatic Play Heaven. I just feel like I'm having a party of everyone's beliefs." Max picked up on this idea, saying, "It's something like Caroline's. It's like a big party of beliefs." Having disagreed sharply with Emily about the genesis of people several months earlier, Max now explained, "The fun thing about studying different beliefs is that they are different."

References

Baumgartner, J.J., & T. Buchanan. 2010. Supporting each child's spirit. *Young Children* (65) 2: 90–95.

Carlsson-Paige, N. 2008. *Taking back childhood: Helping your kids thrive in a fast-paced, media-saturated, violence-filled world.* New York, NY: Penguin.

Coles, R. 1990. *The spiritual life of children.* Boston, MA: Houghton Mifflin.

Copple, C., & S. Bredekamp, eds. 2009. *Developmentally appropriate practice in early childhood programs serving children from birth through age 8.* 3rd ed. Washington, DC: NAEYC.

Derman-Sparks, L., & J.O. Edwards. 2010. *Anti-bias education for young children and ourselves.* Washington, DC: NAEYC.

Eck, D.L. 2002. *A new religious America: How a "Christian country" has become the world's most religiously diverse nation.* San Francisco, CA: HarperOne.

Haynes, C.C., O. Thomas, & J. Ferguson, eds. 2007. *Finding common ground: A First Amendment guide to religion and public education.* Nashville, TN: First Amendment Center.

Katz, L., & S. Chard. 1989. *Engaging children's minds: The project approach.* Norwood, NJ: Ablex.

Mardell, B. 1999. *From basketball to the Beatles: In search of compelling early childhood curriculum.* Portsmouth, NH: Heinemann.

Massachusetts Department of Education. 2001. English language arts curriculum frameworks. www.doe.mass/edu/frame works/ela/0601.pdf

NAEYC. 2007. *NAEYC Early Childhood Program Standards and Accreditation Criteria: The mark of quality in early childhood education.* Rev. ed. Washinhton, DC: Author. www.naeyc.org/torch

Perkins, D. 2009. *Making learning whole: How seven principles of teaching can transform education.* San Francisco: Jossey-Bass.

Project Zero & Reggio Children. 2000. *Making learning visible: Children as individual and group learners.* Reggio Emilia, Italy: Reggio Children.

Critical Thinking

1. How can discussions about spirituality between children help children understand differences between people and create a more "inclusive" school environment?

2. Given the experiences described in this article, what are some benefits that parents and teachers might find through having civil and constructive discussions about young children's beliefs?

Create Central

www.mhhe.com/createcentral

Internet References

Psychology Today.com
http://www.psychologytoday.com/blog/digital-children/200806/origins-religion-in-the-child

Science Direct.com
http://www.sciencedirect.com/science/article/pii/S0049089X07000129

BEN MARDELL, PhD, is a researcher at Project Zero at the Harvard Graduate School of Education and an associate professor of early childhood education at Lesley University, in Cambridge, Massachusetts. He has taught infants, toddlers, preschoolers, and kindergartners. bmardell@lesley.edu. **MONA M. ABO-ZENA,** PhD, is a research associate at the Eliot-Pearson Department of Child Development at Tufts University. She has more than 15 years of teaching, administrative, and board experience in public and religious schools.

Unit 3

UNIT

Prepared by: Chris J. Boyatzis, *Bucknell University*

Social and Emotional Development

One of the truisms about our species is that we are social animals. From birth, each person's life is a constellation of relationships, from family at home to friends in the neighborhood, school, the community, and beyond. This unit addresses how children's social and emotional development is influenced by important relationships with parents, peers, and teachers.

When John Donne in 1623 wrote, "No man is an island, entire of itself . . . any man's death diminishes me, because I am involved in mankind," he implied that all humans are connected to each other and that these connections make us who we are. Early in this century, sociologist C. H. Cooley highlighted the importance of relationships with the phrase "looking-glass self" to describe how people tend to see themselves as a function of how others perceive them. Personality theorist Alfred Adler, also writing in the early twentieth century, claimed that personal strength derived from the quality of one's connectedness to others: the stronger the relationships, the stronger the person. The notion that a person's self-concept arises from relations with others also has roots in developmental psychology. As Jean Piaget

once wrote, "There is no such thing as isolated individuals; there are only relations." The articles in this unit respect these traditions by emphasizing the theme that a child's emotional and social development occurs within the context of relationships.

Another significant milestone of early childhood involves a child's ability to socialize, communicate, begin to understand ethics and morality, and play effectively with peers. Many studies now point to the importance of encouraging children to engage in contemplative behaviors, as well as understanding how culture and healthy peer interaction shape children's socio-emotional well-being and how adults and teachers can serve as models of caring and prosocial behavior for children. Likewise, unfortunately, a variety of genetic and environmental factors also may affect infants and young children who will suffer negative outcomes in later childhood and even adulthood.

The research and stories offer teachers, parents, and others guidance and information of how they might safeguard their students and children in building a strong social-emotional understanding of themselves and others.

Article   Prepared by: Chris J. Boyatzis, *Bucknell University*

Raising a Moral Child

ADAM GRANT

Learning Outcomes

After reading this article, you will be able to:

- Describe the role of different kinds of praise in shaping children's kind and generous behaviors.

- Explain the effect of different kinds of praise on children of different ages.

- Develop a training program for parents or teachers to help them develop effective strategies to help children share.

What does it take to be a good parent? We know some of the tricks for teaching kids to become high achievers. For example, research suggests that when parents praise effort rather than ability, children develop a stronger work ethic and become more motivated.

Yet although some parents live vicariously through their children's accomplishments, success is not the No. 1 priority for most parents. We're much more concerned about our children becoming kind, compassionate and helpful. Surveys reveal that in the United States, parents from European, Asian, Hispanic and African ethnic groups all place far greater importance on caring than achievement. These patterns hold around the world: When people in 50 countries were asked to report their guiding principles in life, the value that mattered most was not achievement, but caring.

Despite the significance that it holds in our lives, teaching children to care about others is no simple task. In an Israeli study of nearly 600 families, parents who valued kindness and compassion frequently failed to raise children who shared those values.

Are some children simply good-natured—or not? For the past decade, I've been studying the surprising success of people who frequently help others without any strings attached. As the father of two daughters and a son, I've become increasingly curious about how these generous tendencies develop.

Genetic twin studies suggest that anywhere from a quarter to more than half of our propensity to be giving and caring is inherited. That leaves a lot of room for nurture, and the evidence on how parents raise kind and compassionate children flies in the face of what many of even the most well-intentioned parents do in praising good behavior, responding to bad behavior, and communicating their values.

By age 2, children experience some moral emotions—feelings triggered by right and wrong. To reinforce caring as the right behavior, research indicates, praise is more effective than rewards. Rewards run the risk of leading children to be kind only when a carrot is offered, whereas praise communicates that sharing is intrinsically worthwhile for its own sake. But what kind of praise should we give when our children show early signs of generosity?

Many parents believe it's important to compliment the behavior, not the child—that way, the child learns to repeat the behavior. Indeed, I know one couple who are careful to say, "That was such a helpful thing to do," instead of, "You're a helpful person."

But is that the right approach? In a clever experiment, the researchers Joan E. Grusec and Erica Redler set out to investigate what happens when we commend generous behavior versus generous character. After 7- and 8-year-olds won marbles and donated some to poor children, the experimenter remarked, "Gee, you shared quite a bit."

The researchers randomly assigned the children to receive different types of praise. For some of the children, they praised the action: "It was good that you gave some of your marbles to those poor children. Yes, that was a nice and helpful thing to do." For others, they praised the character behind the action: "I guess you're the kind of person who likes to help others whenever you can. Yes, you are a very nice and helpful person."

A couple of weeks later, when faced with more opportunities to give and share, the children were much more generous after their character had been praised than after their actions had been. Praising their character helped them internalize it as part of their identities. The children learned who they were from observing their own actions: I am a helpful person. This dovetails with new research led by the psychologist Christopher J. Bryan, who finds that for moral behaviors, nouns work better than verbs. To get 3- to 6-year-olds to help with a task, rather than inviting them "to help," it was 22 to 29 percent more effective to encourage them to "be a helper." Cheating was cut in half when instead of, "Please don't cheat," participants were told, "Please don't be a cheater." When our actions become a reflection of our character, we lean more heavily toward the moral and generous choices. Over time it can become part of us.

Praise appears to be particularly influential in the critical periods when children develop a stronger sense of identity. When the researchers Joan E. Grusec and Erica Redler praised the character of 5-year-olds, any benefits that may have emerged didn't have a lasting impact: They may have been too young to internalize moral character as part of a stable sense of self. And by the time children turned 10, the differences between praising character and praising actions vanished: Both were effective. Tying generosity to character appears to matter most around age 8, when children may be starting to crystallize notions of identity.

Praise in response to good behavior may be half the battle, but our responses to bad behavior have consequences, too. When children cause harm, they typically feel one of two moral emotions: shame or guilt. Despite the common belief that these emotions are interchangeable, research led by the psychologist June Price Tangney reveals that they have very different causes and consequences.

Shame is the feeling that I am a bad person, whereas guilt is the feeling that I have done a bad thing. Shame is a negative judgment about the core self, which is devastating: Shame makes children feel small and worthless, and they respond either by lashing out at the target or escaping the situation altogether. In contrast, guilt is a negative judgment about an action, which can be repaired by good behavior. When children feel guilt, they tend to experience remorse and regret, empathize with the person they have harmed, and aim to make it right.

In one study spearheaded by the psychologist Karen Caplovitz Barrett, parents rated their toddlers' tendencies to experience shame and guilt at home. The toddlers received a rag doll, and the leg fell off while they were playing with it alone. The shame-prone toddlers avoided the researcher and did not volunteer that they broke the doll. The guilt-prone toddlers were more likely to fix the doll, approach the experimenter, and explain what happened. The ashamed toddlers were avoiders; the guilty toddlers were amenders.

If we want our children to care about others, we need to teach them to feel guilt rather than shame when they misbehave. In a review of research on emotions and moral development, the psychologist Nancy Eisenberg suggests that shame emerges when parents express anger, withdraw their love, or try to assert their power through threats of punishment: Children may begin to believe that they are bad people. Fearing this effect, some parents fail to exercise discipline at all, which can hinder the development of strong moral standards.

The most effective response to bad behavior is to express disappointment. According to independent reviews by Professor Eisenberg and David R. Shaffer, parents raise caring children by expressing disappointment and explaining why the behavior was wrong, how it affected others, and how they can rectify the situation. This enables children to develop standards for judging their actions, feelings of empathy and responsibility for others, and a sense of moral identity, which are conducive to becoming a helpful person. The beauty of expressing disappointment is that it communicates disapproval of the bad behavior, coupled with high expectations and the potential for improvement: "You're a good person, even if you did a bad thing, and I know you can do better."

As powerful as it is to criticize bad behavior and praise good character, raising a generous child involves more than waiting for opportunities to react to the actions of our children. As parents, we want to be proactive in communicating our values to our children. Yet many of us do this the wrong way.

In a classic experiment, the psychologist J. Philippe Rushton gave 140 elementary- and middle-school-age children tokens for winning a game, which they could keep entirely or donate some to a child in poverty. They first watched a teacher figure play the game either selfishly or generously, and then preach to them the value of taking, giving, or neither. The adult's influence was significant: Actions spoke louder than words. When the adult behaved selfishly, children followed suit. The words didn't make much difference—children gave fewer tokens after observing the adult's selfish actions, regardless of whether the adult verbally advocated selfishness or generosity. When the adult acted generously, students gave the same amount whether generosity was preached or not—they donated 85 percent more than the norm in both cases. When the adult preached selfishness, even after the adult acted generously, the students still gave 49 percent more than the norm. Children learn generosity not by listening to what their role models say, but by observing what they do.

To test whether these role-modeling effects persisted over time, two months later, researchers observed the children playing the game again. Would the modeling or the preaching influence whether the children gave—and would they even remember it from two months earlier?

The most generous children were those who watched the teacher give but not say anything. Two months later, these children were 31 percent more generous than those who observed the same behavior but also heard it preached. The message from this research is loud and clear: If you don't model generosity, preaching it may not help in the short run, and in the long run, preaching is less effective than giving while saying nothing at all.

People often believe that character causes action, but when it comes to producing moral children, we need to remember that action also shapes character. As the psychologist Karl Weick is fond of asking, "How can I know who I am until I see what I do? How can I know what I value until I see where I walk?"

Critical Thinking

1. Can you think of times in your life when different kinds of feedback about your generous or selfish behavior affected how you viewed yourself and changed your future behavior?

2. Why would it be more effective to say to a child after he was mean to a peer, "You're not a mean person, so don't do that" rather than "That was not a nice thing to do"?

3. Why would different kinds of feedback affect children differently based on their age?

Create Central

www.mhhe.com/createcentral

Internet References

AhaParenting.com
    http://www.ahaparenting.com/_blog/Parenting_Blog/post/What_To_ Say_Instead_of_Praising

ParentingScience.com
    http://www.parentingscience.com/effects-of-praise.html

Psychology Today.com
    http://www.psychologytoday.com/blog/the-power-prime/200909/ parenting-dont-praise-your-children

---

ADAM GRANT is a professor of management and psychology at the Wharton School of the University of Pennsylvania and the author of *Give and Take: Why Helping Others Drives Our Success.*

Article   Prepared by: Chris J. Boyatzis, *Bucknell University*

Why Can Some Kids Handle Pressure While Others Fall Apart?

Po Bronson and Ashley Merryman

Learning Outcomes

After reading this article, you will be able to:

- Explain how different children react to pressure and task demands.

- Describe how the COMT gene and dopamine influence the ability to handle pressure.

- Contrast the "warrior" and "worrier" personality types described in the article.

Noah Muthler took his first state standardized test in third grade at the Spring Cove Elementary School in Roaring Spring, PA. It was a miserable experience, said his mother, Kathleen Muthler. He was a good student in a program for gifted children. But, Muthler said, "he was crying in my arms the night before the test, saying: 'I'm not ready, Mom. They didn't teach us everything that will be on the test.' In fourth grade, he was upset the whole week before the exam. He manifests it physically," his mother said. "He got headaches and stomachaches. He would ask not to go to school." Not a good sleeper anyway, Noah would slip downstairs after an hour tossing in bed and ask his mom to lie down with him until he fell asleep. In fifth grade, the anxiety lasted a solid month before the test. "Even after the test, he couldn't let it go. He would wonder about questions he feared he misunderstood," Muthler said.

So this year, Muthler is opting Noah out of the Pennsylvania System of School Assessment, using a broad religious and ethical exemption. Just knowing he won't be taking the tests in March has put Noah in a better frame of mind about school. "The pressure is off his shoulders now," his mother said. When

he doesn't grasp a concept immediately, he can talk it through without any panic. "He looks forward to science class and math class again," Muthler said. "He wants to be a chemical or nuclear engineer."

Muthler understands Noah's distress; more mysterious is why her son Jacob, who is in eighth grade, isn't the least bit unnerved by the same tests. He, too, is in the gifted program, but that seems to give him breezy confidence, not fear. "You would think he doesn't even care," Muthler marveled. "Noah has the panic and anxiety for both of them." Nevertheless, she will opt out Jacob from the tests, too, to be consistent.

Never before has the pressure to perform on high-stakes tests been so intense or meant so much for a child's academic future. As more school districts strive for accountability, standardized tests have proliferated. The pressure to do well on achievement tests for college is filtering its way down to lower grades, so that even third graders feel as if they are on trial. Students get the message that class work isn't what counts and that the standardized exam is the truer measure. Sure, you did your homework and wrote a great history report—but this test is going to find out how smart you *really* are. Critics argue that all this test-taking is churning out sleep-deprived, overworked, miserable children.

But some children actually do better under competitive, stressful circumstances. Why can Jacob thrive under pressure, while it undoes Noah? And how should that difference inform the way we think about high-stakes testing? An emerging field of research—and a pioneering study from Taiwan—has begun to offer some clues. Like any kind of human behavior, our response to competitive pressure is derived from a complex set of factors—how we were raised, our skills and experience, the hormones that we marinated in as fetuses. There is also a genetic component: One particular gene, referred to as the

COMT gene, could to a large degree explain why one child is more prone to be a worrier, while another may be unflappable, or in the memorable phrasing of David Goldman, a geneticist at the National Institutes of Health, more of a warrior.

Understanding their propensity to become stressed and how to deal with it can help children compete. Stress turns out to be far more complicated than we've assumed, and far more under our control than we imagine. Unlike long-term stress, short-term stress can actually help people perform, and viewing it that way changes its effect. Even for those genetically predisposed to anxiety, the antidote isn't necessarily less competition—it's *more* competition. It just needs to be the right kind.

Every May in Taiwan, more than 200,000 ninth-grade children take the Basic Competency Test for Junior High School Students. This is not just any test. The scores will determine which high school the students are admitted to—or if they get into one at all. Only 39 percent of Taiwanese children make the cut, with the rest diverted to vocational schools or backup private schools. The test, in essence, determines the future for Taiwanese children.

The test is incredibly difficult; answering the multiple-choice questions requires knowledge of chemistry, physics, advanced algebra and geometry, and testing lasts for two days. "Many students go to cram school almost every night to study all the subjects on the test," says Chun-Yen Chang, director of the Science Education Center at National Taiwan Normal University. "Just one or two percentage points difference will drag you from the No. 1 high school in the local region down to No. 3 or 4."

In other words, the exam was a perfect, real-world experiment for studying the effects of genetics on high-stakes competition. Chang and his research team took blood samples from 779 students who had recently taken the Basic Competency Test in three regions of Taiwan. They matched each student's genotype to his or her test score.

The researchers were interested in a single gene, the COMT gene. This gene carries the assembly code for an enzyme that clears dopamine from the prefrontal cortex. That part of the brain is where we plan, make decisions, anticipate future consequences and resolve conflicts. "Dopamine changes the firing rate of neurons, speeding up the brain like a turbocharger," says Silvia Bunge, associate professor of psychology and neuroscience at the University of California, Berkeley. Our brains work best when dopamine is maintained at an optimal level. You don't want too much, or too little. By removing dopamine, the COMT enzyme helps regulate neural activity and maintain mental function.

Here's the thing: There are two variants of the gene. One variant builds enzymes that *slowly* remove dopamine. The other variant builds enzymes that *rapidly* clear dopamine. We all carry the genes for one or the other, or a combination of the two.

In lab experiments, people have been given a variety of cognitive tasks—computerized puzzles and games, portions of I.Q. tests—and researchers have consistently found that, under normal conditions, those with slow-acting enzymes have a cognitive advantage. They have superior executive function and all it entails: they can reason, solve problems, orchestrate complex thought and better foresee consequences. They can concentrate better. This advantage appears to increase with the number of years of education.

The brains of the people with the other variant, meanwhile, are comparatively lackadaisical. The fast-acting enzymes remove too much dopamine, so the overall level is too low. The prefrontal cortex simply doesn't work as well.

On that score alone, having slow-acting enzymes sounds better. There seems to be a trade-off, however, to these slow enzymes, one triggered by stress. In the absence of stress, there is a cognitive advantage. But when under stress, the advantage goes away and in fact reverses itself.

"Stress floods the prefrontal cortex with dopamine," says Adele Diamond, professor of developmental cognitive neuroscience at the University of British Columbia. A little booster hit of dopamine is normally a good thing, but the big surge brought on by stress is too much for people with the slow-acting enzyme, which can't remove the dopamine fast enough. "Much like flooding a car engine with too much gasoline, prefrontal-cortex function melts down," Diamond says.

Other research has found that those with the slow-acting enzymes have higher I.Q.'s, on average. One study of Beijing schoolchildren calculated the advantage to be 10 I.Q. points. But it was unclear if the cognitive advantages they had would stay with them when they were under stress outside the security of the lab environment.

The Taiwan study was the first to look at the COMT gene in a high-stakes, real-life setting. Would the I.Q. advantage hold up, or would the stress undermine performance?

It was the latter. The Taiwanese students with the slow-acting enzymes sank on the national exam. On average, they scored 8 percent lower than those with the fast-acting enzymes. It was as if some of the A students and B students traded places at test time.

"I am not against pressure. Actually, pressure is good [for] someone," Chang commented. "But those who are more vulnerable to stress will be more disadvantaged."

As of 2014, Taiwan will no longer require all students to take the Basic Competency Test, as the country moves to 12-year compulsory education. The system will no longer be built to weed out children, but to keep them all in school. But academically advanced students will still take some kind of entrance exam. And those elite students will still feel the pressure, which, it bears repeating, will hurt some but help others.

"The people who perform best in normal conditions may not be the same people who perform best under stress," Diamond says. People born with the fast-acting enzymes "actually need the stress to perform their best." To them, the everyday is underwhelming; it doesn't excite them enough to stimulate the sharpness of mind of which they are capable. They benefit from that surge in dopamine—it raises the level up to optimal. They are like Superman emerging from the phone booth in times of crisis; their abilities to concentrate and solve problems go up.

Some scholars have suggested that we are all Warriors or Worriers. Those with fast-acting dopamine clearers are the Warriors, ready for threatening environments where maximum performance is required. Those with slow-acting dopamine clearers are the Worriers, capable of more complex planning. Over the course of evolution, both Warriors and Worriers were necessary for human tribes to survive.

In truth, because we all get one COMT gene from our father and one from our mother, about half of all people inherit one of each gene variation, so they have a mix of the enzymes and are somewhere in between the Warriors and the Worriers. About a quarter of people carry Warrior-only genes and a quarter of people Worrier-only.

A number of research studies are looking at COMT, including several involving the American military. Researchers at Brown University have been studying COMT's connection to post-traumatic stress disorder in veterans of the wars in Iraq and Afghanistan. Quinn Kennedy, a research psychologist at the Naval Postgraduate School, is studying how the gene correlates with pilot performance. Douglas C. Johnson, a professor of psychiatry at the University of California, San Diego, is part of a consortium of researchers called the OptiBrain Center, where he is interested in COMT's role in combat performance and well-being.

While the studies are ongoing, the early results show those with Worrier-genes can still handle incredible stress—as long as they are well trained. Even some Navy SEALs have the Worrier genes, so you can literally be a Worrier-gene Warrior. In Kennedy's sample, almost a third of the expert pilots were Worriers—a larger proportion than in the general population.

Kennedy's work is particularly revealing. She puts pilots through a series of six flight-simulator tests, where pilots endure turbulence, oil-pressure problems, iced carburetors and crosswinds while landing. They are kept furiously busy, dialing to new frequencies, flying to new altitudes and headings and punching in transponder codes.

Among recreational pilots with the lowest rating level—trained to fly only in daylight—those with Warrior genes performed best. But that changed with more experience. Among recreational pilots who had the next level of qualification—trained to fly at night using cockpit instruments—the Worriers

far outperformed the Warriors. Their genetically blessed working memory and attention advantage kicked in. And their experience meant they didn't melt under the pressure of their genetic curse.

What this suggests, Kennedy says, is that, for Worriers, "through training, they can learn to manage the particular stress in the specific pilot training, even if it is not necessarily transferred over to other parts of their lives."

So while the single-shot stakes of a standardized exam is particularly ill suited for Worrier genotypes, this doesn't mean that they should be shielded from all challenge. In fact, shielding them could be the worst response, depriving them of the chance to acclimate to recurring stressors. Johnson explains this as a form of stress inoculation: You tax them without overwhelming them. "And then allow for sufficient recovery," he continued. Training, preparation and repetition defuse the Worrier's curse.

There are many psychological and physiological reasons that long-term stress is harmful, but the science of elite performance has drawn a different conclusion about short-term stress. Studies that compare professionals with amateur competitors—whether concert pianists, male rugby or female volleyball players—show that professionals feel just as much anxiety as amateurs. The difference is in how they interpret their anxiety. The amateurs view it as detrimental, while the professionals tend to view stress as energizing. It gets them to focus.

A similar mental shift can also help students in test-taking situations. Jeremy Jamieson, assistant professor of social psychology at the University of Rochester, has done a series of experiments that reveal how the labeling of stress affects performance on academic testing.

The first experiment was at Harvard University with undergraduates who were studying for the Graduate Record Examination. Before taking a practice test, the students read a short note explaining that the study's purpose was to examine the effects of stress on cognition. Half of the students, however, were also given a statement declaring that recent research suggests "people who feel anxious during a test might actually do better." Therefore, if the students felt anxious during the practice test, it said, "you shouldn't feel concerned. . . simply remind yourself that your arousal could be helping you do well."

Just reading this statement significantly improved students' performance. They scored 50 points higher in the quantitative section (out of a possible 800) than the control group on the practice test. Remarkable as that seemed, it is relatively easy to get a result in a lab. Would it affect their actual G.R.E. results? A couple of months later, the students turned in their real G.R.E. scores. Jamieson calculated that the group taught to see anxiety as beneficial in the lab experiment scored 65 points higher than the controls. In ongoing work, Jamieson is replicating the experiment with remedial math students at a Midwestern community college: after they were told to think of stress as beneficial, their grades improved.

At first blush, you might assume that the statement about anxiety being beneficial simply calmed the students, reducing their stress and allowing them to focus. But that was not the case. Jamieson's team took saliva samples of the students, both the day before the practice test to set a base line and right after reading the lines about the new science—just moments before they started the first question. Jamieson had the saliva tested for biomarkers that show the level of activation of the body's sympathetic nervous system—our "fight or flight" response. The experimental group's stress levels were decidedly higher. The biological stress was real, but it had different physiological manifestations and had somehow been transformed into a positive force that drove performance.

If you went to an SAT testing site and could run physiological and neurological scans on the teenagers milling outside the door right before the exam, you would observe very different biomarkers from student to student. Those standing with shoulders hunched, or perhaps rubbing their hands, stamping their feet to get warm, might be approaching what Wendy Berry Mendes and colleagues call a "threat state." According to Mendes, an associate professor of psychology at the University of California, San Francisco, the hallmark of a threat state is vasoconstriction—a tightening of the smooth muscles that line every blood vessel in the body. Blood pressure rises; breathing gets shallow. Oxygenated blood levels drop, and energy supplies are reduced. Meanwhile, a rush of hormones amplifies activity in the brain's amygdala, making you more aware of risks and fearful of mistakes.

At that same test center, you might see students with shoulders back, chest open, putting weight on their toes. They may be in a "challenge state." Hormones activate the brain's reward centers and suppress the fear networks, so the person is excited to start in on the test. In this state, decision making becomes automatic. The blood vessels and lungs dilate. In a different study of stress, Jamieson found that the people told to feel positive about being anxious had their blood flow increase by an average of more than half a liter per minute, with more oxygen and energy coursing throughout the body and brain. Some had up to two liters per minute extra.

Jamieson is frustrated that our culture has such a negative view of stress: "When people say, 'I'm stressed out,' it means, 'I'm not doing well.' It doesn't mean, 'I'm excited—I have increased oxygenated blood going to my brain.'"

As the doors to the test center open, the line between challenge and threat is thin. Probably nothing induces a threat state more than feeling you can't make any mistakes.

Threat physiology can be activated with the sense of being judged, or anything that triggers the fear of disappointing others. As a student opens his test booklet, threat can flare when he sees a subject he has recently learned but hasn't mastered. Or when he sees a problem he has no idea how to solve.

Armando Rodriguez graduated last spring from Bright Star Secondary Charter Academy in Los Angeles, but he is waiting until next fall to start college. He is not taking a gap year to figure out what he wants to do with his life. He's recuperating from knee surgery for a bone condition, spending his days in physical therapy. And what does he miss about being out of school? Competing.

"It's an adrenaline rush—like no other thing." He misses being happy when he wins. He even misses losing. "At least it was a feeling you got," he said. "It made you want to be better, the next time." Without a competitive goal, he feels a little adrift. He finds himself mentally competing with other physical-therapy patients.

Rodriguez recorded a 3.86 G.P.A. his senior year of high school and was a defender for the school soccer team. The knee injury happened during a stint on the school's football team: his doctor had warned that it was too risky to play, but "I just had to try," he said. He used to constantly challenge his friends on quiz grades; it's how they made schoolwork fun.

But when he took the SAT last year, he experienced a different sensation. "My heart was racing," he said. "I had butterflies." Occasionally, he'd look up from his exam to see everyone else working on their own tests: they seemed to be concentrating so hard and answering questions faster than he was. "What if they're doing way better than me?" immediately led to the thought, "These people are smarter than me. All the good schools are going to want them, and not me." Within seconds, he arrived at the worst possible outcome: his hopes of a good college would be gone.

It might seem surprising that the same student can experience competition in such different ways. But this points to what researchers think is the difference between competition that challenges and competition that threatens.

Taking a standardized test is a competition in which the only thing anyone cares about is the final score. No one says, "I didn't do that well, but it was still worth doing, because I learned so much math from all the months of studying." Nobody has ever come out of an SAT test saying, "Well, I won't get into the college I wanted, but that's O.K. because I made a lot of new friends at the Kaplan center." Standardized tests lack the side benefits of competing that normally buffer children's anxiety. When you sign your child up for the swim team, he may really want to finish first, but there are many other reasons to be in the pool, even if he finishes last.

High-stakes academic testing isn't going away. Nor should competition among students. In fact, several scholars have concluded that what students need is more academic competition but modeled on the kinds children enjoy.

David and Christi Bergin, professors of educational and developmental psychology at the University of Missouri, have begun a pilot study of junior high school students participating in math competitions. They have observed that, within a few weeks, students were tackling more complex problems than they would even at the end of a year-long class. Some were even doing college-level math. That was true even for students who didn't like math before joining the team and were forced into it by their parents. Knowing they were going up against other teams in front of an audience, the children took ownership over the material. They became excited about discovering ever more advanced concepts, having realized each new fact was another weapon in their intellectual arsenal.

In-class spelling bees. Science fairs. Chess teams. "The performance is highly motivating," David Bergin says. Even if a child knows her science project won't win the science fair, she still gets that moment to perform. That moment can be stressful and invigorating and scary, but if the child handles it well, it feels like a victory.

"Children benefit from competition they have prepared for intensely, especially when viewed as an opportunity to gain recognition for their efforts and improve for the next time," says Rena Subotnik, a psychologist at the American Psychological Association. Subotnik notes that scholastic competitions can raise the social status of academic work as well as that of the contestants. Competitions like these are certainly not without stress, but the pressure comes in predictable ebbs and flows, broken up by moments of fun and excitement.

Maybe the best thing about academic competitions is that they benefit both Warriors and Worriers equally. The Warriors get the thrilling intensity their minds are suited for, where they can shine. The Worriers get the gradual stress inoculation they need, so that one day they can do more than just tolerate stress—they can embrace it. And through the cycle of preparation, performance and recovery, what they learn becomes ingrained.

It may be difficult to believe, as Jamieson advises, that stress can benefit your performance. We can read it, and we can talk about it, but it's the sort of thing that needs to be practiced, perhaps for years, before it can become a deeply held conviction.

It turns out that Armando Rodriguez was accepted at five colleges. He rallied that day on the SAT. It wasn't his best score—he did better the second time around—but it was not as bad as he feared. Rodriguez had never heard of Jeremy Jamieson. He had never read, or ever been told, that intense stress could be harnessed to perform his best. But he understood it and drew strength from it. In the middle of his downward spiral of panic, he realized something: "I'm in a competition. This is a competition. I've got to beat them."

Critical Thinking

1. How has this article's explanation of how biology helps explain why some kids may handle stress well while others don't changed how you view children or your fellow students? Do you have either a more objective or a more emphathic view of students who can't handle pressure?

2. Based on the article, what strategies could you teach to children—or your fellow students—to cope better with stress in their daily lives or when anticipating stressful events like tests and deadlines?

3. Are you a Warrior or a Worrier? How might you benefit from trying to adapt some qualities of the other type?

Create Central

www.mhhe.com/createcentral

Internet References

Kids Health: Helping Kids Cope with Stress
http://kidshealth.org/parent/emotions/feelings/stress_coping.html

Learning Dynamics: Psychological, Educational, Social Services
http://learningdynamicsinc.org/child-adolescent-counseling

Psychology Foundation of Canada
http://psychologyfoundation.org/index.php/programs/kids-have-stress-too

WebMD
http://www.webmd.com/anxiety-panic/features/school-stress-anxiety-children

---

Po Bronson and **Ashley Merryman** are the authors of *Top Dog: The Science of Winning and Losing.*

Bronson, Po and Merryman, Ashley. "Why Can Some Kids Handle Pressure While Others Fall Apart?" Reprinted by permission of Curtis Brown, Ltd., February 6, 2013.

Article   Prepared by: Chris J. Boyatzis, *Bucknell University*

Don't!
The Secret of Self-Control

Children who are able to pass the marshmallow test enjoy greater success as adults.

JONAH LEHRER

Learning Outcomes

After reading this article, you will be able to:

- Describe the famous marshmallow test and the different ways that children behave in it.

- Analyze the findings from the marshmallow test to determine if it is a good measure of self-control.

- Explain how performance on the marshmallow test is linked to later development and behavior in life.

In the late nineteen-sixties, Carolyn Weisz, a four-year-old with long brown hair, was invited into a "game room" at the Bing Nursery School, on the campus of Stanford University. The room was little more than a large closet, containing a desk and a chair. Carolyn was asked to sit down in the chair and pick a treat from a tray of marshmallows, cookies, and pretzel sticks. Carolyn chose the marshmallow. Although she's now forty-four, Carolyn still has a weakness for those air-puffed balls of corn syrup and gelatine. "I know I shouldn't like them," she says. "But they're just so delicious!" A researcher then made Carolyn an offer: she could either eat one marshmallow right away or, if she was willing to wait while he stepped out for a few minutes, she could have two marshmallows when he returned. He said that if she rang a bell on the desk while he was away he would come running back, and she could eat one marshmallow but would forfeit the second. Then he left the room.

Although Carolyn has no direct memory of the experiment, and the scientists would not release any information about the subjects, she strongly suspects that she was able to delay gratification. "I've always been really good at waiting," Carolyn told me. "If you give me a challenge or a task, then I'm going to find a way to do it, even if it means not eating my favorite food." Her mother, Karen Sortino, is still more certain: "Even as a young kid, Carolyn was very patient. I'm sure she would have waited." But her brother Craig, who also took part in the experiment, displayed less fortitude. Craig, a year older than Carolyn, still remembers the torment of trying to wait. "At a certain point, it must have occurred to me that I was all by myself," he recalls. "And so I just started taking all the candy." According to Craig, he was also tested with little plastic toys—he could have a second one if he held out—and he broke into the desk, where he figured there would be additional toys. "I took everything I could," he says. "I cleaned them out. After that, I noticed the teachers encouraged me to not go into the experiment room anymore."

Footage of these experiments, which were conducted over several years, is poignant, as the kids struggle to delay gratification for just a little bit longer. Some cover their eyes with their hands or turn around so that they can't see the tray. Others start kicking the desk, or tug on their pigtails, or stroke the marshmallow as if it were a tiny stuffed animal. One child, a boy with neatly parted hair, looks carefully around the room to make sure that nobody can see him. Then he picks up an Oreo, delicately twists it apart, and licks off the white cream filling before returning the cookie to the tray, a satisfied look on his face.

Most of the children were like Craig. They struggled to resist the treat and held out for an average of less than three minutes. "A few kids ate the marshmallow right away," Walter Mischel, the Stanford professor of psychology in charge of the experiment, remembers. "They didn't even bother ringing the bell.

Other kids would stare directly at the marshmallow and then ring the bell thirty seconds later." About thirty percent of the children, however, were like Carolyn. They successfully delayed gratification until the researcher returned, some fifteen minutes later. These kids wrestled with temptation but found a way to resist.

The initial goal of the experiment was to identify the mental processes that allowed some people to delay gratification while others simply surrendered. After publishing a few papers on the Bing studies in the early seventies, Mischel moved on to other areas of personality research. "There are only so many things you can do with kids trying not to eat marshmallows."

But occasionally Mischel would ask his three daughters, all of whom attended the Bing, about their friends from nursery school. "It was really just idle dinnertime conversation," he says. "I'd ask them, 'How's Jane? How's Eric? How are they doing in school?'" Mischel began to notice a link between the children's academic performance as teen agers and their ability to wait for the second marshmallow. He asked his daughters to assess their friends academically on a scale of zero to five. Comparing these ratings with the original data set, he saw a correlation. "That's when I realized I had to do this seriously," he says. Starting in 1981, Mischel sent out a questionnaire to all the reachable parents, teachers, and academic advisers of the six hundred and fifty-three subjects who had participated in the marshmallow task, who were by then in high school. He asked about every trait he could think of, from their capacity to plan and think ahead to their ability to "cope well with problems" and get along with their peers. He also requested their S.A.T. scores.

Once Mischel began analyzing the results, he noticed that low delayers, the children who rang the bell quickly, seemed more likely to have behavioral problems, both in school and at home. They got lower S.A.T. scores. They struggled in stressful situations, often had trouble paying attention, and found it difficult to maintain friendships. The child who could wait fifteen minutes had an S.A.T. score that was, on average, two hundred and ten points higher than that of the kid who could wait only thirty seconds.

Carolyn Weisz is a textbook example of a high delayer. She attended Stanford as an undergraduate, and got her PhD in social psychology at Princeton. She's now an associate psychology professor at the University of Puget Sound. Craig, meanwhile, moved to Los Angeles and has spent his career doing "all kinds of things" in the entertainment industry, mostly in production. He's currently helping to write and produce a film. "Sure, I wish I had been a more patient person," Craig says. "Looking back, there are definitely moments when it would have helped me make better career choices and stuff."

Mischel and his colleagues continued to track the subjects into their late thirties—Ozlem Ayduk, an assistant professor of psychology at the University of California at Berkeley, found that low-delaying adults have a significantly higher body-mass index and are more likely to have had problems with drugs—but it was frustrating to have to rely on self-reports. "There's often a gap between what people are willing to tell you and how they behave in the real world," he explains. And so, last year, Mischel, who is now a professor at Columbia, and a team of collaborators began asking the original Bing subjects to travel to Stanford for a few days of experiments in an fMRI machine. Carolyn says she will be participating in the scanning experiments later this summer; Craig completed a survey several years ago, but has yet to be invited to Palo Alto. The scientists are hoping to identify the particular brain regions that allow some people to delay gratification and control their temper. They're also conducting a variety of genetic tests, as they search for the hereditary characteristics that influence the ability to wait for a second marshmallow.

If Mischel and his team succeed, they will have outlined the neural circuitry of self-control. For decades, psychologists have focussed on raw intelligence as the most important variable when it comes to predicting success in life. Mischel argues that intelligence is largely at the mercy of self-control: even the smartest kids still need to do their homework. "What we're really measuring with the marshmallows isn't will power or self-control," Mischel says. "It's much more important than that. This task forces kids to find a way to make the situation work for them. They want the second marshmallow, but how can they get it? We can't control the world, but we can control how we think about it."

Walter Mischel is a slight, elegant man with a shaved head and a face of deep creases. He talks with a Brooklyn bluster and he tends to act out his sentences, so that when he describes the marshmallow task he takes on the body language of an impatient four-year-old. "If you want to know why some kids can wait and others can't, then you've got to think like they think," Mischel says.

Mischel was born in Vienna, in 1930. His father was a modestly successful businessman with a fondness for café society and Esperanto, while his mother spent many of her days lying on the couch with an ice pack on her forehead, trying to soothe her frail nerves. The family considered itself fully assimilated, but after the Nazi annexation of Austria, in 1938, Mischel remembers being taunted in school by the Hitler Youth and watching as his father, hobbled by childhood polio, was forced to limp through the streets in his pajamas. A few weeks after the takeover, while the family was burning evidence of their Jewish ancestry in the fireplace, Walter found a long-forgotten certificate of U.S. citizenship issued to his maternal grandfather decades earlier, thus saving his family.

The family settled in Brooklyn, where Mischel's parents opened up a five-and-dime. Mischel attended New York University, studying poetry under Delmore Schwartz and Allen Tate, and taking studio-art classes with Philip Guston. He also became fascinated by psychoanalysis and new measures of personality, such as the Rorschach test. "At the time, it seemed like a mental X-ray machine," he says. "You could solve a person by showing them a picture." Although he was pressured to join his uncle's umbrella business, he ended up pursuing a PhD in clinical psychology at Ohio State.

But Mischel noticed that academic theories had limited application, and he was struck by the futility of most personality science. He still flinches at the naïveté of graduate students who based their diagnoses on a battery of meaningless tests. In 1955, Mischel was offered an opportunity to study the "spirit possession" ceremonies of the Orisha faith in Trinidad, and he leapt at the chance. Although his research was supposed to involve the use of Rorschach tests to explore the connections between the unconscious and the behavior of people when possessed, Mischel soon grew interested in a different project. He lived in a part of the island that was evenly split between people of East Indian and of African descent; he noticed that each group defined the other in broad stereotypes. "The East Indians would describe the Africans as impulsive hedonists, who were always living for the moment and never thought about the future," he says. "The Africans, meanwhile, would say that the East Indians didn't know how to live and would stuff money in their mattress and never enjoy themselves."

Mischel took young children from both ethnic groups and offered them a simple choice: they could have a miniature chocolate bar right away or, if they waited a few days, they could get a much bigger chocolate bar. Mischel's results failed to justify the stereotypes—other variables, such as whether or not the children lived with their father, turned out to be much more important—but they did get him interested in the question of delayed gratification. Why did some children wait and not others? What made waiting possible? Unlike the broad traits supposedly assessed by personality tests, self-control struck Mischel as potentially measurable.

In 1958, Mischel became an assistant professor in the Department of Social Relations at Harvard. One of his first tasks was to develop a survey course on "personality assessment," but Mischel quickly concluded that, while prevailing theories held personality traits to be broadly consistent, the available data didn't back up this assumption. Personality, at least as it was then conceived, couldn't be reliably assessed at all. A few years later, he was hired as a consultant on a personality assessment initiated by the Peace Corps. Early Peace Corps volunteers had sparked several embarrassing international incidents—one mailed a postcard on which she expressed disgust at the sanitary habits of her host country—so the Kennedy Administration wanted a screening process to eliminate people unsuited for foreign assignments. Volunteers were tested for standard personality traits, and Mischel compared the results with ratings of how well the volunteers performed in the field. He found no correlation; the time-consuming tests predicted nothing. At this point, Mischel realized that the problem wasn't the tests—it was their premise. Psychologists had spent decades searching for traits that exist independently of circumstance, but what if personality can't be separated from context? "It went against the way we'd been thinking about personality since the four humors and the ancient Greeks," he says.

While Mischel was beginning to dismantle the methods of his field, the Harvard psychology department was in tumult. In 1960, the personality psychologist Timothy Leary helped start the Harvard Psilocybin Project, which consisted mostly of self-experimentation. Mischel remembers graduate students' desks giving way to mattresses, and large packages from Ciba chemicals, in Switzerland, arriving in the mail. Mischel had nothing against hippies, but he wanted modern psychology to be rigorous and empirical. And so, in 1962, Walter Mischel moved to Palo Alto and went to work at Stanford.

There is something deeply contradictory about Walter Mischel—a psychologist who spent decades critiquing the validity of personality tests—inventing the marshmallow task, a simple test with impressive predictive power. Mischel, however, insists there is no contradiction. "I've always believed there are consistencies in a person that can be looked at," he says. "We just have to look in the right way." One of Mischel's classic studies documented the aggressive behavior of children in a variety of situations at a summer camp in New Hampshire. Most psychologists assumed that aggression was a stable trait, but Mischel found that children's responses depended on the details of the interaction. The same child might consistently lash out when teased by a peer, but readily submit to adult punishment. Another might react badly to a warning from a counsellor, but play well with his bunkmates. Aggression was best assessed in terms of what Mischel called "if-then patterns." If a certain child was teased by a peer, then he would be aggressive.

One of Mischel's favorite metaphors for this model of personality, known as interactionism, concerns a car making a screeching noise. How does a mechanic solve the problem? He begins by trying to identify the specific conditions that trigger the noise. Is there a screech when the car is accelerating, or when it's shifting gears, or turning at slow speeds? Unless the mechanic can give the screech a context, he'll never find the broken part. Mischel wanted psychologists to think like mechanics, and look at people's responses under particular conditions. The challenge was devising a test that accurately simulated something relevant to the behavior being predicted. The search for a meaningful test of personality led Mischel to revisit, in 1968, the protocol he'd used on young children in Trinidad nearly a decade earlier. The experiment seemed especially relevant now that he had three young daughters of his own. "Young kids are pure id," Mischel says. "They start off unable to wait for anything—whatever they want they need. But then, as I watched my own kids, I marvelled at how they gradually learned how to delay and how that made so many other things possible."

A few years earlier, in 1966, the Stanford psychology department had established the Bing Nursery School. The classrooms were designed as working laboratories, with large one-way mirrors that allowed researchers to observe the children. In February, Jennifer Winters, the assistant director of the school, showed me around the building. While the Bing is still an active center of research—the children quickly learn to ignore the students scribbling in notebooks—Winters isn't sure that Mischel's marshmallow task could be replicated today. "We recently tried to do a version of it, and the kids were very excited about having food in the game room," she says. "There are so many allergies and peculiar diets today that we don't do many things with food."

Mischel perfected his protocol by testing his daughters at the kitchen table. "When you're investigating will power in a four-year-old, little things make a big difference," he says. "How big should the marshmallows be? What kind of cookies work best?" After several months of patient tinkering, Mischel came up with an experimental design that closely simulated the difficulty of delayed gratification. In the spring of 1968, he conducted the first trials of his experiment at the Bing. "I knew we'd designed it well when a few kids wanted to quit as soon as we explained the conditions to them," he says. "They knew this was going to be very difficult."

At the time, psychologists assumed that children's ability to wait depended on how badly they wanted the marshmallow. But it soon became obvious that every child craved the extra treat. What, then, determined self-control? Mischel's conclusion, based on hundreds of hours of observation, was that the crucial skill was the "strategic allocation of attention." Instead of getting obsessed with the marshmallow—the "hot stimulus"—the patient children distracted themselves by covering their eyes, pretending to play hide-and-seek underneath the desk, or singing songs from "Sesame Street." Their desire wasn't defeated—it was merely forgotten. "If you're thinking about the marshmallow and how delicious it is, then you're going to eat it," Mischel says. "The key is to avoid thinking about it in the first place."

In adults, this skill is often referred to as metacognition, or thinking about thinking, and it's what allows people to outsmart their shortcomings. (When Odysseus had himself tied to the ship's mast, he was using some of the skills of metacognition: knowing he wouldn't be able to resist the Sirens' song, he made it impossible to give in.) Mischel's large data set from various studies allowed him to see that children with a more accurate understanding of the workings of self-control were better able to delay gratification. "What's interesting about four-year-olds is that they're just figuring out the rules of thinking," Mischel says. "The kids who couldn't delay would often have the rules backwards. They would think that the best way to resist the marshmallow is to stare right at it, to keep a close eye on the goal. But that's a terrible idea. If you do that, you're going to ring the bell before I leave the room."

According to Mischel, this view of will power also helps explain why the marshmallow task is such a powerfully predictive test. "If you can deal with hot emotions, then you can study for the S.A.T. instead of watching television," Mischel says. "And you can save more money for retirement. It's not just about marshmallows."

Subsequent work by Mischel and his colleagues found that these differences were observable in subjects as young as nineteen months. Looking at how toddlers responded when briefly separated from their mothers, they found that some immediately burst into tears, or clung to the door, but others were able to overcome their anxiety by distracting themselves, often by playing with toys. When the scientists set the same children the marshmallow task at the age of five, they found that the kids who had cried also struggled to resist the tempting treat.

The early appearance of the ability to delay suggests that it has a genetic origin, an example of personality at its most predetermined. Mischel resists such an easy conclusion. "In general, trying to separate nature and nurture makes about as much sense as trying to separate personality and situation," he says. "The two influences are completely interrelated." For instance, when Mischel gave delay-of-gratification tasks to children from low-income families in the Bronx, he noticed that their ability to delay was below average, at least compared with that of children in Palo Alto. "When you grow up poor, you might not practice delay as much," he says. "And if you don't practice then you'll never figure out how to distract yourself. You won't develop the best delay strategies, and those strategies won't become second nature." In other words, people learn how to use their mind just as they learn how to use a computer: through trial and error.

But Mischel has found a shortcut. When he and his colleagues taught children a simple set of mental tricks—such as pretending that the candy is only a picture, surrounded by an imaginary frame—he dramatically improved their self-control.

The kids who hadn't been able to wait sixty seconds could now wait fifteen minutes. "All I've done is given them some tips from their mental user manual," Mischel says. "Once you realize that will power is just a matter of learning how to control your attention and thoughts, you can really begin to increase it."

Marc Berman, a lanky graduate student with an easy grin, speaks about his research with the infectious enthusiasm of a freshman taking his first philosophy class. Berman works in the lab of John Jonides, a psychologist and neuroscientist at the University of Michigan, who is in charge of the brain-scanning experiments on the original Bing subjects. He knows that testing forty-year-olds for self-control isn't a straightforward proposition. "We can't give these people marshmallows," Berman says. "They know they're part of a long-term study that looks at delay of gratification, so if you give them an obvious delay task they'll do their best to resist. You'll get a bunch of people who refuse to touch their marshmallow."

This meant that Jonides and his team had to find a way to measure will power indirectly. Operating on the premise that the ability to delay eating the marshmallow had depended on a child's ability to banish thoughts of it, they decided on a series of tasks that measure the ability of subjects to control the contents of working memory—the relatively limited amount of information we're able to consciously consider at any given moment. According to Jonides, this is how self-control "cashes out" in the real world: as an ability to direct the spotlight of attention so that our decisions aren't determined by the wrong thoughts.

Last summer, the scientists chose fifty-five subjects, equally split between high delayers and low delayers, and sent each one a laptop computer loaded with working-memory experiments. Two of the experiments were of particular interest. The first is a straightforward exercise known as the "suppression task." Subjects are given four random words, two printed in blue and two in red. After reading the words, they're told to forget the blue words and remember the red words. Then the scientists provide a stream of "probe words" and ask the subjects whether the probes are the words they were asked to remember. Though the task doesn't seem to involve delayed gratification, it tests the same basic mechanism. Interestingly, the scientists found that high delayers were significantly better at the suppression task: they were less likely to think that a word they'd been asked to forget was something they should remember.

In the second, known as the Go/No Go task, subjects are flashed a set of faces with various expressions. At first, they are told to press the space bar whenever they see a smile. This takes little effort, since smiling faces automatically trigger what's known as "approach behavior." After a few minutes, however,

subjects are told to press the space bar when they see frowning faces. They are now being forced to act against an impulse. Results show that high delayers are more successful at not pressing the button in response to a smiling face.

When I first started talking to the scientists about these tasks last summer, they were clearly worried that they wouldn't find any behavioral differences between high and low delayers. It wasn't until early January that they had enough data to begin their analysis (not surprisingly, it took much longer to get the laptops back from the low delayers), but it soon became obvious that there were provocative differences between the two groups. A graph of the data shows that as the delay time of the four-year-olds decreases, the number of mistakes made by the adults sharply rises.

The big remaining question for the scientists is whether these behavioral differences are detectable in an fMRI machine. Although the scanning has just begun—Jonides and his team are still working out the kinks—the scientists sound confident. "These tasks have been studied so many times that we pretty much know where to look and what we're going to find," Jonides says. He rattles off a short list of relevant brain regions, which his lab has already identified as being responsible for working-memory exercises. For the most part, the regions are in the frontal cortex—the overhang of brain behind the eyes—and include the dorsolateral prefrontal cortex, the anterior prefrontal cortex, the anterior cingulate, and the right and left inferior frontal gyri. While these cortical folds have long been associated with self-control, they're also essential for working memory and directed attention. According to the scientists, that's not an accident. "These are powerful instincts telling us to reach for the marshmallow or press the space bar," Jonides says. "The only way to defeat them is to avoid them, and that means paying attention to something else. We call that will power, but it's got nothing to do with the will."

The behavioral and genetic aspects of the project are overseen by Yuichi Shoda, a professor of psychology at the University of Washington, who was one of Mischel's graduate students. He's been following these "marshmallow subjects" for more than thirty years: he knows everything about them from their academic records and their social graces to their ability to deal with frustration and stress. The prognosis for the genetic research remains uncertain. Although many studies have searched for the underpinnings of personality since the completion of the Human Genome Project, in 2003, many of the relevant genes remain in question. "We're incredibly complicated creatures," Shoda says. "Even the simplest aspects of personality are driven by dozens and dozens of different genes." The scientists have decided to focus on genes in the dopamine pathways, since those neurotransmitters are believed to regulate both motivation and attention. However, even if minor coding differences influence delay ability—and that's a likely possibility—Shoda doesn't expect to discover these differences: the sample size is simply too small.

In recent years, researchers have begun making house visits to many of the original subjects, including Carolyn Weisz, as they try to better understand the familial contexts that shape self-control. "They turned my kitchen into a lab," Carolyn told me. "They set up a little tent where they tested my oldest daughter on the delay task with some cookies. I remember thinking, I really hope she can wait."

While Mischel closely follows the steady accumulation of data from the laptops and the brain scans, he's most excited by what comes next. "I'm not interested in looking at the brain just so we can use a fancy machine," he says. "The real question is what can we do with this fMRI data that we couldn't do before?" Mischel is applying for an N.I.H. grant to investigate various mental illnesses, like obsessive-compulsive disorder and attention-deficit disorder, in terms of the ability to control and direct attention. Mischel and his team hope to identify crucial neural circuits that cut across a wide variety of ailments. If there is such a circuit, then the same cognitive tricks that increase delay time in a four-year-old might help adults deal with their symptoms. Mischel is particularly excited by the example of the substantial subset of people who failed the marshmallow task as four-year-olds but ended up becoming high-delaying adults. "This is the group I'm most interested in," he says. "They have substantially improved their lives."

Mischel is also preparing a large-scale study involving hundreds of schoolchildren in Philadelphia, Seattle, and New York City to see if self-control skills can be taught. Although he previously showed that children did much better on the marshmallow task after being taught a few simple "mental transformations," such as pretending the marshmallow was a cloud, it remains unclear if these new skills persist over the long term. In other words, do the tricks work only during the experiment or do the children learn to apply them at home, when deciding between homework and television?

Angela Lee Duckworth, an assistant professor of psychology at the University of Pennsylvania, is leading the program. She first grew interested in the subject after working as a high-school math teacher. "For the most part, it was an incredibly frustrating experience," she says. "I gradually became convinced that trying to teach a teenager algebra when they don't have self-control is a pretty futile exercise." And so, at the age of thirty-two, Duckworth decided to become a psychologist. One of her main research projects looked at the relationship between self-control and grade-point average. She found that the ability to delay gratification—eighth graders were given a choice between a dollar right away or two dollars the following week—was a far better predictor of academic performance than I.Q. She said that her study shows that "intelligence is really important, but it's still not as important as self-control."

Last year, Duckworth and Mischel were approached by David Levin, the co-founder of KIPP, an organization of sixty-six public charter schools across the country. KIPP schools are known for their long workday—students are in class from 7:25 A.M. to 5 P.M.—and for dramatic improvement of inner-city students' test scores. (More than eighty percent of eighth graders at the KIPP academy in the South Bronx scored at or above grade level in reading and math, which was nearly twice the New York City average.) "The core feature of the KIPP approach is that character matters for success," Levin says. "Educators like to talk about character skills when kids are in kindergarten—we send young kids home with a report card about 'working well with others' or 'not talking out of turn.' But then, just when these skills start to matter, we stop trying to improve them. We just throw up our hands and complain."

Self-control is one of the fundamental "character strengths" emphasized by KIPP—the KIPP academy in Philadelphia, for instance, gives its students a shirt emblazoned with the slogan "Don't Eat the Marshmallow." Levin, however, remained unsure about how well the program was working—"We know how to teach math skills, but it's harder to measure character strengths," he says—so he contacted Duckworth and Mischel, promising them unfettered access to KIPP students. Levin also helped bring together additional schools willing to take part in the experiment, including Riverdale Country School, a private school in the Bronx; the Evergreen School for gifted children, in Shoreline, Washington; and the Mastery Charter Schools, in Philadelphia.

For the past few months, the researchers have been conducting pilot studies in the classroom as they try to figure out the most effective way to introduce complex psychological concepts to young children. Because the study will focus on students between the ages of four and eight, the classroom lessons will rely heavily on peer modelling, such as showing kindergartners a video of a child successfully distracting herself during the marshmallow task. The scientists have some encouraging preliminary results—after just a few sessions, students show significant improvements in the ability to deal with hot emotional states—but they are cautious about predicting the outcome of the long-term study. "When you do these large-scale educational studies, there are ninety-nine uninteresting reasons the study could fail," Duckworth says. "Maybe a teacher doesn't show the video, or maybe there's a field trip on the day of the testing. This is what keeps me up at night."

Mischel's main worry is that, even if his lesson plan proves to be effective, it might still be overwhelmed by variables the scientists can't control, such as the home environment.

He knows that it's not enough just to teach kids mental tricks—the real challenge is turning those tricks into habits, and that requires years of diligent practice. "This is where your parents are important," Mischel says. "Have they established rituals that force you to delay on a daily basis? Do they encourage you to wait? And do they make waiting worthwhile?" According to Mischel, even the most mundane routines of childhood—such as not snacking before dinner, or saving up your allowance, or holding out until Christmas morning—are really sly exercises in cognitive training: we're teaching ourselves how to think so that we can outsmart our desires. But Mischel isn't satisfied with such an informal approach. "We should give marshmallows to every kindergartner," he says. "We should say, 'You see this marshmallow? You don't have to eat it. You can wait. Here's how.'"

Critical Thinking

1. When do children develop the capacity for self-control, and how do psychological and neurological development affect this capacity?

2. Does self-control in childhood predict later behavior and achievement? If so, in what ways?

3. Some of the most valuable insights about child development have resulted from simple experiments with common materials. What is the marshmallow test? If you were to conduct similar studies, how would you revise the procedure or materials?

4. In what ways did the marshmallow test measure not only children's self-control but their obedience to authority or reaction to novel situations?

Create Central

www.mhhe.com/createcentral

Internet References

AhaParenting.com
http://www.ahaparenting.com/_blog/Parenting_Blog/post/Help_Your_Child_Develop_Self_Control

AboutOurKids.org
http://www.aboutourkids.org/articles/about_discipline_helping_children_develop_selfcontrol

KidsHealth.org
http://kidshealth.org/parent/emotions/behavior/self_control.html

Article   Prepared by: Chris J. Boyatzis, *Bucknell University*

The Moral Life of Babies

PAUL BLOOM

Learning Outcomes

After reading this article, you will be able to:

• Describe the methods and findings from the studies to test morality in young children.

• Evaluate the conclusion that young children have a moral sense.

• Explain how traits can be passed from one generation to the next.

Not long ago, a team of researchers watched a 1-year-old boy take justice into his own hands. The boy had just seen a puppet show in which one puppet played with a ball while interacting with two other puppets. The center puppet would slide the ball to the puppet on the right, who would pass it back. And the center puppet would slide the ball to the puppet on the left . . . who would run away with it. Then the two puppets on the ends were brought down from the stage and set before the toddler. Each was placed next to a pile of treats. At this point, the toddler was asked to take a treat away from one puppet. Like most children in this situation, the boy took it from the pile of the "naughty" one. But this punishment wasn't enough—he then leaned over and smacked the puppet in the head.

This incident occurred in one of several psychology studies that I have been involved with at the Infant Cognition Center at Yale University in collaboration with my colleague (and wife), Karen Wynn, who runs the lab, and a graduate student, Kiley Hamlin, who is the lead author of the studies. We are one of a handful of research teams around the world exploring the moral life of babies.

Like many scientists and humanists, I have long been fascinated by the capacities and inclinations of babies and children. The mental life of young humans not only is an interesting topic in its own right, it also raises—and can help answer—fundamental questions of philosophy and psychology, including how biological evolution and cultural experience conspire to shape human nature. In graduate school, I studied early language development and later moved on to fairly traditional topics in cognitive development, like how we come to understand the minds of other people—what they know, want and experience.

But the current work I'm involved in, on baby morality, might seem like a perverse and misguided next step. Why would anyone even entertain the thought of babies as moral beings? From Sigmund Freud to Jean Piaget to Lawrence Kohlberg, psychologists have long argued that we begin life as amoral animals. One important task of society, particularly of parents, is to turn babies into civilized beings—social creatures who can experience empathy, guilt and shame; who can override selfish impulses in the name of higher principles; and who will respond with outrage to unfairness and injustice. Many parents and educators would endorse a view of infants and toddlers close to that of a recent Onion headline: "New Study Reveals Most Children Unrepentant Sociopaths." If children enter the world already equipped with moral notions, why is it that we have to work so hard to humanize them?

A growing body of evidence, though, suggests that humans do have a rudimentary moral sense from the very start of life. With the help of well-designed experiments, you can see glimmers of moral thought, moral judgment and moral feeling even in the first year of life. Some sense of good and evil seems to be bred in the bone. Which is not to say that parents are wrong to concern themselves with moral development or that their interactions with their children are a waste of time. Socialization is critically important. But this is not because babies and young children lack a sense of right and wrong; it's because the sense of right and wrong that they naturally possess diverges in important ways from what we adults would want it to be.

Smart Babies

Babies seem spastic in their actions, undisciplined in their attention. In 1762, Jean-Jacques Rousseau called the baby "a perfect idiot," and in 1890, William James famously described a baby's mental life as "one great blooming, buzzing confusion." A sympathetic parent might see the spark of consciousness in a baby's large eyes and eagerly accept the popular claim that babies are wonderful learners, but it is hard to avoid the impression that they begin as ignorant as bread loaves. Many developmental psychologists will tell you that the ignorance of human babies extends well into childhood. For many years, the conventional view was that young humans take a surprisingly long time to learn basic facts about the physical world (like that objects continue to exist once they are out of sight) and basic facts about people (like that they have beliefs and desires and goals)—let alone how long it takes them to learn about morality.

I am admittedly biased, but I think one of the great discoveries in modern psychology is that this view of babies is mistaken.

A reason this view has persisted is that, for many years, scientists weren't sure how to go about studying the mental life of babies. It's a challenge to study the cognitive abilities of any creature that lacks language, but human babies present an additional difficulty, because, even compared to rats or birds, they are behaviorally limited: they can't run mazes or peck at levers. In the 1980s, however, psychologists interested in exploring how much babies know began making use of one of the few behaviors that young babies can control: the movement of their eyes. The eyes are a window to the baby's soul. As adults do, when babies see something that they find interesting or surprising, they tend to look at it longer than they would at something they find uninteresting or expected. And when given a choice between two things to look at, babies usually opt to look at the more pleasing thing. You can use "looking time," then, as a rough but reliable proxy for what captures babies' attention: what babies are surprised by or what babies like.

The studies in the 1980s that made use of this methodology were able to discover surprising things about what babies know about the nature and workings of physical objects—a baby's "naïve physics." Psychologists—most notably Elizabeth Spelke and Renée Baillargeon—conducted studies that essentially involved showing babies magic tricks, events that seemed to violate some law of the universe: you remove the supports from beneath a block and it floats in midair, unsupported; an object disappears and then reappears in another location; a box is placed behind a screen, the screen falls backward into empty space. Like adults, babies tend to linger on such scenes—they look longer at them than at scenes that are identical in all regards except that they don't violate physical laws. This suggests that babies have expectations about how objects should behave. A vast body of research now suggests that—contrary to what was taught for decades to legions of psychology undergraduates—babies think of objects largely as adults do, as connected masses that move as units, that are solid and subject to gravity and that move in continuous paths through space and time.

Other studies, starting with a 1992 paper by my wife, Karen, have found that babies can do rudimentary math with objects. The demonstration is simple. Show a baby an empty stage. Raise a screen to obscure part of the stage. In view of the baby, put a Mickey Mouse doll behind the screen. Then put another Mickey Mouse doll behind the screen. Now drop the screen. Adults expect two dolls—and so do 5-month-olds: if the screen drops to reveal one or three dolls, the babies look longer, in surprise, than they do if the screen drops to reveal two.

A second wave of studies used looking-time methods to explore what babies know about the minds of others—a baby's "naïve psychology." Psychologists had known for a while that even the youngest of babies treat people different from inanimate objects. Babies like to look at faces; they mimic them, they smile at them. They expect engagement: if a moving object becomes still, they merely lose interest; if a person's face becomes still, however, they become distressed.

But the new studies found that babies have an actual understanding of mental life: they have some grasp of how people think and why they act as they do. The studies showed that, though babies expect inanimate objects to move as the result of push-pull interactions, they expect people to move rationally in accordance with their beliefs and desires: babies show surprise when someone takes a roundabout path to something he wants. They expect someone who reaches for an object to reach for the same object later, even if its location has changed. And well before their 2nd birthdays, babies are sharp enough to know that other people can have false beliefs. The psychologists Kristine Onishi and Renée Baillargeon have found that 15-month-olds expect that if a person sees an object in one box, and then the object is moved to another box when the person isn't looking, the person will later reach into the box where he first saw the object, not the box where it actually is. That is, toddlers have a mental model not merely of the world but of the world as understood by someone else.

These discoveries inevitably raise a question: If babies have such a rich understanding of objects and people so early in life, why do they seem so ignorant and helpless? Why don't they put their knowledge to more active use? One possible answer is that these capacities are the psychological equivalent of physical traits like testicles or ovaries, which are formed in infancy and then sit around, useless, for years and years. Another possibility is that babies do, in fact, use their knowledge from Day 1, not for action but for learning. One lesson from the study of artificial intelligence (and from cognitive science more generally) is that an empty head learns nothing: a system that is capable of rapidly absorbing information needs to have some prewired understanding of what to pay attention to and what generalizations to make. Babies might start off smart, then, because it enables them to get smarter.

Nice Babies

Psychologists like myself who are interested in the cognitive capacities of babies and toddlers are now turning our attention to whether babies have a "naïve morality." But there is reason to proceed with caution. Morality, after all, is a different sort of affair than physics or psychology. The truths of physics and psychology are universal: objects obey the same physical laws everywhere; and people everywhere have minds, goals, desires and beliefs. But the existence of a universal moral code is a highly controversial claim; there is considerable evidence for wide variation from society to society.

In the journal *Science,* a couple of months ago, the psychologist Joseph Henrich and several of his colleagues reported a cross-cultural study of 15 diverse populations and found that people's propensities to behave kindly to strangers and to punish unfairness are strongest in large-scale communities with market economies, where such norms are essential to the smooth functioning of trade. Henrich and his colleagues concluded that much of the morality that humans possess is a consequence of the culture in which they are raised, not their innate capacities.

At the same time, though, people everywhere have *some* sense of right and wrong. You won't find a society where people don't have some notion of fairness, don't put some value on loyalty and kindness, don't distinguish between acts of cruelty and innocent mistakes, don't categorize people as nasty or nice. These universals make evolutionary sense. Since natural selection works, at least in part, at a genetic level, there is a logic to being instinctively kind to our kin, whose survival and well-being promote the spread of our genes. More than that, it is often beneficial for humans to work together with other humans, which means that it would have been adaptive to evaluate the niceness and nastiness of other individuals. All this is reason to consider the innateness of at least basic moral concepts.

In addition, scientists know that certain compassionate feelings and impulses emerge early and apparently universally in human development. These are not moral concepts, exactly, but they seem closely related. One example is feeling pain at the pain of others. In his book "The Expression of the Emotions in Man and Animals," Charles Darwin, a keen observer of human nature, tells the story of how his first son, William, was fooled by his nurse into expressing sympathy at a very young age: "When a few days over 6 months old, his nurse pretended to cry, and I saw that his face instantly assumed a melancholy expression, with the corners of his mouth strongly depressed."

There seems to be something evolutionarily ancient to this empathetic response. If you want to cause a rat distress, you can expose it to the screams of other rats. Human babies, notably, cry more to the cries of other babies than to tape recordings of their *own* crying, suggesting that they are responding to their awareness of someone else's pain, not merely to a certain pitch of sound. Babies also seem to want to assuage the pain of others: once they have enough physical competence (starting at about 1 year old), they soothe others in distress by stroking and touching or by handing over a bottle or toy. There are individual differences, to be sure, in the intensity of response: some babies are great soothers; others don't care as much. But the basic impulse seems common to all. (Some other primates behave similarly: the primatologist Frans de Waal reports that chimpanzees "will approach a victim of attack, put an arm around her and gently pat her back or groom her." Monkeys, on the other hand, tend to shun victims of aggression.)

Some recent studies have explored the existence of behavior in toddlers that is "altruistic" in an even stronger sense—like when they give up their time and energy to help a stranger accomplish a difficult task. The psychologists Felix Warneken and Michael Tomasello have put toddlers in situations in which an adult is struggling to get something done, like opening a cabinet door with his hands full or trying to get to an object out of reach. The toddlers tend to spontaneously help, even without any prompting, encouragement or reward.

Is any of the above behavior recognizable as moral conduct? Not obviously so. Moral ideas seem to involve much more than mere compassion. Morality, for instance, is closely related to notions of praise and blame: we want to reward what we see as good and punish what we see as bad. Morality is also closely connected to the ideal of impartiality—if it's immoral for you to do something to me, then, all else being equal, it is immoral for me to do the same thing to you. In addition, moral principles are different from other types of rules or laws: they cannot, for instance, be overruled solely by virtue of authority. (Even a 4-year-old knows not only that unprovoked hitting is wrong but also that it would continue to be wrong even if a teacher said that it was O.K.) And we tend to associate morality with the possibility of free and rational choice; people *choose* to do good or evil. To hold someone responsible for an act means that we believe that he could have chosen to act otherwise.

Babies and toddlers might not know or exhibit any of these moral subtleties. Their sympathetic reactions and motivations—including their desire to alleviate the pain of others—may not be much different in kind from purely nonmoral reactions and motivations like growing hungry or wanting to void a full bladder. Even if that is true, though, it is hard to conceive of a moral system that didn't have, as a starting point, these empathetic capacities. As David Hume argued, mere rationality can't be the foundation of morality, since our most basic desires are neither rational nor irrational. "Tis not contrary to reason," he wrote, "to prefer the destruction of the whole world to the scratching of my finger." To have a genuinely moral system, in other words, some things first have to matter, and what we see in babies is the development of *mattering*.

Moral-Baby Experiments

So what do babies really understand about morality? Our first experiments exploring this question were done in collaboration with a postdoctoral researcher named Valerie Kuhlmeier (who is now an associate professor of psychology at Queen's University in Ontario). Building on previous work by the psychologists David and Ann Premack, we began by investigating what babies think about two particular kinds of action: helping and hindering.

Our experiments involved having children watch animated movies of geometrical characters with faces. In one, a red ball would try to go up a hill. On some attempts, a yellow square got behind the ball and gently nudged it upward; in others, a green triangle got in front of it and pushed it down. We were interested in babies' expectations about the ball's attitudes—what would the baby expect the ball to make of the character who helped it and the one who hindered it? To find out, we then showed the babies additional movies in which the ball either approached the square or the triangle. When the ball approached the triangle (the hinderer), both 9- and 12-month-olds looked longer than they did when the ball approached the square (the helper). This was consistent with the interpretation that the former action surprised them; they expected the ball to approach the helper. A later study, using somewhat different stimuli, replicated the finding with 10-month-olds, but found that 6-month-olds seem to have no expectations at all. (This effect is robust only when the animated characters have faces; when they are simple faceless figures, it is apparently harder for babies to interpret what they are seeing as a social interaction.)

This experiment was designed to explore babies' expectations about social interactions, not their moral capacities per se. But if you look at the movies, it's clear that, at least to adult eyes, there is some latent moral content to the situation: the triangle is kind of a jerk; the square is a sweetheart. So we set out to investigate whether babies make the same judgments about the characters that adults do. Forget about how babies expect the ball to act toward the other characters; what do babies themselves think about the square and the triangle? Do they prefer the good guy and dislike the bad guy?

Here we began our more focused investigations into baby morality. For these studies, parents took their babies to the Infant Cognition Center, which is within one of the Yale psychology buildings. (The center is just a couple of blocks away from where Stanley Milgram did his famous experiments on obedience in the early 1960s, tricking New Haven residents into believing that they had severely harmed or even killed strangers with electrical shocks.) The parents were told about what was going to happen and filled out consent forms, which described the study, the risks to the baby (minimal) and the benefits to the baby (minimal, though it is a nice-enough experience). Parents often asked, reasonably enough, if they would learn how their baby does, and the answer was no. This sort of study provides no clinical or educational feedback about individual babies; the findings make sense only when computed as a group.

For the experiment proper, a parent will carry his or her baby into a small testing room. A typical experiment takes about 15 minutes. Usually, the parent sits on a chair, with the baby on his or her lap, though for some studies, the baby is strapped into a high chair with the parent standing behind. At this point, some of the babies are either sleeping or too fussy to continue; there will then be a short break for the baby to wake up or calm down, but on average this kind of study ends up losing about a quarter of the subjects. Just as critics describe much of experimental psychology as the study of the American college undergraduate who wants to make some extra money or needs to fulfill an Intro Psych requirement, there's some truth to the claim that this developmental work is a science of the interested and alert baby.

In one of our first studies of moral evaluation, we decided not to use two-dimensional animated movies but rather a three-dimensional display in which real geometrical objects, manipulated like puppets, acted out the helping/hindering situations: a yellow square would help the circle up the hill; a red triangle would push it down. After showing the babies the scene, the experimenter placed the helper and the hinderer on a tray and brought them to the child. In this instance, we opted to record not the babies' looking time but rather which character they reached for, on the theory that what a baby reaches for is a reliable indicator of what a baby wants. In the end, we found that 6- and 10-month-old infants overwhelmingly preferred the helpful individual to the hindering individual. This wasn't a subtle statistical trend; just about all the babies reached for the good guy.

(Experimental minutiae: What if babies simply like the color red or prefer squares or something like that? To control for this, half the babies got the yellow square as the helper; half got it as the hinderer. What about problems of unconscious cueing and unconscious bias? To avoid this, at the moment when the two characters were offered on the tray, the parent had his or her eyes closed, and the experimenter holding out the characters and recording the responses hadn't seen the puppet show, so he or she didn't know who was the good guy and who the bad guy.)

One question that arose with these experiments was how to understand the babies' preference: did they act as they did because they were attracted to the helpful individual or because they were repelled by the hinderer or was it both? We explored this question in a further series of studies that introduced a neutral character, one that neither helps nor hinders. We found that, given a choice, infants prefer a helpful character to a neutral one and prefer a neutral character to one who hinders. This finding indicates that both inclinations are at work—babies are drawn to the nice guy and repelled by the mean guy. Again, these results were not subtle; babies almost always showed this pattern of response.

Does our research show that babies believe that the helpful character is *good* and the hindering character is *bad?* Not necessarily. All that we can safely infer from what the babies reached for is that babies prefer the good guy and show an aversion to the bad guy. But what's exciting here is that these preferences are based on how one individual treated another, on whether one individual was helping another individual achieve its goals or hindering it. This is preference of a very special sort; babies were responding to behaviors that adults would describe as nice or mean. When we showed these scenes to much older kids—18-month-olds—and asked them, "Who was nice? Who was good?" and "Who was mean? Who was bad?" they responded as adults would, identifying the helper as nice and the hinderer as mean.

To increase our confidence that the babies we studied were really responding to niceness and naughtiness, Karen Wynn and Kiley Hamlin, in a separate series of studies, created different sets of one-act morality plays to show the babies. In one, an individual struggled to open a box; the lid would be partly opened but then fall back down. Then, on alternating trials, one puppet would grab the lid and open it all the way, and another puppet would jump on the box and slam it shut. In another study (the one I mentioned at the beginning of this article), a puppet would play with a ball. The puppet would roll the ball to another puppet, who would roll it back, and the first puppet would roll the ball to a different puppet who would run away with it. In both studies, 5-month-olds preferred the good guy—the one who helped to open the box; the one who rolled the ball back—to the bad guy. This all suggests that the babies we studied have a general appreciation of good and bad behavior, one that spans a range of actions.

A further question that arises is whether babies possess more subtle moral capacities than preferring good and avoiding bad. Part and parcel of adult morality, for instance, is the idea that good acts should meet with a positive response and bad acts with a negative response—justice demands the good be rewarded and the bad punished. For our next studies, we turned our attention back to the older babies and toddlers and

tried to explore whether the preferences that we were finding had anything to do with moral judgment in this mature sense. In collaboration with Neha Mahajan, a psychology graduate student at Yale, Hamlin, Wynn and I exposed 21-month-olds to the good guy/bad guy situations described above, and we gave them the opportunity to reward or punish either by giving a treat to, or taking a treat from, one of the characters. We found that when asked to give, they tended to choose the positive character; when asked to take, they tended to choose the negative one.

Dispensing justice like this is a more elaborate conceptual operation than merely preferring good to bad, but there are still-more-elaborate moral calculations that adults, at least, can easily make. For example: Which individual would you prefer—someone who rewarded good guys and punished bad guys or someone who punished good guys and rewarded bad guys? The same amount of rewarding and punishing is going on in both cases, but by adult lights, one individual is acting justly and the other isn't. Can babies see this, too?

To find out, we tested 8-month-olds by first showing them a character who acted as a helper (for instance, helping a puppet trying to open a box) and then presenting a scene in which this helper was the target of a good action by one puppet and a bad action by another puppet. Then we got the babies to choose between these two puppets. That is, they had to choose between a puppet who rewarded a good guy versus a puppet who punished a good guy. Likewise, we showed them a character who acted as a hinderer (for example, keeping a puppet from opening a box) and then had them choose between a puppet who rewarded the bad guy versus one who punished the bad guy.

The results were striking. When the target of the action was itself a good guy, babies preferred the puppet who was nice to it. This alone wasn't very surprising, given that the other studies found an overall preference among babies for those who act nicely. What was more interesting was what happened when they watched the bad guy being rewarded or punished. Here they chose the punisher. Despite their overall preference for good actors over bad, then, babies are drawn to bad actors when those actors are punishing bad behavior.

All of this research, taken together, supports a general picture of baby morality. It's even possible, as a thought experiment, to ask what it would be like to see the world in the moral terms that a baby does. Babies probably have no conscious access to moral notions, no idea why certain acts are good or bad. They respond on a gut level. Indeed, if you watch the older babies during the experiments, they don't act like impassive judges—they tend to smile and clap during good events and frown, shake their heads and look sad during the naughty events (remember the toddler who smacked the bad puppet).

The babies' experiences might be cognitively empty but emotionally intense, replete with strong feelings and strong desires. But this shouldn't strike you as an altogether alien experience: while we adults possess the additional critical capacity of being able to consciously reason about morality, we're not otherwise that different from babies—our moral feelings are often instinctive. In fact, one discovery of contemporary research in social psychology and social neuroscience is the powerful emotional underpinning of what we once thought of as cool, untroubled, mature moral deliberation.

Is This the Morality We're Looking For?

What do these findings about babies' moral notions tell us about adult morality? Some scholars think that the very existence of an innate moral sense has profound implications. In 1869, Alfred Russel Wallace, who along with Darwin discovered natural selection, wrote that certain human capacities—including "the higher moral faculties"—are richer than what you could expect from a product of biological evolution. He concluded that some sort of godly force must intervene to create these capacities. (Darwin was horrified at this suggestion, writing to Wallace, "I hope you have not murdered too completely your own and my child.")

A few years ago, in his book "What's So Great About Christianity," the social and cultural critic Dinesh D'Souza revived this argument. He conceded that evolution can explain our niceness in instances like kindness to kin, where the niceness has a clear genetic payoff, but he drew the line at "high altruism," acts of entirely disinterested kindness. For D'Souza, "there is no Darwinian rationale" for why you would give up your seat for an old lady on a bus, an act of nice-guyness that does nothing for your genes. And what about those who donate blood to strangers or sacrifice their lives for a worthy cause? D'Souza reasoned that these stirrings of conscience are best explained not by evolution or psychology but by "the voice of God within our souls."

The evolutionary psychologist has a quick response to this: To say that a biological trait evolves for a purpose doesn't mean that it always functions, in the here and now, for that purpose. Sexual arousal, for instance, presumably evolved because of its connection to making babies; but of course we can get aroused in all sorts of situations in which baby-making just isn't an option—for instance, while looking at pornography. Similarly, our impulse to help others has likely evolved because of the reproductive benefit that it gives us in certain contexts—and it's not a problem for this argument that some acts of niceness that people perform don't provide this sort of

benefit. (And for what it's worth, giving up a bus seat for an old lady, although the motives might be psychologically pure, turns out to be a coldbloodedly smart move from a Darwinian standpoint, an easy way to show off yourself as an attractively good person.)

The general argument that critics like Wallace and D'Souza put forward, however, still needs to be taken seriously. The morality of contemporary humans really does outstrip what evolution could possibly have endowed us with; moral actions are often of a sort that have no plausible relation to our reproductive success and don't appear to be accidental byproducts of evolved adaptations. Many of us care about strangers in faraway lands, sometimes to the extent that we give up resources that could be used for our friends and family; many of us care about the fates of nonhuman animals, so much so that we deprive ourselves of pleasures like rib-eye steak and veal scaloppine. We possess abstract moral notions of equality and freedom for all; we see racism and sexism as evil; we reject slavery and genocide; we try to love our enemies. Of course, our actions typically fall short, often far short, of our moral principles, but these principles do shape, in a substantial way, the world that we live in. It makes sense then to marvel at the extent of our moral insight and to reject the notion that it can be explained in the language of natural selection. If this higher morality or higher altruism were found in babies, the case for divine creation would get just a bit stronger.

But it is not present in babies. In fact, our initial moral sense appears to be biased toward our own kind. There's plenty of research showing that babies have within-group preferences: 3-month-olds prefer the faces of the race that is most familiar to them to those of other races; 11-month-olds prefer individuals who share their own taste in food and expect these individuals to be nicer than those with different tastes; 12-month-olds prefer to learn from someone who speaks their own language over someone who speaks a foreign language. And studies with young children have found that once they are segregated into different groups—even under the most arbitrary of schemes, like wearing different colored T-shirts—they eagerly favor their own groups in their attitudes and their actions.

The notion at the core of any mature morality is that of impartiality. If you are asked to justify your actions, and you say, "Because I wanted to," this is just an expression of selfish desire. But explanations like "It was my turn" or "It's my fair share" are potentially moral, because they imply that anyone else in the same situation could have done the same. This is the sort of argument that could be convincing to a neutral observer and is at the foundation of standards of justice and law. The philosopher Peter Singer has pointed out that this notion of impartiality can be found in religious and philosophical systems of morality, from the golden rule in Christianity to the teachings of Confucius to the political philosopher John Rawls's landmark theory of justice. This is an insight that emerges within communities of intelligent, deliberating and negotiating beings, and it can override our parochial impulses.

The aspect of morality that we truly marvel at—its generality and universality—is the product of culture, not of biology. There is no need to posit divine intervention. A fully developed morality is the product of cultural development, of the accumulation of rational insight and hard-earned innovations. The morality we start off with is primitive, not merely in the obvious sense that it's incomplete but in the deeper sense that when individuals and societies aspire toward an enlightened in which all beings capable of reason and suffering are on an equal footing, where all people are equal—they are fighting with what children have from the get-go. The biologist Richard Dawkins was right, then, when he said at the start of his book *The Selfish Gene,* "Be warned that if you wish, as I do, to build a society in which individuals cooperate generously and unselfishly toward a common good, you can expect little help from biological nature." Or as a character in the Kingsley Amis novel *One Fat Englishman* puts it, "It was no wonder that people were so horrible when they started life as children."

Morality, then, is a synthesis of the biological and the cultural, of the unlearned, the discovered and the invented. Babies possess certain moral foundations—the capacity and willingness to judge the actions of others, some sense of justice, gut responses to altruism and nastiness. Regardless of how smart we are, if we didn't start with this basic apparatus, we would be nothing more than amoral agents, ruthlessly driven to pursue our self-interest.

But our capacities as babies are sharply limited. It is the insights of rational individuals that make a truly universal and unselfish morality something that our species can aspire to.

Critical Thinking

1. Given the information in this article, would you conclude that babies have a moral life? What qualifications or reservations would you have?

2. In what ways could the various findings cited in this article be used to argue that morality is determined by "nature"? In what ways could they support the "naurture" argument?

Create Central

www.mhhe.com/createcentral

Internet References

EarlyChildhoodNews.com
> http://www.earlychildhoodnews.com/earlychildhood/article_view.aspx?ArticleID=118

International Centre for Educators' Styles
> http://www.icels-educators-for-learning.ca/index.php?option=com_content&view=article&id=48&Itemid=62

PsychologyToday.com
> http://www.psychologytoday.com/blog/child-myths/200911/learning-right-wrong-how-does-morality-develop

---

PAUL BLOOM is a professor of psychology at Yale. His new book, *How Pleasure Works,* will be published next month.

Article

Prepared by: Chris J. Boyatzis, *Bucknell University*

Same Place, Different Experiences: Bringing Individual Differences to Research in Child Care

DEBORAH A. PHILLIPS, NATHAN A. FOX, AND MEGAN R. GUNNAR

Learning Outcomes

After reading this article, you will be able to:

- Justify why it is important to pay attention to individual differences in development.

- Describe the role of reactivity to stress and temperament in children's individual differences.

Research on child care has focused on how various features of care, notably the timing and amount of exposure, type and stability of care, and level of quality, affect the typical course of development (Lamb & Ahnert, 2006; Phillips & Lowenstein, in press; Phillips, McCartney, & Sussman, 2006). In this article, we argue that the next wave of child-care research needs to draw upon insights from research on temperament, and even newer evidence regarding stress reactivity, to explicate how individual differences interact with features of child care to produce distinct patterns of outcomes for different children.

During the infant day-care debate of the mid-1980s, temperament was repeatedly mentioned as an important moderating influence to be examined in future research (see Fein & Fox, 1988). Belsky (1988) noted the need to understand the characteristics of the "50 percent or more of the infants" who, in his review of the extant literature, established secure relationships with their mothers "despite" early exposure to child care. He and other commentators (Clarke-Stewart, 1988; Phillips, McCartney, Scarr, & Howes, 1987; Sroufe, 1988) pointed specifically to infant temperament as an especially promising

variable to pursue to gain a more nuanced understanding of within-group differences in the effects of infant child care. Nevertheless, the contribution of temperament to the evolving portrait of child-care effects has remained a relatively neglected issue, perhaps because the driving questions for so much of this research over the past 20 years have been *whether* and *under what conditions* of care—not *for whom*—child care confers risk or protection. It is this neglect that we seek to remedy.

Child-Care Risks and Benefits

At the outset, a brief summary of what current evidence tells us about *whether* and *under what conditions* child-care experiences affect early development is warranted insofar as this evidence sets the stage for our focus on the *for whom* question. This evidence now indicates that early nonparental care environments sometimes pose risks to young children and sometimes confer benefits, but most often they play a less powerful—albeit significant and cumulative—role in the context of other potent influences, such as the quality of parental care (National Institute of Child Health and Human Development Early Child Care Research Network [NICHD ECCRN], 2006; Phillips et al., 2006). Efforts to explain these divergent effects have focused on identifying the conditions of care that affect children's social development because this is the behavioral domain for which mixed outcomes have been reported most frequently.

Extensive evidence indicates that higher *quality* of child care increases the odds of positive social skills and adjustment, while higher *amounts* of child care contribute to elevated (albeit non-clinical) levels of externalizing behavior, including aggression, noncompliance, risk taking, and impulsivity (NICHD ECCRN, 2006; Phillips & Lowenstein, in press; Phillips et al., 2006). Recent longitudinal findings from the NICHD Study of Early Child Care and Youth Development indicate that this pattern holds up through age 15 years (Belsky et al., 2007; NICHD ECCRN, 2005). Other attempts to discern the conditions under which child care elevates the odds of negative social behavior have pointed to the contribution of type of care and, specifically, time in center-based care (Belsky et al., 2007; NICHD ECCRN, 2005). Some have speculated that the proximal or active ingredient behind these effects is the social opportunities and challenges posed by peer groups (Fabes, Hanish, & Martin, 2003), and emerging evidence lends support to this possibility. As Crockenberg (2003) has noted, however, the relatively small effect sizes in these studies make it clear that only some children display heightened externalizing behavior in response to child care, thus highlighting the pressing question of who these children are. Unfortunately, these studies rarely examined the mediating role played by children's temperaments, and when they did, significant findings did not emerge. They also relied almost exclusively on parental and teacher reports of temperament, which limited their conclusions. This body of research is therefore unable to shed much light on the question of which children are most sensitive to variation in quality and quantity of child care.

Why the *for Whom* Question?

We argue that this mixed pattern of evidence points to the need to go beyond examination of the type, quantity, and quality of care to understand how the day-to-day experiences of individual children in the same child-care settings might differ, thus leading to different outcomes for different children. Two interrelated strands of evidence are especially pertinent in this context. The first strand involves preliminary evidence that child-care influences vary with certain temperamental dispositions in young children (Fox, Henderson, Rubin, Calkins, & Schmidt, 2001; Watamura, Donzella, Alwin, & Gunnar, 2003), especially tendencies toward negative emotional reactivity, inhibition, and social reticence. The second strand implicates child-care experiences in the early development of physiological processes that govern the regulation of stress (Geoffroy, Cote, Parent, & Seguin, 2006; Vermeer & van IJzendoorn, 2006). Considered together, these two strands of research create an exciting opportunity to revisit how the field approaches questions of individual differences among infants and children in response to child care. They also carry the potential to bring evidence from child-care research to bear on pressing questions regarding how early social experiences get "under the skin" to affect the paths that children follow toward problematic or promising futures.

Temperament and Child Care

It is now well established that individual differences in patterns of emotional reactivity to novelty early in infancy are associated with subsequent social outcomes (Fox, Henderson, Marshall, Nichols, & Ghera, 2005; Kagan, Snidman, & Arcus, 1998). Negative emotional reactivity in early infancy, characterized by high levels of crying and motor arousal during presentation of novel sensory stimuli, appears to be a precursor to behavioral inhibition and social reticence. Positive reactivity, characterized by high motor arousal in the absence of negative emotion, is associated with a pattern of behavioral exuberance that, if not tempered by strong regulatory control, can manifest itself in externalizing behaviors (Rothbart & Bates, 2006).

Efforts to understand the influence of rearing environments on the development of children with varying temperamental profiles have focused almost exclusively on the home environment and parenting (Degnan, Henderson, Fox, & Rubin, 2008; Hane, Cheah, Rubin, & Fox, 2008). Only recently have examinations of the influence of nonparental child care on children with varying temperaments begun to emerge, driven by questions about whether links between child care and developmental outcomes are more pronounced for children with particular temperamental profiles and whether child-care experiences play a role in the discontinuities that are often seen in the expression of temperament over time. The answer that is emerging, in both cases, is yes.

Both the amount of child care and the quality of care have been found to affect children with different temperaments in different ways, with both positive and negative impacts being reported in the literature. With regard to the amount of care, greater exposure to child care has been associated with increased internalizing behavior for children characterized by their mothers as, or observed to be, fearful of novelty, but not for their unfearful peers (Crockenberg & Leerkes, 2005; De Shipper, Tavecchio, van IJzendoorn, & van Zeijl, 2004). Crockenberg and Leerkes (2005) further reported that long hours in child care led to more externalizing behavior for children observed to be more easily frustrated by limits and that this effect was restricted to children attending child-care centers, which raises the issue of peer influences that has become salient within the child-care literature more broadly. Others, however, have reported positive associations between exposure to child care and social behavior among children with more emotionally reactive temperaments. In one case, longer hours in care predicted fewer internalizing symptoms in 5-year-olds characterized as temperamentally positive in infancy (Almas, Phillips, & Fox, 2009); in another, exposure to child care with peers during the toddler years differentiated behaviorally inhibited children who became less inhibited over time from those who displayed greater stability in this temperamental style (Fox et al., 2001).

Variation in child-care quality also appears to have differing consequences for children with different temperamental profiles. Pluess and Belsky (2009) found that the teacher-rated social development of preschool- and kindergarten-age children who were portrayed by their mothers as temperamentally difficult during infancy was more susceptible to variation in the quality of child care—but not to variation in the amount of care—than was the case for children who were not difficult as infants. Results just emerging from a collaboration between Phillips and Fox indicate that toddlers characterized as high in temperamental fear at 4 months of age were, compared to their less reactive peers, more sensitive to variation in the quality of their child-care experiences defined in terms of both positive peer interactions (Almas et al., in press) and caregiver sensitivity-warmth and an overall positive emotional climate (Phillips et al., 2010). Almas and colleagues (in press) found that more positive peer interactions in child care at 24 months were associated with *less* wariness around unfamiliar peers in the lab at 36 months of age for these children, but not for their temperamentally more typical peers. Phillips and colleagues (2010) found that higher quality caregiving was uniquely associated with less isolation from peers in child care at age 24 months for the children characterized by negative reactivity as infants. Children characterized by positive reactivity were also less isolated from peers under conditions of higher quality care. This evidence is reminiscent of prior findings that the quality of peer interactions experienced by infants who were rated high in social fear was more positive among those in high-quality care and more negative among infants in low-quality care than was the case for their peers who were rated low in social fear (Volling & Feagans, 1995).

These findings clearly implicate child care as an important environment to consider in research on the developmental pathways followed by children with differing temperamental profiles. They also indicate that temperament contributes to individual differences in response to both the amount and quality of child care that children experience. In both cases, the results point particularly to children characterized by negative emotionality, inhibition, and social fear as a group who may be especially sensitive to variation in features of child care. At this point, however, the findings are mixed with regard to which dimensions of child care matter most for children at the more reactive ends of the temperament spectrum.

The Regulation of Stress and Child Care

Turning to the second strand of research on child care, we call attention to the activity of the hypothalamic–pituitary–adrenal (HPA) system, which regulates physiological and behavioral responses to stress. Recent research clearly suggests that some children react to child care as a stressful experience. This evidence, in turn, is directly pertinent to efforts to understand which children, under what conditions, are most likely to respond this way and what behavioral processes these responses set in motion. We start with a brief summary of the role of cortisol as an influence on early development.

The HPA system produces cortisol, a steroid hormone that plays critical roles in adaptation to stressors (Gunnar & Quevedo, 2007). The impact of elevated levels of cortisol on neural development depends, in part, on the neural systems that are activated in response to given stressors. Research on animals shows that when cortisol is elevated in conjunction with events stimulating fear and anxiety, it supports the laying down of threat memories and affects plasticity in brain regions coordinating anxious, fearful behavior (Roozendaal, McEwen, & Chattarji, 2009). Cortisol's impact on the brain also reflects activity of corticotropin-releasing hormone (CRH). This neuropeptide is produced not only in the hypothalamus (where it regulates the cascade of events that ultimately increase cortisol production by the adrenal glands) but also in brain systems that support fear and anxiety (e.g., amygdala) and the orchestration of behavioral and sympathetic fight-flight responses.

Interactions between cortisol, CRH, and other neurochemical systems activated in response to perceived threat have been shown in animal studies to bias developing organisms toward heightened defensive rather than exploratory responses to novel or ambiguous situations, including social encounters (Joels & Baram, 2009). Thus, it is hypothesized that repeated or prolonged activation of the HPA axis and CRH in the context of adverse or threatening care experiences may increase the functioning of brain systems underlying fear and anxiety and impair the development of brain systems involved in memory and behavior regulation. Explicit links to enduring behavioral consequences, however, remain to be documented. These neurological, regulatory effects are expected to be more marked during periods of rapid brain development, such as the first years of life, when children are also adjusting to child care (Gunnar & Quevedo, 2007).

With respect to child care, several studies in both the United States and abroad indicate that children in child care exhibit higher cortisol levels (due largely to rising levels over the course of the day) than they do on days spent at home. Both meta-analyses (Geoffroy et al., 2006; Vermeer & van IJzendoorn, 2006) and recent data (Dettling, Gunnar, & Donzella, 1999; Gunnar, Kryzer, van Ryzin, & Phillips, 2010) suggest that this pattern is more notable in toddlers and younger preschoolers than in older preschoolers and school-aged children. It is also more pronounced among children in full-day care (Geoffroy et al., 2006; Vermeer & van IJzendoorn, 2006) and those in poorer quality care (Dettling, Parker, Lane, Sebanc, & Gunnar,

2000; Gunnar et al., 2010; Legendre, 2003; Sims, Guilfoyle, & Parry, 2006; Watamura, Kryzer, & Robertson, 2009). Intrusive, overcontrolling caregiver–child interactions (Gunnar et al., 2010), as well as daily schedules characterized by long periods of both provider-directed, structured activities and frequent full-group transitions (Sims et al., 2006), have been associated with larger rises in cortisol over the child-care day. Notably, these are also child-care conditions that are known to be associated with poorer socioemotional outcomes for young children. Unfortunately, to date, there are no long-term longitudinal studies linking variation in child-care quality with both behavioral and neurobiological responding among children in care. Moreover, there is some evidence that elevated cortisol levels at child care (relative to home) resolve themselves with age and exposure to care (Ouellet-Morin et al., 2010).

In an initial attempt to better understand concurrent relations among child-care quality, cortisol elevations, and children's behavior in child care, we (Gunnar et al., 2010) recently examined preschool-aged children in family child-care settings. As in other studies, we found that cortisol levels were higher at child care than at home, rose from morning to afternoon at child care, and were particularly high by late afternoon at child care. Four of 10 children met criteria that indicate a significant stress response of the HPA axis. Cortisol elevations were associated with both child-care quality and children's behavior. Specifically, cortisol rose more over the day in family child-care homes in which children received more intrusive, overcontrolling care. For girls, anxious–vigilant behavior was associated with larger rises in cortisol; for boys, angry–aggressive behavior was associated with the rise in cortisol. A 6-month follow-up study addressed the question of the longer term consequences of these altered cortisol patterns associated with early child-care experience (Gunnar, Kryzer, van Ryzin, & Phillips, in press). The rise in cortisol at Time 1 was associated with higher levels of anxious–vigilant behavior in child care and with more internalizing symptoms at Time 2. However, these associations emerged only among children who, at Time 1, were observed (laboratory assessment) to display, and were rated by parent and caregivers as having, behaviorally inhibited temperaments.

This pattern of findings raises the possibility that children's temperaments play a role in their neurobiological and behavioral adaptation to child care. Not only have children with differing temperaments been found to react differently to variation in the amount and quality of child care, as reviewed earlier, but certain temperaments have been implicated in studies of cortisol responses among children in child care. Specifically, while not found consistently (Watamura, Sebanc, & Gunnar, 2002), there is a tendency for children who, according to observation or teacher or parent reports, display social fearfulness, negative emotional temperaments, and poorer self-control to show relatively larger rises in cortisol levels over the course of the day in

child care than do their more temperamentally easy-going peers (Dettling et al., 1999, 2000; Tout, de Haan, Kipp Campbell, & Gunnar, 1998; Watamura et al., 2003).

What might underlie the relation between temperament and stress reactivity in the context of child care? Our speculation leads us to the role of social evaluative threat in the activation of the HPA system. Social evaluative threat, which includes being rejected, ignored, or worried about making mistakes and being thought badly of, is a very potent trigger of fear and anxiety, and thus of stress, in adults and children (Dickerson & Kemeny, 2004; van Goozen, Fairchild, Snoek, & Harold, 2007). In that child-care environments confront young children with the challenge of negotiating relations with other children at a stage when peer skills are just developing, they may be more stressful for certain children. For children with more negative, inhibited temperaments, the experience of child care may provide more frequent opportunities for the activation of social fearfulness, which characterizes children with this temperamental disposition. For children who tend toward aggressive behavior, child care may pose experiences of social threat that arise from negative peer interactions.

Longer hours in care likely play a role insofar as the challenges of negotiating peer interactions, which are especially daunting for children with these more reactive temperaments, become even more taxing over the course of the child-care day. Quality of care adds to this equation insofar as the caregivers' ability to provide emotional support and buffer children from peer-related sources of stress (e.g., isolation, rejection, aggression) probably contributes to whether or not these children, in particular, experience child care as stressful. Speculation that these issues will be more salient in settings with larger groups of children (Belsky et al., 2007; Legendre, 2003) requires additional exploration, given that they appear to be operational in small family day-care settings, as well (Gunnar et al., 2010, in press). To come full circle, then, current evidence suggests that the features of child care that we have highlighted need to be examined in conjunction with children's temperaments and experiences of stress to best capture the processes that render child care either a positive or negative experience for young children.

Implications for Child-Care Research

The evidence we have reviewed raises the possibility that the emergence and nature of both negative and positive socialemotional effects associated with child care depend on the interplay between children's individual differences, notably those associated with temperament and stress reactivity, and the circumstances of their child care, particularly with regard to the social challenges these settings pose to young children and how well the children are supported by the adults who care for them in their efforts to manage these challenges. This assertion is consistent with both the biological sensitivity to context theory (Boyce & Ellis, 2005) and with the differential susceptibility hypothesis (Belsky, 1997; Belsky & Pluess, 2009). While the differential susceptibility hypothesis focuses on genes and temperamental dispositions, and the biological sensitivity to context theory emphasizes physiological reactivity to stress as a trait that enhances sensitivity to context, they are both consistent with the argument that children at the extremes of the temperament spectrum will be more sensitive to variations in environmental conditions. Accordingly, children with more reactive temperaments would be hypothesized not only to experience more stress and negative outcomes than other children do when rearing conditions are poor but also to experience less stress and better outcomes when rearing conditions are especially supportive.

At the outset, we argued that emerging evidence at the intersection of stress reactivity, temperament, and child care holds the potential to advance understanding of the factors that converge to render child care a beneficial or risky context for young children. We further asserted that this question needs to be approached from an individual differences perspective, for which notions of biological sensitivity to context are especially pertinent. Guided by this general perspective, we call for four lines of research.

First, to make predictions about the effects of child care on children with different temperaments, there is a need for increased specificity to the measurement of temperament and with that, better description of which aspects of temperament are involved in shaping the trajectories of social and emotional development for children with varying child-care experiences. In this context, it is essential to have more refined information about the composition of the child-care peer group (with regard to temperamental and behavioral dispositions) and more refined observations of both how children with different temperaments negotiate peer interactions and how caregivers either support or fail to support these efforts. Further, it will be important to examine the possibility that high-quality caregiving entails somewhat different strategies for the withdrawn, inhibited child than it does for the approach-driven, exuberant child.

Second, longitudinal studies are needed to understand how children who begin care with differing temperamental dispositions change over time in child care as a function of their experiences with both child-care providers and other children. This will necessarily entail sampling children in different types of care, with differing peer demands and wide variation in the quality of caregiving. Further, this work needs to take the children's age and history of child-care experience into account.

Third, longitudinal studies that integrate assessments of temperament and stress reactivity (i.e., cortisol levels) are needed to advance understanding of how these two facets of development—one a biologically based disposition and the other a physiological reaction to environmental conditions—interact to influence children's social-emotional, regulatory, and cognitive responses to child care in the short and long term. Here again, specific observations of how children who vary in temperament and stress reactivity deploy coping strategies when confronted with challenging social encounters—and are facilitated or undermined by their caregivers—will be an important element of this work.

Finally, we urge efforts to examine the role that temperament, as well as other indicators of biological risk (e.g., special needs status), plays in conjunction with indicators of environmental risk, such as poverty and low parental education or literacy, in influencing the developmental impacts of child care. Such efforts would have huge payoffs (see, e.g., Corapci, 2008).

Our hope is that these new directions for research on child care, focused on questions of individual differences, will ultimately lead to greater understanding of the children for whom we should have the greatest concern and, accordingly, who we have the greatest potential to help, as they experience the challenges and opportunities posed by their early histories of exposure to child care.

References

Almas, A., Phillips, D., & Fox, N. (2009). *The moderating role of temperamental reactivity in the associations between non-maternal childcare during toddlerhood and children's internalizing and externalizing behavior at 5 years of age.* Unpublished manuscript, University of Maryland.

Almas, A., Phillips, D., Henderson, H., Hane, A., Degnan, K., & Fox, N. (in press). The relations between infant negative reactivity, non-maternal childcare, and children's interactions with familiar and unfamiliar peers. *Social Development.*

Belsky, J. (1988). The "effects" of infant day care reconsidered. *Early Childhood Research Quarterly, 3,* 235–272.

Belsky, J. (1997). Variation in susceptibility to rearing influences: An evolutionary argument. *Psychological Inquiry, 8,* 182–186.

Belsky, J., & Pluess, M. (2009). Beyond diathesis stress: Differential susceptibility to environmental influences. *Psychological Bulletin, 135,* 885–908.

Belsky, J., Vandell, D. L., Burchinal, M., Clarke-Stewart, K. A., McCartney, K., Owen, M. T., et al. (2007). Are there long-term effects of early child care? *Child Development, 78,* 681–701.

Boyce, W. T., & Ellis, B. J. (2005). Biological sensitivity to context: I. An evolutionary developmental theory of the origins and functions of stress reactivity. *Development and Psychopathology, 17,* 271–301.

Clarke-Stewart, K. A. (1988). "The 'effects' of infant day care reconsidered" reconsidered. *Early Childhood Research Quarterly, 3,* 293–318.

Corapci, F. (2008). The role of child temperament on Head Start preschoolers' social competence in the context of cumulative risk. *Journal of Applied Developmental Psychology, 29,* 1–16.

Crockenberg, S. C. (2003). Rescuing the baby from the bathwater: How gender and temperament influence how child care affects child development. *Child Development, 74,* 1034–1038.

Crockenberg, S. C., & Leerkes, E. M. (2005). Infant temperament moderates associations between childcare type and quantity and externalizing and internalizing behaviors at 2½ years. *Infant Behavior and Development, 28,* 20–35.

Degnan, K. A., Henderson, H. A., Fox, N. A., & Rubin, K. H. (2008). Predicting social wariness in middle childhood: The moderating roles of childcare history, maternal personality, and maternal behavior. *Social Development, 17,* 471–487.

De Shipper, J. C., Tavecchio, L. W. C., van IJzendoorn, M. H., & van Zeijl, J. (2004). Goodness-of-fit in center day care: Relations of temperament, stability, and quality of care with the child's adjustment. *Early Childhood Research Quarterly, 19,* 257–272.

Dettling, A. C., Gunnar, M. R., & Donzella, B. (1999). Cortisol levels of young children in full-day childcare centers: Relations with age and temperament. *Psychoneuroendocrinology, 24,* 519–536.

Dettling, A., Parker, S. W., Lane, S., Sebanc, A., & Gunnar, M. R. (2000). Quality of care and temperament determine whether cortisol levels rise over the day for children in full-day child care. *Psychoneuroendocrinology, 25,* 819–836.

Dickerson, S. S., & Kemeny, M. E. (2004). Acute stressors and cortisol responses: A theoretical integration and synthesis of laboratory research. *Psychological Bulletin, 130,* 355–391.

Fabes, R. A., Hanish, L. D., & Martin, C. L. (2003). Children at play: The role of peers in understanding the effects of child care. *Child Development, 74,* 1039–1043.

Fein, G., & Fox, N. (Guest Eds.). (1988). Special Issue: Infant day care. *Early Childhood Research Quarterly, 3*(3).

Fox, N. A., Henderson, H. A., Marshall, P. J., Nichols, K. E., & Ghera, M. M. (2005). Behavioral inhibition: Linking biology and behavior within a developmental framework. *Annual Review of Psychology, 56,* 235–262.

Fox, N. A., Henderson, H. A., Rubin, K. H., Calkins, S. D., & Schmidt, L. A. (2001). Continuity and discontinuity of behavioral inhibition and exuberance: Psychophysiological and behavioral influences across the first four years of life. *Child Development, 72,* 1–21.

Geoffroy, M.-C., Cote, S. M., Parent, S., & Seguin, J. R. (2006). Daycare attendance, stress, and mental health. *Canadian Journal of Psychiatry, 51,* 607–615.

Gunnar, M. R., Kryzer, E., van Ryzin, M. J., & Phillips, D. A. (2010). The rise in cortisol in family day care: Associations with aspects of care quality, child behavior, and child sex. *Child Development, 81,* 853–870.

Gunnar, M. R., Kryzer, E., van Ryzin, M. J., & Phillips, D. A. (in press). The import of the cortisol rise at child care differs as a function of behavioral inhibition. *Developmental Psychology.*

Gunnar, M. R., & Quevedo, L. (2007). The neurobiology of stress and development. *Annual Review of Psychology, 58,* 145–173.

Hane, A. A., Cheah, C., Rubin, K. H., & Fox, N. A. (2008). The role of maternal behavior in the relation between shyness and social reticence in early childhood and social withdrawal in middle childhood. *Social Development, 17,* 795–811.

Joels, M., & Baram, T. Z. (2009). The neurosymphony of stress. *Nature Review Neuroscience, 10,* 459–466.

Kagan, J., Snidman, N., & Arcus, D. (1998). Childhood derivates of high and low reactivity in infancy. *Child Development, 69,* 1483–1493.

Lamb, M. E., & Ahnert, L. (2006). Nonparental child care: Context, concepts, correlates, and consequences. In W. Damon & R. M. Lerner (Series Eds.) & K. A. Renninger & I. E. Sigel (Vol. Eds.), *Handbook of child psychology: Vol. 4. Child psychology in practice* (6th ed., pp. 950–1016). Hoboken, NJ: Wiley.

Legendre, A. (2003). Environmental features influencing toddlers' bioemotional reactions in day care centers. *Environment and Behavior, 35,* 523–549.

National Institute of Child Health and Human Development Early Child Care Research Network. (2005). Early child care and children's development in the primary grades: Results from the NICHD Study of Early Child Care. *American Educational Research Journal, 43,* 537–570.

National Institute of Child Health and Human Development Early Child Care Research Network. (2006). *Child care and child development. Results from the NICHD Study of Early Child Care and Youth Development.* New York: Guildford.

Ouellet-Morin, I., Tremblay, R. E., Boivin, M., Meaney, M., Kramer, M., & Cote, S. M. (2010). Diurnal cortisol secretion at home and in child care: A prospective study of 2-year old toddlers. *Journal of Child Psychology and Psychiatry, 51,* 295–303.

Phillips, D., Crowell, N., Sussman, A. L., Fox, N., Hane, A., Gunnar, M., et al. (2010). *Child care and children's temperaments: A story of moderation.* Manuscript submitted for publication.

Phillips, D., & Lowenstein, A. (in press). Structure and goals of preschool educational settings. *Annual Review of Psychology.*

Phillips, D., McCartney, K., Scarr, S., & Howes, C. (1987). Selective review of infant day care research: A cause for concern. *Zero to Three, 7,* 18–21.

Phillips, D., McCartney, K., & Sussman, A. (2006). Child care and early development. In K. McCartney & D. Phillips (Eds.), *Handbook of early childhood development* (pp. 471–489). Malden, MA: Blackwell.

Pluess, M., & Belsky, J. (2009). Differential susceptibility to rearing experience: The case of childcare. *Journal of Child Psychology and Psychiatry, 50,* 396–404.

Roozendaal, B., McEwen, B. S., & Chattarji, S. (2009). Stress, memory and the amygdale. *Natural Review of Neuroscience, 10,* 423–433.

Rothbart, M. K., & Bates, J. E. (2006). Temperament. In W. Damon & R. Lerner (Series Eds.) & N. Eisenberg (Vol. Ed.), *Handbook of child psychology: Vol. 3. Social, emotional, and personality development* (pp. 99–166). Hoboken, NJ: Wiley.

Sims, M., Guilfoyle, A., & Parry, T. S. (2006). Children's cortisol levels and quality of child care provision. *Child: Care, Health, and Development, 32,* 453–466.

Sroufe, L. A. (1988). A developmental perspective on day care. *Early Childhood Research Quarterly, 3,* 283–292.

Tout, K., de Haan, M., Kipp Campbell, E. K., & Gunnar, M. R. (1998). Social behavior correlates of cortisol activity in child care: Gender differences and time of day effects. *Child Development, 69,* 1247–1262.

van Goozen, S. H., Fairchild, G., Snoek, H., & Harold, G. T. (2007). The evidence for neurobiological model of childhood antisocial behavior. *Psychological Bulletin, 133,* 149–182.

Vermeer, H. J., & van IJzendoorn, M. H. (2006). Children's elevated cortisol levels at daycare: A review and meta-analysis. *Early Childhood Research Quarterly, 21,* 390–401.

Volling, B., & Feagans, L. (1995). Infant day care and children's social competence. *Infant Behavior and Development, 18,* 177–188.

Watamura, S. E., Donzella, B., Alwin, J., & Gunnar, M. R. (2003). Morning to afternoon increases in cortical concentrations for infants and toddlers at child care: Age differences and behavioral correlates. *Child Development, 74,* 1006–1020.

Watamura, S. E., Kryzer, E. M., & Robertson, S. S. (2009). Cortisol patterns at home and child care: Afternoon differences and evening recovery in children attending very high quality full-day center-based child care. *Journal of Applied Developmental Psychology, 30,* 475–485.

Watamura, S. E., Sebanc, A. M., & Gunnar, M. R. (2002). Rising cortisol at childcare: Relations with nap, rest, and temperament. *Developmental Psychobiology, 40,* 33–42.

Critical Thinking

1. How does this article help us move beyond the traditional approaches to studying how child care affects children? How does this article help you appreciate the need to study individual differences between children?

2. Why are children's temperament and reactivity to stress so important for shaping how they respond to, and are affected by, child care?

Create Central

www.mhhe.com/createcentral

Internet References

Ability Path.org

http://www.abilitypath.org/areas-of-development/social—emotional/behavior-and-discipline/articles/behavior-individualdifferences.html

Education.com

http://www.education.com/reference/article/individual-differences-children

Article

Prepared by: Ellen N. Junn, *California State University, Dominguez Hills*

The Role of Neurobiological Deficits in Childhood Antisocial Behavior

STEPHANIE H. M. VAN GOOZEN, GRAEME FAIRCHILD, AND GORDON T. HAROLD

Learning Outcomes

After reading this article, you will be able to:

- Evaluate and assess the extent to which genes and the environment influence the development and maintenance of antisocial behavior in children. Summarize and recommend interventions that may help reduce antisocial behavior in children. Cite supportive evidence on the efficacy of the various interventions.

- Recommend possible changes in medical practice or training that would assist physicians and child specialists in better diagnosing and treating children with antisocial behavior, conduct disorder, or oppositional defiant disorder.

- Understand the role that early experiences and family adversity play in antisocial behavior.

- Analyze the theoretical model relating early social adversity to later antisocial behavior problems

- Explain how stress impacts individual differences in antisocial behavior

A ntisocial behavior is a significant social and clinical concern. Every year, more than 1.6 million people are killed as a result of violence, and many more suffer from physical or mental health problems stemming from violence (World Health Organization, 2002). Antisocial behavior committed by youths is an issue of particular concern. A recent survey showed that citizens of European nations see themselves as having "significant" difficulties with antisocial behavior and that the problem is above all associated with people under 25 years of age ("Bad behaviour," 2006).

The term *antisocial behavior* refers to the fact that people who are on the receiving end of the behavior are disadvantaged by it and that social norms and values are violated. Not only aggression but also activities such as theft, vandalism, lying, truancy, running away from home, and oppositional behaviors are involved.

Most normally developing children will occasionally exhibit negative and disobedient behavior toward adults and engage in lying, fighting, and bullying other children. When antisocial behavior forms a pattern that goes beyond the "normal" realm and starts to have adverse effects on the child's functioning, psychiatrists tend to make a diagnosis of conduct disorder (CD) or oppositional defiant disorder (ODD; American Psychiatric Association, 1994). These disorders are relatively common in children, with estimated prevalences ranging from 5 to 10 percent. The extent to which these disorders can be treated via therapy is limited, and, as a result, these children are at risk for a host of negative outcomes in adolescence and adulthood, including dropping out of school, criminality unemployment, dependence on welfare, and substance abuse (Hill & Maughan, 2001).

There is a growing consensus that both child-specific (i.e., genetic, temperamental) and social (e.g., early adversity) factors contribute to the development and maintenance of antisocial behavior, although most research has focused on identifying specific contextual factors that impinge on the developing child. For example, negative life events, family stress, and parental relationship problems have been associated with antisocial-behavior problems in children. However, there is increasing evidence that factors organic to individual children exacerbate the risk of antisocial behavior to those who live with social adversity. Here, we review evidence relating to the role of neurobiological factors in accounting for the link between early adversity and childhood antisocial behavior and propose that consideration of biological factors underlying this stress–distress link significantly advances understanding of the mechanisms explaining individual differences in the etiology of antisocial behavior.

Research suggests that neurobiological deficits related to the functioning of the stress systems in children with CD are linked to antisocial behavior. We argue that familial factors (e.g., genetic influences, early adversity) are linked to negative outcomes through the mediating and transactional interplay with neurobiological deficits (see Figure 1) and propose that stress hyporeactivity is an index of persistent and serious antisocial behavior.

Stress-Response Systems

There are clear indications that stress plays an important role in explaining individual differences in antisocial behavior. The systems involved in the regulation of stress are the neuroendocrine hypothalamic-pituitary-adrenal (HPA) axis and the psychophysiological autonomic nervous system (ANS). Cortisol is studied in relation to HPA-axis activation, and heart rate (HR) and skin-conductance (SC) responses are used as markers of ANS (re)activity.

The starting point of our approach is that antisocial individuals are less sensitive to stress. This can be deduced from the fact that antisocial individuals engage in risky or dangerous behavior more often than other people do and seem less deterred by its possible negative consequences. There are two explanations for the proposed relationship between lower stress sensitivity and antisocial behavior. One theory claims that antisocial individuals are fearless (Raine, 1996). A lack of fear leads to antisocial behavior because individuals are less sensitive to the negative consequences of their own or other people's behavior in general and to the receipt of punishment in particular. The implications for treatment are clear: Antisocial individuals will have problems learning the association between behavior and punishment, such that pointing out the negative consequences of behavior, or punishing unacceptable behavior, is likely to have little or no effect.

The second explanation focuses on stress thresholds and sensation-seeking behavior (Zuckerman, 1979) and argues that antisocial individuals have elevated thresholds for stress. They are more easily bored and less easily put off by situations that normal people find stressful or dangerous.

What evidence is there that dysfunctional stress systems play a role in antisocial behavior? Several studies (e.g., Virkkumen, 1985) have found that antisocial adults have low resting levels of cortisol, SC, and HR. There is also evidence of inverse relationships between these physiological variables and the severity of the behavioral problems shown. Studies investigating the relation between biological stress parameters and antisocial behavior have also been performed in children (e.g., van Goozen et al., 1998), and the predicted (inverse) relations have been found.

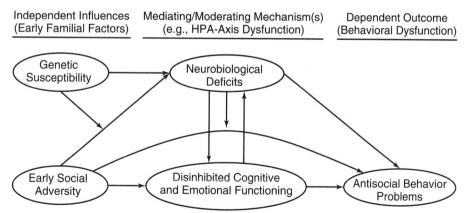

Figure 1 Theoretical model relating early social adversity to later antisocial behavior problems. It is hypothesized that this relationship is explained by the underlying mediating and moderating role of neurobiological factors. The dashed rolled lines emanating from genetic susceptibility to neurobiological deficits and from neurobiological deficits to antisocial behavior problems represent an indirect (or mediating) pathway between these factors. The bold line emanating from genetic susceptibility to the pathway linking early social adversity to neurobiological deficits and the dashed-dotted line from neurobiological deficits to the pathway linking early social adversity to antisocial behavior problems represent proposed moderating influences from each source variable (i.e., genetic susceptibility and neurobiological deficits). A moderating influence is the equivalent of statistical interaction between two theoretical constructs. Bold and dashed-dotted lines in all other instances represent direct and indirect pathways linking primary theoretical constructs. For a full exposition of this model, see van Goosen, Fairchild, Snoek, and Harold (2007).

Stress variables can also predict antisocial behavior over time. Raine, Venables, and Mednick (1997) measured HR in more than 1,700 three-year-old children. Aggressive behavior was assessed at age 11. Raine et al. found that low resting HR at age 3 predicted aggressive behavior at age 11. In a study of criminals' sons (who are at risk of becoming delinquent), Brenman et al. (1997) found that boys who did not become delinquent had higher HR and SC than did boys who became delinquent. The authors concluded that the boys in the former group were biologically protected by their heightened autonomic responsivity.

Studies of youths who engage in antisocial behavior show that they, like antisocial adults, have less reactive stress systems than do youths who do not engage in antisocial behavior. The question is whether the same applies to children with serious antisocial behavior who have been diagnosed with CD or ODD.

Stress Studies in CD Children

Most studies collect stress data under resting conditions rather than during stress exposure. Antisocial individuals might be different from normal individuals in two respects: A low resting stress level could result in failing to avoid, or even approaching, stressful situations and low stress reactivity implies that one is more fearless and cares less about possible negative consequences.

Our studies use a paradigm in which psychosocial stress is evoked by exposing children to frustration, provocation, and competition (e.g., van Goozen et al., 1998). The participant competes against a fictitious videotaped "opponent" who behaves in an antagonistic manner. The participant and opponent perform computerized tasks on which they can earn points. The participant is told that the person who earns the most points will receive an attractive prize. Some tasks are impossible to complete, which induces frustration. HR and SC are measured continuously, and cortisol is collected repeatedly in saliva.

CD children show lower HR, SC, and cortisol reactivity to stress than do normal children. Although CD children appear to be less affected at a biological level, they react more angrily and aggressively to provocation than do non-CD children and report feeling quite upset. It is known that CD children are impulsive, have hostile appraisal patterns, and engage in conflictual situations. It is striking that this pattern of appraisal and behavior is not accompanied by contextually appropriate somatic changes.

Genetic factors likely play a role in the functioning of the HPA axis and ANS. There is also evidence that stressful events—by which we mean serious stressors like neglect and traumatization—play an important role in "programming" the stress systems, particularly the HPA axis. This evidence comes mainly from nonhuman animal studies, but the neurobiological consequences of the types of severe stress that can be manipulated in animal studies also occur in humans.

Early Experience and Family Adversity

Physical and biological problems during important phases in development (e.g., birth complications, stress or illness during pregnancy), together with early adversity (e.g., malnutrition, neglect, abuse), contribute importantly to the development of personality and psychopathology. There is increasing evidence that interactions between biological and environmental factors affect the developing brain (Huizink, Mulder, & Buitelaar, 2004).

Nonhuman animal studies show that stressors in early life can have permanent effects on the functioning of the HPA axis, resulting in altered basal and stress-reactivity levels. For example, Liu et al. (1997) varied the amount of licking and grooming behavior in mothers of newborn rats. In adulthood, offspring who had been exposed to normal maternal care were more capable of handling stress than were rats that had received less care. The former also expressed more stress-hormone receptors in the hippocampus, an area important for stress regulation, than did rats that had received less care. Thus, maternal behavior had a direct and lasting effect on the development of the stress systems of the offspring.

Such conclusions are based on data from nonhuman animals, and for obvious reasons, it is difficult to conduct similar studies on humans. However, evidence from a handful of studies involving institutionalized children suggests that the processes at work are similar (Carlson & Earls, 1997; Gunnar, Morison, Chisolm, & Schuder, 2001).

Antisocial children are more likely to come from adverse rearing environments involving atypical caregiver–child interactions (Rutter & Silberg, 2002). It is known that CD children are more likely to experience compromised pre- or perinatal development due to maternal smoking, poor nutrition, or exposure to alcohol and/or drugs. It is possible that these factors have affected such children's stress-response systems and resulted in children with a difficult temperament.

Stress Hyporeactivity as a Mediating Factor

We have suggested that physiological hyporeactivity may reflect an inability to generate visceral signals to guide behavior and, in particular, to regulate anger and reactive aggression (van Goozen, Fairchild, Snoek, & Harold, 2007). Evidence from nonhuman animals indicates that abolishing the hormonal response to stress may impair processing of social signals and lead to abnormal patterns of aggression (Haller, Halász, Mikics, & Kruk, 2004). These studies also showed that abnormal aggressive behavior can be prevented by mimicking the hormonal response normally seen during aggressive encounters. These findings have clear parallels with abnormal aggression in humans, in the sense that the behavior is not only excessive but also often risky, badly judged, and callous.

We have proposed an integrative theoretical model linking genetic factors, early adversity, cognitive and neurobiological regulatory mechanisms, and childhood antisocial behavior (van Goozen et al., 2007; see Figure 1). Interactions between genetic predispositions and the environment in which they are expressed appear to be crucial in the etiology of antisocial-behavior problems. A genetic predisposition toward antisocial behavior may be expressed in adverse rearing environments in which the child receives harsh or inconsistent discipline or is exposed to high levels of interparental conflict or marital breakdown (Moffitt, 2005). It is likely that the origin of antisocial behavior in young children lies in this combination of a difficult temperament and a harsh environment in which there is ineffective socialization: A difficult child elicits harsh, inconsistent, and negative socialization behaviors, as a result of which a difficult temperament develops into antisocial behavior (Lykken, 1995). Conversely, the effects of a genetic predisposition may be minimized if the child is raised in an environment in which the parents express warmth or adopt a consistent, authoritative parenting style.

Some children are born with a more easygoing temperament than others. In cases of "hard-to-manage" children, a child's genotype can evoke negative behavior from the environment because genetic influences lead the individual to create, seek out, or otherwise end up in environments that match the genotype (Rutter & Silberg, 2002). These active, evocative gene–environment processes are extremely important in understanding the development and continuity of antisocial behavior (Moffitt, 2005). Social factors occurring independently of the child's genetic makeup or temperament can serve as contributory factors (Harold, Aitken, & Shelton, 2008).

We noted above that early brain development is vulnerable to the effects of environmental stress (Huizink et al., 2004) and that CD children are likely to have been exposed to early stress. A down regulation of the stress-response system in the face of chronic stress in early life would be an adaptive mechanism, avoiding chronic arousal and excessive energy expenditure that could ultimately result in serious pathophysiological consequences. Given what we know about the background of CD children, it is plausible that these processes have occurred.

We propose that physiological hyperactivity is a mediating and/or moderating factor for persistent and severe antisocial behavior and that the effects of variations in genetic makeup and early adversity on childhood antisocial behavior occur via this deficit. The primary pathway by which familial factors are linked to antisocial outcome is the reciprocal interplay with neurobiological deficits and resulting disinhibited cognitive (e.g., impulsivity, hostile bias) and emotional (e.g., increased anger) processing, with the latter serving as the psychological gateway through which neurobiological deficits find their expression in antisocial behavior.

Conclusion

Antisocial behavior in children can be persistent and difficult to treat. Although behavioral interventions have been shown to be effective in milder forms of problem behavior, they have limited effectiveness in more seriously disturbed children (Hill & Maughan, 2001).

At present, we do not know what causes the pattern of neurobiological impairments observed in antisocial children, although it is clear that genetic factors are involved (Caspi et al., 2002). An important line of research suggests that psychosocial adversity affects brain development. Knowing that many CD children have problematic backgrounds, it seems possible that exposure to severe stress has had an effect on the development of their stress systems. Longitudinal research in high-risk children is needed to shed more light on this issue.

Future interventions and treatments should benefit from a neurobiological approach: Neurobiological assessment of high-risk children could indicate whether their deficits are such that interventions involving "empathy induction" or "learning from punishment," for example, are unlikely to work. In such cases, pharmacological interventions could be considered as a treatment option. An important line of future research is to establish whether CD children with attenuated stress (re)activity would be more effectively treated by using pharmacological therapies that reinstate normal HPA-axis functioning.

Current interventions for childhood antisocial behavior have limited success because we lack knowledge of the cognitive–emotional problems of these children and their neurobiological bases. We also fail to assess the environmental risk factors that affect individual neurodevelopment. Furthermore, available treatment options do not target the individual's specific neurobiological vulnerabilities. It seems prudent to identify subgroups of children in whom different causal processes initiate and maintain behavioral problems. This should result in a better match between patient and treatment.

A final point is that the understandable tendency to focus on persistence of antisocial behavior runs the risk of overlooking the fact that a substantial proportion of antisocial children do not grow up to be antisocial adults (with prevalence rates for antisocial children who persist into adulthood ranging from 35 to 75 percent). Neurobiological factors could also account for this: Promising data from a handful of studies show that neurobiological factors differ between children who persist in and desist from antisocial behavior (Brennan et al., 1997; van de Wiel, van Goozen, Matthys, Snoek, & van Engeland, 2004). Expanding on this research base is essential if we are to reach a more adequate understanding of the causes, course, and consequences of childhood antisocial behavior and, most importantly, devise effective ways of reducing the negative consequences for society.

Recommended Reading

Hill, J., & Maughan, B. (2001). *Conduct disorders in childhood and adolescence.* Cambridge, UK: Cambridge University Press. A clearly written and comprehensive review for readers who wish to expand their knowledge on conduct disorders in youngsters.

Moffitt, T.E. (2005). The new look of behavioral genetics in developmental psychopathology: Gene–environment interplay in antisocial behaviors. *Psychological Bulletin, 131,* 533–554. Explains and discusses the gene–environment interplay in antisocial behavior in more detail.

van Goozen, S.H.M., Fairchild, G., Snoek, H., & Harold, G.T. (2007). The evidence for a neurobiological model of childhood antisocial behavior. *Psychological Bulletin, 133,* 149–182. Discusses the neurobiological basis of antisocial behavior in greater detail than the current paper.

References

American Psychiatric Association. (1994). *Diagnostic and statistical manual of mental disorders* (4th ed.). Washington, DC: Author.

Bad behaviour 'worst in Europe'. (2006). BBC News. Downloaded April 30, 2008, from http://news.bbc.co.uk/l/hi/uk/4751315.stm

Brennan, P.A., Raine, A., Schulsinger, F., Kirkegaard-Sorensen, L., Knop, J., Hutchings, B., et al. (1997). Psychophysiological protective factors for male subjects at high risk for criminal behavior. *American Journal of Psychiatry, 154,* 853–855.

Carlson, M., & Earls, F. (1997). Psychological and neuroendocrinological sequelae of early social deprivation in institutionalized children in Romania. *Annals of the New York Academy of Sciences, 807,* 419–428.

Caspi, A., McClay J., Moffitt, T.E., Mill, J., Martin, J., Craig, I.W., et al. (2002). Role of the genotype in the cycle of violence in maltreated children. *Science, 297,* 851–854.

Gunnar, M.R., Morison, S.J., Chisholm, K., & Schuder, M. (2001). Salivary cortisol levels in children adopted from Romanian orphanages. *Development and Psychopathology, 13,* 611–628.

Harold, G.T, Aitken, J.J., & Shelton, K.H. (2008). Inter-parental conflict and children's academic attainment: A longitudinal analysis. *Journal of Child Psychology and Psychiatry, 48,* 1223–1232.

Haller, J., Halász, J., Mikics, E., & Kruk, M.R. (2004). Chronic glucocorticoid deficiency-induced abnormal aggression, autonomic hypoarousal, and social deficit in rats. *Journal of Neuroendocrinology, 16,* 550–557.

Hill, J., & Maughan, B. (2001). *Conduct disorders in childhood and adolescence.* Cambridge, UK: Cambridge University Press.

Huizink, A.C., Mulder, E.J.H., & Buitelaar, J.K. (2004). Prenatal stress and risk for psychopathology: Specific effects or induction of general susceptibility. *Psychological Bulletin, 130,* 115–142.

Liu, D., Diorio, J., Tannenbaum, B., Caldji, C., Francis, D., Freedman, A., et al. (1997). Maternal care, hippocampal glucocorticoid receptors, and hypothalamic-pituitary-adrenal responses to stress. *Science, 277,* 1659–1662.

Lykken, D.T (1995). *The antisocial personalities.* Hillsdale, NJ: Erlbaum.

Moffitt, T.E. (2005). The new look of behavioral genetics in developmental psychopathology: Gene–environment interplay in antisocial behaviors. *Psychological Bulletin, 131,* 533–554.

Raine, A. (1996). Autonomic nervous system activity and violence. In D.M. Stoff & R.B. Cairns (Eds.), *Aggression and violence: Genetic, neurobiological and biological perspectives* (pp. 145–168). Mahwah, NJ: Erlbaum.

Raine, A., Venables, P.H., & Mednick, S.A. (1997). Low resting heart rate at age 3 years predisposes to aggression at age 11 years: Evidence from the Mauritius Child Health Project. *Journal of the American Academy of Child and Adolescent Psychiatry, 36,* 1457–1464.

Rutter, M., & Silberg, J. (2002). Gene–environment interplay in relation to emotional and behavioral disturbance. *Annual Review of Psychology, 53,* 463–490.

van de Wiel, N.M.H., van Goozen, S.H.M., Matthys, W., Snoek, H., & van Engeland, H. (2004). Cortisol and treatment effect in children with disruptive behavior disorders: A preliminary study. *Journal of the American Academy of Child and Adolescent Psychiatry, 43,* 1011–1018.

van Goozen, S.H.M., Fairchild, G., Snoek, H., & Harold, G.T. (2007). The evidence for a neurobiological model of childhood antisocial behaviour. *Psychological Bulletin, 133,* 149–182.

van Goozen, S.H.M., Matthys, W., Cohen-Kettenis P.T, Gispen-de Wied, C., Wiegant, V.M., & van Engeland, H. (1998). Salivary cortisol and cardiovascular activity during stress in oppositional-defiant disorder boys and normal controls. *Biological Psychiatry, 43,* 531–539.

Virkkunen, M. (1985). Urinary free cortisol secretion in habitually violent offenders. *Acta Psychiatrica Scandinavica, 72,* 40–44.

World Health Organization. (2002). In E.G. Krug, L.L. Dahlman, J.A. Mercy, A.B. Zwi, & R. Lozano (Eds.), *World report on violence and health.* Geneva, Switzerland: Author.

Zuckerman, M. (1979). *Sensation seeking: Beyond the optimum level of arousal.* Hillsdale, NJ: Erlbaum.

Critical Thinking

1. Several highly visible cases of tragic school violence across the country have been traced to incidences of antisocial behavior in school. According to this article, what factors might have contributed toward making some children antisocial?

2. Suppose you are the parent of a young child who has been diagnosed with conduct disorder (CD) or oppositional defiant disorder (ODD). Based on this article, does this mean that your child will grow up to be an antisocial adult? What interventions (both behavioral and pharmacological) might be available to you for your child and how effective might these be?

3. Imagine you are a director or principal in a school with preschoolers or young children. Over the past year, the number of young children being diagnosed with possible conduct disorders in your school has doubled. Given the information in this article, what specific steps would you take to assist these children and families that would involve your teachers, the parents, and the surrounding medical community?

4. Based on this article, support your arguments with evidence and information involving early biological factors and the neurobiological stress-response systems (e.g., early physical adversity such as birth complications, temperament, lower resting stress levels, stronger negative response reactivity, and higher sensation-seeking behavior). Explain how social and environmental factors also can exacerbate or mediate these more biological factors.

Create Central

www.mhhe.com/createcentral

Internet References

GlobalPost.com
http://everydaylife.globalpost.com/characteristics-antisocial-behavior-children-5090.html
NCBI National Center for Biotechnology Information.org
http://www.ncbi.nlm.nih.gov/pubmed/17201574

Article   Prepared by: Ellen N. Junn, *California State University, Dominguez Hills*

Is Your Child Gay?

If your son likes sissy stuff or your daughter shuns feminine frocks, he or she is more likely to buck the heterosexual norm. But predicting sexual preference is still an inexact science.

JESSE BERING

Learning Outcomes

After reading this article, you will be able to:

- Understand how forms of play may act indicators of sexual orientation.
- Comprehend the difference between assessing sexual orientation with prospective and retrospective models.

We all know the stereotypes: an unusually light, delicate, effeminate air in a little boy's step, an interest in dolls, makeup, princesses and dresses, and a strong distaste for rough play with other boys. In little girls, there is the outwardly boyish stance, perhaps a penchant for tools, a square-jawed readiness for physical tussles with boys, and an aversion to all the perfumed, delicate trappings of femininity.

These behavioral patterns are feared, loathed and often spoken of directly as harbingers of adult homosexuality. It is only relatively recently, however, that developmental scientists have conducted controlled studies to identify the earliest and most reliable signs of adult homosexuality. In looking carefully at the childhoods of gay adults, researchers are finding an intriguing set of behavioral indicators that homosexuals seem to have in common. Curiously enough, the age-old homophobic fears of many parents reflect some genuine predictive currency.

J. Michael Bailey and Kenneth J. Zucker, both psychologists, published a seminal paper on childhood markers of homosexuality in 1995. Bailey and Zucker examined sex-typed behavior—that long, now scientifically canonical list of innate sex differences in the behaviors of young males versus young females. In innumerable studies, scientists have documented that these sex differences are largely impervious to learning.

They are also found in every culture examined. Of course, there are exceptions to the rule; it is only when comparing the aggregate data that sex differences leap into the stratosphere of statistical significance.

The most salient differences are in the domain of play. Boys engage in what developmental psychologists refer to as "rough-and-tumble play." Girls prefer the company of dolls to a knee in the ribs. Toy interests are another key sex difference, with boys gravitating toward toy machine guns and monster trucks and girls orienting toward baby dolls and hyperfeminized figurines. Young children of both sexes enjoy pretend play, but the roles within the fantasy context are gender-segregated by age two. Girls enact the role of, say, cooing mothers, ballerinas or fairy princesses and boys prefer to be soldiers and superheroes. Not surprisingly, therefore, boys naturally select other boys for playmates and girls would much rather play with other girls.

So on the basis of some earlier, shakier research, along with a good dose of common sense, Bailey and Zucker hypothesized that homosexuals would show an inverted pattern of sex-typed childhood behaviors—little boys preferring girls as playmates and becoming infatuated with their mother's makeup kit; little girls strangely enamored of field hockey or professional wrestling—that sort of thing. Empirically, the authors explain, there are two ways to investigate this hypothesis, with either a prospective or retrospective study. Using the prospective method, young children displaying sex-atypical patterns are followed into adolescence and early adulthood so that their sexual orientation can be assessed at maturity.

This method is not terribly practical for several reasons. Given that a small proportion of the population is homosexual, prospective studies require a large number of children. This approach also takes a long time, around 16 years. Finally, not a lot of parents are likely to volunteer their children. Right or wrong, this is a sensitive topic, and usually it is only children who present significant sex-atypical behaviors who are brought into clinics and whose cases are made available to researchers.

Rough-and-Tumble Girls

For example, in a 2008 study, psychologist Kelley Drummond and her colleagues interviewed 25 adult women who were referred by their parents for assessment at a mental health clinic when they were between three and 12 years old. At the time, all these girls had several diagnostic indicators of gender identity disorder. They might have strongly preferred male playmates, insisted on wearing boys' clothing, favored rough-and-tumble play, stated that they would eventually grow a penis or refused to urinate in a sitting position. Although only 12 percent of these women grew up to be gender dysphoric (the uncomfortable sense that your biological sex does not match your gender), the odds of these women reporting a bisexual or homosexual orientation were up to 23 times higher than would occur in a general sample of young women. Not all tomboys become lesbians, of course, but these data suggest that lesbians often have a history of cross-sex-typed behaviors.

And the same holds for gay men. Bailey and Zucker, who conducted a retrospective study in which adults answered questions about their past, revealed that 89 percent of randomly sampled gay men recalled cross-sex-typed childhood behaviors exceeding the heterosexual median.

Critics have argued that participants' memories may be distorted to fit with societal expectations and stereotypes. But in a clever study published in 2008 in *Developmental Psychology*, evidence from childhood home videos validated this retrospective method. People blindly coded child targets on the latter's sex-typical behaviors, as shown on the screen. The authors found that "those targets who, as adults, identified themselves as homosexual were judged to be gender nonconforming as children."

Numerous studies have since replicated this general pattern, revealing a strong link between childhood deviations from gender role norms and adult sexual orientation. There is also evidence of a "dosage effect": the more gender-nonconforming characteristics there are in childhood, the more likely it is that a homosexual or bisexual orientation will be present in adulthood.

Not all little boys who like to wear dresses grow up to be gay, nor do all little girls who despise dresses become lesbians. Many will be straight, and some, let's not forget, will be transsexuals. I was rather androgynous, showing a mosaic pattern of sex-typical and atypical behaviors. In spite of my parents' preferred theory that I was simply a young Casanova, Zucker and

Bailey's findings may account for that old Polaroid snapshot in which 11 of the 13 other children at my seventh birthday party are little girls. But I wasn't an overly effeminate child, was never bullied as a "sissy" and, by the time I was 10, was indistinguishably as annoying, uncouth and wired as my close male peers.

On the Monkey Bars

In fact, by age 13, I was deeply socialized into masculine norms. I took to middle school wrestling as a rather scrawny 80-pound eighth grader, and in so doing, ironically became all too conscious of my homosexual orientation.

Cross-cultural data show that prehomosexual boys are more attracted to solitary sports such as swimming, cycling and tennis than they are to rougher contact sports such as football and soccer; they are also less likely to be childhood bullies. In any event, I distinctly recall being with the girls on the monkey bars during recess in second grade while the boys were in the field playing football and looking over at them, thinking to myself how that was rather strange. I wondered why anyone would want to act that way.

Researchers readily concede that there are quite likely multiple—and no doubt extremely complicated—developmental routes to adult homosexuality. Heritable, biological factors interact with environmental experiences to produce sexual orientation. Because the data often reveal very early emerging traits in prehomosexuals, children who show pronounced sex-atypical behaviors may have more of a genetic loading to their homosexuality, whereas gay adults who were sex-typical as children might trace their homosexuality more directly to particular childhood experiences.

Then we arrive at the most important question of all. Why do parents worry so much about whether their child may or may not be gay? All else being equal, I suspect we would be hard-pressed to find parents who would actually prefer their offspring to be homosexual. Evolutionarily, parental homophobia is a no-brainer: gay sons and lesbian daughters are not likely to reproduce (unless they get creative).

But bear this in mind, parents, there are other ways for your child to contribute to your overall genetic success than humdrum sexual reproduction. I don't know how much money or residual fame is trickling down to, say, k. d. lang, Elton John and Rachel Maddow's close relatives, but I can only imagine that these straight kin are far better off in terms of their own reproductive opportunities than they would be without a homosexual dangling so magnificently on their family trees. So cultivate your little prehomosexual's native talents, and your ultimate genetic payoff could, strangely enough, be even larger with one very special gay child than it would be if 10 mediocre straight offspring leaped from your loins.

If researchers eventually perfect the forecasting of adult sexual orientation in children, would parents want to know? I can say as a once prehomosexual pipsqueak that some preparation on the part of others would have made it easier on me, rather than constantly fearing rejection or worrying about some careless slipup leading to my "exposure." It would have at least avoided all those awkward, incessant questions during my teenage years about why I wasn't dating a nice pretty girl (or questions from the nice pretty girl about why I was dating her and rejecting her advances).

And another thing: it must be pretty hard to look into your prehomosexual toddler's limpid eyes, brush away the cookie crumbs from her cheek and toss her out on the streets for being gay.

Critical Thinking

1. According to the author, how can you tell if a young child is gay?

2. Suppose you are a parent and you observe your child exhibiting sex-atypical behavior. How do you react to your child, and why?

3. Does the article's author have a personal bias? Do his personal anecdotes influence your interpretation of the findings or understanding of children's sexuality?

4. What role might environmental experiences play in the development of sexual orientation?

5. Do the research findings in this article suggest a strong genetic link to homosexuality? Why or why not?

Create Central

www.mhhe.com/createcentral

Internet References

Advocates for Youth.org
http://www.advocatesforyouth.org/pu

Parenting.com
http://www.parenting.com/article/could-your-child-be-gay

PFLAG.org
http://community.pflag.org/Page.aspx?pid=194&srcid=-2

Article

Prepared by: Chris J. Boyatzis, *Bucknell University*

To Help a Shy Child, Listen

Perri Klass

Learning Outcomes

After reading this article, you will be able to:

- Explain the role of temperament in how children react to the world and handle new situations.

- Describe effective strategies that teachers and parents could use to help shy children adapt and cope with new surroundings.

Toward the end of the summer, I was seeing a middle-school girl for a physical. The notes from a clinic visit last spring said she was a good student but didn't talk enough in class. So I asked her: Is this still a problem for you?

I'm shy, she said. I'm just shy.

Should I have turned to her mother and suggested—a counselor? An academic evaluation? Should I have probed further? How do you feel in school, do you have some friends, is anybody bullying you?

Or should I have said: Lots of people are shy. It's one of the healthy, normal styles of being human.

All of these responses, together, would have been correct. A child who is being bullied or bothered may be anxious about drawing attention to herself; a child who doesn't ever talk in class may be holding back because some learning problem is getting in the way, making her self-conscious. So you do need to listen—especially to a child who talks less rather than more—and find ways to ask questions. Are you happy, anxious, afraid?

But shyness is also part of the great and glorious range of the human normal. Two years ago, Kathleen Merikangas, a senior investigator at the National Institute of Mental Health, and her colleagues published a study of 10,000 older children, ranging from 13 to 18 years old. "We found that about half of kids in America describe themselves as shy," she told me.

Common though it may be, our schools—and our broader culture—do not always celebrate the reserved and retiring.

"Children who are shy, who don't raise their hand, who don't talk in class, are really penalized in this society," Dr. Merikangas said.

I have heard it said that temperament was invented by the first parent to have a second child—that's when parents realize that children come wired with many of the determinants of disposition and personality. What worked with Baby 1 doesn't necessarily work with Baby 2. The analysis of temperament has been a topic of discussion in pediatrics and psychology for decades.

"Temperament is the largely inborn set of behaviors that are the style with which a person functions, not to be confused with their motivation or their developmental status and abilities," said Dr. William B. Carey, a clinical professor of pediatrics at the Children's Hospital of Philadelphia and the author of *Understanding Your Child's Temperament*.

Shyness reflects a child's place on the temperamental continuum, the part of it that involves dealing with new and unfamiliar circumstances. And starting a new school year may be hard on those who find new situations more difficult and more full of anxiety. What most children need is time to settle in, support from parents and teachers, and sometimes help making connections and participating in class.

If a child is not more comfortable after a month or so, parents should look at whether more help is needed, said Anne Marie Albano, director of the Columbia University Clinic for Anxiety and Related Disorders. Treatment usually involves cognitive behavioral strategies to help the child cope with anxiety.

All ranges of temperament have their uncomfortable, or even pathological, outer zones. Just as there are children whose rambunctious eagerness to participate makes trouble for them in school or signals the presence of other problems, there are children whose silence is a shout for help.

I'm struck by the parallels between the ways we discuss shyness and the ways we discuss impulsivity and hyperactivity. In both cases, there is concern about the risk of "pathologizing" children who are well within the range of normal and worry that we are too likely to medicate outliers. By this thinking, children who would once have been considered shy and quiet too often get antidepressants, just as children who would once have been considered lively and rambunctious too often get A.D.H.D. medications.

But the most important question is whether children are in distress. Dr. Merikangas's study distinguished between the common trait of shyness and the psychiatric diagnosis of social phobia. Over all, about 5 percent of the adolescents in the study were severely restricted by social anxiety; they included some who described themselves as shy and some who did not. The authors questioned whether the debate about the "medicalization" of shyness might be obscuring the detection of the distinct signs of social phobia.

For parents who simply want to help a shy child cope with, for example, a brand new classroom full of brand new people, consider rehearsing, scripting encounters and interactions. "The best thing they can do is do a role play and behavioral rehearsal ahead of time," said Steven Kurtz, a senior clinician at the Child Mind Institute in Manhattan. Parents should "plan on rewarding the bravery."

But don't take over. "The danger point is rescuing too soon, too often, too much, so the kids don't develop coping mechanisms," said Dr. Kurtz.

Cognitive behavioral therapy relies on "successive approximations," in which children slowly close in on the behaviors they are hoping to achieve. In that spirit, a parent might arrange to meet another parent on the way to school, so a shy child can walk with another and bond. A teacher might look for the right partner to pair up with a shy child for cooperative activities in the classroom.

"Probably the worst thing to do is to say, 'Don't be shy. Don't be quiet,'" Dr. Merikangas told me. This is not about trying to change the child's temperament. It's about respecting and honoring temperament and variation and helping children navigate the world with their own instruments.

Critical Thinking

1. What would you do to help a shy child adjust to a new classroom? What are some suggestions you could give parents and teachers to help shy children adapt?

2. Do you think shyness is valued and desired in American culture? Why might we want or encourage children to be outgoing?

Create Central

www.mhhe.com/createcentral

Internet References

Ask Dr. Sears
http://www.askdrsears.com/topics/parenting/child-rearing-and-development/8-ways-help-shy-child

Better Health Channel
http://www.betterhealth.vic.gov.au/bhcv2/bhcarticles.nsf/pages/Shyness_and_children

Healthy Children.org
http://www.healthychildren.org/English/ages-stages/gradeschool/Pages/Shyness-in-Children.aspx

ShakeYourShyness.com
http://www.shakeyourshyness.com/parentingshychildren.htm

WebMD.org
http://www.webmd.com/parenting/features/parent-shy-child

Article   Prepared by: Chris J. Boyatzis, *Bucknell University*

Certain Television Fare Can Help Ease Aggression in Young Children, Study Finds

CATHERINE SAINT LOUIS

Learning Outcomes

After reading this article, you will be able to:

- Describe the research studies in the article that test whether watching TV leads to better or worse behavior.

- Design a new study with greater variety of TV shows to determine which lead to more aggression or prosocial behavior.

- Explain to parents how watching TV shows with their own children can help their children better comprehend what they see.

Experts have long known that children imitate many of the deeds—good and bad—that they see on television. But it has rarely been shown that changing a young child's viewing habits at home can lead to improved behavior.

In a study published on Monday in the journal *Pediatrics*, researchers reported the results of a program designed to limit the exposure of preschool children to violence-laden videos and television shows and increase their time with educational programming that encourages empathy. They found that the experiment reduced the children's aggression toward others, compared with a group of children who were allowed to watch whatever they wanted.

"Here we have an experiment that proposes a potential solution," said Dr. Thomas N. Robinson, a professor of pediatrics at Stanford, who was not involved in the study. "Giving this intervention—exposing kids to less adult television, less aggression on television and more prosocial television—will have an effect on behavior."

While the research showed "a small to moderate effect" on the preschoolers' behavior, he added, the broader public health impact could be "very meaningful."

The new study was a randomized trial, rare in research on the effects of media on children. The researchers, at Seattle Children's Research Institute and the University of Washington, divided 565 parents of children aged 3 to 5 into two groups. Both were told to track their children's media consumption in a diary that the researchers assessed for violent, didactic and prosocial content, which they defined as showing empathy, helping others and resolving disputes without violence.

The control group was given advice only on better dietary habits for children. The second group of parents were sent program guides highlighting positive shows for young children. They also received newsletters encouraging parents to watch television with their children and ask questions during the shows about the best ways to deal with conflict. The parents also received monthly phone calls from the researchers, who helped them set television-watching goals for their preschoolers.

The researchers surveyed the parents at six months and again after a year about their children's social behavior. After six months, parents in the group receiving advice about television-watching said their children were somewhat less aggressive with others, compared with those in the control group. The children who watched less violent shows also scored higher on measures of social competence, a difference that persisted after one year.

Low-income boys showed the most improvement, though the researchers could not say why. Total viewing time did not differ between the two groups.

"The take-home message for parents is it's not just about turning off the TV; it's about changing the channel," said Dr. Dimitri A. Christakis, the lead author of the study and a professor of pediatrics at the University of Washington.

"We want our children to behave better," Dr. Christakis said, "and changing their media diet is a good way to do that."

Until she began participating in Dr. Christakis's trial, Nancy Jensen, a writer in Seattle, had never heard of shows like Nickelodeon's *Wonder Pets!,* featuring cooperative team players, and NBC's *My Friend Rabbit,* with its themes of loyalty and friendship.

At the time, her daughter Elizabeth, then 3, liked *King of the Hill,* a cartoon comedy geared toward adults that features beer and gossip. In hindsight, she said, the show was "hilariously funny, but completely inappropriate for a 3-year-old."

These days, she consults Common Sense Media, a nonprofit advocacy group in San Francisco, to make sure that the shows her daughter watches have some prosocial benefit. Elizabeth, now 6, was "not necessarily an aggressive kid," Ms. Jensen said. Still, the girl's teacher recently commended her as very considerate, and Ms. Jensen believes a better television diet is an important reason.

The new study has limitations, experts noted. Data on both the children's television habits and their behavior was reported by their parents, who may not be objective. And the study focused only on media content in the home, although some preschool-aged children are exposed to programming elsewhere.

Children watch a mix of "prosocial but also antisocial media," said Marie-Louise Mares, an associate professor of communications at the University of Wisconsin, Madison. "Merely being exposed to prosocial media doesn't mean that kids take it that way."

Even educational programming with messages of empathy can be misunderstood by preschoolers, with negative consequences. A study published online in November in *The Journal of Applied Developmental Psychology* found that preschoolers shown educational media were more likely to engage in certain forms of interpersonal aggression over time.

Preschoolers observe relationship conflict early in a television episode but do not always connect it to the moral lesson or resolution at the end, said Jamie M. Ostrov, the lead author of the November study and an associate professor of psychology at the University of Buffalo.

Preschoolers watch an estimated 4.1 hours of television and other screen time daily, according to a 2011 study. Dr. Ostrov advised parents to watch television with their young children and to speak up during the relationship conflicts that are depicted. Citing one example, Dr. Ostrov counseled parents to ask children, "What could we do differently here?" to make it clear that yelling at a sibling is not acceptable.

He also urged parents to stick with age-appropriate programming. A 3-year-old might misunderstand the sibling strife in the PBS show *Arthur,* he said, or stop paying attention before it is resolved.

Critical Thinking

1. What kinds of learning mechanisms help explain why TV shows may affect children's behavior?

2. Do you have memories of watching TV shows with your parents or other adults? Was there any discussion about the rightness or wrongness of behaviors displayed by characters, and if so, how did it affect your understanding or behavior?

3. How might you justify showing violent TV shows to classrooms of school children? What kind of curriculum might you design to help foster "media literacy" in children and help them critically view TV content?

Create Central

www.mhhe.com/createcentral

Internet References

American Academy of Child and Adolescent Psychiatry.org
http://www.aacap.org/AACAP/Families_and_Youth/Facts_for_Families/Facts_for_Families_Pages/Children_And_Wat_54.aspx

Kid's Health.org
http://kidshealth.org/parent/positive/family/tv_affects_child.html

Mayo Clinic.org
http://www.mayoclinic.org/healthy-living/childrens-health/in-depth/children-and-tv/art-20047952

University of Michigan Health System
http://www.med.umich.edu/yourchild/topics/tv.htm

Unit 4

UNIT

Prepared by: Chris J. Boyatzis, *Bucknell University*

Parenting and Family Issues

Few people today realize that the potential freedom to choose parenthood—deciding whether to become a parent, deciding when to have children, or deciding how many children to have—is a development due to the advent of reliable methods of contraception and other recent sociocultural changes. Moreover, unlike any other significant job to which we may aspire, few, if any, of us will receive any formal training or information about the lifelong responsibility of parenting. For most of us, our behavior is generally based on our own conscious and subconscious recollections of how we were parented as well as on our observations of the parenting practices of others around us. In fact, our society often behaves as if the mere act of producing a baby automatically confers upon the parents an innate parenting ability, furthermore, that a family's parenting practices should remain private and not be subjected to scrutiny or criticism by outsiders.

Given this climate, it is not surprising that misconceptions about many parenting practices persist. Only within the last 60 years or so have researchers turned their lenses on the scientific study of the family. Social, historical, cultural, and economic forces also have dramatically changed the face of the American family today. In fact, the vast majority of parents today never take courses or learn of the research on parenting. This unit helps present some of the research on the many complex factors related to successful parenting.

One of the most fundamental achievements of infancy is for the baby to develop a strong attachment to a parent or primary adult caregiver. With the growing numbers of parents in two-parent working households, coping with the demands of full-time employment and childcare, researchers are now studying the impact that childcare has on the short- and long-term consequences of childcare.

Moreover, many first marriages in the United States today will end in divorce. Researchers today are studying the effects of divorce and making recommendations that might improve children's adjustment to divorce.

"Spare the rod or spoil the child" is an oft-heard retort used to justify spanking children for misbehaving. Even today, a majority of parents in the United States admit to relying on spanking as a form of discipline for their children, and many do not view spanking as inappropriate. Researchers are beginning to understand the negative effects of spanking for children and are advocating the use of other more effective forms of discipline.

Finally, the powerful role that siblings, families, morality, and other influences such as media play on child growth and development, also represent other fast-growing and fruitful areas of research and intervention.

Article   Prepared by: Chris J. Boyatzis, *Bucknell University*

Why Fathers Really Matter

JUDITH SHULEVITZ

Learning Outcomes

After reading this article, you will be able to:

- Comprehend how a man's health can have an impact on his future child.

- Evaluate the role that genetics plays in the health of children.

Motherhood begins as a tempestuously physical experience but quickly becomes a political one. Once a woman's pregnancy goes public, the storm moves outside. Don't pile on the pounds! Your child will be obese. Don't eat too little, or your baby will be born too small. For heaven's sake, don't drink alcohol. Oh, please: you can sip some wine now and again. And no matter how many contradictory things the experts say, don't panic. Stress hormones wreak havoc on a baby's budding nervous system.

All this advice rains down on expectant mothers for the obvious reason that mothers carry babies and create the environments in which they grow. What if it turned out, though, that expectant fathers molded babies, too, and not just by way of genes?

Biology is making it clearer by the day that a man's health and well-being have a measurable impact on his future children's health and happiness. This is not because a strong, resilient man has a greater likelihood of being a fabulous dad—or not only for that reason—or because he's probably got good genes. Whether a man's genes are good or bad (and whatever "good" and "bad" mean in this context), his children's bodies and minds will reflect lifestyle choices he has made over the years, even if he made those choices long before he ever imagined himself strapping on a Baby Bjorn.

Doctors have been telling men for years that smoking, drinking, and recreational drugs can lower the quality of their sperm. What doctors should probably add is that the health of unborn children can be affected by what and how much men eat; the toxins they absorb; the traumas they endure; their poverty or powerlessness; and their age at the time of conception. In other words, what a man needs to know is that his life experience leaves biological traces on his children. Even more astonishingly, those children may pass those traces along to their children.

Before I began reading up on fathers and their influence on future generations, I had a high-school-biology-level understanding of how a man passes his traits on to his child. His sperm and the mother's egg smash into each other, his sperm tosses in one set of chromosomes, the egg tosses in another, and a child's genetic future is set for life. Physical features: check. Character: check. Cognitive style: check. But the pathways of inheritance, I've learned, are subtler and more varied than that. Genes matter, and culture matters, and how fathers behave matters, too.

Lately scientists have become obsessed with a means of inheritance that isn't genetic but isn't nongenetic either. It's epigenetic. "Epi," in Greek, means "above" or "beyond." Think of epigenetics as the way our bodies modify their genetic makeup. Epigenetics describes how genes are turned on or off, in part through compounds that hitch on top of DNA—or else jump off it—determining whether it makes the proteins that tell our bodies what to do.

In the past decade or so, the study of epigenetics has become so popular it's practically a fad. Psychologists and sociologists particularly like it because gene expression or suppression is to some degree dictated by the environment and plays at least as large a role as genes do in the development of a person's temperament, body shape, and predisposition to disease. I've become obsessed with epigenetics because it strikes me as both game-changing and terrifying. Our genes can be switched on or off by three environmental factors, among other things: what we ingest (food, drink, air, toxins); what we experience (stress, trauma); and how long we live.

Epigenetics means that our physical and mental tendencies were not set in stone during the Pleistocene age, as evolutionary psychology sometimes seems to claim. Rather, they're shaped by the life we lead and the world we live in right now. Epigenetics proves that we are the products of history, public as well as private, in parts of us that are so intimately ours that few people ever imagined that history could reach them. (One person who did imagine it is the French 18th-century naturalist Jean-Baptiste Lamarck, who believed that acquired traits could be inherited. Twentieth-century Darwinian genetics dismissed Lamarckism as laughable, but because of epigenetics, Lamarckism is staging a comeback.)

The best-known example of the power of nutrition to affect the genes of fathers and sons comes from a corner of northern Sweden called Overkalix. Until the 20th century, Overkalix was cut off from the rest of the world, unreachable by road, train, or even, in wintertime, boat, because the frozen Baltic Sea could not be crossed. Thus, when there were bad harvests in Overkalix, the children starved, and when there were good harvests, they stuffed themselves.

More than a decade ago, three Swedish researchers dug up records from Overkalix going back to 1799 in order to correlate its children's health data with records of regional harvests and other documents showing when food was and wasn't available. What the researchers learned was extremely odd. They found that when boys ate badly during the years right before puberty, between the ages of 9 and 12, their sons, as adults, had lower than normal rates of heart disease. When boys ate all too well during that period, their grandsons had higher rates of diabetes.

When the study appeared in 2002, a British geneticist published an essay speculating that how much a boy ate in prepuberty could permanently reprogram the epigenetic switches that would govern the manufacture of sperm a few years later. And then, in a process so intricate that no one agrees yet how it happens but probably has something to do with the germline (the reproductive cells that are handed down to children, and to children's children), those reprogrammed switches are transferred to his sons and his sons' sons.

A decade later, animal studies confirm that a male mammal's nutritional past has a surprisingly strong effect on his offspring. Male rats that are starved before they're mated produce offspring with less blood sugar and altered levels of corticosterone (which protects against stress) and insulin-like growth factor 1 (which helps babies develop).

Southeast Asian men who chew betel nuts, a snack that contains a chemical affecting metabolic functioning, are more likely to have children with weight problems and heart disease.

Animal studies have shown that the effects of betel nut consumption by a male may extend to his grandchildren.

Environmental toxins leave even more florid traces on grandchildren and great-grandchildren. Vinclozin, a fungicide that used to be sprayed all over America (it's less common now), is what's known as an endocrine disrupter; it blocks the production of testosterone. Male rats whose mothers receive a fat dose of vinclozin late in their pregnancy are highly likely to be born with defective testicles and reduced fertility. These problems seem to reappear in up to four generations of male rats after the mother is poisoned.

That food and poison change us is not all that surprising, even if it is surprising how far down the change goes. What is unexpected are the psychological dimensions of epigenetics. To learn more about these, I visited the Mount Sinai Medical Center laboratory of Dr. Eric Nestler, a psychiatrist who did a discomfiting study on male mice and what he calls "social defeat." His researchers put small normal field mice in cages with big, nasty retired breeders, and let the big mice attack the smaller mice for about five minutes a day. If a mean mouse and a little mouse were pried apart by means of a screen, the torturer would claw at the screen, trying to get at his victim. All this subjected the field mouse to "a horrendous level of stress," Dr. Nestler told me. This process was repeated for 10 days, with a different tormentor placed in each cage every day. By the time the torture stopped, about two-thirds of the field mice exhibited permanent and quantifiable symptoms of the mouse equivalents of depression, anxiety, and post-traumatic stress disorder. The researchers then bred these unhappy mice with normal females. When their pups grew up, they tended to overreact to social stress, becoming so anxious and depressed that they wouldn't even drink sugar water. They avoided other mice as much as they could.

Dr. Nestler is not sure exactly how the mouse fathers' trauma communicates itself to their offspring. It may be via sperm, or it may be through some more complicated dance of nature and nurture that involves not only sperm but also other factors. When instead of letting the "defeated" mice mate, Dr. Nestler's researchers killed them, harvested their sperm, and impregnated the female mice through artificial means, the offspring were largely normal. Perhaps the sperm was harvested at the wrong stage in the process, says Dr. Nestler. Or maybe the female mouse picked up some signal when she had sex with the dysfunctional male mouse, some telltale pheromone or squeak, that made her body withhold nutrition and care from his pups. Females have been known to not invest in the spawn of non-optimal males, an outcome that makes perfect evolutionary sense—why waste resources on a loser?

When it comes to the epigenetics of aging, however, there is little question that the chemical insults and social setbacks of everyday life distill themselves in sperm. A woman is born with all the eggs she'll ever carry. By the time a man turns 40, on the other hand, his gonad cells will have divided 610 times to make spermatozoa. By the time he's in his 50s, that number goes up to 840. Each time those cells copy themselves, mistakes may appear in the DNA chain. Some researchers now think that a percentage of those mistakes reflects not just random mutations but experience-based epigenetic markings that insinuate themselves from sperm to fetus and influence brain development. Another theory holds that aging gonad cells are more error-prone because the parts of the DNA that should have spotted and repaired any mistakes have been epigenetically tamped down. In any case, we now know that the children of older fathers show more signs of schizophrenia, autism, and bipolar disorder than children of younger ones.

In a meta-analysis of a population study of more than a million people published last year, Christina Hultman of the Karolinska Institute of Sweden concluded that children of men older than 50 were 2.2 times as likely to have autism as children of 29-year-olds, even after the study had factored out mothers' ages and known risk factors for autism. By the time the men passed 55, the risk doubled to 4.4 times that of 29-year-olds. Can the aging of the parent population explain the apparent spike in autism cases? A study published last month in *Nature* that used whole-genome sequencing on 78 Icelandic families made the strongest case to date that as fathers age, mutations in their sperm spike dramatically. Some of the mutations found by the researchers in Reykjavik have been linked to autism and schizophrenia in children.

In his Washington Heights laboratory at the New York State Psychiatric Institute, Jay Gingrich, a professor of psychobiology, compares the pups of young male mice (3 months old or so) to those of old male mice (12 to 14 months old). The differences between the pups, he told me, weren't "earth-shattering"—they weighed about the same and there weren't big gaps in their early development. But discrepancies appeared when the mice grew up. The adult offspring of the older fathers had less adventuresome personalities; they also reacted to loud noises in unusual ways that paralleled reactions evinced by schizophrenics who heard similar sounds.

Still, Dr. Gingrich said, "the differences were subtle" until he decided to pool the data on their behavior and graph it on a bell curve. A "vast majority" of the children of the older mice were "completely normal," he said, which meant their score fell under the upside-down parabola of the curve. The real differences came at the tails or skinny ends of the bell curve. There was about a sixfold increase in likelihood that one of the "abnormal outliers," mice with cognitive or behavioral handicaps, "would come from an older father." Conversely, the super-high-performing mice were about six times more likely to come

from a younger father. "I'm an inherently skeptical person," Dr. Gingrich told me, but he was impressed by these results.

One unanswered question about autism and schizophrenia is how they crop up in generation after generation; after all, wildly dysfunctional individuals don't usually flourish romantically. "I think we're going to have to consider that advanced paternal age, with its epigenetic effects, may be a way of explaining the mysteries of schizophrenia and autism, insofar as the rates of these disorders have maintained themselves—and autism may be going up," Dr. Gingrich said. "From a cruel Darwinian perspective, it's not clear how much success these folks have at procreating, or how else these genes maintain themselves in the population."

When you're an older mother, you get used to the sidelong glances of sonogram technicians, the extra battery of medical tests, the fear that your baby has Down syndrome, the real or imagined hints from younger mothers that you're having children so late because you care more about professional advancement than family. But as the research on paternal inheritance piles up, the needle of doubt may swing at least partway to fathers. "We're living through a paradigm shift," said Dolores Malaspina, a professor of psychiatry at New York University who has done pioneering work on older fathers and schizophrenia. Older mothers no longer need to shoulder all the blame: "It's the aging man who damages the offspring."

Aging, though, is only one of the vicissitudes of life that assault a man's reproductive vitality. Think of epigenetics as having ushered in a new age of sexual equality, in which both sexes have to worry about threats to which women once felt uniquely exposed. Dr. Malaspina remembers that before she went to medical school, she worked in a chemical plant making radioactive drugs. The women who worked there came under constant, invasive scrutiny, lest the toxic workplace contaminate their eggs. But maybe, Dr. Malaspina points out, the plant managers should have spared some concern for the men, whose germlines were just as susceptible to poisoning as the women's, and maybe even more so. The well-being of the children used to be the sole responsibility of their mothers. Now fathers have to be held accountable, too. Having twice endured the self-scrutiny and second-guessing that goes along with being pregnant, I wish them luck.

Critical Thinking

1. What biological and genetic processes in fathers may affect their offspring?
2. How might these effects be passed on over multiple generations?
3. Why should we be concerned about how fathers' age and health may affect their reproductive health?

Create Central

www.mhhe.com/createcentral

Internet References

Child Welfare.gov

https://www.childwelfare.gov/pubs/usermanuals/fatherhood/chaptertwo.cfm

Parents.com

http://www.parents.com/parenting/better-parenting/style/the-role-of-fathers-with-daughters-and-sons

Zero to Three.org

http://www.zerotothree.org/about-us/funded-projects/parenting-resources/podcast/daddy-papi-papa-or-baba.html

JUDITH SHULEVITZ is the science editor for *The New Republic*.

Article   Prepared by: Chris J. Boyatzis, *Bucknell University*

Parent Training Can Improve Kids' Behavior

INGRID WICKELGREN

Learning Outcomes

After reading this article, you will be able to:

- Comprehend how Parent–Child Interaction Therapy (PCIT) affects the parent–child relationship.

- Assess which situations may be best suited for Parent–Child Interaction Therapy (PCIT) while considering where the boundary line is drawn between needing or not needing this type of therapy.

On a Thursday in early August, psychologist Steven Kurtz is preparing one of his clients, Maria, for a therapy session. A calm, cheerful woman with long, dark hair, Maria has been in training at the Child Mind Institute in New York City with her six-year-old son, Ryan (not his real name), for months to ready him for this day. Her goal seems simple: to coax Ryan to obey a simple command. But Ryan does not take direction well.

Maria and Ryan are undertaking a brand of parent training called Parent–Child Interaction Therapy (PCIT) designed to correct oppositional behavior in children. Until now, Maria has let Ryan pick their activities. Today, for the first time, Maria will choose something to do.

One command at a time, Kurtz tells Maria. She practices: "Can you give me the blue piece?" The psychologist corrects her: "Give me the blue piece." Commands must be direct, to avoid any implication of a choice. Praise immediately if he obeys, Kurtz advises; when he does not, say: "If you don't hand me the blue piece, you have to sit in the time-out chair." If he gets off the chair, Mom's line is: "You got off the chair before I said you could. If you get off the chair again, you will have to go to the time-out room."

"Like the Lord's Prayer, the words are always the same." Kurtz explains. "Spoken with the same intonation."

Kurtz removes the bins for storing toys now in the room; they are more likely to be used as weapons than for cleanup, he reasons. Another issue is Ryan. He is at a computer downstairs and feels like staying there. When Maria drags the thin, dark-haired boy into the room, he is scowling. "This is boring!" he shouts.

Kurtz explains the new rules to Ryan. "Until now, you've been choosing the activities." Today, Kurtz says, "Mom is going to take turns with you."

"Hey—I have this car. I have this car!" the boy interrupts. He is holding one of the toy cars in the room. Kurtz continues: "When Mom chooses the activity, it's very important that you follow her directions. If you don't, she is going to tell you to go in this chair. If you stay in this chair, you get to go back and play with her again. If you don't, you have to go in this room." He gestures toward the door of a narrow enclosure in one corner of the room. "No, I will stay in here!" Ryan yells.

Kurtz exits and sets up shop in a small observation room behind a wall of one-way glass. Kurtz can watch the pair, but they cannot see him. Maria will listen to his directions through an earbud she is wearing.

Maria tells Ryan that their special time is beginning. "Would you like to pick an activity?" she asks. Ryan is throwing toys around the room. "Hold off on all instructions until later," Kurtz advises. "What is he doing?" The therapy calls for narrating a child's actions, to show interest and help focus a child's attention on a task. "Right now he's playing with the cars," Maria says.

Cars are flying around the room. Bang! Crash! Bang! Maria does not scold, shout or even look at Ryan. She stares straight ahead. "Look for that split second he does something you like," Kurtz advises. "When he stops throwing . . . for a second . . ."

Most young children willfully disobey or throw tantrums from time to time. Yet when every routine task—fastening a seatbelt, holding hands at the corner, getting dressed—ignites a confrontation, parents often seek help. Designed for kids who are two to seven years old, PCIT changes the way parents respond to their children. It strengthens the bond between parent and child while providing consistent rules and incentives for cooperation.

Rather than treating a disorder, PCIT is aimed more broadly at disruptive behavior, which can range from talking back to severe aggression. The most common mental health concern for young children, disruptive behavior is a feature of several different diagnoses, including oppositional defiant disorder (ODD)—extreme disobedience and hostility toward authority figures—and conduct disorder, in which kids flaunt rules, fight, lie, steal and engage in other alarmingly bad behavior.

Ryan has attention-deficit hyperactivity disorder (ADHD), which often spurs conduct problems. He is not so much driven to defiance as he is inexorably drawn to whatever is most alluring at the moment—a television show, hot chocolate, a playground, even sleep. His need to pursue his current activity causes him to refuse conflicting requests or demands. Every morning Maria had forcibly pulled Ryan out of bed and dressed him. When Ryan's grandmother had taken care of him after school and turned off the TV, Ryan angrily threw all the available books and toys onto the floor.

More than 100 research articles, including eight randomized trials, have demonstrated that PCIT is highly effective in ameliorating such reactions, and the gains are lasting. The stakes go beyond family dynamics. Little kids with significant behavior problems are at high risk of serious antisocial behavior later on. "Previous research is very clear: if early child behavior problems are not corrected, they are likely to escalate to behaviors that are more destructive and intractable," says Jennifer Wyatt Kaminski, a developmental psychologist at the Centers for Disease Control and Prevention. "Preventing risky and violent behavior in adolescents is an important public health issue."

Because of its scientific backing, PCIT is gaining international recognition and making rapid headway into clinics in pockets of the country—principally, Delaware, California, the Carolinas, Pennsylvania, Oklahoma and Iowa—where large-scale training programs are in effect. The therapy most likely will become more widely disseminated when PCIT International, an organization established in 2009, rolls out its planned protocol for certifying therapists. Certification will make it possible for interested parents to find qualified therapists on the Internet.

Recent adaptations have retrofitted the approach to suit older children, and—taking advantage of its emphasis on parenting skills—to prevent relapse in abusive parents. PCIT offers useful tactics, too, for controlling more moderate forms of troublesome behavior in children. "It is a way to change your vocabulary and speak to your kids in a positive manner," says Joshua Masse, a clinical psychologist at Delaware's Division of Prevention and Behavioral Health Services. Kurtz adds, "This is the manual that parents should be given."

"Your Imagination Flies Like Your Robot"

PCIT got its start in the early 1970s, when Sheila M. Eyberg was a clinical psychology intern at the Oregon Health Sciences University. She treated behavior problems with play therapy, in which a therapist coaches a child to describe his or her emotions during playtime, as a route toward self-acceptance. Eyberg noticed that her charges "seemed to calm down, 'self-correct,' and try to please me," she wrote in *PCIT Pages: The Parent–Child Interaction Therapy Newsletter* in 2004. But, she penned, "their parents were not reporting similar experiences at home. Nor were they reporting changes in their children's behaviors." Instead of bonding with their parents, the kids were connecting with Eyberg.

Psychologist Constance Hanf, also then at O.H.S.U., was piloting an approach that addressed these concerns. She was training mothers to act as therapists for their children, who had developmental disabilities. A key target of Hanf's program was the parent–child bond. According to attachment theory, that bond provides a secure base from which a child can explore the world and helps that child control his or her emotions. In Hanf's therapy, parents built that connection while playing a game of the child's choosing. As one of Hanf's students, Eyberg constructed PCIT around her teacher's scaffold.

Last summer Laura (not her real name), a fun-loving young mother, gave a textbook demonstration of this element of PCIT during one of her therapy sessions. Her son, whom I will call Gabriel, a small six-year-old with light brown, curly hair, had just created a robot out of magnets.

"Oh, you choose to play with the magnets!" Laura says. "Beautiful robot. I love it."

"Now it's a castle," Gabriel says of his creation. Gabriel has ODD.

"It's so smart—you converted a robot into a castle," his mother says.

Gabriel sticks out his tongue. "You're sticking out your tongue," Laura narrates.

"People hate him so he started to transform," Gabriel says of his robot.

"That's very smart," his mother compliments. "Thank you for telling me the whole story." Gabriel starts speaking in a funny, robotic voice. Laura copies him.

"Your imagination flies like your robot," Laura says. "You can come up with different designs like this. It's amazing to me."

Laura describes and imitates Gabriel's actions, repeats what he says—all of which let the child lead—and acts happy and relaxed. Laura's behavioral descriptions also show she is interested, demonstrate proper speech and help Gabriel stay focused on the task. Laura frequently praises the boy, telling him exactly what she likes about what he is doing. In addition, parents are told to ignore minor misbehavior, so that the child learns that only behaving appropriately earns him attention. Laura has met the criteria for mastery: in five minutes, she issues five behavioral descriptions, five reflections, 15 praises, and fewer than three commands, questions and criticisms.

The second phase of PCIT, which Maria and Ryan were just starting, is directed at limit setting and discipline. It is also based on Hanf's therapy, which included a component geared toward controlling behavior. Parents guide a child with clear instructions and consistent consequences, such as praise for compliance and time-out for disobedience. Parents graduate from this phase when three quarters of their commands are direct and the child complies with all of them.

Laura is close. Gabriel complies with some but not all of her requests. When Laura says she wants to do a puzzle, Gabriel protests: "I am tired of listening! I don't want to do this. Can we go out?" Gabriel does not work on the puzzle for long, but he does eventually agree to sit next to Laura and put the pieces away—and he never needs to sit in the time-out chair, although Laura threatens to put him there.

Gabriel and Laura have already come a long way. Earlier in the year, Gabriel had been very unhappy and angry. He acted aggressively toward Laura and refused to obey her. "Get ready for bed or get ready for school . . . to get him to do anything was very, very hard," Laura recalls. Now Gabriel complies with her requests much more often. "When I ask him to turn off the iPad, he hands it to me," Laura says. "He knows that if he doesn't, there's a consequence."

In one landmark test of the therapy, published in 1998, Eyberg, now at the University of Florida, and her colleagues gave PCIT to 22 families of three- to six-year-old children with ODD and assigned 27 others to a waitlist. The parents who received treatment interacted with their children more positively, praising them more and criticizing them less, than those on the waitlist. The children of the parents who participated in PCIT, in turn, were more likely to do what was asked of them. These parents noted large improvements at home as well, rating their child's behavior within the normal range, on average, by the end of treatment. Many of these kids no longer qualified for a diagnosis of ODD. A 2003 study revealed that the treated children became even easier to handle in the following three to six years, perhaps because children and parents reinforce one another's good behavior over time.

In a 2007 meta-analysis (statistical review) of 13 studies of PCIT, psychologists Rae Thomas and Melanie J. Zimmer-Gembeck, both

then at Griffith University in Australia, confirmed that the therapy is linked to significantly improved parenting and reduced negative behavior in kids. It boosts warmth from parents, decreases their hostility and reduces their stress. It also diminishes aggression and oppositional behavior among children.

The success of PCIT is thought to stem, in part, from its emphasis on rehearsal of a particularly relevant set of skills. In a meta-analysis of 77 investigations of parent-training programs published in 2008, Kaminski and her colleagues found that requiring parents to practice the appropriate actions with their children during the training sessions seemed to be critical to correcting parent behavior. Kaminski's team also noted that parent proficiency tended to improve whenever moms and dads were taught to talk to their kids about emotions and to effectively listen to them. In addition, the researchers identified the two essential elements to boosting children's behavior ratings: instructing parents to interact positively with their children—expressing enthusiasm and following the child's lead—and to respond consistently to a child's actions.

Child Protection

Sometimes the child is not the problem; the parent is. Parenting education and training has been a staple in child welfare for decades. Typically parents discuss their experiences and strategies in groups, but such conversations often fail to change the family dynamic, and parental neglect or abuse persists.

In the early 2000s, Mark Chaffin, a child abuse researcher at the University of Oklahoma Health Sciences Center, wanted to test PCIT with such parents on the grounds that teaching skills might be more effective than discussing concepts. The state child welfare system sent him 110 adults who had been reported multiple times for physical abuse of their children. The parents received 12 to 14 one-hour sessions at the university's large PCIT center. In addition, Chaffin required these mothers and fathers to participate in a motivational exercise. "If your five-year-old is driving you crazy, you are fairly motivated," Chaffin explains. "But we were concerned that people coming from child welfare would not be happy to be sent to a program." In Chaffin's program, parents were asked to consider their parenting goals and whether their actions aligned with those goals.

The combination approach worked. More than two years later, only 19 percent of the parents who had received both PCIT and the motivational interview had been reported again for abuse—compared with 49 percent of those who had been assigned to a standard parenting group, according to a 2004 study by Chaffin and his colleagues. "We got large effect sizes in reduction of child welfare recidivism," something that is hard to budge, Chaffin says.

In a follow-up trial published in 2011, Chaffin's team extended these results to more severe cases of abuse and neglect and a more realistic therapeutic setting: a small inner-city agency under contract with the state's child welfare system. Among 192 parents who had averaged six prior referrals to child welfare, a motivational interview along with PCIT led to a recidivism rate of around 17 percent two and a half years later, compared with about 65 percent for those who received standard group therapy along with a motivational interview. "Even if you are motivated, typical group therapy doesn't give you a lot of benefit," Chaffin concludes.

The children involved in Chaffin's studies ranged from four to 12 years old, so he and his colleagues adapted the treatment to older kids. Time-outs were replaced with logical consequences—such as taking away objects that a child is actively misusing—and loss of privileges. And praise was less demonstrative. Instead of exclaiming "What a nice tower!" to a child playing Legos, a father might challenge his 11-year-old son to a tower-building race. "Oh, you're killing me!" the dad might praise. In a 2012 case study, Eyberg and her colleagues also found that PCIT greatly improved the newly aggressive and oppositional behavior of an 11-year-old who had suffered a traumatic brain injury from a gunshot wound.

"Please Hand Me the Pink Doughnut"

PCIT holds useful lessons for more ordinary circumstances as well: ignore bad behavior, praise good; tell a child what *to* do rather than what *not* to do; phrase commands as such, not as questions or suggestions. Indeed, Eyberg and her colleagues found that two abbreviated versions of the technique significantly improved the behavior of 30 three- to six-year-olds whom their mothers had characterized as having moderate behavior problems. Both a four-session group intervention and written materials describing how to practice PCIT garnered similar benefits, suggesting that hands-on coaching may not be necessary in milder cases.

Back at the Child Mind Institute, Ryan has calmed down but balks at the suggestion that he play his mother's game. Soon he is sent to the time-out chair, but he will not sit there voluntarily and gets up repeatedly. Then, before he can be moved to the time-out room, he kicks his mother and pushes *her* into the room, locking her inside, and then knocks over all the big metal chairs. Kurtz intervenes.

For more than an hour, Ryan goes from the time-out room to the time-out chair and back again, crying and protesting. "I'll kill you! I'll kill you! You're nuts!" he shouts. Maria remains calm. She smiles and laughs to help ease the tension.

Finally, Ryan elects to stay in the chair, so Maria attempts a command. She tells Ryan to come sit next to her. "To do what?" he challenges. He is sent back to the chair. Yet again he stays there, whimpering. Twenty minutes later, in response to a period of relative silence, Maria says. "You're sitting quietly. Are you ready to come and sit with me?" "Yes." He walks over to her, sobbing softly.

"Okay. Please hand me the pink doughnut." He finds the pink doughnut from a smattering of plastic toys spread out on the table—and hands it to her.

"Thank you for doing what I told you." She pets his face and smiles. He is still teary.

"Now please hand me the banana." He does.

"Yay! Good listening." She kisses him. Ryan brings his mom one more item, a plastic potato chip, before Kurtz ends the session.

That afternoon Ryan passed another milestone. When Kurtz enters the room, Maria flashes a wide smile. She gives Kurtz a thumbs-up, and the two exchange a high five. Ryan does not feel like celebrating, however. "I had a very hard day," he sighs.

This article was originally published with the title "Behave!."

Critical Thinking

1. Is there truly a need for children to obey their parents' every word? What might be some of the cons that come along with such obedience?
2. Do you think it would be beneficial for every parent to go through a parent training course to learn how to interact with their children? How might it change the parent–child dynamic?

Create Central

www.mhhe.com/createcentral

Internet References

First 5 LA
   http://www.first5la.org/Parent-Child-Interaction-Therapy
Good Therapy.org
   http://www.goodtherapy.org/parent-child-interaction-therapy.html
Parent-Child Interaction Therapy.org
   http://www.pcit.org

INGRID WICKELGREN is an editor at *Scientific American Mind* and author of the blog Streams of Consciousness at ScientificAmerican.com.

Article

Prepared by: Chris J. Boyatzis, *Bucknell University*

Evidence of Infants' Internal Working Models of Attachment

SUSAN C. JOHNSON, CAROL S. DWECK, AND FRANCES S. CHEN

Learning Outcomes

After reading this article, you will be able to:

- Describe in detail the habituation procedure that the researchers used to measure infants' internal working models.

- Distinguish between characteristics of securely and insecurely attached infants.

- Explain to parents who might not understand psychological experiments and research why a baby's looking time at a visual stimulus like "non-responsive" ovals could in fact reveal what is going on inside the baby's head.

Nearly half a century ago, psychiatrist John Bowlby proposed that the instinctual behavioral system that underpins an infant's attachment to his or her mother is accompanied by "internal working models" of the social world—models based on the infant's own experience with his or her caregiver (Bowlby, 1958, 1969/1982). These mental models were thought to mediate, in part, the ability of an infant to use the caregiver as a buffer against the stresses of life, as well as the later development of important self-regulatory and social skills.

Hundreds of studies now testify to the impact of caregivers' behavior on infants' behavior and development: Infants who most easily seek and accept support from their parents are considered secure in their attachments and are more likely to have received sensitive and responsive caregiving than insecure infants; over time, they display a variety of socioemotional advantages over insecure infants (Cassidy & Shaver, 1999). Research has also shown that, at least in older children and adults, individual differences in the security of attachment are indeed related to the individual's representations of social relations (Bretherton & Munholland, 1999). Yet no study has ever directly assessed internal working models of attachment in infancy. In the present study, we sought to do so.

Method

Using a visual habituation technique, we tested expectations of caregivers' responsiveness in 10 securely and 11 insecurely attached 12- to 16-month-old infants (mean age = 403 days; 13 females). Attachment security was measured in the lab using the Strange Situation (Ainsworth, Blehar, Waters, & Wall, 1978).

Following Bowlby (1958, 1969/1982) and Ainsworth (Ainsworth et al., 1978), we predicted that different experiences with their own primary caregivers would lead infants to construct different internal working models, including different expectations of caregivers' responsiveness. Thus, we expected that secure infants, compared with insecure infants, would look longer at a display of an unresponsive caregiver (relatively unexpected) relative to a display of a responsive caregiver (relatively expected).

Given recent demonstrations of the abstractness and generality of infants' reasoning about agents (Gergely, Nádasdy, Csibra, & Bíró, 1995; Johnson, 2003; Kuhlmeier, Wynn, & Bloom, 2003), we chose to test infants' expectations with displays of animated geometric characters, rather than actual people. Infants were habituated to a video of two animated ellipses enacting a separation event. The large "mother" and small "child" appeared together at the bottom of a steep incline and then the mother traveled halfway up the incline to a small plateau. As the mother came to rest there, the child below began to cry, an event depicted by a slight pulsation and bouncing and an actual human infant cry. The animation then paused, allowing the participant to look at the scene as long as he or she desired. Once the participant looked away, the sequence was repeated until his or her visual attention to the event declined to half of its initial amount, as measured by the duration of the participant's looks. When an infant reached this criterion of habituation, each of two test outcomes was shown twice. Each test outcome opened with the mother still positioned halfway up the incline, as the child continued to cry. In the *responsive* outcome, the mother returned to the child. In the *unresponsive* outcome, the mother continued up the slope, away from the child. The order in which the outcomes were presented was counterbalanced. Interest in each outcome was measured by looking time.

The Strange Situation sessions of all 21 infants were blind-coded by the third author after training at the Institute of Child Development's Attachment Workshop. A second blind coder, the first author, scored 10 randomly selected sessions. The coders' agreement was 90%, and kappa was .83.

The visual looking times of all infants were coded on-line by an observer blind to attachment status and test event. A second blind observer, also on-line, coded the looking times of 13 of the infants, achieving 93% agreement and a kappa of .82.

Results

Mean looking times for the last three trials of habituation and each outcome were calculated for each infant (see Figure 1). Securely attached infants looked for 5.9 s ($SD = 4.1$) at the last three habituation events, 10.2 s ($SD = 8.9$) at the unresponsive-caregiver outcome, and 7.3 s ($SD = 7.0$) at the responsive-caregiver outcome. The comparable times in insecurely attached infants were 5.4 s ($SD = 2.9$), 6.6 s ($SD = 3.5$), and 8.0 s ($SD = 5.4$). Preliminary analyses showed no effect of gender or order of presentation on looking times in the outcome trials.

A mixed analysis of variance with attachment status (secure, insecure) and outcome (responsive, unresponsive) as variables revealed no differences between secure and insecure infants in the overall amount of time that they looked at the test displays, $F(1, 19) = 0.31$, n.s., and no differences between the overall looking times (secure and insecure infants combined) to responsive versus unresponsive outcomes, $F(1, 19) = 0.48$, n.s. However, as predicted, infants' relative interest in the two outcomes did vary by group. Secure infants looked relatively longer at the unresponsive outcome than the responsive outcome compared with the insecure infants, $F(1, 19) = 4.76$, $p = .042$.[1] These results constitute direct positive evidence that infants' own personal attachment experiences are reflected in abstract mental representations of social interactions.

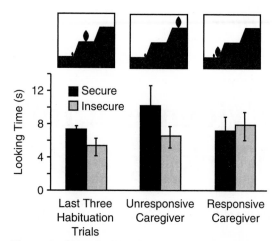

Figure 1 Mean looking times (in seconds) to habituation and test events among secure and insecure infants. Standard error bars are shown. Each illustration depicts the final scene in the video corresponding to the graph below. The large oval represents the "mother" and the small oval represents the "child."

The current method opens a new window onto the nature of internal working models of attachment. In addition, these representations can now be traced as they emerge, well before existing behavioral measures of attachment can be employed. The literature on attachment has shown the profound impact of early experience. The method used in the present study provides a means of looking into the mind upon which that experience has left its imprint.

Note

1. Results of additional analyses converged. One-tailed, pair-wise comparisons revealed a significant effect of outcome within the secure group, $t(9) = 1.99$, $p < .04$, but not the insecure group. Also, 7 of the 10 secure infants looked longer at the unresponsive than at the responsive outcome, whereas 7 of the 11 insecure infants showed the opposite result, $p < .07$, Mann-Whitney test. The looking behaviors of the two subtypes of insecure infants (6 avoidant, 5 resistant) did not differ.

References

Ainsworth, M.D.S., Blehar, M.C., Waters, E., & Wall, S. (1978). *Patterns of attachment: A psychological study of the strange situation.* Hillsdale, NJ: Erlbaum.

Bowlby, J. (1958). The nature of the child's ties to his mother. *International Journal of Psychoanalysis, 39,* 350.

Bowlby, J. (1982). *Attachment and loss: Vol. 1. Attachment.* New York: Basic Books. (Original work published 1969)

Bretherton, I., & Munholland, K.A. (1999). Internal working models revisited. In J. Cassidy & P.R. Shaver (Eds.), *Handbook of attachment: Theory, research, and clinical applications* (pp. 89–111). New York: Guilford Press.

Cassidy, J., & Shaver, P.R. (Eds.). (1999). *Handbook of attachment: Theory, research, and clinical applications.* New York: Guilford Press.

Gergely, G., Nádasdy, Z., Csibra, G., & Bíró, S. (1995). Taking the intentional stance at 12 months of age. *Cognition, 56,* 165–193.

Johnson, S.C. (2003). Detecting agents. *Philosophical Transactions of the Royal Society B, 358,* 549–559.

Kuhlmeier, V.A., Wynn, K., & Bloom, P. (2003). Attribution of dispositional states by 12-month-olds. *Psychological Science, 14,* 402–408.

Critical Thinking

1. What is the evidence from this experiment for the notion that infants, in fact, possess internal working models of attachment?

2. What were the key differences between securely attached and insecurely attached infants' responses to the visual stimuli?

3. What are some ways that you would modify the experiment if you were to replicate it?

Create Central

www.mhhe.com/createcentral

Internet References

Early Childhood News.com

http://www.earlychildhoodnews.com/earlychildhood/article_view.aspx?ArticleId=716

Child Welfare Information Gateway, U.S. Department of Health and Human Services

https://www.childwelfare.gov/can/factors/nurture_attach.cfm

U.S. Department of Health and Human Services.org

http://aspe.hhs.gov/daltcp/reports/inatrpt.htm

SUSAN C. JOHNSON, CAROL S. DWECK, and FRANCES S. CHEN Stanford University.

Article   Prepared by: Chris J. Boyatzis, *Bucknell University*

Parental Divorce and Children's Adjustment

JENNIFER E. LANSFORD

Learning Outcomes

After reading this article, you will be able to:

- Assess and summarize the research on the effects of divorce on children's adjustment in terms of child's age, sex of child, ethnicity, family income, and interpersonal conflict. Given these outcomes, what recommendations would you make to parents who are considering divorce but want to reduce the negative effects on their children?

- Evaluate and discuss the effects of genetics versus environment on children's adjustment to divorce in terms of interparental conflict, parenting practices, parents' psychological well-being and adjustment, and genetic factors.

- Compare and contrast the differential effects of divorce versus remarriage on children's short- and long-term adjustment. Analyze and identify any common themes or factors that may explain and integrate children's outcomes across both family transitions.

In the United States, between 43% and 50% of first marriages end in divorce (U.S. Census Bureau, 2004), and 50% of American children will experience their parents' divorce (National Center for Health Statistics, 2008). Given the large number of families affected by divorce each year, parents, clinicians, and policymakers alike are concerned with understanding how experiencing parental divorce affects children's adjustment. Indeed, many parents considering divorce ask whether they should stay together for the sake of their children.

Key questions in the research literature have focused on whether divorce per se affects children's adjustment and, if so, why and how. The literature has at times portrayed two extreme positions on whether divorce affects children's adjustment (Cherlin, 1999). The first extreme position holds that the long-term effects of divorce on children are quite debilitating and that children carry a lasting negative burden years after the divorce in terms of mental health and interpersonal relationships (e.g., Glenn, 2001; Popenoe, 1993, 2003; Wallerstein, Lewis, & Blakeslee, 2000). This work has drawn criticism for methodological (e.g., reliance on small samples of clinical populations) and ideological reasons. For example, Coontz (1992) points out that many condemnations of divorce and nontraditional families stem from misguided perceptions of family life in previous decades and that myths about family life in the past reflected reality for only a small subset of middle-class European Americans. At the opposite extreme is the position that divorce has no measurable long-term effects on children (e.g., Harris, 1998). This extreme has been criticized because it appears to conflict with hundreds of empirical studies to the contrary.

Between these two extremes, most researchers have come to the conclusion that divorce has some negative effects on children's adjustment but that these effects may be small in magnitude and not universal. For example, in a meta-analysis of 92 studies conducted in the 1950s through 1980s, Amato and Keith (1991b) reported that 70% of studies found lower well-being for children whose parents had divorced than for children whose parents had not divorced; the median effect size was .14 of a standard deviation. Conduct problems and father–child relationship outcomes showed the largest effect sizes, and psychological adjustment and self-concept outcomes showed the smallest effect sizes (Amato & Keith, 1991b). Amato (2001) updated the meta-analysis using 67 studies published in the 1990s. Although 88% of the effects suggested lower well-being for children whose parents divorced than for children whose parents did not divorce, only 42% of the effects were significant (Amato, 2001). There has been considerable debate in the literature regarding the extent to which these effects are attributable to divorce per se or to correlated factors such as exposure to interparental conflict.

The main purpose of this review is to provide an overview of the nuances represented in the patterns of findings regarding links between parental divorce and children's short and long-term adjustment. First, I consider how divorce is related to several different aspects of children's adjustment. Second, I examine the timing of divorce, demographic characteristics, children's adjustment prior to the divorce, and stigmatization as moderators of the links between divorce and children's adjustment. Third, I examine income, interparental conflict, parenting, and parents' well-being as mediators of relations between divorce and children's adjustment. Fourth, I describe the caveats and limitations of the research literature. Finally, I consider the notable policies related to grounds for divorce, child support, and child custody in light of how they might affect children's adjustment to their parents' divorce.

Indicators of Children's Adjustment

Although findings regarding whether and how parental divorce is related to children's adjustment are not always clear in the literature, there is agreement among most researchers that children experiencing parental divorce are at risk for a variety of negative developmental outcomes (see Cherlin, 1999, for a review). However, the magnitude of these effects appears to depend on the indicators of adjustment under consideration, and some studies find no differences on particular outcomes between children whose parents divorce and those whose parents stay together (Ruschena, Prior, Sanson, & Smart, 2005). Externalizing behaviors, internalizing problems, academic achievement, and quality of social relationships are frequently included indicators of adjustment in the divorce literature. Studies that have examined these indicators of adjustment at discrete time points provide some evidence that children whose parents have divorced have more externalizing and internalizing problems, lower academic achievement, and more problematic social relationships than do children whose parents have not divorced (e.g., Cherlin et al., 1991; Emery, Waldron, Kitzmann, & Aaron, 1999).

Meta-analyses have revealed that divorce has larger effects on relationships with nonresidential fathers and externalizing behaviors than it does on internalizing problems or academic achievement (Amato, 2001; Amato & Keith, 1991b). In the earlier meta-analysis (Amato & Keith, 1991b), divorce was found to have larger effects on academic achievement than on internalizing problems, but in the later meta-analysis (Amato, 2001), divorce was found to have larger effects on internalizing problems than on academic achievement. In these meta-analyses,

effect sizes depended on the methodological sophistication of the studies under consideration. More methodologically sophisticated studies (e.g., those with multiple-item scales and control variables) showed smaller effect sizes than did less methodologically sophisticated studies. Methodologically unsophisticated studies may overestimate the effects of divorce on children. For example, if socioeconomic status is not controlled, children who have experienced divorce and are living with a single mother may show worse adjustment than do children who are living with two parents in part because of the confounding effect of having fewer economic resources in single-mother families.

A problem with relying on indicators of adjustment measured at a single point in time is that these indicators are likely to look worse if they are assessed in close temporal proximity to the time of the divorce, but they show improvement over time because the short-term effects of divorce tend to look worse than the long-term effects. The examination of developmental trajectories of adjustment has several advantages over the examination of adjustment at discrete points in time. The examination of trajectories makes it possible to track change over time from before the divorce occurs to some period following the divorce. The inclusion of predivorce adjustment in these models is important because of evidence that children whose parents eventually divorce show poorer adjustment prior to the divorce than do children whose parents do not divorce (e.g., Cherlin, Chase-Lansdale, & McRae, 1998; Doherty & Needle, 1991). Links between parental divorce and children's adjustment are often attenuated or eliminated by controlling for predivorce adjustment. For example, Sun and Li (2001) used longitudinal data from a nationally representative sample and found that differences in academic achievement between children whose parents divorced and children whose parents stayed together could be accounted for almost entirely by children's academic achievement and family functioning prior to the divorce.

Although one can control for prior adjustment in analyses predicting subsequent adjustment at a discrete point in time, such analyses do not allow for an examination of how these effects continue to develop over time. Children often have more short-term adjustment difficulties immediately after their parents' divorce, but these difficulties may lessen in severity or disappear following an initial adjustment period (Chase-Lansdale & Hetherington, 1990). Studying trajectories of adjustment that extend from before the parents' divorce to a period well after the divorce will provide a more complete picture of children's long-term adjustment.

To overcome the limitations of cross-sectional approaches, Cherlin et al. (1998) followed a large sample of children born in 1958 in Great Britain prospectively from childhood to the age of 33. Prior to their parents' divorce, individuals whose parents eventually divorced had more internalizing and externalizing problems than did individuals whose parents did not divorce. However, divorce itself also contributed to higher levels of long-term internalizing and externalizing problems into adulthood. It is important to note that their findings suggested that some of the effects of divorce during childhood may not manifest themselves shortly after the divorce and that they may not become apparent until adolescence or adulthood. The gap between groups of individuals whose parents had and had not divorced widened over the course of several years from childhood to adulthood. Cherlin et al. (1998) suggested that parental divorce may curtail educational achievement or disrupt social relationships in ways that are not apparent until children try to enter the labor market, marry, or have children of their own.

In a sample of American children followed from before kindergarten through Grade 10, Malone et al. (2004) used latent change score models to examine trajectories of teacher-rated externalizing behavior over time. Parental divorce was unrelated to girls' externalizing behavior trajectories, regardless of the timing of divorce. Parental divorce was related to boys' externalizing trajectories differently depending on the timing of the divorce. In particular, parental divorce during elementary school was related to an increase in boys' externalizing behaviors that began in the year of the divorce and persisted for years afterward. Parental divorce during middle school was related to an increase in boys' externalizing behaviors in the year of the divorce that declined below baseline levels in the year following the divorce and persisted into subsequent years.

Several studies also address whether parental divorce during childhood relates to long-term effects on adults' own romantic relationships and their relationships with their parents later in life. Intergenerational studies suggest that parental divorce doubles the risk that one's own marriage will end in divorce, in part because individuals whose parents have divorced are less likely to view marriage as a lifelong commitment (Amato & DeBoer, 2001); the risk is exacerbated if both spouses experienced their parents' divorce (Hetherington & Elmore, 2004). There is also evidence that intergenerational transmission of divorce is mediated by interpersonal skill deficits (e.g., communication patterns not conducive to supporting a long-term intimate relationship) that make it more difficult for individuals whose parents have divorced to sustain their own intimate relationships (Amato, 1996). In addition to being at greater risk for difficulties in romantic relationships, adults whose parents divorced have lower quality relationships with their parents (particularly fathers) during adulthood, on average (Lye, 1996). However, these associations depend on the parents' marital quality prior to the divorce, the gender of the parent, and the gender of the adult child (Booth & Amato, 1994; Orbuch, Thornton, & Cancio, 2000).

To summarize, research suggests that children whose parents have divorced have higher levels of externalizing behaviors and internalizing problems, lower academic achievement, and more problems in social relationships than do children whose parents have not divorced. But, the magnitude of these effects is attenuated after controlling for children's adjustment prior to the divorce and other potential confounds. Furthermore, even though children whose parents divorce have worse adjustment on average than do children whose parents stay together, most children whose parents divorce do not have long-term negative outcomes. For example, in their longitudinal study of a representative sample of 17,414 individuals in Great Britain who were followed from ages 7 to 23, Chase-Lansdale, Cherlin, and Kiernan (1995) reported that the likelihood of scoring in the clinical range on the Malaise Inventory, which measures a wide range of adult emotional disorders, was 11% for young adults who had experienced their parents' divorce and 8% for young adults who had not experienced their parents' divorce. Nevertheless, analyses using data from this sample after they were followed to age 33 led Cherlin et al. (1998) to conclude that the adjustment gap between individuals who had and had not experienced parental divorce widened over time and that although part of the effect of parental divorce could be attributed to factors prior to the divorce, experiencing parental divorce during childhood was related to worse mental health when the offspring were in their 20s and 30s.

Hetherington and Kelly (2002) concluded that 25% of individuals whose parents divorce have serious long-term social, emotional, or psychological problems in adulthood in comparison with 10% of individuals whose parents have stayed together; still, this means that 75% of individuals whose parents divorce do not have serious long-term impairment during adulthood. Even studies that do find long-term effects of divorce generally report that the effect sizes are small. For example, Allison and Furstenberg (1989) used longitudinal data from a nationally representative sample and concluded that although divorce was related to behavior problems, psychological distress, and low academic achievement, the effect sizes for divorce were smaller than those found for gender differences (but larger than those found for several other demographic variables). Amato (2003) concluded that about 10% of children whose parents divorce grow up to have poorer psychological well-being than would have been predicted if their parents had stayed together, 18% of children whose parents divorce have more marital discord as adults than do children whose parents stayed together, and 35% of children whose parents divorce have worse relationships with their fathers than do children whose parents stayed together. Laumann-Billings and Emery (2000) caution that researchers and clinicians may reach different conclusions regarding the long-term effects of divorce because researchers often study psychological or behavioral problems, whereas clinicians often are faced with clients' subjective impressions of their psychological distress (which may not be manifest in psychological or behavioral disorders). Taken together, these findings indicate that the majority of children whose parents divorce do not have long-term adjustment problems, but the risk of externalizing behaviors, internalizing problems, poorer academic achievement, and problematic social relationships is greater for children whose parents divorce than for those whose parents stay together. Different children may manifest adjustment problems in different ways. Future research should adopt a more person-centered approach to investigate whether, for example, those children whose grades are dropping are the same children whose internalizing or externalizing problems are increasing following their parents' divorce.

Moderators of Links between Divorce and Children's Adjustment

Despite the research suggesting that divorce is related to children's adjustment, there is considerable evidence that these effects do not operate in the same way for all children. Links between divorce and children's adjustment are moderated by several factors, including children's age at the time of their parents' divorce, children's age at the time of the study, the length of time since the divorce, children's demographic characteristics (gender, race/ethnicity), children's adjustment prior to the divorce, and stigmatization of divorce (by location or historical period).

Children's Age at Divorce, Age at the Time of the Study, and Length of Time Since Divorce

Studies have shown mixed results with respect to how the timing of divorce affects children's adjustment (see Hetherington, Bridges, & Insabella, 1998). Hetherington (1989) suggests that, in comparison with older children, young children may be less capable of realistically assessing the causes and consequences of divorce, may feel more anxious about abandonment, may be more likely to blame themselves, and may be less able to take advantage of resources outside the family to cope with the divorce. All of these factors may contribute to findings that young children experience more problems after their parents divorce than do children who are older when the divorce occurs (Allison & Furstenberg, 1989). Note that this conclusion applies specifically to divorce; other findings suggest that adjusting

to parents' remarriage may be harder for adolescents than for younger children (Hetherington, Stanley-Hagan, & Anderson, 1989). It may be that divorce has effects on particular outcomes that are salient during the developmental period during which the divorce occurs. For example, academic achievement, identity development, and emerging romantic relationships may be affected by divorce that occurs during adolescence because these domains of functioning are developmentally salient then.

A methodological problem is that in many studies, children's reported age reflects their age at the time of the study rather than their age at the time of their parents' divorce. Amato (2001) noted this lack of availability of children's age at the time of the divorce as a limitation in his meta-analysis. The most common approach is to study children in a particular developmental stage (e.g., early childhood, middle childhood, adolescence) and compare the adjustment of children whose parents have divorced with the adjustment of children whose parents have not divorced. A drawback of this strategy is that the length of time between the parents' divorce and the time of the assessment will vary considerably across the sample. Lansford et al. (2006) addressed this limitation by using the time of parental divorce as an anchor point and modeling trajectories of adjustment over a period from 1 year prior to the divorce to 3 years after the divorce. This approach makes it possible to compare children at comparable points of time in relation to their parents' divorce. Lansford et al. (2006) also analyzed a matched group of children whose parents did not divorce. Results suggested that parental divorce occurring from kindergarten to Grade 5 exerted more adverse effects on internalizing and externalizing problems than did parental divorce occurring from Grades 6 to 10, whereas parental divorce occurring from Grades 6 to 10 exerted more adverse effects on grades.

Children's Demographic Characteristics

Researchers have attempted to understand how children's demographic characteristics (primarily gender and race) may moderate the link between parental divorce and children's adjustment. Early research findings suggested that parental divorce was related to more adjustment difficulties for boys than girls but that parents' remarriage was related to more adjustment difficulties for girls than for boys (see Hetherington, Cox, & Cox, 1985). However, recent findings have been more mixed; there is no consistent pattern regarding whether divorce has more adverse effects on girls or boys. Some studies report that boys have more adjustment problems following parental divorce than do girls (Morrison & Cherlin, 1995; Shaw, Emery, & Tuer, 1993). Other studies report that girls have more adjustment problems following parental divorce than do boys (Allison & Furstenberg, 1989). Still other studies report no gender differences (e.g., Amato & Cheadle, 2005; Sun & Li, 2002). There is also evidence that the particular outcomes affected by parental divorce may differ by gender. For example, early childbearing has been found to be associated with parental divorce for girls, and more unemployment has been found to be associated with parental divorce for boys (McLanahan, 1999). In their meta-analysis, Amato and Keith (1991b) found no gender differences except that boys whose parents divorced had a harder time adjusting socially than did girls.

It has been proposed that parental divorce may have a less negative effect on African American children than on European American children (Jeynes, 2002). Specifically, researchers have suggested that because African American children tend to experience less of a decrease in household income following parents' divorce and there is a greater norm for single parenthood in the African American community (Cherlin, 1998; Laosa, 1988), these factors may mitigate the effects of divorce on African American youth. Research assessing these effects has produced mixed results, but a meta-analysis of 37 studies investigating links between parental divorce and adults' well-being found that effect sizes were smaller for African Americans than for European Americans (Amato & Keith, 1991a), which is consistent with the hypothesis that divorce would have a less negative effect on African American children than for European American children.

Children's Adjustment Prior to the Divorce

Some evidence suggests that children whose parents eventually divorce already have more adjustment problems many years before the divorce (Cherlin et al., 1998). Genetic or other environmental factors may be contributing to these adjustment problems, and the children's adjustment may have appeared to be just as problematic even if the parents had not divorced. Chase-Lansdale et al. (1995) found a steeper increase in adjustment problems after parental divorce for children who were well-adjusted prior to the divorce than for children with predivorce adjustment problems (or for children whose parents did not divorce). However, the long-term adjustment of children with predivorce adjustment problems was worse than it was for children who were better adjusted prior to the divorce (Chase-Lansdale et al., 1995). Controlling for children's adjustment prior to their parents' divorce greatly reduces differences between children whose parents divorce and those whose parents stay together (Cherlin et al., 1991).

Children with positive attributes such as attractiveness, easy temperament, and social competence are also more resilient following their parents' divorce (Hetherington et al., 1989).

In part, this may be because children with such attributes are more likely to have strong support networks outside the family (e.g., from teachers or peers) and to evoke positive responses from others. In an epidemiological sample of 648 children who were initially assessed when they were 1–10 years old and assessed again 8 years later, Kasen, Cohen, Brook, and Hartmark (1996) found significant interactions between temperament assessed in the first 10 years of life and family structure in the prediction of subsequent adjustment. In particular, the risk of oppositional defiant disorder was exacerbated for children who had early affective problems and were living with a single mother or in a stepfamily; the authors speculated that the stress of adjusting to new living arrangements may have overwhelmed the coping capacities of these already vulnerable children. On the other hand, Kasen et al. (1996) also found that the risk of overanxiety disorder was reduced for children (especially boys) who were socially immature early in life and were living with a single mother; the authors speculated that needing to play more "adult" roles in a single-parent family may have enhanced the social skills of previously immature children. Thus, children's adjustment can moderate the effects of divorce on subsequent adjustment.

Stigmatization

At a societal level, stigmatization has been considered as a potential moderator of the link between parents' divorce and children's adjustment. Divorce would be expected to have more detrimental effects for children in societal contexts in which family forms other than two-parent biological families are stigmatized than it would in societies that are more accepting of diverse family forms. There is some empirical support for this perspective. For example, Amato and Keith's (1991b) meta-analysis revealed smaller effect sizes for some outcomes in more recent studies than in studies from earlier decades, suggesting that the effects of divorce became less pronounced over time from the 1950s to the 1980s. Amato and Keith also reported that studies conducted outside the United States on average found more problems with conduct, psychological adjustment, and both mother–child and father–child relationships than did studies conducted in the United States. One explanation for these findings is that divorce is less stigmatized in the United States than in many other countries (Amato & Keith, 1991b). On the other hand, Amato (2001) found that although the adjustment of children whose parents had and had not divorced became increasingly similar over time from the 1950s to the 1980s, the gap between these two groups began to increase again in the 1990s (Reifman, Villa, Amans, Rethinam, & Telesca, 2001, reached a similar conclusion). It is not clear that stigmatization increased again over this same time period.

Mediators of Links between Divorce and Children's Adjustment

Most researchers no longer simply compare the adjustment of children whose parents have and have not divorced. Instead, researchers have adopted more complex models of how divorce may be related to children's adjustment and now investigate moderators as described previously or analyze their data to understand the mechanisms through which divorce might affect children's adjustment. Several scholars have argued that processes occurring in all types of families are more important than family structure in relation to the well-being of children and adolescents (e.g., Dunn, Deater-Deckard, Pickering, & O'Connor, 1998; Lansford, Ceballo, Abbey, & Stewart, 2001). Taking family process and other mediating variables into account attenuates the association between the experience of parental divorce and children's adjustment (e.g., Amato & Keith, 1991b; Mechanic & Hansell, 1989). It is also important to keep in mind that divorce can be conceptualized more as a process than as a discrete event, with the family processes leading up to and following the divorce being an integral part of the divorce itself.

Income

In a review of five theoretical perspectives on why marital transitions may be related to children's adjustment, Hetherington et al. (1998) found some support for an economic disadvantage perspective suggesting that a drop in household income often accompanies divorce and mediates the link between parents' divorce and children's adjustment. Twenty-eight percent of single mothers and 11% of single fathers live in poverty in comparison with 8% of two-parent families (Grall, 2007). Following their parents' divorce, children most often live with single mothers who do not have the same financial resources they did prior to the divorce, especially if they are not receiving regular child-support payments from nonresidential fathers. This sometimes necessitates a change for the worse in housing, neighborhoods, and schools. These economic hardships and their sequelae can lead to behavioral and emotional problems in children. For example, Guidubaldi, Cleminshaw, Perry, and McLoughlin (1983) surveyed children whose parents had and had not divorced and found differences between them on 27 out of 34 outcomes before controlling for income, but only found 13 differences between them after controlling for income, suggesting that income plays an important role but does not account for all of the effect of divorce on children's adjustment. Furthermore, children's adjustment often worsens rather than improves following remarriage and its accompanying increase in economic resources (Hetherington et al., 1989).

Taken together, these findings suggest that income is important, but there is more contributing to children's adjustment problems following divorce than a decrease in household income.

Interparental Conflict

Interparental conflict has received substantial empirical attention. There is consistent evidence that high levels of interparental conflict have negative and long-lasting implications for children's adjustment (Davies & Cummings, 1994; Grych & Fincham, 1990). Amato (1993) and Hetherington et al. (1998) found more support for a parental conflict perspective on why divorce is related to children's adjustment than for any other theoretical perspective that has been proposed to account for this link. Averaging across measures in their review, children in high-conflict, intact families scored .32 standard deviation below children in low-conflict, intact families and .12 standard deviation below children in divorced families on measures of adjustment, suggesting that exposure to high levels of conflict was more detrimental to children than was parental divorce (Hetherington et al., 1998). To illustrate, using data from the National Survey of Families and Households, Vandewater and Lansford (1998) found that when interparental conflict and family structure (married and never divorced vs. divorced and not remarried) were considered simultaneously after controlling for family demographic covariates and children's prior adjustment, high interparental conflict was related to more externalizing behaviors, internalizing problems, and trouble with peers, but family structure was not significantly related to child outcomes. The finding that children whose parents divorce look worse before the divorce than do comparable children whose parents do not divorce is also consistent with this perspective; worse adjustment prior to the divorce could be accounted for, in part, by exposure to interparental conflict.

If divorce leads to a reduction in children's exposure to interparental conflict, one might expect that their adjustment would improve. Indeed, this issue is at the heart of parents' question of whether they should stay in a conflicted marriage for the sake of the children. In an important longitudinal investigation of this issue, Amato, Loomis, and Booth (1995) found that children's problems decrease when parents in a high-conflict marriage divorce (which encompassed 30%–49% of divorces), whereas children's problems increase when parents in a low-conflict marriage divorce. Booth and Amato (2001) examined correlates of divorce for low-conflict couples and found that factors such as less integration in the community, having fewer friends, not owning a home, and having more positive attitudes toward divorce were related to an increased likelihood of divorce; the authors suggest that because these factors may be less salient to children than conflict between their parents, the divorce may come as more of an unwelcome and unexpected shock, accounting for the more negative effects of divorce on children from low-conflict families than those seen in children from high-conflict families.

Researchers have moved beyond monolithic characterizations of conflict into descriptions of particular types of conflict and specific aspects of interparental conflict that may be especially detrimental to children. Overt conflict may be physical or verbal and includes behaviors and emotions such as belligerence, contempt, derision, screaming, insulting, slapping, threatening, and hitting; exposure to overt conflict has been linked to children's externalizing problems (Buehler et al., 1998). Covert conflict may include passive-aggressive techniques such as trying to get the child to side with one parent, using the child to get information about the other parent, having the child carry messages to the other parent, and denigrating the other parent in the presence of the child; covert conflict has been linked more to internalizing problems than to externalizing problems (Buehler et al., 1998). Amato and Afifi (2006) found that the feeling of being caught between parents even into young adulthood was associated with high-conflict marriages but not with divorce and that it was related to more internalizing problems and worse parent–child relationships. Thus, children whose parents divorce may have better long-term adjustment than do children whose parents remain in high-conflict marriages if divorce enables children to escape from exposure to conflict and feelings of being caught between their parents.

Parenting

Another mechanism that has been proposed many times in the literature as an explanation for the links between parental divorce and children's adjustment is the disruption in parenting practices that may occur following divorce. Divorce can make it more difficult for parents to monitor and supervise children effectively (Buchanan, Maccoby, & Dornbusch, 1996; McLanahan & Sandefur, 1994), to discipline consistently (Hetherington, Cox, & Cox, 1979), and to provide warmth and affection (Forehand, Thomas, Wierson, & Brody, 1990; Hetherington & Stanley-Hagan, 1999). After divorce, parent–child conflict often increases, and family cohesion decreases (Short, 2002).

As with studies of children's adjustment showing that children whose parents eventually divorce have significantly more predivorce adjustment problems than do children whose parents do not divorce, parents who eventually divorce have been found to have more problematic parenting practices as long as 8–12 years before the divorce than do parents who do not divorce (Amato & Booth, 1996; Shaw et al., 1993). Parenting problems contribute to children's adjustment problems in all types of family structures. Several studies provide evidence

that controlling for the quality of parenting attenuates the link between parental divorce and children's adjustment (Amato, 1986; Amato & Gilbreth, 1999; Simons, Whitbeck, Beaman, & Conger, 1994; Tschann, Johnson, & Wallerstein, 1989; Videon, 2002). For example, in a study of mothers and their sons in Grades 1–3, Martinez and Forgatch (2002) found that mothers' encouragement of academic skills mediated the relation between marital transitions and boys' academic achievement and that a more general indicator of effective parenting mediated the link between marital transitions and externalizing and internalizing problems.

Some studies have investigated whether contact with the non-custodial parent and the quality of this relationship also mediate the link between parental divorce and children's adjustment. In a meta-analysis of 63 studies, Amato and Gilbreth (1999) found that improved child adjustment (academic achievement and fewer externalizing and internalizing problems) was unrelated to frequency of contact with nonresident fathers but was associated with nonresident fathers' payment of child support, authoritative parenting, and feelings of father–child closeness.

Parents' Well-Being

Yet another possible mediator of the link between parental divorce and children's adjustment is parents' well-being. Marital conflict and divorce increase parents' depression, anxiety, and stress, which decrease parents' ability to parent well and may in turn negatively affect children's adjustment. Mothers' history of delinquent behavior has also been found to account for much of the link between parental divorce and children's externalizing behaviors (Emery et al., 1999). These relations are complicated. Through assortative mating, parents with problems such as depression, substance use, or antisocial behavior are at risk of selecting spouses with similar problems (Maes et al., 1998). These parental risk factors increase marital conflict and divorce (Merikangas, 1984). Children may share some of these parental characteristics genetically or through shared environmental experiences.

Caveats

Because children cannot be randomly assigned to family structure groups, studies of links between parents' divorce and children's adjustment are necessarily correlational. Despite researchers' attempts to control for potential confounds, it is possible that uncontrolled variables account for associations between divorce and adjustment. Two large bodies of research that present important caveats for understanding links between parental divorce and children's adjustment are studies of children's adjustment in stepfamilies and studies of genetic effects.

Remarriage and Stepfamilies

Much of the literature comparing the adjustment of children whose parents have or have not divorced is complicated by the fact that children are often exposed not only to one marital transition (i.e., their biological parents' divorce) but to multiple marital transitions (e.g., the initial divorce plus subsequent remarriages and divorces). If these multiple transitions are not taken into account, children's adjustment to divorce may be confounded with children's adjustment to remarriage and possibly multiple divorces. The present review focuses on parental divorce rather than stepfamilies, but several excellent reviews provide nuanced information about children's adjustment following their parents' remarriage (e.g., Dunn, 2002; Hetherington & Clingempeel, 1992; Hetherington et al., 1999).

Genetic Effects

Recent research has attempted to estimate the relative contributions of genes and environments in accounting for the likelihood that parents will divorce and the adjustment of their children following the divorce (Neiderhiser, Reiss, & Hetherington, 2007). Lykken (2002) presents evidence that a monozygotic twin has a 250% increase in risk of divorcing if his or her cotwin has divorced. Furthermore, divorce is more concordant between monozygotic than dizygotic twins (McGue & Lykken, 1992). These findings support the role of genetics as a risk factor for divorce, but Jocklin, McGue, and Lykken (1996) further specified the personality mechanisms through which this effect occurs. That is, they found between 30% and 42% of the heritability of divorce to be associated with the heritability of the personality characteristics of positive emotionality, negative emotionality, and less constraint, which were, in turn, associated with divorce (Jocklin et al., 1996).

Research also has begun to examine genotype–environment interactions to understand under what environmental conditions genes may express themselves. An important question is whether the genetic contributions to divorce also account for the poorer adjustment of children whose parents have divorced or whether experiencing parental divorce contributes above and beyond the genetic risks. In a longitudinal study of 398 biological and adoptive families, O'Connor, Caspi, DeFries, and Plomin (2000) found that children who experienced their biological parents' divorce by the age of 12 had higher levels of behavior problems and substance use and lower levels of achievement and social adjustment than did children whose biological parents did not divorce. Children who experienced their adoptive parents' divorce by the age of 12 also had higher levels of behavior problems and substance use than did children who did not experience their adoptive parents' divorce, but these two groups of adopted children did not differ on achievement or social adjustment. These findings suggest the importance of gene–environment interactions in contributing to achievement and social adjustment and suggest the importance of the environment in accounting for links between parental divorce and children's behavior problems and substance use (O'Connor et al., 2000).

Using a high-risk sample in Australia, D'Onofrio et al. (2005) compared the offspring of adult twins on externalizing, internalizing, and substance-use problems and concluded that environmental (rather than genetic) effects of divorce accounted for the higher rates of problems among the group that experienced their parents' divorce. In a further elaboration of the process involved in genetic versus environmental effects, D'Onofrio et al. (2006) found that the experience of divorce was related to earlier age of first intercourse and more emotional and educational problems, whereas earlier use of drugs and likelihood of cohabitation were predicted by genetic and other selection factors. Using a children of twins design with a population-based American sample, D'Onofrio et al. (2007) found that genetic and other selection factors, rather than divorce per se, accounted for differences in internalizing problems, whereas substance use was not accounted for by genetic factors. The reasons for the discrepancies between the findings from these studies are not clear. However, although the precise nature of which genetic or environmental factors contribute to distinct developmental outcomes is not clear from the research to date, it is apparent that genetic and environmental contributions both shape whether individuals will eventually divorce and, if they do, how their children may adjust to the divorce.

Divorce Laws and Policies

The questions of whether family structure per se affects children's adjustment and, if so, why and how it does so are important in informing policy because one can adjust policy to influence different proximal mechanisms that may affect children's adjustment. At one level, answers to questions related to whether and how divorce affects children's adjustment also influence how hard it should be for parents to divorce in the first place (e.g., determining if it is better to stay in a conflicted marriage for the sake of the children). States differ in terms of requirements related to waiting periods, counseling, the length of separation needed prior to divorce, and other factors that affect how hard it is to get a divorce in a given state. Despite shifts in rates immediately after a new policy is implemented, the difficulty of divorcing and rates of divorce are for the most part unrelated after this initial phase (Wolfers, 2003), so policies are unlikely to influence how many parents divorce over the long run.

At another level, understanding children's adjustment following divorce is important for implementing policies that can help children once their parents have decided to divorce. For example, if divorce increases children's risk for externalizing behaviors because it results in more limited financial resources available to children and, in turn, the risks of dangerous neighborhoods associated with lower SES, then a reasonable policy response would be to make noncustodial parents more responsible for child-support payments. Similarly, state policies may minimize or exacerbate interparental conflict, with implications for children's adjustment. Key policy issues related to children's adjustment involve the divorce process (e.g., grounds for divorce), custody decisions, and financial support of children. Each category of policies is reviewed below.

Grounds for Divorce

The primary distinction of importance related to grounds for divorce involves whether fault is considered in the divorce proceedings. If fault is considered, then divorce is granted only if one spouse is determined to be "guilty" (of adultery, physically or sexually abusing the spouse or a child, abandoning the home for at least a year, or other serious offenses) and the other spouse is determined to be "innocent" (Nakonezny, Shull, & Rodgers, 1995). The consent of the "innocent" spouse is needed to grant the divorce, and divorce is not granted if both spouses are "guilty." In theory, the innocent spouse is awarded alimony, child support, and property in a fault-based divorce. If fault is not considered, both spouses do not need to provide consent, and alimony, child support, and property are no longer awarded according to fault but according to needs and the ability to pay.

No-fault grounds for divorce were enacted in all 50 states between the 1950s and 1980s, and all 50 states now allow no-fault divorces. However, only 15 states have entirely eliminated fault-based divorces (Grounds for Divorce, n.d.). In the other 35 states, one may choose between a no-fault divorce and a fault-based divorce. The most common reasons for selecting a fault-based divorce are to avoid a longer waiting period often required for a no-fault divorce or to obtain a larger share of the marital assets or more alimony. A main concern related to children's adjustment is that proving guilt and innocence in a fault-based divorce tends to perpetuate acrimony and conflict between the parents, which may lead to worse outcomes for their children.

Child Custody Policies

Child custody policies include several guidelines that determine with whom the child lives following divorce, how time is divided in joint custody situations, and visitation rights. The most frequently applied custody guideline is the "best interests of the child" standard, which takes into account the parents' preferences, the child's preferences, the interactions between parents and children, children's adjustment, and all

family members' mental and physical health (see Kelly, 1994). Recently, the approximation rule has been proposed as an alternative to the best interests of the child standard because of concerns that the latter does not provide enough concrete guidance and leaves too many factors to be evaluated at the discretion of individual judges (American Law Institute, 2002). The approximation rule holds that custody should be awarded to each parent to approximate the amount of time each spent in providing care for the children during the marriage. Opinions range from support of the approximation rule as an improvement over the best interests of the child standard (Emery, Otto, & O'Donohue, 2005) to criticisms that the approximation rule would lead to biases against fathers and be less sensitive to the needs of individual families than is the best interests of the child standard (Warshak, 2007). Regardless of the custody standard applied, custody disputes that are handled through mediation rather than litigation have been found to be related to more involvement of the nonresidential parent in the child's life, without increasing interparental conflict (Emery, Laumann-Billings, Waldron, Sbarra, & Dillon, 2001; Emery, Sbarra, & Grover, 2005).

A distinction is made between legal custody, which involves making decisions regarding the child, and physical custody, which involves daily living arrangements. The most common arrangement following divorce is for parents to share joint legal custody but for mothers to have sole physical custody. Several studies have investigated whether children's adjustment is related to custody arrangements following their parents' divorce. Using data from a large national sample, Downey and Powell (1995) found few differences between the adjustment of children whose fathers had custody following divorce and those whose mothers had custody. For the few outcomes in which differences did emerge, children appeared somewhat better adjusted in paternal custody families if income was left uncontrolled, but after controlling for income, children appeared somewhat better adjusted in maternal custody families (Downey & Powell, 1995).

Major benefits of joint custody include the access to financial resources and other resources that a second parent can provide and the more frequent and meaningful contact that is possible between both parents and the child (Bender, 1994). The major concerns raised with respect to joint custody are that it may prolong children's exposure to conflict between parents with acrimonious relationships and reduce stability that is needed for children's positive adjustment (Johnston, 1995; Twaite & Luchow, 1996). In a meta-analysis of 33 studies comparing joint physical or legal custody with sole maternal custody, Bauserman (2002) concluded that children in joint custody (either physical or legal) had fewer externalizing and internalizing problems and better academic achievement and social relationships than did children in sole maternal custody. Parents with joint custody reported having less past and current conflict than did parents with sole custody, but the findings regarding better adjustment of children in joint custody held after controlling for interparental conflict. Nevertheless, caution is warranted, because there are a wide array of factors affecting the selection of joint versus sole custody that can plausibly explain differences in adjustment for children in these different custody situations. An additional methodological concern is that only 11 of the 33 studies included in Bauserman's meta-analysis were published—21 were unpublished dissertations and 1 was another unpublished manuscript. Therefore, the majority of the studies included in the meta-analyses have not passed the rigor of peer review. The finding that joint physical and joint legal custody were equally associated with better child adjustment is consistent with the finding from Amato and Gilbreth's (1999) meta-analysis that there was little relation between children's adjustment and the frequency with which they had contact with their father. Amato and Gilbreth (1999) found that the quality of children's relationship with their father is a more important predictor of children's adjustment than is frequency of contact. If joint physical or legal custody promotes more positive father–child relationships, this might account for the more positive adjustment of children in joint custody reported by Bauserman (2002).

Child-Support Policies and Enforcement

Child-support policies involve a diverse set of factors related to ensuring that noncustodial parents provide financial support for their children. States vary in their statutory criteria for child support: whether the state can take a percentage of the noncustodial parent's wages, formulas for child support, discretion to have payment made directly to the court, and long-arm statutes. Historically, public assistance played an important role in the economic status of divorced mothers and children (see Garfinkel, Melli, & Robertson, 1994, for a review). Guidelines of "reasonableness" were used by states to determine noncustodial parents' responsibility to pay child support. Local judges used budgets submitted by custodial parents in conjunction with the ability of the noncustodial parent to pay (based on income and other factors), but awards differed considerably from court to court, and the child-support awards were generally too small to pay for a fair share of rearing the children (Garfinkel et al., 1994).

Federal legislation in 1984, 1988, and 1996 provided numerical formulas to guide decisions about child-support awards, authorized states to withhold the noncustodial parent's wages to make child-support payments, and implemented other changes to make it easier for custodial parents to obtain a support award and for courts to enforce those awards (see Roberts,

1994). For example, some states will not issue driver's licenses, vehicle registrations, or state-issued permits to individuals who are behind in child-support payments. Nevertheless, only 57% of custodial parents have a child-support award, and only 47% of those receive full payments (Grall, 2007). Whether custodial parents receive payments is still highly dependent on noncustodial parents' motivation and ability to pay (Thomas & Sawhill, 2005).

In addition to policies specifically focused on child-support payments, policies related to alimony and distribution and maintenance of property also affect the financial resources available to children following divorce. Long-term alimony is no longer as common as it was in the past, except in situations with extenuating circumstances (e.g., a spouse has health problems that prohibit work; Katz, 1994). More common is short-term alimony or rehabilitative alimony, which is provided for a limited period of time during which the spouse receiving alimony (usually the wife) goes to school or gains other skills to enable her to return to the workforce (Katz, 1994). In determining how property is divided following divorce, both monetary and nonmonetary factors are typically considered. Over time, the nonmonetary contributions of parents who stay home with children and the economic needs of children have been given greater consideration in changing statutory laws affecting the distribution of assets following divorce. To the extent that they affect the financial resources available to children, policies involving child support, alimony, and distribution of property following divorce can be important for children's postdivorce adjustment.

Summary

In contrast to the necessity of correlational studies on effects of divorce itself, it is possible to collect experimental data to examine the effects of policies related to divorce. This will be an important direction for future research. Some data could come from natural experiments (e.g., comparing children in states with a particular policy of interest to children in states with a different policy). Other data could come from true experiments in which some children are randomly assigned to interventions being evaluated and other children are randomly assigned to the state's status quo (evaluations along these lines have been conducted in relation to different methods of determining child-support payments, such as in New York's Child Assistance Program; Hamilton, Burstein, & Long, 1998). Policy evaluations have the potential to lead to recommendations for a set of standards that could improve children's adjustment following their parents' divorce by making the divorce process less acrimonious and the decisions regarding finances and custody as conducive to children's well-being as possible.

Summary and Conclusions

In this article, I reviewed the research literature on links between parental divorce and children's adjustment. First, I considered evidence regarding how divorce is related to children's externalizing behaviors, internalizing problems, academic achievement, and social relationships. Research suggests that children whose parents have divorced have higher levels of externalizing behaviors and internalizing problems, lower academic achievement, and more problems in social relationships than do children whose parents have not divorced. However, even though children whose parents divorce have worse adjustment on average than do children whose parents do not divorce, most children whose parents divorce do not have long-term negative outcomes.

Second, I examined children's age at the time of the divorce, age at the time of the study, length of time since the divorce, demographic characteristics, children's adjustment prior to the divorce, and stigmatization as moderators of the links between divorce and children's adjustment. There is evidence that, for behavioral outcomes, children who are younger at the time of their parents' divorce may be more at risk than are children who are older at the time of the divorce, but for academic outcomes and social relationships (particularly with romantic partners), adolescents whose parents divorce may be at greater risk than are younger children. The evidence is inconclusive regarding whether girls or boys are more affected by divorce, but there is some evidence that European American children are more negatively affected by divorce than are African American children. Children who have adjustment difficulties prior to divorce are more negatively affected by divorce than are children who are functioning well before the divorce. In cultural and historical contexts in which divorce is stigmatized, children may show worse adjustment following divorce than they do in contexts where divorce is not stigmatized.

Third, I examined income, interparental conflict, parenting, and parents' well-being, as mediators of relations between divorce and children's adjustment. All four of these mediators attenuate the link between parental divorce and children's adjustment difficulties. Interparental conflict has received the most empirical support as an important mediator.

Fourth, I noted the caveats of the research literature. This review focused on the relation between divorce and children's adjustment, but stepfamily formation and subsequent divorces are often part of the experience of children whose biological parents divorce. Recent work using adoption and twin designs demonstrates the importance of both genetics and environments (and their interaction) in predicting the likelihood of divorce and children's adjustment following parental divorce.

Fifth, I considered notable policies related to grounds for divorce, child custody, and child support in light of how they might affect children's adjustment to their parents' divorce. Policies that reduce interparental conflict and provide economic security to children have the potential to benefit children's adjustment. Evaluating whether particular policies are related to children's adjustment following their parents' divorce has the potential to inform future policymaking.

It is important to end this review by emphasizing that not all children experience similar trajectories before or after experiencing their parents' divorce. Thus, trajectories of adjustment that may be typical of many children may not be exhibited by an individual child. Furthermore, what initially appear to be effects of divorce are likely to be a complex combination of parent, child, and contextual factors that precede and follow the divorce in conjunction with the divorce itself.

References

Allison, P.D., & Furstenberg, F.F., Jr. (1989). How marital dissolution affects children: Variations by age and sex. *Developmental Psychology, 25,* 540–549.

Amato, P.R. (1986). Marital conflict, the parent–child relationship, and child self-esteem. *Family Relations, 35,* 403–410.

Amato, P.R. (1993). Children's adjustment to divorce: Theories, hypotheses, and empirical support. *Journal of Marriage and the Family, 55,* 23–38.

Amato, P.R. (1996). Explaining the intergenerational transmission of divorce. *Journal of Marriage and the Family, 58,* 628–640.

Amato, P.R. (2001). Children of divorce in the 1990s: An update of the Amato and Keith (1991) meta-analysis. *Journal of Family Psychology, 15,* 355–370.

Amato, P.R. (2003). Reconciling divergent perspectives: Judith Wallerstein, quantitative family research, and children of divorce. *Family Relations, 52,* 332–339.

Amato, P.R., & Afifi, T.D. (2006). Feeling caught between parents: Adult children's relations with parents and subjective well-being. *Journal of Marriage and the Family, 68,* 222–235.

Amato, P.R., & Booth, A. (1996). A prospective study of divorce and parent–child relationships. *Journal of Marriage and the Family, 58,* 356–365.

Amato, P.R., & Cheadle, J. (2005). The long reach of divorce: Divorce and child well-being across three generations. *Journal of Marriage and the Family, 67,* 191–206.

Amato, P.R., & DeBoer, D.D. (2001). The transmission of marital instability across generations: Relationship skills or commitment to marriage? *Journal of Marriage and the Family, 63,* 1038–1051.

Amato, P.R., & Gilbreth, J.G. (1999). Nonresident fathers and children's well-being: A meta-analysis. *Journal of Marriage and the Family, 61,* 557–573.

Amato, P.R., & Keith, B. (1991a). Parental divorce and adult well-being: A meta-analysis. *Journal of Marriage and the Family, 53,* 43–58.

Amato, P.R., & Keith, B. (1991b). Parental divorce and the well-being of children: A meta-analysis. *Psychological Bulletin, 110,* 26–46.

Amato, P.R., Loomis, L.S., & Booth, A. (1995). Parental divorce, marital conflict, and offspring well-being during early adulthood. *Social Forces, 73,* 895–915.

American Law Institute. (2002). *Principles of the law of family dissolution: Analysis and recommendations.* Newark, NJ: Matthew Bender.

Bauserman, R. (2002). Child adjustment in joint-custody versus sole-custody arrangements: A meta-analytic review. *Journal of Family Psychology, 16,* 91–102.

Bender, W.N. (1994). Joint custody: The option of choice. *Journal of Divorce and Remarriage, 21,* 115–131.

Booth, A., & Amato, P.R. (1994). Parental marital quality, parental divorce, and relations with parents. *Journal of Marriage and the Family, 56,* 21–34.

Booth, A., & Amato, P.R. (2001). Parental predivorce relations and offspring postdivorce well-being. *Journal of Marriage and the Family, 63,* 197–212.

Buchanan, C.M., Maccoby, E.E., & Dornbusch, S.M. (1996). *Adolescents after divorce.* Cambridge, MA: Harvard University Press.

Buehler, C., Krishnakumar, A., Stone, G., Anthony, C., Pemberton, S., Gerard, J., et al. (1998). Interparental conflict styles and youth problem behaviors: A two-sample replication study. *Journal of Marriage and the Family, 60,* 119–132.

Chase-Lansdale, P.L., Cherlin, A.J., & Kiernan, K.K. (1995). The long-term effects of parental divorce on the mental health of young adults: A developmental perspective. *Child Development, 66,* 1614–1634.

Chase-Lansdale, P.L., & Hetherington, E.M. (1990). The impact of divorce on life-span development: Short and long term effects. In P.B. Baltes, D.L. Featherman, & R.M. Lerner (Eds.), *Life-span development and behavior* (pp. 105–150). Hillsdale, NJ: Erlbaum.

Cherlin, A.J. (1998). Marriage and marital dissolution among Black Americans. *Journal of Comparative Family Studies, 29,* 147–158.

Cherlin, A.J. (1999). Going to extremes: Family structure, children's well-being, and social science. *Demography, 36,* 421–428.

Cherlin, A.J., Chase-Lansdale, P.L., & McRae, C. (1998). Effects of parental divorce on mental health throughout the life course. *American Sociological Review, 63,* 239–249.

Cherlin, A.J., Furstenberg, F.F., Chase-Lansdale, P.L., Kiernan, K.E., Robins, P.K., Morrison, D.R., et al. (1991). Longitudinal studies of effects of divorce on children in Great Britain and the United States. *Science, 252,* 1386–1389.

Coontz, S. (1992). *The way we never were: American families and the nostalgia trap.* New York: Basic Books.

Davies, P.T., & Cummings, E.M. (1994). Marital conflict and child adjustment: An emotional security hypothesis. *Psychological Bulletin, 116,* 387–411.

Doherty, W.J., & Needle, R.H. (1991). Psychological adjustment and substance use among adolescents before and after parental divorce. *Child Development, 62,* 328–337.

D'Onofrio, B.M., Turkheimer, E., Emery, R.E., Maes, H.H., Silberg, J., & Eaves, L.J. (2007). A children of twins study of parental divorce and offspring psychopathology. *Journal of Child Psychology and Psychiatry, 48,* 667–675.

D'Onofrio, B.M., Turkheimer, E., Emery, R.E., Slutske, W.S., Heath, A.C., Madden, P.A., et al. (2005). A genetically informed study of marital instability and its association with offspring psychopathology. *Journal of Abnormal Psychology, 114,* 570–586.

D'Onofrio, B.M., Turkheimer, E., Emery, R.E., Slutske, W.S., Heath, A.C., Madden, P.A., et al. (2006). A genetically informed study of the processes underlying the association between parental marital instability and offspring adjustment. *Developmental Psychology, 42,* 486–499.

Downey, D., & Powell, B. (1995). Do children in single-parent households fare better living with same-sex parents? *Journal of Marriage and the Family, 55,* 55–71.

Dunn, J. (2002). The adjustment of children in stepfamilies: Lessons from community studies. *Child and Adolescent Mental Health, 7,* 154–161.

Dunn, J., Deater-Deckard, K., Pickering, K., & O'Connor, T.G. (1998). Children's adjustment and prosocial behaviour in step-, single-parent, and non-stepfamily settings: Findings from a community study. *Journal of Child Psychology and Psychiatry, 39,* 1083–1095.

Emery, R.E., Laumann-Billings, L., Waldron, M.C., Sbarra, D.A., & Dillon, P. (2001). Child custody mediation and litigation: Custody, contact, and coparenting 12 years after initial dispute resolution. *Journal of Consulting and Clinical Psychology, 69,* 323–332.

Emery, R.E., Otto, R.K., & O'Donohue, W.T. (2005). A critical assessment of child custody evaluations: Limited science and a flawed system. *Psychological Science in the Public Interest, 6,* 1–29.

Emery, R.E., Sbarra, D., & Grover, T. (2005). Divorce mediation: Research and reflections. *Family Court Review, 43,* 22–37.

Emery, R.E., Waldron, M., Kitzmann, K.M., & Aaron, J. (1999). Delinquent behavior, future divorce or nonmarital childbearing, and externalizing behavior among offspring: A 14-year prospective study. *Journal of Family Psychology, 13,* 568–579.

Forehand, R., Thomas, A.M., Wierson, M., & Brody, G. (1990). Role of maternal functioning and parenting skills in adolescent functioning following parental divorce. *Journal of Abnormal Psychology, 99,* 278–283.

Garfinkel, I., Melli, M.S., & Robertson, J.G. (1994). Child support orders: A perspective on reform. *Future of Children, 4,* 84–100.

Glenn, N. (2001). Is the current concern about American marriage warranted? *Virginia Journal of Social Policy and the Law,* 5–47.

Grall, T.S. (2007). *Custodial mothers and fathers and their child support: 2005.* Washington, DC: U.S. Bureau of the Census.

Grounds for Divorce. (n.d.). Retrieved March 1, 2008, from www.divorcelawinfo.com/Pages/grounds.html

Grych, J.H., & Fincham, F.D. (1990). Marital conflict and children's adjustment: A cognitive-contextual framework. *Psychological Bulletin, 108,* 267–290.

Guidubaldi, J., Cleminshaw, H.K., Perry, J.D., & McLoughlin, C.S. (1983). The impact of parental divorce on children: Report of the nationwide NASP study. *School Psychology Review, 12,* 300–323.

Hamilton, W.L., Burstein, N.R., & Long, D. (1998). *Using incentives in welfare reform: The New York State Child Assistance Program.* Cambridge, MA: Abt Associates.

Harris, J.R. (1998). *The nurture assumption: Why children turn out the way they do.* New York: Free Press.

Hetherington, E.M. (1989). Coping with family transitions: Winners, losers, and survivors. *Child Development, 60,* 1–14.

Hetherington, E.M., Bridges, M., & Insabella, G.M. (1998). What matters? What does not? Five perspectives on the association between marital transitions and children's adjustment. *American Psychologist, 53,* 167–184.

Hetherington, E.M., & Clingempeel, W.G. (1992). Coping with marital transitions: A family systems perspective. *Monographs of the Society for Research in Child Development, 57* (2–3, Serial No. 227).

Hetherington, E.M., Cox, M., & Cox, R. (1979). Stress and coping in divorce: A focus on women. In J.E. Gullahorn (Ed.), *Psychology and women: In transition* (pp. 95–128). Washington, DC: V. H. Winston & Sons.

Hetherington, E.M., Cox, M., & Cox, R. (1985). Long-term effects of divorce and remarriage on the adjustment of children. *Journal of the American Academy of Child Psychiatry, 24,* 518–530.

Hetherington, E.M., & Elmore, A.M. (2004). The intergenerational transmission of couple instability. In P.L. Chase-Lansdale, K. Kiernan, & R.J. Friedman (Eds.), *Human development across lives and generations: The potential for change* (pp. 171–203). New York: Cambridge University Press.

Hetherington, E.M., Henderson, S.H., Reiss, D., Anderson, E.R., Bridges, M., Chan, R.W., et al. (1999). Adolescent siblings in stepfamilies: Family functioning and adolescent adjustment. *Monographs of the Society for Research in Child Development, 64* (4).

Hetherington, E.M., & Kelly, J. (2002). *For better or worse.* New York: Norton.

Hetherington, E.M., & Stanley-Hagan, M. (1999). The adjustment of children with divorced parents: A risk and resiliency perspective. *Journal of Child Psychology and Psychiatry, 40,* 129–140.

Hetherington, E.M., Stanley-Hagan, M., & Anderson, E.R. (1989). Marital transitions: A child's perspective. *American Psychologist, 44,* 303–312.

Jeynes, W. (2002). *Divorce, family structure, and the academic success of children.* New York: Haworth Press.

Jocklin, V., McGue, M., & Lykken, D.T. (1996). Personality and divorce: A genetic analysis. *Journal of Personality and Social Psychology, 71,* 288–299.

Johnston, J.R. (1995). Research update: Children's adjustment in sole custody compared to joint custody families and principles for custody decision making. *Family and Conciliation Courts Review, 33,* 415–425.

Kasen, S., Cohen, P., Brook, J.S., & Hartmark, C. (1996). A multiple-risk interaction model: Effects of temperament and divorce on psychiatric disorders in children. *Journal of Abnormal Child Psychology, 24,* 121–150.

Katz, S.N. (1994). Historical perspective and current trends in the legal process of divorce. *Future of Children, 4,* 44–62.

Kelly, J.B. (1994). The determination of child custody. *Future of Children, 4,* 121–142.

Lansford, J.E., Ceballo, R., Abbey, A., & Stewart, A.J. (2001). Does family structure matter? A comparison of adoptive, two parent biological, single mother, stepfather, and stepmother households. *Journal of Marriage and the Family, 63,* 840–851.

Lansford, J.E., Malone, P.S., Castellino, D.R., Dodge, K.A., Pettit, G.S., & Bates, J.E. (2006). Trajectories of internalizing, externalizing, and grades for children who have and have not experienced their parents' divorce. *Journal of Family Psychology, 20,* 292–301.

Laosa, L.M. (1988). Ethnicity and single parenting in the United States. In E.M. Hetherington & J.D. Arasteh (Eds.), *Impact of divorce, single parenting, and stepparenting on children* (pp. 23–49). Hillsdale, NJ: Erlbaum.

Laumann-Billings, L., & Emery, R.E. (2000). Distress among young adults from divorced families. *Journal of Family Psychology, 14,* 671–687.

Lye, D.N. (1996). Adult child–parent relationships. *Annual Review of Sociology, 22,* 79–102.

Lykken, D.T. (2002). How relationships begin and end: A genetic perspective. In A.L. Vangelisti, H.T. Reis, & M.A. Fitzpatrick (Eds.), *Stability and change in relationships* (pp. 83–102). New York: Cambridge University Press.

Maes, H.H.M., Neale, M.C., Kendler, K.S., Hewitt, J.K., Silberg, J.L., Foley, D.L., et al. (1998). Assortative mating for major psychiatric diagnoses in two population-based samples. *Psychological Medicine, 28,* 1389–1401.

Malone, P.S., Lansford, J.E., Castellino, D.R., Berlin, L.J., Dodge, K.A., Bates, J.E., et al. (2004). Divorce and child behavior problems: Applying latent change score models to life event data. *Structural Equation Modeling, 11,* 401–423.

Martinez, C.R., Jr., & Forgatch, M.S. (2002). Adjusting to change: Linking family structure transitions with parenting and boys' adjustment. *Journal of Family Psychology, 16,* 107–117.

McGue, M., & Lykken, D.T. (1992). Genetic influence on risk of divorce. *Psychological Science, 3,* 368–373.

McLanahan, S.S. (1999). Father absence and the welfare of children. In E.M. Hetherington (Ed.), *Coping with divorce, single parenting, and remarriage: A risk and resiliency perspective* (pp. 117–145). Hillsdale, NJ: Erlbaum.

McLanahan, S., & Sandefur, G. (1994). *Growing up with a single parent.* Cambridge, MA: Harvard University Press.

Mechanic, D., & Hansell, S. (1989). Divorce, family conflict, and adolescents' well-being. *Journal of Health and Social Behavior, 30,* 105–116.

Merikangas, K.R. (1984). Divorce and assortative mating among depressed patients. *American Journal of Psychiatry, 141,* 74–76.

Morrison, D.R., & Cherlin, A.J. (1995). The divorce process and young children's well-being: A prospective analysis. *Journal of Marriage and the Family, 57,* 800–812.

Nakonezny, P.A., Shull, R.D., & Rodgers, J.L. (1995). The effect of no-fault divorce law on the divorce rate across the 50 states and its relation to income, education, and religiosity. *Journal of Marriage and the Family, 57,* 477–488.

National Center for Health Statistics. (2008). Marriage and divorce. Retrieved March 3, 2008, from www.cdc.gov/nchs/fastats/divorce.htm

Neiderhiser, J.M., Reiss, D., & Hetherington, E.M. (2007). The nonshared environment in adolescent development (NEAD) project: A longitudinal family study of twins and siblings from adolescence to young adulthood. *Twin Research and Human Genetics, 10,* 74–83.

O'Connor, T.G., Caspi, A., DeFries, J.C., & Plomin, R. (2000). Are associations between parental divorce and children's adjustment genetically mediated? An adoption study. *Developmental Psychology, 36,* 429–437.

Orbuch, T.L., Thornton, A., & Cancio, J. (2000). The impact of marital quality, divorce, and remarriage on the relationships between parents and their children. *Marriage and Family Review, 29,* 221–246.

Popenoe, D. (1993). American family decline, 1960–1990: A review and appraisal. *Journal of Marriage and the Family, 55,* 527–542.

Popenoe, D. (2003). Can the nuclear family be revived? In M. Coleman & L. Ganong (Eds.), *Points and counterpoints: Controversial relationship and family issues in the 21st century* (pp. 218–221). Los Angeles: Roxbury Publishing.

Reifman, A., Villa, L.C., Amans, J.A., Rethinam, V., & Telesca, T.Y. (2001). Children of divorce in the 1990s: A meta-analysis. *Journal of Divorce and Remarriage, 36,* 27–36.

Roberts, P.G. (1994). Child support orders: Problems with enforcement. *Future of Children, 4,* 101–120.

Ruschena, E., Prior, M., Sanson, A., & Smart, D. (2005). A longitudinal study of adolescent adjustment following family transitions. *Journal of Child Psychology and Psychiatry, 46,* 353–363.

Shaw, D.S., Emery, R.E., & Tuer, M.D. (1993). Parental functioning and children's adjustment in families of divorce: A prospective study. *Journal of Abnormal Child Psychology, 21,* 119–134.

Short, J.L. (2002). The effects of parental divorce during childhood on college students. *Journal of Divorce and Remarriage, 38,* 143–156.

Simons, R.L., Whitbeck, L.B., Beaman, J., & Conger, R.D. (1994). The impact of mothers' parenting, involvement by nonresidential fathers, and parental conflict on the adjustment of adolescent children. *Journal of Marriage and the Family, 56,* 356–374.

Sun, Y., & Li, Y. (2001). Marital disruption, parental investment, and children's academic achievement: A prospective analysis. *Journal of Family Issues, 22,* 27–62.

Sun, Y., & Li, Y. (2002). Children's well-being during parents' marital disruption process: A pooled time-series analysis. *Journal of Marriage and the Family, 64,* 472–488.

Thomas, A., & Sawhill, I. (2005). For love and money? The impact of family structure on family income. *Future of Children, 15,* 57–74.

Tschann, J.M., Johnson, J.R., & Wallerstein, J.S. (1989). Family processes and children's functioning during divorce. *Journal of Marriage and the Family, 51,* 431–444.

Twaite, J.A., & Luchow, A.K. (1996). Custodial arrangements and parental conflict following divorce: The impact on children's adjustment. *Journal of Psychiatry and Law, 24,* 53–75.

U.S. Census Bureau. (2004). Detailed tables: Number, timing and duration of marriages and divorces, 2004. Washington, DC: Author. Retrieved March 3, 2008, from www.census.gov/population/www/socdemo/marr-div/2004detailed_tables.html

Vandewater, E.A., & Lansford, J.E. (1998). Influences of family structure and parental conflict on children's well-being. *Family Relations, 47,* 323–330.

Videon, T.M. (2002). The effects of parent-adolescent relationships and parental separation on adolescent well-being. *Journal of Marriage and the Family, 64,* 489–503.

Wallerstein, J.S., Lewis, J.M., & Blakeslee, S. (2000). *The unexpected legacy of divorce: A 25 year landmark study.* New York: Hyperion.

Warshak, R.A. (2007). The approximation rule, child development research, and children's best interests after divorce. *Child Development Perspectives, 1,* 119–125.

Wolfers, J. (2003). Did unilateral divorce laws raise divorce rates? A reconciliation and new results. National Bureau of Economic Research Working Paper No. 10014. Retrieved March 1, 2008, from www.nber.org/papers/w10014

Critical Thinking

1. A significant number of children in the United States will experience the divorce of their parents. Think of a child or children who have experienced their parents' divorce. Explain how divorce impacts children at different ages and by gender. Describe factors that can ameliorate the negative effects of divorce.

2. If your parents divorced, at what age were you, how did it make you feel, and explain how you coped with the divorce. Did your parents' divorce influence your feelings about marriage and divorce? If you were married with children and felt the need to get a divorce and you have children, explain what you could do to reduce the negative impact to your children.

3. Find out whether you live in a state that still permits determining fault as grounds for a divorce. Evaluate the pros and cons of proceeding with a divorce based on fault in terms of benefits and negative consequences on both parents and children involved in this type of legal divorce proceeding. Given the research data, explain how you would counsel parents contemplating a fault-based divorce?

4. Critique the legal and public policy positions regarding the determination of child custody, child-support, and alimony in light of the research regarding child outcomes.

5. Your best friend is considering remarriage and has full custody of a fifth grade son and a daughter who is a sophomore in high school. She has been a single mother who is struggling with a part-time job for two years and had a turbulent and difficult first marriage to a husband who is now largely absent. She has asked for your advice on what to expect in terms of her children's reactions if she remarries. Based on the research in this article, how would you counsel and advise her?

6. Do you think attitudes about divorce are changing in the United States? Explain and cite data. Contrast U.S. attitudes toward divorce with other countries and speculate on how these societal or culturally based attitudes may affect children's adjustment to divorce.

Create Central

www.mhhe.com/createcentral

Internet References

American Psychological Association
http://www.apa.org/about/gr/issues/cyf/divorce.aspx

The Future of Children Princeton Brookings.org
http://futureofchildren.org/publications/journals/article/index.xml?journalid=63&articleid=415&sectionid=2841

Healthy Children.org
http://www.healthychildren.org/English/family-life/family-dynamics/types-of-families/Pages/Adjusting-to-Divorce.aspx

The Role of Parental Control in Children's Development in Western and East Asian Countries by Eva M. Pomerantz and Qian Wang

139

Article

Prepared by: Ellen N. Junn, *California State University, Dominguez Hills*

The Role of Parental Control in Children's Development in Western and East Asian Countries

Eva M. Pomerantz and Qian Wang

Learning Outcomes

After reading this article, you will be able to:

- Define "universalism" as it functions in the field of psychology and offer evidence that challenges universalist assumptions.

- Differentiate between mechanisms and effects in understanding psychological phenomena.

- Explain how cultural values and beliefs about parenting influence how parents discipline their children in the United States and in East Asian countries.

- Describe how parental control is a kind of family dynamic that is important for children's good outcomes, but too little or too much control can lead to developmental problems.

There is a wealth of evidence from Western countries, such as the United States, that when parents exert control over children by intruding, pressuring, or dominating them in terms of their thoughts, feelings, and behavior, children suffer psychologically (for a review, see Pomerantz & Thompson, 2008). In contrast, when parents support children's autonomy by allowing them freedom of choice, supporting their initiative, and adopting their perspective, children in the West benefit. Initially, the assumption was that such effects are universal. However, beginning in the 1990s, it was suggested that several aspects of the culture in East Asian countries, such as China, make children more accepting of parental control so that the negative effects are not as strong as they are in Western countries (e.g., Chao, 1994; Iyengar & Lepper, 1999). Because

control is considered one of the most influential dimensions of parenting (Maccoby & Martin, 1983), there has been much debate over the effects of parental control in East Asian (vs. Western) countries. As a consequence, there is now a sizable body of research, conducted mainly in the United States and China, from which it is possible to gain significant insights about similarities and differences in the effects of parental control in Western and East Asian countries.

Parental Control

In theory and research on parenting, the term "control" is often used to refer to parental intrusiveness, pressure, or domination, with the inverse being parental support of autonomy (Grolnick & Pomerantz, 2009). The focus of much research has been psychological control, or parents' regulation of children's feelings and thoughts (e.g., Barber, Stolz, & Olsen, 2005). Psychological control is frequently contrasted with behavioral control, defined as parents' regulation of what children do. Behavioral control commonly includes parental guidance, monitoring, and rule setting. As such, it does not necessarily entail intrusiveness, pressure, or domination; indeed, behavioral control has positive, rather than negative, effects on children's psychological development (Grolnick & Pomerantz, 2009). The debate about the effects of parental control in the West and East Asia has centered on control in the intrusive sense, with little attention to distinguishing between its targets—that is, whether parents are attempting to regulate children's psychology or behavior (Wang, Pomerantz, & Chen, 2007). We follow suit here, by focusing on parental control that is intruding, pressuring, or dominating, regardless of whether parents are attempting to regulate children's psychology or behavior.

Universalist Perspectives

Much of the research so far has been guided by the idea that parental control undermines children's sense of autonomy, thereby interfering with their psychological development (e.g., Barber et al., 2005). In the context of self-determination theory, Deci and Ryan (1985) argue that there is a universal need for autonomy and that satisfaction of this need is essential to optimal psychological functioning. These investigators make the case that controlling environments detract from feelings of autonomy, regardless of culture. Thus, when parents exert control over children, for instance by making decisions for them about personal issues (e.g., who to be friends with), children suffer, as they feel they do not have control over their lives. Such a universalist perspective is also evident in parental acceptance–rejection theory, which holds that parental control may negatively influence children by conveying rejection—for example, when parents withdraw love because children have not met their expectations, children may feel that parents no longer care about them. Parental acceptance–rejection theory postulates that children's feelings of being rejected (vs. accepted) by parents play a role in their development regardless of culture, because relatedness is universally important (e.g., Rohner, Khaleque, & Cournoyer, 2004).

Culture-Specific Perspectives

The major principle behind culture-specific perspectives is that Western and East Asian countries have distinct cultures that shape the effects of parental control on children's development leading the effects to be less negative in East Asian contexts. Iyengar and Lepper (1999), for instance, contend that when East Asian parents exert control over children by making decisions for them about personal issues, it does not have detrimental effects; taking on their parents' decisions as their own provides children with an opportunity to harmonize with parents, something that in East Asia is prioritized over autonomy, given the heightened cultural orientation toward interdependence. In a somewhat different vein, because East Asian notions about parents' role in children's development—such as the Chinese concept of *guan*, which means to govern as well as to care for—involve parental control with the ultimate aim of supporting children, parental control may not be experienced as rejecting by children (Chao, 1994). As parental control is more common in East Asia than in the West (e.g., Wang et al., 2007), it has also been suggested that East Asian parents may exert control more deliberately and calmly, with less negative effect, because control does not violate, and is even part of, "good parenting" (e.g., Grusec, Rudy, & Martini, 1997).

Empirical Evidence

The culture-specific perspectives arose in part in response to a series of findings from the 1990s showing that authoritarian (vs. authoritative) parenting has a greater negative effect on American children of European heritage than it does on American children of Asian heritage in terms of academic functioning (e.g., grades) but not necessarily in terms of emotional functioning (e.g., depressive symptoms; e.g., Steinberg, Lamborn, Darling, Mounts, & Dornbusch, 1994). Unfortunately, conclusions about the dissimilarity of the effects of parental control in Western and East Asian countries cannot be made from such data, because authoritarian parenting is an amalgamation of multiple dimensions of parenting including control, structure, and acceptance. Thus, it is unclear if it is parental control that drives the difference (or absence of difference) in the effects of authoritarian parenting; it could be one of the other dimensions or the interaction between two or more of the dimensions.

The research on the effects of authoritarian parenting on children of European and Asian heritage in the United States was followed by research on the effects specifically of parental control in Western and East Asian countries. Hasebe, Nucci, and Nucci (2004) found that parents making decisions for children about personal issues was associated with dampened emotional functioning among American and Japanese high-school children. Similarly, Barber et al. (2005) documented positive associations between parental psychological control and adolescents' depression and delinquency in a variety of countries including the United States, Germany, China, and India. Because these studies used concurrent designs in which parental control and children's psychological functioning were examined at a single point in time, the findings cannot provide insight into whether parental control precedes dampened psychological functioning among children similarly in Western and East Asian contexts; determining whether it does is critical in drawing conclusions about the role of parental control in children's psychological development in the two regions.

Research following children over time in the United States and China sheds light on this issue. The more parents make decisions for children about personal issues as children enter adolescence, the more children's emotional functioning suffers 2 years later, adjusting for their earlier functioning; notably, the size of the effects in the United States and China do not differ (Qin, Pomerantz, & Wang, 2009). A comparable pattern is evident for psychological control (Wang et al., 2007): During early adolescence, such control predicts children's dampened emotional functioning 6 months later, taking into account children's earlier emotional functioning, similarly in the United

States and China. Conversely, parental support of children's autonomy (e.g., encouraging them to express their opinions) predicts better subsequent emotional functioning among children in both countries, albeit with a stronger effect for positive, but not negative, emotional functioning in the United States. Parental support of children's autonomy also predicts children's enhanced grades over time similarly in the two countries, but its effect on children's motivation (e.g., investment in school) is stronger in the United States.

Moderating Contexts

Although parental control appears to interfere with children's psychological functioning similarly in the West and East Asia, there may be some contexts in which it may do so to a greater extent in Western countries. Because the identification of such contexts represents a second step in elucidating whether the effects of parental control differ in the two regions, there is limited evidence on this issue. However, the existing evidence is suggestive of several circumstances under which the effects of parental control are stronger in the West. First, almost all of the research has been conducted in areas that are in or near urban centers. Given that such areas in East Asia have been increasingly exposed to Western values in the past few decades, it is unclear to what extent the findings are generalizable to rural areas. Indeed, parental control may play a stronger undermining role in urban areas than in rural areas, given that children, particularly boys, in urban China feel less of a sense of obligation to parents (Fuligni & Zhang, 2004) and are also more averse to conflict with parents than are their counterparts in rural areas (Zhang & Fuligni, 2006). Stronger effects of parental control in urban (versus rural) areas may also exist in the West, however, given cultural variability by geographical area in the West (e.g., Plaut, Markus, & Lachman, 2002).

Second, differences in the strength of the effects of parental control in Western and East Asian countries may exist, as reflected in the extent to which parents decrease their control as children mature. Perhaps because of the West's heightened orientation toward independence and its less hierarchical structure (Triandis, 1994), American parents decrease their control (i.e., refraining from making decisions for their children about personal issues) more than do Chinese parents as children progress through the early adolescent years (Qin et al., 2009). As Western children expect this decrease in parental control more than East Asian children do (Feldman & Rosenthal, 1991), their psychological functioning may be influenced more by the extent to which their parents "loosen the reins" during these years. As shown in Figure 1, when American parents relinquish control by making fewer decisions for children about personal issues as children enter adolescence, children have better emotional

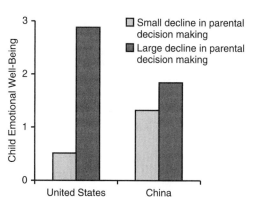

Figure 1 The effects of change over time in parental decision making on child emotional well-being during early adolescence in the United States and China (adapted from Qin, Pomerantz, & Wang, 2009). In the United States, the larger the decline in parental (vs. child) decision making about personal issues as children progressed through the seventh and eighth grades (adjusting for such decision making at the beginning of seventh grade), the better the children's emotional well-being at the end of eighth grade (adjusting for such well-being at the beginning of seventh grade). In China, there was a similar pattern, but it was significantly smaller.

functioning; although such a trend is also evident in China, it is substantially weaker (Qin et al., 2009). It is possible that Chinese children benefit more from a decline in parental control in later adolescence, when it may be more normative. Unfortunately, similarities and differences in how Western and East Asian children move through development have not been comprehensively documented.

Third, the effects of parental control over children's academic learning may be stronger in the West than in East Asia. In Confucian teaching, which is central in East Asian culture, learning is viewed as a moral endeavor in which individuals take on the lifelong task of constantly improving themselves (Li, 2005). Access to education is also more limited, but has greater financial impact, in East Asia (Pomerantz, Ng, & Wang, 2008). Given the moral and practical importance of children's learning, East Asian children may be particularly accepting of parental control when it comes to academics. Although the effects of parental control in the academic area have not been compared to the effects in other areas, there is some suggestive evidence. When European American children believe their mothers have made decisions for them about an academic task, they spend less time and perform more poorly on the task than they do when they make the decisions themselves; however, the reverse is true of Asian American children (Iyengar & Lepper, 1999). Research conducted in China, however, suggests this is the case only when children feel they have positive relationships with their mothers (Bao & Lam, 2008); it may be that children's sense of connectedness to their parents allows children to internalize parents' goals.

Fourth, parental control may take many forms, but the major focus of the comparative research has been on parents making decisions for children about personal issues and their exertion of psychological control over children. These forms of control may be at the extreme end of the continuum. It is possible that less extreme forms, such as providing assistance when children do not request it or hovering over children as they work on something, are more open to interpretation by children in terms of the extent to which they are seen to violate their autonomy or convey rejection. Consequently, culture may play a greater part in how such forms of control are interpreted, leading Western children to hold more negative views of less extreme forms of control than do East Asian children and thus to suffer more when their parents use them. For example, because the West is oriented more toward independence than is East Asia, Western children may see parents' hovering as children complete their homework as more of a violation of their autonomy than might their East Asian counterparts, who may instead interpret such behavior as an expression of parents' love.

Underlying Mechanisms

Fully elucidating the effects of parental control in Western and East Asian countries involves identifying not only the circumstances that may lead to differences in the strength of effects but also the mechanisms underlying the effects. It is necessary to consider the possibility that similar effects reflect different processes. Given different cultural orientations toward independence and interdependence, for example, dampened feelings of autonomy may account for the negative effects of parental control to a greater extent among children in the West, whereas heightened feelings of rejection may account for them to a greater extent among children in East Asia. Under circumstances when there are differences in the effects, the differences need to be unpacked: For example, do they reflect differences in children's interpretation of parental control? In this vein, Chao's (1994) suggestion that parental control has less negative effects among East Asian (vs. Western) children because they view parents' attempts to regulate them as an act of love should be examined. And if differences in how children interpret parental control underlie differences in its effects, is this due, at least in part, to differences in how parents exert control—for instance, in the extent to which parents accompany control with negative affect, as suggested by Grusec et al. (1997)?

Conclusions

In line with universalist perspectives, when parents exert control over children by intruding, pressuring, or dominating them, children suffer, whether they live in the West or East Asia. This undermining role, however, may not be uniform; its strength may differ in the two regions in some contexts. The negative effects of parental control are stronger in the West than in East Asia when parents fail to decrease it as children enter adolescence; parental control may also have stronger effects in the West when it is exerted over academics than in other areas of children's lives. These potential contextual forces, as well as others such as the extremity of control, need more direct investigation—something that may be accomplished as the focus moves away from asking *whether* the effects of parental control are stronger in the West than in East Asia to asking *when* they may be stronger, and *why*. Despite these lingering issues, the findings to date are consistent with self-determination theory's (Deci & Ryan, 1985) notion that there is a universal need for autonomy whose fulfillment may be undermined by controlling environments. Hence, recommendations that parents limit their intrusiveness in children's lives are likely to be useful both in the West and in East Asia.

Recommended Readings

Chao, R.K. (1994). (See References). One of the first papers to suggest why parental control may not have as negative effects in East Asia as it does in the West.

Greenfield, P.M., Keller, H., Fuligni, A.J., & Maynard, A. (2003). Cultural pathways through universal development. *Annual Review of Psychology, 54,* 461–490. This paper provides a full discussion of issues of culture in children's development, including that of the differential effects of parental control.

Grolnick, W.S. (2003). *The psychology of parental control: How well-meant parenting backfires.* Mahwah, NJ: Erlbaum. A clearly written, user-friendly, and relatively comprehensive review for readers who wish to expand their knowledge of the effects of parental control.

Lansford, J.E., Chang, L., Dodge, K.A., Malone, P.A., Oburu, P., Palmerus, K., et al. (2005). Physical discipline and children's adjustment: Cultural normativeness as a moderator. *Child Development, 76,* 1234–1246. An innovative study that illustrates original research about the differential effects of parents' physical discipline in multiple countries.

Wang, Q., Pomerantz, E.M., & Chen, H. (2007). (See References). A representative study that illustrates original research about the differential effects of parental control in the United States and China.

References

Bao, X.-H., & Lam, S.-F. (2008). Who makes the choice? Rethinking the role of autonomy and relatedness in Chinese children's motivation. *Child Development, 79,* 269–283.

Barber, B.K., Stolz, H.E., & Olsen, J.A. (2005). *Parental support, psychological control, and behavioral control: Assessing relevance across time, culture, and method* (Monographs of the Society for Research in Child Development, Serial No. 282, Vol. 70, No. 2). Boston: Blackwell.

Chao, R.K. (1994). Beyond parental control and authoritarian parenting style: Understanding Chinese parenting through the cultural notion of training. *Child Development, 65,* 1111–1119.

Deci, E.L., & Ryan, R.M. (1985). *Intrinsic motivation and self-determination in human behavior.* New York: Plenum.

Feldman, S.S., & Rosenthal, D.A. (1991). Age expectations of behavioural autonomy in Hong Kong, Australian and American Youth: The influence of family variables and adolescents' values. *International Journal of Psychology, 26,* 1–23.

Fuligni, A.J., & Zhang, W. (2004). Attitudes toward family obligation among adolescents in contemporary urban and rural China. *Child Development, 75,* 180–192.

Grolnick, W.S., & Pomerantz, E.M. (2009). Issues and challenges in studying parental control: Toward a new conceptualization. *Child Development Perspectives, 2,* 165–171.

Grusec, J.E., Rudy, D., & Martini, T. (1997). Parenting cognitions and child outcomes: An overview and implications for children's internalization of values. In J.E. Grusec & L. Kuczynski (Eds.), *Parenting and children's internalization of values: A handbook of contemporary theory* (pp. 259–282). Hoboken, NJ: Wiley.

Hasebe, Y., Nucci, L., & Nucci, M.S. (2004). Parental control of the personal domain and adolescent symptoms of psychopathology: A cross-national study in the United States and Japan. *Child Development, 75,* 815–828.

Iyengar, S.S., & Lepper, M.R. (1999). Rethinking the value of choice: A cultural perspective on intrinsic motivation. *Journal of Personality and Social Psychology, 76,* 349–366.

Li, J. (2005). Mind or virtue: Western and Chinese beliefs about learning. *Current Directions in Psychological Science, 14,* 190–194.

Maccoby, E.E., & Martin, J. (1983). Socialization in the context of the family: Parent child interaction. In E.M. Hetherington (Ed.), *Handbook of child psychology: Vol. 4. Socialization, personality, and social development* (4th ed., pp. 1–101). New York: Wiley.

Plaut, V.C., Markus, H.R., & Lachman, M.E. (2002). Place matters: Consensual features and regional variation in American well-being and self. *Journal of Personality and Social Psychology, 83,* 160–184.

Pomerantz, E.M., Ng, F.F., & Wang, Q. (2008). Culture, parenting, and motivation: The case of East Asia and the United States. In M.L. Maehr, S.A. Karabenick, & T.C. Urdan (Eds.), *Advances in motivation and achievement: Social psychological perspectives* (Vol. 15, pp. 209–240). Bingley, England: Emerald Group Publishing.

Pomerantz, E.M., & Thompson, R.A. (2008). Parents' role in children's personality development: The psychological resource principle. In O.P. John, R.W. Robins, & L.A. Pervin (Eds.), *Handbook of personality: Theory and research* (Vol. 3, pp. 351–374). New York: Guilford.

Qin, L., Pomerantz, E.M., & Wang, Q. (2009). Are gains in decision-making autonomy during early adolescence beneficial for emotional functioning? The case of the United States and China. *Child Development, 80,* 1705–1721.

Rohner, R.P., Khaleque, A., & Cournoyer, D.E. (2004). Cross-national perspectives on parental acceptance-rejection theory. *Marriage and Family Review, 35,* 85–105.

Steinberg, L., Lamborn, S.D., Darling, N., Mounts, N.S., & Dornbusch, S. (1994). Over-time changes in adjustment and competence among adolescents from authoritative, authoritarian, indulgent, and neglectful homes. *Child Development, 65,* 754–770.

Triandis, H.C. (1994). *Culture and social behavior.* New York: McGraw-Hill.

Wang, Q., Pomerantz, E.M., & Chen, H. (2007). The role of parents' control in early adolescents' psychological functioning: A longitudinal investigation in the United States and China. *Child Development, 78,* 1592–1610.

Zhang, W., & Fuligni, A.J. (2006). Authority, autonomy, and family relationships among adolescents in urban and rural China. *Journal of Research on Adolescence, 16,* 527–537.

Critical Thinking

1. How would you expect children to respond to parental control in India? What would be the best way to find out?

2. What were the "contextual factors" that were at work in this article? What are some other contextual factors that might play a part in determining the effects of parental control?

Create Central

www.mhhe.com/createcentral

Internet References

McClellandInstitute.Arizona.edu

http://mcclellandinstitute.arizona.edu/sites/mcclellandinstitute.arizona.edu/files/ResearchLink_2.1_Russell_AsianFam.pdf

Cultural Differences in Parenting Practices: What Asian American Families Can Teach Us

http://McClellandInstitute.arizona.edu

Parenting.com

http://www.parenting.com/blogs/show-and-tell/kate-parentingcom/chinese-vs-western-parenting

ParentingScience.com

http://www.parentingscience.com/chinese-parenting.html

From *Current Directions in Psychological Science*, October 2009, pp. 285–289. Copyright © 2009 by the Association for Psychological Science. Reprinted by permission of Sage Publications via Rightslink.

Article   Prepared by: Ellen N. Junn, *California State University, Dominguez Hills*

The Case Against Spanking

Physical Discipline Is Slowly Declining as Some Studies Reveal Lasting Harms for Children

BRENDAN L. SMITH

Learning Outcomes

After reading this article, you will be able to:

- Consider the environment that children grow up in and how that environment can lead to more or less spanking.

- Develop a program that could be used in working with parents to educate them on alternative techniques of working with their children.

- Understand how cultural relativism influences the prevalence of spanking in the family scene.

A growing body of research has shown that spanking and other forms of physical discipline can pose serious risks to children, but many parents aren't hearing the message. "It's a very controversial area even though the research is extremely telling and very clear and consistent about the negative effects on children," says Sandra Graham-Bermann, PhD, a psychology professor and principal investigator for the Child Violence and Trauma Laboratory at the University of Michigan. "People get frustrated and hit their kids. Maybe they don't see there are other options."

Many studies have shown that physical punishment—including spanking, hitting and other means of causing pain—can lead to increased aggression, antisocial behavior, physical injury and mental health problems for children. Americans' acceptance of physical punishment has declined since the 1960s, yet surveys show that two-thirds of Americans still approve of parents spanking their kids.

But spanking doesn't work, says Alan Kazdin, PhD, a Yale University psychology professor and director of the Yale Parenting Center and Child Conduct Clinic. "You cannot punish out these behaviors that you do not want," says Kazdin, who served as APA president in 2008. "There is no need for corporal punishment based on the research. We are not giving up an effective technique. We are saying this is a horrible thing that does not work."

Evidence of Harm

On the international front, physical discipline is increasingly being viewed as a violation of children's human rights. The United Nations Committee on the Rights of the Child issued a directive in 2006 calling physical punishment "legalized violence against children" that should be eliminated in all settings through "legislative, administrative, social and educational measures." The treaty that established the committee has been supported by 192 countries, with only the United States and Somalia failing to ratify it.

Around the world, 30 countries have banned physical punishment of children in all settings, including the home. The legal bans typically have been used as public education tools, rather than attempts to criminalize behavior by parents who spank their children, says Elizabeth Gershoff, PhD, a leading researcher on physical punishment at the University of Texas at Austin.

"Physical punishment doesn't work to get kids to comply, so parents think they have to keep escalating it. That is why it is so dangerous," she says.

After reviewing decades of research, Gershoff wrote the Report on Physical Punishment in the United States: *What Research Tells Us About Its Effects on Children*, published in 2008 in conjunction with Phoenix Children's Hospital. The report recommends that parents and caregivers make every effort to avoid physical punishment and calls for the banning of physical discipline in all U.S. schools. The report has been endorsed by dozens of organizations, including the American Academy of Pediatrics, American Medical Association and Psychologists for Social Responsibility.

After three years of work on the APA Task Force on Physical Punishment of Children, Gershoff and Graham-Bermann wrote a report in 2008 summarizing the task force's recommendations. That report recommends that "parents and caregivers reduce and potentially eliminate their use of any physical punishment as a disciplinary method." The report calls on psychologists and other professionals to "indicate to parents that physical punishment is not an appropriate, or even a consistently effective, method of discipline."

"We have the opportunity here to take a strong stand in favor of protecting children," says Graham-Bermann, who chaired the task force.

APA's Committee on Children, Youth and Families (CYF) and the Board for the Advancement of Psychology in the Public Interest unanimously approved a proposed resolution last year based on the task force recommendations. It states that APA supports "parents' use of non-physical methods of disciplining children" and opposes "the use of severe or injurious physical punishment of any child." APA also should support additional research and a public education campaign on "the effectiveness and outcomes associated with corporal punishment and non-physical methods of discipline," the proposed resolution states. After obtaining feedback from other APA boards and committees in the spring of 2012, APA's Council of Representatives will consider adopting the resolution as APA policy.

Preston Britner, PhD, a child developmental psychologist and professor at the University of Connecticut, helped draft the proposed resolution as co-chair of CYF. "It addresses the concerns about physical punishment and a growing body of research on alternatives to physical punishment, along with the idea that psychology and psychologists have much to contribute to the development of those alternative strategies," he says.

More than three decades have passed since APA approved a resolution in 1975 opposing corporal punishment in schools and other institutions, but it didn't address physical discipline in the home. That resolution stated that corporal punishment can "instill hostility, rage and a sense of powerlessness without reducing the undesirable behavior."

Research Findings

Physical punishment can work momentarily to stop problematic behavior because children are afraid of being hit, but it doesn't work in the long term and can make children more aggressive, Graham-Bermann says.

A study published last year in *Child Abuse and Neglect* revealed an intergenerational cycle of violence in homes where physical punishment was used. Researchers interviewed parents and children aged 3 to 7 from more than 100 families. Children who were physically punished were more likely to endorse hitting as a means of resolving their conflicts with peers and siblings. Parents who had experienced frequent physical punishment during their childhood were more likely to believe it was acceptable, and they frequently spanked their children. Their children, in turn, often believed spanking was an appropriate disciplinary method.

The negative effects of physical punishment may not become apparent for some time, Gershoff says. "A child doesn't get spanked and then run out and rob a store," she says. "There are indirect changes in how the child thinks about things and feels about things."

As in many areas of science, some researchers disagree about the validity of the studies on physical punishment. Robert Larzelere, PhD, an Oklahoma State University professor who studies parental discipline, was a member of the APA task force who issued his own minority report because he disagreed with the scientific basis of the task force recommendations. While he agrees that parents should reduce their use of physical punishment, he says most of the cited studies are correlational and don't show a causal link between physical punishment and long-term negative effects for children.

"The studies do not discriminate well between non-abusive and overly severe types of corporal punishment," Larzelere says. "You get worse outcomes from corporal punishment than from alternative disciplinary techniques only when it is used more severely or as the primary discipline tactic."

In a meta-analysis of 26 studies, Larzelere and a colleague found that an approach they described as "conditional spanking" led to greater reductions in child defiance or anti-social behavior than 10 of 13 alternative discipline techniques, including reasoning, removal of privileges and time out (*Clinical Child and Family Psychology Review*, 2005). Larzelere defines conditional spanking as a disciplinary technique for 2- to 6-year-old children in which parents use two open-handed swats on the buttocks only after the child has defied milder discipline such as time out.

Gershoff says all of the studies on physical punishment have some shortcomings. "Unfortunately, all research on parent discipline is going to be correlational because we can't randomly assign kids to parents for an experiment. But I don't think we have to disregard all research that has been done," she says. "I can just about count on one hand the studies that have found anything positive about physical punishment and hundreds that have been negative."

Teaching New Skills

If parents aren't supposed to hit their kids, what nonviolent techniques can help with discipline? The Parent Management Training program headed by Kazdin at Yale is grounded in research on applied behavioral analysis. The program teaches parents to use positive reinforcement and effusive praise to reward children for good behavior.

Kazdin also uses a technique that may sound like insanity to most parents: Telling toddlers to practice throwing a tantrum. Parents ask their children to have a pretend tantrum without one undesirable element, such as hitting or kicking. Gradually, as children practice controlling tantrums when they aren't angry, their real tantrums lessen, Kazdin says.

Remaining calm during a child's tantrums is the best approach, coupled with time outs when needed and a consistent discipline plan that rewards good behavior, Graham-Bermann says. APA offers the Adults & Children Together Against Violence program, which provides parenting skills classes through a nationwide research-based program called Parents Raising Safe Kids. The course teaches parents how to avoid violence through anger management, positive child discipline and conflict resolution.

Parents should talk with their children about appropriate means of resolving conflicts, Gershoff says. Building a trusting relationship can help children believe that discipline isn't arbitrary or done out of anger.

"Part of the problem is good discipline isn't quick or easy," she says. "Even the best of us parents don't always have that kind of patience."

Critical Thinking

1. Why do you think some parents spank their children? What factors, ranging from parents' personalities and children-rearing beliefs to children's qualities, may lead to more or less spanking?

2. There is ample research suggesting that spanking has negative effects on children, but many parents nevertheless spank their children. Is this a problem? Should parents' child-rearing and disciplinary practices be informed or shaped by what social science has learned? Why might parents' behavior not be affected by social science findings?

3. Aside from social science, are there moral, ethical, or religious reasons why parents should, or should not, spank their children?

Create Central

www.mhhe.com/createcentral

Internet References

American Psychological Association.org
   http://www.apa.org/monitor/2012/04/spanking.aspx
Journal of American Medical Association Pediatrics.
   http://archpedi.jamanetwork.com/article.aspx?articleid=518458
Project No Spank.net
   http://nospank.net

BRENDAN L. SMITH is a writer in Washington, D.C.

From *Monitor on Psychology*, April 2012. Copyright © 2012 by American Psychological Association. Reproduced with permission. No further reproduction or distribution without written permission from the American Psychological Association.

Article   Prepared by: Chris J. Boyatzis, *Bucknell University*

Sibling Experiences in Diverse Family Contexts

Shirley McGuire and Lilly Shanahan

Learning Outcomes

After reading this article, you will be able to:

- Design a lesson plan for social workers and therapists who are just beginning to work with culturally diverse families.

- Describe how siblings' lives seem similar yet different in families with different cultural backgrounds.

In the United States, siblings are children's most constant social companions and provide a proximal and long-lasting context for development (Cicirelli, 1995; McHale & Crouter, 1996). The field of sibling research has grown considerably in recent years, showing that siblings can advance one another's social, emotional, and cognitive development in the context of their relationship (Brody, 2004; Dunn, 2007). We use the ecological perspective (e.g., Bronfenbrenner & Morris, 1998) to examine sibling experiences in family environments that are diverse in terms of their structure and ethnicity. We emphasize that micro-level sibling experiences and their meaning in children's development are embedded in macrocontexts; that is, sibling experiences are intricately linked with family context and cultural values across and within societies (see also Weisner, 1993).

Sibling Experiences Are Embedded in Layers of Ecological Context

Sibling experiences have been studied using a variety of conceptual models, including behavior genetics, socialization and social learning theory, risk and resilience perspectives, and, broadly speaking, family and developmental systems models. Here, we use the broad umbrella of the ecological perspective on development (e.g., Bronfenbrenner & Morris, 1998) because it subsumes elements of many of these perspectives, has been commonly used in sibling research (e.g., East, Weisner, & Reyes, 2006; McHale & Crouter, 1996) and highlights the role of context in children's development. Indeed, the ecological perspective describes multiple embedded layers of context, ranging from microsystems (e.g., daily settings and relationships) to mesosystems (e.g., connections among microsystems such as the school–home interface) and macrosystems (e.g., societal and cultural beliefs). Ecological layers that are close to the individual both shape and are shaped by more distant, macrosystemic layers.

The importance of the macrosystem for understanding sibling experiences has been illustrated in cross-cultural research (Cicirelli, 1994; Nuckolls, 1993; Zukow, 1989). Families in the United States hold some expectations about sibling experiences, such as equal or fair parental treatment of siblings (Kowal & Kramer, 1997), but overall, siblings in U.S. society, compared with siblings in some non-Western societies, may have fewer clearly defined roles, such as caregiving, or economic obligations. In fact, U.S. siblings bear few legal rights and responsibilities for one another (Dwyer, 2006). This lack of legally prescribed sibling roles, and the overall diversity within U.S. society, may mean that within-society subcultures and contexts play an integral role in shaping the sibling experience and its influence on child development. In the next section, we review sibling experiences in families that vary by ethnicity and family structure (Fields, 2003a, 2003b; McLoyd, Cauce, Takeuchi, & Wilson, 2000; Parke, 2004) and discuss emerging family contexts in additional macrolevel niches (Weisner, 1993).

Siblings in Ethnically and Structurally Diverse Family Contexts

Sibling research has focused almost exclusively on sibling processes in maritally intact European American families and has only recently explored sibling experiences in diverse family structures. Newer studies of African American and Mexican American siblings provide insight into sibling dynamics in other ecological niches in the United States. We begin by reviewing research conducted on school-age and teenage siblings in primarily two-parent European American families.

European American Families

Sibling relationship research using two-parent, maritally intact European American families has been reviewed in detail elsewhere, along with studies of families of primarily European background in the United Kingdom and Canada (e.g., Brody, 1998, 2004; Dunn, 1996, 2007; Noller, 2005). Here, we outline three main lines of research that have been conducted on siblings in these family contexts. The first has examined the role of structural characteristics of the sibling dyad, including birth order, sex constellation, age gap, and genetic relatedness in children's development. With respect to birth order, parents tend to expect firstborns to conform to parental rules and expectations more than they do for laterborns (e.g., Sulloway, 1996). Mixed-sex sibling constellations provide opportunities for sex-typed treatment by parents, as illustrated by the finding that younger brothers with older sisters spent significantly less time doing housework than did younger sisters with older brothers (e.g., McHale, Crouter, & Whiteman, 2003). Regarding age gap, younger siblings with close-in-age older siblings may have increased access to older peers, who may, in turn, provide socialization for antisocial behaviors (e.g., Snyder, Bank, & Burraston, 2005). Genetic relatedness of the sibling dyad appears to contribute to relationship quality, with monozygotic twins experiencing closer, more trusting, and less hostile relationships compared with dizygotic twins and full siblings (McGuire, Segal, Gill, Whitlow, & Clausen, 2010; Reiss, Neiderhiser, Hetherington, & Plomin, 2000).

A second line of research has investigated relationship dynamics. At the dyadic level, similarities among siblings in terms of age and sex may foster both sibling differentiation (i.e., sibling differences in terms of personality and activity involvement; e.g., Feinberg & Hetherington, 2000; Shanahan, Kim, McHale, & Crouter, 2007) and social learning (e.g., sibling similarities in antisocial or empathic behaviors; Slomkowski, Rende, Conger, Simons, & Conger, 2001; Whiteman, McHale, & Crouter, 2007). Furthermore, sibling collusion (i.e., coercive

sibling interactions) may contribute to the development of antisocial and risky sexual behaviors (Bullock & Dishion, 2002). Longitudinal studies reveal both stability and mean-level changes in sibling relationship quality across childhood and adolescence (e.g., Kim, McHale, Osgood, & Crouter, 2006; see Dunn, Slomkowski, & Beardsall, 1994, for British sample). At the family-systemic level, research on parents' differential treatment of siblings has shown that having a less positive or more negative relationship with parents than one's sibling does is linked with lower self-esteem and higher levels of internalizing and externalizing behaviors (e.g., McGuire, Dunn, & Plomin, 1995; McGuire, 2001; Shanahan, McHale, Crouter, & Osgood, 2008; see Jenkins, Rasbash, & O'Connor, 2003, for Canadian sample).

A third line of research has examined sibling experiences in a variety of ecological contexts within the European American community. For instance, sibling relationship processes in families with a disabled child differ from those in families with nondisabled children. Although parents tend to treat a child with a disability more "favorably" than they do the other children in the family, such differential treatment does not necessarily translate into sibling conflict and poor adjustment for the nondisabled children (McHale & Pawletko, 1992). A sibling's disability may "legitimize" differential treatment in the eyes of the nondisabled sibling (McHale & Pawletko, 1992), and siblings who appraise differential treatment as fair may have positive sibling relationships and adjustment despite being treated nonpreferentially (Kowal & Kramer, 1997).

The importance of family context for understanding sibling dynamics has been further explored using studies of European American families from varying family structures, including divorced families and stepfamilies. One finding is that sibling relationships influence, and are influenced by, the conflict and ambivalence typically found in disrupted families. For example, conflict between parents tends to have a spillover effect, increasing sibling hostility and emotional distance (e.g., Hetherington & Clingempeel, 1992; Hetherington, Henderson, & Reiss, 1999). Siblings often experience decreases in mutual engagement following divorce and during the beginning stages of remarriage. Sibling hostility typically increases when a stepfamily is constituted but declines as children get older and spend more time together.

Siblings may also serve a buffering role during their parents' marital transitions, possibly compensating for a lack of parental availability and warmth. But studies on families of European background in the United States, the United Kingdom, and Canada suggest that both spillover and compensation processes may depend on the dyad sex constellation, dyad type (e.g., full siblings, half-siblings, or stepsiblings), and macrolevel influences (Anderson, 1999; Anderson & Rice, 1992; Dunn et al., 1999). For example, females provide more comfort to siblings, particularly to sisters, than do males (e.g., Gass, Jenkins, & Dunn, 2007; Kempton, Armistead, Wierson, & Forehand, 1991). Furthermore, unlike the pattern in the United States, in a U.K. sample, sibling relationship qualities in stepfamilies did not differ from those in nondivorced families, possibly because families in the United Kingdom receive greater government assistance during marital transitions, alleviating parental and child stress (Deater-Deckard, Dunn, & Lussier, 2002; Dunn et al., 1999). Thus, taking macrolevel economic and cultural factors into account when examining sibling experiences across family structures may help in understanding the specific processes that trigger conflict spillover or compensation in the sibling relationship (Conger & Conger, 1996; Larson & Almeida, 1999).

Finally, other intricacies of sibling life in divorced and remarried families still need to be documented, including the effects of visitation arrangements, the differential involvement of biological parents in siblings' and stepsiblings' lives, the relationship between the newly formed families after divorce, the implications of romantic attraction between genetically unrelated stepsiblings, and the redefining of sibling relationships after the dissolution of a second marriage (e.g., Bernstein, 1997; Drapeau, Simard, & Beaudry, 2000; Hetherington et al., 1999; Kaplan, Ade-Ridder, & Hennon, 1991). In addition, some of the issues discussed in this section may also apply to siblings from never-married families, another understudied (but growing) family structure (Fields, 2003b).

African American Families

Recent research on African American families has examined sibling experiences in two-parent and single-parent family structures. These studies have begun to provide insight into sibling processes that may transcend ecological niches or that are specific to some family contexts. For instance, cluster analyses using sibling warmth and hostility measures revealed different sibling relationship types in two separate samples of two-parent families, one consisting of African American families from working- and middle-class backgrounds (McHale, Whiteman, Kim, & Crouter, 2007) and the other of European American families from similar economic circumstances (McGuire, McHale, & Updegraff, 1996). In both studies, researchers crossed measures of sibling negativity and positivity and found three types of relationships: a "high-negativity" group, a "high-warmth" group, and an "emotionally distant" group. In addition, high sibling negativity was associated with children's depression and risky behavior, and positive parent–child relationships were linked with high sibling positivity in the African American families (McHale et al., 2007), as well as in European American families in another study (Kim, McHale, Crouter, & Osgood, 2007).

Researchers have also identified important factors that may influence sibling dynamics specifically in African American families (McHale et al., 2007). For example, maternal experiences with racism were linked with sibling negativity, parental spirituality was linked with higher sibling warmth, and lower ethnic identity in the children was linked with sibling emotional distance.

Many African American siblings are raised by single mothers (Fields, 2003b), and studying these families can help test links among sibling experiences, family stress, economic hardship, and children's development. For example, in a study involving rural African American single-mother families, older siblings had both direct and indirect influences on their younger siblings. Older siblings' competence was directly linked with younger siblings' self-regulation and, indirectly via its positive link, to maternal psychological functioning and, in turn, quality of parenting (Brody, Kim, Murry, & Brown, 2003). Furthermore, as sibling support increased, sibling similarity in externalizing behaviors also increased (Brody, Kim, Murry, & Brown, 2005). This finding is consistent with some previous work on European American siblings suggesting that antisocial siblings with a supportive relationship may become "partners in crime" and socialize each other in delinquent behavior (Rowe & Gulley, 1992; Slomkowski et al., 2001). However, correlations among siblings' problem behaviors may be amplified in disadvantaged neighborhoods (Brody et al., 2003). In terms of developmental assets, a parenting style that combines high levels of control and monitoring with support and involvement (i.e., a no-nonsense style) and maintains a strong bond with extended family members provides significant sources of social capital, particularly for children of single African American mothers (Burton, 1995; McLoyd et al., 2000; Parke, 2004; Taylor, 2001).

The roles of prejudice, discrimination, racial identity, and spirituality in sibling dynamics and family life need to be examined in studies of African American siblings (e.g., Garcia Coll et al., 1996). Such research could increase understanding of siblings' roles in one another's racial socialization and experiences of discrimination. It could also, in turn, reveal links between child development and societal experiences. Furthermore, sibling dynamics need to be explored in Black immigrant families, and families that have siblings who vary in race and color (e.g., American Psychological Association, Task Force on Resilience and Strength in Black Children and Adolescents, 2008). Successful prevention and intervention programs for African American families increase understanding of the role of family-systemic mechanisms, including sibling modeling and mentoring, for positive adjustment in African American youth (e.g., Brody, Kogan, Chen, & Murry, 2008).

Mexican American Families

Studies of siblings in Mexican American families have also focused on two-parent and single-parent families. Research suggests that adolescents' sibling relationships in two-parent families are characterized by both warmth and conflict (Updegraff, McHale, Whiteman, Thayer, & Delgado, 2005), which is consistent with studies of siblings in African American and European American families. In addition, positive sibling relationships in Mexican American families have been found to be linked with child well-being; this result is consistent with findings from other family contexts with the exception of families with antisocial children (e.g., Brody et al., 2003; Dunn & McGuire, 1992; East & Khoo, 2005; McHale et al., 2007; Updegraff et al., 2005).

Unlike the case with European American and African American families, understanding sibling experiences in Mexican American families requires an appreciation of the immigrant experience (Portes & Rumbaut, 1990), including the culture of origin, acculturation levels, and the nativity (i.e., first, second, or third generation) of the family members. For instance, upon arriving in the United States, immigrant children have to negotiate a balance between valuing their culture of origin and becoming immersed into the mainstream U.S. culture (e.g., Balls Organista, Marin, & Chun, 2009; Chun, 2006). Indeed, because children typically overcome linguistic and cultural barriers quickly, they may have to serve as cultural brokers for less acculturated siblings and parents. Furthermore, because of the family's lack of economic resources and social support, older siblings in immigrant families commonly take on caregiving and parenting roles (e.g., Fuligni, Yip, & Tseng, 2002; see also Walsh, Shulman, Bar-On, & Tsur, 2006).

The meaning of sibling experiences may vary depending on cultural values related to the importance of family (Marín & Marín, 1991; Updegraff et al., 2005). For example, preferential treatment of a sibling by a parent is often linked with adjustment problems for children in European American samples (McGuire, 2001). However, in a sample of Mexican American families, older siblings who embraced the cultural value of familism, which emphasizes support, interdependence, and loyalty among family members, were not more likely to have higher levels of depressive symptoms and risky behaviors when their parents regularly treated a younger sibling preferentially (McHale, Updegraff, Shanahan, Crouter, & Killoren, 2005). In the same sample, both older and younger siblings who reported high familism were more likely to report using solution-oriented and non-confrontational strategies to resolve sibling conflicts than were siblings reporting low familism (Killoren, Thayer, & Updegraff, 2008). Both strategies involve promoting harmony in relationships and may be in line with the collectivist values promoted in Mexican culture,

whereas the controlling strategies typically found in studies of European American siblings may be more consistent with individualistic values found in U.S. culture (Killoren et al., 2008; see also Gabrielidis, Stephan, Ybarra, Dos Santos Pearson, & Villareal, 1997).

In Mexico, families typically have many children, along with a large extended family, and treat siblings in sex-typed ways (Cauce & Domenech-Rodriguez, 2002). One study found that when parents were more enculturated with Mexican culture than with Anglo culture, older sisters with younger brothers were granted significantly fewer privileges in the household than were older brothers with younger sisters (McHale et al., 2005). Furthermore, the same study found that children in Mexican American families with close ties to Mexican culture tended to spend many of their nonschool hours with siblings and cousins (Updegraff et al., 2005), and older sisters in these families tended to serve as caregivers for younger siblings (Cauce & Domenech-Rodriguez, 2002; Vega, 1990). Thus, families' cultural values, gender constellation, and sibship size are important contexts for sibling dynamics in Mexican-origin families, and sibling studies provide a window into links between child development and cultural values.

Teenage childbearing is common in Mexican American families (Martin et al., 2007). Studies by East and colleagues (which also included African American families) have shown that sisters' caregiving extends to teenage siblings' offspring in these families (East, 1998; East & Khoo, 2005; East et al., 2006). Results of these studies suggest that caring for young nieces and nephews results in both developmental costs (e.g., higher stress and lower grades) and benefits (e.g., higher life satisfaction and lower school dropout rate). Furthermore, taking care of young nieces and nephews in low-income, single-mother families was linked with high sibling warmth and increased levels of maturity among younger sisters. When older sisters were dominant or sibling conflict was high, however, younger siblings were at increased risk of early sexual behavior, pregnancy, and drug use.

Taken together, the findings in our review of families from different structures and ethnicities suggest that some correlates of sibling experiences, such as parental stress, economic strain, racism, and acculturation, are specific to certain ecological niches. Highlighting findings that appear to be consistent across contexts is tempting. For instance, studies have found that sibling positivity is associated with healthy development and resilience, especially for sister–sister pairs. Still, even this result may differ in unexplored family contexts, such as Asian American families and adoptive families. Furthermore, sibling positivity may need to be defined differently for boys and girls and in families of different cultural backgrounds. Consequently, we prefer to be cautious when discussing possible "universal" sibling processes. Instead, we encourage understanding processes *within* contexts defined by structure, ethnicity, and culture (e.g., Garcia Coll et al., 1996).

Emerging Family Contexts

In this section, we discuss a selection of four U.S. family contexts, the study of which will further the understanding of sibling experiences and ethnic and structural family diversity.

Other Ethnic-Minority Families

Sibling experiences in other nonimmigrant ethnically diverse families (e.g., Native American families) have been largely neglected, but research on them could provide additional insight into the roles of discrimination, economic disadvantage, cultural values, and risk and resilience in children's development. In addition, no large studies of sibling or family experiences in the 28 Asian American subgroups in the United States have been conducted (Parke, 2004). Such studies are needed not only to understand sibling experiences and the acculturation process in other immigrant populations but also to learn about the role of family obligations in siblings' lives (Fuligni et al., 2002). Additional studies should examine sibling experiences in the context of ethnically diverse families living in extended, multigeneration, and multiethnic households (Burton, 1995; Taylor, 2001).

Lesbian and Gay Families

From 1990 to 2000, there was a 314 percent increase in the number of households headed by same-sex partners, with gay and lesbian families living in 99.3 percent of U.S. counties at the turn of the century (Smith & Gates, 2001). Exploring sibling experiences in families headed by same-sex partners would further the understanding of links among marginalization, family context, and sibling experiences (Patterson, 2000; Patterson & D'Augelli, 1998). And comparing these experiences in terms of whether or not the families live in states that allow same-sex marriage could help illuminate the joint influence of macrocontextual (e.g., laws and policies) and microcontextual influences (e.g., marriage) on sibling experiences. In addition, researchers could test hypotheses about the role of parental gender in links between parental differential treatment and children's development, connections which have been investigated only in heterosexual-headed households (e.g., McHale et al., 2005; Shanahan, McHale, Crouter, & Osgood, 2007). Studies of the experiences of sexual-minority individuals in their family of origin would shed light on the role of sibling relationships in identity and relationship development, especially given that a significant number of youth initially come out to their brothers and sisters (e.g., Allen & Demo, 1995; D'Augelli & Hershberger, 1993; Gottlieb, 2005; Savin-Williams, 1998).

Adoptive Families

Behavioral genetic studies of siblings in adoptive families have examined genetic and environmental contributions to sibling relationship quality (e.g., Rende, Slomkowski, Stocker, Fulker, & Plomin, 1992; Stocker & Dunn, 1994) and to the differences between adopted and nonadopted siblings in adjustment and family experiences (e.g., McGue et al., 2007; Sharma, McGue, & Benson, 1998). Still, little is known about the nature of sibling processes in families with adopted children. In addition, research on sibling placement in adoptive or foster-care families would advance understanding of sibling contributions to risk and resilience during stressful transitions (Hegar, 2005; Linares, Li, Shrout, Brody, & Pettit, 2007). Studies of families with internationally adopted children could illuminate the role of siblings in the development of children's ethnic and racial identity and acculturation processes in multiethnic families (Lee, Grotevant, Hellerstedt, Gunnar, & the Minnesota International Adoption Project Team, 2006).

Assisted Reproductive Technology

A more recent development in evolving family structures is the increasing use of assisted reproductive technology (ART). Golombok (2006) has reviewed research on parenting and child development in families that used ART, and most of this research has focused on singletons in order to avoid the complications associated with multiple births. Studies of families with twins and other multiples conceived through ART would further the literature on genetic contributions to sibling relationship quality (McGuire et al., 2010). Within-family studies of naturally conceived children suggest that there would be sibling differences in parenting experiences and children's outcomes in these families (e.g., Shanahan et al., 2008). In addition, family types have been evolving with the use of ART, including heterosexual women choosing to become single parents and lesbian or gay partners choosing to start a family together (Golombok, 2006).

Conclusions

Sibling experiences provide a context for child development, a context that can differ at many levels within and across societies. Our review of studies of sibling experiences in ethnically and structurally diverse families points to the importance of context at multiple levels, from sex composition of the dyads to family structure to family policy to cultural beliefs. Sibling relationships are embedded in larger ecological niches. Diverse and evolving family contexts, even within societies, must be considered when describing the sibling experience and developing and testing theories of sibling dynamics. In addition, more sibling research is needed on families with complex structures and diverse ethnic and racial backgrounds to increase understanding of key developmental influences such as family stability, economic hardship, discrimination, and acculturation.

References

Allen, K. R., & Demo, D. H. (1995). The families of lesbians and gay men: A new frontier in family research. *Journal of Marriage and the Family, 57,* 1–17.

American Psychological Association, Task Force on Resilience and Strength in Black Children and Adolescents. (2008). *Resilience in African American children and adolescents: A vision for optimal development.* Washington, DC: American Psychological Association.

Anderson, E. R. (1999). Sibling, half-sibling, and stepsibling relationships in remarried families. In E. M. Hetherington, S. H. Henderson, & D. Reiss (Eds.), *Adolescent siblings in stepfamilies: Family functioning and the adolescent adjustment.* Monographs for the Society for Research in Child Development, *64*(Serial No. 259, pp. 1–222).

Anderson, E. R., & Rice, A. M. (1992). Sibling relationships during remarriage. In E. M. Hetherington & W. G. Clingempeel (Eds.), *Coping with marital transitions: A family systems perspective.* Monographs for the Society for Research in Child Development, *57*(Serial No. 227, pp. 1–242).

Balls Organista, P., Marin, G., & Chun, K. M. (2009). *Psychology of ethnic groups in the U.S.* Thousand Oaks, CA: Sage.

Bernstein, A. C. (1997). Stepfamilies from siblings' perspectives. *Marriage & Family Review, 26,* 153–175.

Brody, G. H. (1998). Sibling relationship quality: Its causes and consequences. *Annual Review of Psychology, 49,* 1–24.

Brody, G. H. (2004). Siblings' direct and indirect contributions to child development. *Current Directions in Psychological Science, 13,* 124–212.

Brody, G. H., Ge, X., Kim, S. Y., Murry, V. M., Simons, R. L., Gibbons, F. X., et al. (2003). Neighborhood disadvantage moderates associations of parenting and older sibling problem attitudes and behavior with conduct disorders in African American children. *Journal of Consulting and Clinical Psychology, 71,* 211–222.

Brody, G. H., Kim, S., Murry, V. B., & Brown, A. C. (2003). Longitudinal direct and indirect pathways linking older sibling competence to the development of younger sibling competence. *Developmental Psychology, 39,* 618–628.

Brody, G. H., Kim, S., Murry, V. M., & Brown, A. C. (2005). Longitudinal links among parenting, self-presentations to peers, and the development of externalizing and internalizing symptoms in African American siblings. *Development and Psychopathology, 17,* 185–205.

Brody, G. H., Kogan, S. M., Chen, Y., & Murry, V. M. (2008). Long-term effects of the strong African American families program on youths' conduct problems. *Journal of Adolescent Health, 43,* 474–481.

Bronfenbrenner, U., & Morris, P. A. (1998). The ecology of developmental processes. In R. M. Lerner (Ed.), *Handbook of child psychology: Theoretical model of human development* (Vol. 1, 5th ed., pp. 993–1028). New York: Wiley.

Bullock, B. M., & Dishion, T. J. (2002). Sibling collusion and problem behavior in early adolescence: Toward a process model for family mutuality. *Journal of Abnormal Child Psychology, 30,* 143–153.

Burton, L. M. (1995). Intergenerational patterns of providing care in African-American families with teenage childbearers: Emerging patterns in an ethnographic study. In V. L. Bengtson, K. W. Schaie, & L. M. Burton (Eds.), *Intergenerational relations: Effects of social change* (pp. 79–125). New York: Springer.

Cauce, A. M., & Domenech-Rodriguez, M. (2002). Latino families: Myths and realities. In J. M. Contreras, K. A. Kerns, & A. M. Neal-Barnett (Eds.), *Latino children and families in the United States* (pp. 5–25). Westport, CT: Praeger.

Chun, K. M. (2006). Conceptual and measurement issues in family acculturation research. In M. H. Bornstein & L. R. Cote (Eds.), *Acculturation and parent–child relationships: Measurement and development* (pp. 63–78). Mahwah, NJ: Erlbaum.

Cicirelli, V. G. (1994). Sibling relationships in cross-cultural perspective. *Journal of Marriage and the Family, 56,* 7–20.

Cicirelli, V. G. (1995). *Sibling relationships across the life span.* New York: Plenum.

Conger, R. D., & Conger, K. J. (1996). Sibling relationships. In R. L. Simons (Ed.), *Understanding differences between divorced and intact families* (pp. 104–121). Thousand Oaks, CA: Sage.

D'Augelli, A. R., & Hershberger, S. L. (1993). Lesbian, gay and bisexual youth in community settings: Personal challenges and mental health problems. *American Journal of Community Psychology, 21,* 421–448.

Deater-Deckard, K., Dunn, J., & Lussier, G. (2002). Sibling relationships and social-emotional adjustment in different family contexts. *Social Development, 11,* 571–590.

Drapeau, S., Simard, M., & Beaudry, M. (2000). Siblings in family transitions. *Family Relations, 49,* 77–85.

Dunn, J. (1996). Siblings: The first society. In N. Vanzetti & S. Duck (Eds.), *A lifetime of relationships* (pp. 105–124). Belmont, CA: Thomson Brooks/Cole.

Dunn, J. (2007). Siblings and socialization. In J. Grusec & P. D. Hastings (Eds.), *Handbook of socialization: Theory and research* (pp. 309–327). New York: Guilford.

Dunn, J., Deater-Deckard, K., Pickering, K., Golding, J., & the ALSPAC Study Team. (1999). Siblings, parents, and partners: Family relationships within a longitudinal community study. *Journal of Child Psychology and Psychiatry, 40,* 1025–1037.

Dunn, J., & McGuire, S. (1992). Sibling and peer relationships in childhood. *Journal of Child Psychology and Psychiatry, 33,* 67–105.

Dunn, J., Slomkowski, C., & Beardsall, L. (1994). Sibling relationships from the preschool period through middle childhood and early adolescence. *Developmental Psychology, 30,* 315–324.

Dwyer, J. G. (2006). *The relationship rights of children.* New York: Cambridge University Press.

East, P. L. (1998). Impact of adolescent childbearing on families and younger siblings: Effects that increase younger siblings' risk for early pregnancy. *Applied Developmental Science, 2,* 62–74.

East, P. L., & Khoo, S. K. (2005). Longitudinal pathways linking family factors and sibling relationship qualities to adolescence substance use and sexual risk behaviors. *Journal of Family Psychology, 19,* 571–580.

East, P. L., Weisner, T. S., & Reyes, B. T. (2006). Youths' caretaking of their adolescent sisters' children: Its costs and benefits for youths' development. *Applied Developmental Science, 10*(2), 86–95.

Feinberg, M. E., & Hetherington, E. M. (2000). Sibling differentiation in adolescence: Implications for behavioral genetic theory. *Child Development, 71,* 1512–1524.

Fields, J. (2003a). *America's families and living arrangements: 2003* (Current Population Reports, P20-553). Washington, DC: U.S. Census Bureau.

Fields, J. (2003b). *Children's living arrangements and characteristics: March 2002* (Current Population Reports, P20-547). Washington, DC: U.S. Census Bureau.

Fuligni, A. J., Yip, T., & Tseng, V. (2002). The impact of family obligation on the daily activities and psychological well-being of Chinese American adolescents. *Child Development, 73,* 302–314.

Gabrielidis, C., Stephan, W. G., Ybarra, O., Dos Santos Pearson, V. M., & Villareal, L. (1997). Preferred styles of conflict resolution: Mexico and the United States. *Journal of Cross-Cultural Psychology, 28,* 661–677.

Garcia Coll, C., Crnic, K., Lamberty, G., Wasik, B. H., Jenkins, R., Garcia, H. V., et al. (1996). An integrative model for the study of developmental competencies in minority children. *Child Development, 67,* 1891–1914.

Gass, K., Jenkins, J., & Dunn, D. (2007). Are sibling relationships protective? A longitudinal study. *Journal of Child Psychology and Psychiatry, 48,* 167–175.

Golombok, S. (2006). New family forms. In A. Clarke-Stewart & J. Dunn (Eds.), *Families count: Effects on child and adolescent development* (pp. 273–298). New York: Cambridge University Press.

Gottlieb, A. R. (2005). *Side by side: On having a gay or lesbian sibling.* New York: Harrington Park Press.

Hegar, R. L. (2005). Sibling placement in foster care and adoption: An overview of international research. *Children and Youth Services Review, 27,* 717–739.

Hetherington, E. M., & Clingempeel, W. G. (1992). Coping with marital transitions: A family systems perspective. *Monographs for the Society for Research in Child Development, 57*(Serial No. 227).

Hetherington, E. M., Henderson, S. H., & Reiss, D. (1999). Adolescent siblings in stepfamilies: Family functioning and the adolescent adjustment. *Monographs for the Society for Research in Child Development, 64*(Serial No. 259).

Jenkins, J. M., Rasbash, J., & O'Connor, T. G. (2003). The role of the shared family context in differential parenting. *Developmental Psychology, 39,* 99–113.

Kaplan, L., Ade-Ridder, L., & Hennon, C. B. (1991). Issues of split custody: Siblings separated by divorce. *Journal of Divorce and Remarriage, 16,* 253–274.

Kempton, T., Armistead, L., Wierson, M., & Forehand, R. (1991). Presence of a sibling as a potential buffer following parental divorce: An examination of young adolescents. *Journal of Clinical Child Psychology, 20,* 434–438.

Killoren, S. E., Thayer, S. M., & Updegraff, K. A. (2008). Conflict resolution between Mexican origin adolescent siblings. *Journal of Marriage and Family, 70,* 1200–1212.

Kim, J., McHale, S. M., Crouter, A. C., & Osgood, D. W. (2007). Longitudinal linkages between sibling relationships and adjustment from middle childhood through adolescence. *Developmental Psychology, 43,* 960–973.

Kim, J., McHale, S. M., Osgood, D. W., & Crouter, A. C. (2006). Longitudinal course and family correlates of sibling relationships from childhood through adolescence. *Child Development, 77,* 1746–1761.

Kowal, A., & Kramer, L. (1997). Children's understanding of parental differential treatment. *Child Development, 68,* 113–126.

Larson, R. W., & Almeida, D. M. (1999). Emotional transmission in the daily lives of families: A new paradigm for studying family process. *Journal of Marriage and the Family, 61,* 5–20.

Lee, R. M., Grotevant, H. D., Hellerstedt, W. L., Gunnar, M. R., & the Minnesota International Adoption Project Team. (2006). Cultural socialization in families with internationally adopted children. *Journal of Family Psychology, 20,* 571–580.

Linares, L. O., Li, M., Shrout, P. E., Brody, G. H., & Pettit, G. S. (2007). Placement shift, sibling relationship quality, and child outcomes in foster care: A controlled study. *Journal of Family Psychology, 21,* 736–743.

Marín, G., & Marín, B. (1991). *Research with Hispanic populations.* Newbury Park, CA: Sage.

Martin, J. A., Hamilton, B. E., Sutton, P. D., Ventura, S. J., Menacker, F., Kirmeyer, S., et al. (2007). *Births: Final data for 2005 National vital statistics reports* (Vol. 56, No. 6). Hyattsville, MD: National Center for Health Statistics.

McGue, M., Keyes, M., Sharma, A., Elkins, I., Legrand, L., Johnson, W., et al. (2007). The environments of adopted and non-adopted youth: Evidence on range restriction from the sibling interaction and behavior study (SIBS). *Behavior Genetics, 37,* 449–462.

McGuire, S. (2001). Nonshared environment research: What is it and where is it going? *Marriage and Family Review, 33*(1), 31–57.

McGuire, S., Dunn, J., & Plomin, R. (1995). Maternal differential treatment of siblings and children's behavioral problems: A longitudinal study. *Development and Psychopathology, 7,* 515–528.

McGuire, S., McHale, S., & Updegraff, K. A. (1996). Children's perceptions of the sibling relationship during middle childhood:

Connections within and between family relationships. *Personal Relationships, 3,* 229–239.

McGuire, S., Segal, N. L., Gill, P., Whitlow, B., & Clausen, J. M. (2010). Siblings and trust. In K. Rotenberg (Ed.), *Interpersonal trust during childhood and adolescence* (pp. 133–154). Cambridge, UK: Cambridge University Press.

McHale, S. M., & Crouter, A. C. (1996). The family contexts of children's sibling relationships. In G. H. Brody (Ed.), *Sibling relationships: Their causes and consequences* (pp. 173–195). Westport, CT: Ablex.

McHale, S. M., Crouter, A. C., & Whiteman, S. D. (2003). The family contexts of gender development in childhood and adolescence. *Social Development, 12,* 125–148.

McHale, S. M., & Pawletko, T. M. (1992). Differential treatment of siblings in two family contexts. *Child Development, 63,* 68–81.

McHale, S. M., Updegraff, K. A., Shanahan, L., Crouter, A. C., & Killoren, S. E. (2005). Gender, culture, and family dynamics: Differential treatment of siblings in Mexican American families. *Journal of Marriage and the Family, 67,* 1259–1274.

McHale, S. M., Whiteman, S. D., Kim, J., & Crouter, A. C. (2007). Characteristics and correlates of sibling relationships in two-parent African American families. *Journal of Family Psychology, 21,* 227–235.

McLoyd, V. C., Cauce, A. M., Takeuchi, D., & Wilson, L. (2000). Marital processes and parental socialization in families of color: A decade review of research. *Journal of Marriage and the Family, 62,* 1070–1093.

Noller, P. (2005). Sibling relationships in adolescence: Learning and growing together. *Personal Relationships, 12,* 1–22.

Nuckolls, C. W. (1993). *Siblings in South Asia: Brothers and sisters in cultural context.* New York: Guilford.

Parke, R. D. (2004). Development in the family. *Annual Review Psychology, 55,* 365–399.

Patterson, C. (2000). Family relationship of lesbians and gay men. *Journal of Marriage and the Family, 62,* 1052–1069.

Patterson, C. J., & D'Augelli, A. R. (Eds.). (1998). *Lesbian, gay and bisexual identities in families: Psychological perspectives.* New York: Oxford University Press.

Portes, A., & Rumbaut, G. R. (1990). *Immigrant America: A portrait.* Berkeley: University of California Press.

Reiss, D., Neiderhiser, J. M., Hetherington, E. M., & Plomin, R. (2000). *The relationship code.* Cambridge, MA: Harvard University Press.

Rende, R. D., Slomkowski, C. L., Stocker, C., Fulker, D. W., & Plomin, R. (1992). Genetic and environmental influences on maternal and sibling interaction in middle childhood: A sibling adoption study. *Developmental Psychology, 28,* 484–490.

Rowe, D., & Gulley, B. (1992). Sibling effects on substance abuse and delinquency. *Criminology, 30,* 217–233.

Savin-Williams, R. C. (1998). The disclosure to families of same-sex attractions by lesbian, gay, and bisexual youths. *Journal of Research on Adolescence, 8,* 49–68.

Shanahan, L., Kim, J., McHale, S. M., & Crouter, A. C. (2007). Sibling similarities and differences in time use: A pattern-analytic, within-family approach. *Social Development, 16,* 662–681.

Shanahan, L., McHale, S. M., Crouter, A. C., & Osgood, D. W. (2007). Warmth with mothers and fathers from middle childhood to late adolescence: Within- and between-families comparisons. *Developmental Psychology, 43,* 551–563.

Shanahan, L., McHale, S. M., Crouter, A. C., & Osgood, D. W. (2008). Parents' differential treatment and youth depressive symptoms and sibling relationships: Longitudinal linkages. *Journal of Marriage and the Family, 70,* 480–495.

Sharma, A. R., McGue, M. K., & Benson, P. L. (1998). The psychological adjustment of United States adopted adolescents and their nonadopted siblings. *Child Development, 69,* 791–802.

Slomkowski, C., Rende, R., Conger, K. J., Simons, R. L., & Conger, R. D. (2001). Sisters, brothers, and delinquency: Evaluating social influence during early and middle adolescence. *Child Development, 72,* 271–283.

Smith, D. M., & Gates, G. J. (2001). Gay and lesbian families in the United States: Same-sex unmarried partnered household: A Human Rights Campaign Report. Retrieved April 28, 2008, from www.urban.org/url.cfm?ID51000491

Snyder, J., Bank, L., & Burraston, B. (2005). The consequences of antisocial behavior in older male siblings for younger brothers and sisters. *Journal of Family Psychology, 19,* 643–653.

Stocker, C., & Dunn, J. (1994). Sibling relationships in childhood and adolescence. In J. C. DeFries, R. Plomin, & D. W. Fulker (Eds.), *Nature and nurture during middle childhood* (pp. 214–232). Malden, MA: Blackwell.

Sulloway, F. J. (1996). *Born to rebel: Birth order, family dynamics, and creative lives.* New York: Pantheon Books.

Taylor, R. (2001). *Minority families in the US: A multicultural perspective* (3rd ed.). Upper Saddle River, NJ: Prentice Hall.

Updegraff, K. A., McHale, S. M., Whiteman, S. D., Thayer, S. M., & Delgado, M. Y. (2005). Adolescent sibling relationships in Mexican American families: Exploring the role of familism. *Journal of Family Psychology, 19,* 512–522.

Vega, W. A. (1990). Hispanic families in the 1980s: A decade of research. *Journal of Marriage and the Family, 52,* 1015–1024.

Walsh, S., Shulman, S., Bar-On, Z., & Tsur, A. (2006). The role of parentification and family climate in adaptation among immigrant adolescents in Israel. *Journal of Research on Adolescence, 16,* 321–350.

Weisner, T. S. (1993). Overview: Sibling similarity and difference in different cultures. In C. W. Nuckolls (Ed.), *Siblings in South Asia: Brothers and sisters in cultural context* (pp. 1–17). New York: Guilford.

Whiteman, S. D., McHale, S. M., & Crouter, A. C. (2007). Competing processes of siblings influence: Observational learning and sibling deidentification. *Social Development, 16,* 642–661.

Zukow, P. G. (1989). *Sibling interaction across cultures: Theoretical and methodological issues.* New York: Springer-Verlag.

Critical Thinking

1. Why is it important to consider ethnic and cultural issues in our attempt to understand how siblings matter in children's lives? What are some similarities and differences in sibling dynamics and impact across different ethnic groups in the United States?

2. How does the experience of racism and prejudice influence sibling dynamics in African American families?

3. What are some new "emerging" kinds of families that need to be studied more to understand sibling experiences in different families?

Create Central

www.mhhe.com/createcentral

Internet References

Huffington Post.com
http://www.huffingtonpost.com/2014/01/27/older-siblings-improve-kids-vocabulary_n_4674430.html

National Center for Biotechnology Information.gov
http://www.ncbi.nlm.nih.gov/pubmed/3286666

Article Prepared by: Chris J. Boyatzis, *Bucknell University*

Daddy Track: The Case for Paternity Leave

It makes men more involved at home, women more involved at work, and workplaces friendlier for all parents.

LIZA MUNDY

Learning Outcomes

After reading this article, you will be able to:

- Describe the variety of father-leave policies in different countries and U.S. states.

- Evaluate the impact of paternity leave on men's involvement in childcare, women's labor force employment, and gender equity at home.

- Understand how and why paternity-leave laws and policies are changing over time.

When Chris Renshaw told his co-workers that he was planning to take six weeks of paternity leave, they responded with overwhelming support. "It's definitely looked at in a good light," says Renshaw, 28, who lives in Northern California and was taking infant-care classes to hone his diapering and baby-bathing skills. "People have said, 'That's a great idea—take as much as you can. It's time that you can be with your child.'"

This would hardly be surprising if Renshaw worked for one of the legions of progressive tech companies in the Bay Area, but he's a firefighter. His decision to take paternity leave, and his fellow firefighters' enthusiastic reaction, is a sign of a new phase in our never-ending quest for work–life harmony.

As usual, California is at the vanguard of this shift. While the federal Family and Medical Leave Act has long granted up to 12 weeks of unpaid leave to mothers and fathers in large and medium-size workplaces, in 2002, California became the first U.S. state to guarantee six weeks of *paid* leave for mothers and fathers alike, financed by a small payroll-tax contribution from eligible workers. Since then, Rhode Island and New Jersey have followed suit with four and six paid weeks, respectively, while other states are taking steps toward similar policies.* In Silicon Valley, many tech giants have gone above and beyond the government mandate: Google offers men seven weeks of paid leave; Yahoo, eight; and Reddit and Facebook, a generous 17.

Paternity leave has also begun to enter the corporate and cultural mainstream. According to a study by the Boston College Center for Work and Family, which surveyed men in a number of *Fortune* 500 companies, most new fathers now take at least some time off after the birth of a baby, though few depart the workplace for more than two weeks. In England, Prince William took two weeks' leave from his job as a military search-and-rescue helicopter pilot when his son, George, was born. Even Major League Baseball has formalized paternity leave—albeit three days' worth—for players, partnering with Dove's line for men in a pro-fatherhood campaign called Big League Dads.

But here's what men may not realize: While paid paternity leave may feel like an unexpected gift, the biggest beneficiaries aren't men, or even babies. In the long run, the true beneficiaries of paternity leave are women, and the companies and nations that benefit when women advance. In October, the World Economic Forum released its latest global gender-gap report, showing that countries with the strongest economies are those that have found ways to further women's careers, close the gender pay gap, and keep women—who in most nations are now better educated than men—tethered to the workforce after they become mothers. One strikingly effective strategy used by the highest-ranking countries is paternity leave, which, whatever else it may accomplish, is a brilliant and ambitious form of social engineering: a behavior-modification tool that has been shown to boost male participation in the household, enhance female participation in the labor force, and promote gender equity in both domains.

The genius of paternity leave is that it shapes domestic and parenting habits as they are forming. While most mothers in the United States now work, many women still see their careers suffer after they became parents, in part because they end up shouldering the bulk of the domestic load—a phenomenon the sociologist Arlie Hochschild has dubbed the "second shift." A 2007 study found that 60 percent of professional women who stopped working reported that they were largely motivated by their husbands' unavailability to share housework and child-care duties. Paternity leave is a chance to intervene at what one study called "a crucial time of renegotiation": those early, sleep-deprived weeks of diaper changes and midnight feedings, during which couples fall into patterns that turn out to be surprisingly permanent.

Maternity leave, on the other hand, has mostly medical origins. As early as the late 19th century in certain countries, taking a leave of absence was compulsory before and after birth. After World War II, some European countries used compulsory-leave policies to funnel women from the factories and offices they'd filled during the war back into what was seen as their proper domestic sphere. But the medical benefits are real; by the 1970s, as the ranks of working women rose, maternity leave was increasingly understood as a way to safeguard the health of women and children, giving mothers time to recover from childbirth and take babies to those early, frequent doctor appointments. Studies have confirmed that when women take maternity leave, babies get breast-fed longer and infant-mortality rates go down.

In recent decades, the rationale has expanded, thanks in part to adoptive parents who made the sensible case that not giving birth to your child doesn't invalidate the need to spend intimate time with a small, vulnerable person who has just joined your family. This crusade helped pave the way for dads, encouraging the idea that leave is as much about forming attachments as recovering from medical trauma. California's six weeks are known as "bonding leave" (mothers who give birth can add this to a period of paid disability leave).

Somewhat paradoxically, paternity leave has also evolved as a way for progressive countries to correct for an overly enthusiastic embrace of paid leave for mothers. We tend to think of Scandinavia and northern Europe as exemplars of work–family balance, but a tangle of warring policies in these regions has led to a few backfires. In their pursuit of an egalitarian workplace

(and higher fertility rates), countries like Sweden and Germany have at times offered women more than a year of maternity leave—sometimes quite a bit more—a strategy that can fortify the glass ceiling rather than shatter it. Anticipating that women will disappear for long periods of time, managers become reluctant to hire them into senior positions, and female workers are shunted (or shunt themselves) into lower-paying sectors. Among labor economists, overly long maternity leaves are now recognized as creating a barrier to pay equity. At home, meanwhile, long leaves result in women doing most of the housework and child care.

Some countries began recalibrating, shortening leave for women and offering "neutral leave" that could be taken by either parent—but which became de facto maternity leave. So policy makers decided to make men an offer they would feel ashamed to refuse. Norway, Iceland, Germany, Finland, and several other countries offered a variety of incentives to nudge men to take leave. Some countries offered them more money, which helped men feel that they were financially supporting their families even when they were at home. Many also adopted a "use it or lose it" approach, granting each family a total amount of leave, a certain portion of which could be used only by fathers.

The brilliance of "daddy days," as this solution came to be known, is that, rather than feeling stigmatized for taking time off from their jobs, many men now feel stigmatized if they don't. The economist Ankita Patnaik, who has studied Quebec's implementation of such a policy, told me that "families felt they were wasting something" if the father didn't take leave. In 2006, Quebec increased the financial benefits for paid leave and offered five weeks that could be taken only by fathers. "That's what really made a difference," Patnaik told me. "Now dads might feel bad for not taking leave—your baby loses this time with parents." Since then, the percentage of Quebecois fathers taking paternity leave has skyrocketed, from about 10 percent in 2001 to more than 80 percent in 2010.

The policy has achieved many of the hoped-for long-term outcomes, chief among them more fluidity in who does what around the house. Previous studies found that fathers who take paternity leave are more likely, a year or so down the road, to change diapers, bathe their children, read them bedtime stories, and get up at night to tend to them. Patnaik's study confirmed this; looking at time-use diaries, she found that men who were eligible for the new leave—whether or not they took it—ended up spending more time later on routine chores like shopping and cooking.

If these changes sound minor, they aren't. As men have taken on more domestic work over the past 20 or so years, they have gravitated toward the fun stuff, like hanging out with the kids, rather than the boring but inescapable duties, like boiling the ravioli or vacuuming Cheerios out of the family-room carpet. The University of Oregon sociologist Scott Coltrane has noted that when men share "routine repetitive chores," women feel they are being treated fairly and are less likely to become depressed.

In Quebec, women whose husbands were eligible for the new leave were more likely to return to their original employers and were more likely to work full-time, resulting in their spending "considerably" more hours on paid work. (When women work full-time, it alters the home division of labor more than when they work part-time.) And as women were spending more time working for pay, men were spending less: the Quebec paternity-leave policy resulted in a small but long-term decrease in fathers' time at work.

This finding hints at the possibility that paternity leave could erode the fabled "fatherhood wage premium." In the early 20th century, employers explicitly and even proudly paid married men more than they paid single men—and much more than they paid women—in recognition of the fact that husbands were the conduit by which families got fed. Even after employers dropped these formal policies, fathers have continued to enjoy a wage bonus, because they are seen as being more motivated and reliable, because they work longer hours, or both. But Patnaik's study suggests that paternity leave might give men a new mind-set, prompting them to trade more money for more time at home, more flexibility, or both. In this way, it could make men behave more like women.

Which points to a core goal of many workplace-equity policies: spreading the parenthood stigma around. Widespread paternity-leave plans raise the possibility that bosses will stop looking askance at the résumé of a 20-something female applicant, or at least apply the same scrutiny to a similar male applicant.

While it's too soon to tell whether California's, New Jersey's, and Rhode Island's paid-paternity-leave programs will be as transformative as Quebec's, the early signs are positive. Since California instituted its program, the percentage of "bonding leaves" claimed by men has risen from 18.7 in 2005 and 2006 to 31.3 in 2012 and 2013. A study by the economist Eileen Appelbaum and the sociologist Ruth Milkman showed that initial concerns that the California law would be a "job killer" were unfounded and that workplaces have figured out effective and creative ways to cover for leave-taking parents. The biggest hurdle seems to be getting the word out, particularly among lower-income families that could benefit enormously from the program. (Part of the beauty of the California policy is that it extends leave to men in non-white-collar jobs.)

News stories and conventional wisdom suggest that men still feel judged when they take paternity leave, so I was struck, while speaking with a New York City dads' group, by

how many of its members had received positive reinforcement from bosses and colleagues after announcing their decision to take leave. A different study by the Boston College Center for Work and Family has found that for men, joining the "parents club" tends to have positive professional consequences: fathers are more readily permitted to adjust their work hours than are mothers, who are often viewed as less committed and less promotable. The study also found that men tend not to ask for formal work–life policies; they use "stealth" methods instead, like slipping out to coach soccer practice. Part of the leniency toward working dads, of course, may be due to the fact that they simply haven't asked for much.

But now they're asking. Rich Gallagher, who works in public relations in New York, had a supportive employer when he took his first leave. But he'd switched jobs by the time his second child was born, and found that taking time off "soured" his standing and won him dirty looks from colleagues. He left that job, and even now that he doesn't need paternity leave anymore, he looks at potential employers' leave policies as a benchmark for whether they are committed to work–life balance.

Most men who take leave, it's important to note, don't take anything close to six weeks, and many are obliged to use vacation time for part or all of whatever time they do take. In the United States, we are only just starting to wrap our minds around longer paternity leave. "Two weeks for men may be the best we can hope for in the medium term," says Scott Behson, a management professor at Fairleigh Dickinson University, who blogs about fatherhood. He suggests a compromise in which men receive two weeks of paid leave, followed by a flexible schedule that would enable them to take a paid day or two off each week. Companies like Deloitte, which offers three to eight weeks of paid paternity leave, are finding that many men prefer to stagger their time off, taking a few weeks when the baby is born, for example, and then more time when their wives go back to work.

Options like these may help to address the somewhat surprising fact that, regardless of whatever plaudits or premiums they may or may not enjoy in the office, working fathers increasingly report feeling more work–family conflict than working mothers do. A 2011 report concluded that the most-conflicted men are those who are stuck working long hours yet feel they should be at home.

In another sign of how paternity leave can narrow the gap between working mothers and fathers, more than one man I spoke with had made a decision long familiar to mothers who find themselves trapped in the office after bedtime too many nights. Upon the birth of his first child, Lance Somerfeld planned to take paternity leave from his teaching job at a big elementary school in the Bronx. He looked forward to being home, and his wife's career was going well. As they thought about the future, they reckoned that child-care costs would eat up most of his after-tax salary, so he decided to extend his leave indefinitely. When Somerfeld informed the school that he would not be returning, at least not anytime soon, his principal went on the PA system and announced, "Mr. Somerfeld will be leaving us next year to become a modern man!"

Critical Thinking

1. Why might "daddy time" after a child's birth promote fathers' greater involvement with childcare?

2. What are some obstacles, from personal to professional to cultural, that could impede fathers' willingness to take advantage of paternity leave?

3. Regardless of your gender, if you have children now or in the future, what do you envision regarding "daddy time" in your family? How might it influence you personally?

Create Central

www.mhhe.com/createcentral

Internet References

Baby Center.com

http://www.babycenter.com/0_paternity-leave-what-are-the-options-for-dads_8258.bc

Human Impact Partners

http://workfamilyca.org/resources/HIPFactSheet_2011.pdf

The Future of Children.org

http://futureofchildren.org/publications/journals/article/index.xml?journal id=44&articleid=191&sectionid=1254

http://futureofchildren.org/publications/journals/article/index.xml?journal id=76&articleid=557&sectionid=3855

Article   Prepared by: Chris J. Boyatzis, *Bucknell University*

Why Parents Need to Let Their Children Fail

A new study explores what happens to students who aren't allowed to suffer through setbacks.

Jessica Lahey

Learning Outcomes

After reading this article, you will be able to:

- Discuss the implications of parental overprotectiveness and how the child is affected by it.

- Understand why it is so important for children to receive autonomy in their learning experience.

Thirteen years ago, when I was a relatively new teacher, stumbling around my classroom on wobbly legs, I had to call a student's mother to inform her that I would be initiating disciplinary proceedings against her daughter for plagiarism, and that furthermore, her daughter would receive a zero for the plagiarized paper.

"You can't do that. She didn't do anything wrong," the mother informed me, enraged.

"But she did. I was able to find entire paragraphs lifted off of web sites," I stammered.

"No, I mean *she* didn't do it. I did. *I* wrote her paper."

I don't remember what I said in response, but I'm fairly confident I had to take a moment to digest what I had just heard. And what would I do, anyway? Suspend the mother? Keep her in for lunch detention and make her write "I will not write my daughter's papers using articles plagiarized from the Internet" one hundred times on the board? In all fairness, the mother submitted a defense: her daughter had been stressed out, and she did not want her to get sick or overwhelmed.

In the end, my student received a zero and I made sure she re-wrote the paper. Herself. Sure, I didn't have the authority to discipline the student's mother, but I have done so many times in my dreams.

While I am not sure what the mother gained from the experience, the daughter gained an understanding of consequences, and I gained a war story. I don't even bother with the old reliables anymore: the mother who "helps" a bit too much with the child's math homework, the father who builds the student's science project. Please. Don't waste my time.

The stories teachers exchange these days reveal a whole new level of overprotectiveness: parents who raise their children in a state of helplessness and powerlessness, children destined to an anxious adulthood, lacking the emotional resources they will need to cope with inevitable setback and failure.

I believed my accumulated compendium of teacher war stories were pretty good—until I read a study out of Queensland University of Technology, by Judith Locke, et al., a self-described "examination by parenting professionals of the concept of overparenting."

Overparenting is characterized in the study as parents' "misguided attempt to improve their child's current and future personal and academic success." In an attempt to understand such behaviors, the authors surveyed psychologists, guidance counselors, and teachers. The authors asked these professionals if they had witnessed examples of overparenting, and left space for descriptions of said examples. While the relatively small sample size and questionable method of subjective self-reporting cast a shadow on the study's statistical significance, the examples cited in the report provide enough ammunition for a year of dinner parties.

Some of the examples are the usual fare: a child isn't allowed to go to camp or learn to drive, a parent cuts up a 10-year-old's food or brings separate plates to parties for a 16-year-old because he's a picky eater. Yawn. These barely rank a "Tsk, tsk" among my colleagues. And while I pity those kids, I'm not that worried. They will go out on their own someday and recover from their overprotective childhoods.

What worry me most are the examples of overparenting that have the potential to ruin a child's confidence and undermine an education in independence. According to the authors, parents guilty of this kind of overparenting "take their child's perception as truth, regardless of the facts," and are "quick to believe their child over the adult and deny the possibility that their child was at fault or would even do something of that nature."

This is what we teachers see most often: what the authors term "high responsiveness and low demandingness" parents. These parents are highly responsive to the perceived needs and issues of their children, and don't give their children the chance to solve their own problems. These parents "rush to school at the whim of a phone call from their child to deliver items such as forgotten lunches, forgotten assignments, forgotten uniforms" and "demand better grades on the final semester reports or threaten withdrawal from school." One study participant described the problem this way:

> I have worked with quite a number of parents who are so overprotective of their children that the children do not learn to take responsibility (and the natural consequences) of their actions. The children may develop a sense of entitlement and the parents then find it difficult to work with the school in a trusting, cooperative and solution focused manner, which would benefit both child and school.

These are the parents who worry me the most—parents who won't let their child learn. You see, teachers don't just teach reading, writing, and arithmetic. We teach responsibility, organization, manners, restraint, and foresight. These skills may not get assessed on standardized testing, but as children plot their journey into adulthood, they are, by far, the most important life skills I teach.

I'm not suggesting that parents place blind trust in their children's teachers; I would never do such a thing myself. But children make mistakes, and when they do, it's vital that parents remember that the educational benefits of consequences are a gift, not a dereliction of duty. Year after year, my "best" students—the ones who are happiest and successful in their lives—are the students who were allowed to fail, held responsible for missteps, and challenged to be the best people they could be in the face of their mistakes.

I'm done fantasizing about ways to make that mom from 13 years ago see the light. That ship has sailed, and I did the best I could for her daughter. Every year, I reassure some parent, "This setback will be the best thing that ever happened to your child," and I've long since accepted that most parents won't believe me. That's fine. I'm patient. The lessons I teach in middle school don't typically pay off for years, and I don't expect thank-you cards.

I have learned to enjoy and find satisfaction in these day-to-day lessons and in the time I get to spend with children in need of an education. But I fantasize about the day I will be trusted to teach my students how to roll with the punches, find their way through the gauntlet of adolescence, and stand firm in the face of the challenges—challenges that have the power to transform today's children into resourceful, competent, and confident adults.

Critical Thinking

1. As a teacher, how would you work with a child whose parents were overly intrusive on his or her learning experience?
2. What are the benefits of allowing children to learn on their own? Is there benefit of having parental involvement?

Create Central

www.mhhe.com/createcentral

Internet References

Frank Porter Graham Child Development Institute
   http://fpg.unc.edu/emphasis-area/physical-and-social-health
Mental Help.net
   http://www.mentalhelp.net/poc/view_doc.php?id=1326&type=book&cn=28
The Effects of Intrusive Parenting: The Long Term Effects of Denying Children Their Independence
   http://voices.yahoo.com/the-effects-intrusive-parenting-6659550.html

Unit 5

UNIT

Prepared by: Chris J. Boyatzis, *Bucknell University*

Cultural and Societal Influences

Social scientists and developmental psychologists have come to realize that children are influenced by a multitude of complex social forces. This unit presents articles that illuminate how children and adolescents are influenced by broad factors such as economics, culture, politics, the media, and technology. These influences also affect the family, which is a major context of child development, and many children are now faced with more family challenges than ever.

In addition, analysis of exceptional or atypical children gives the reader a more comprehensive account of child development.

Some children must cope with special psychological, emotional, and cognitive challenges such as ADHD, autism, and chronic illness. Such children are often misunderstood and mistreated and pose special challenges.

In this unit, we provide a wide variety of articles that will shed light on the new research, implications, and practical interventions that parents, educators, and others might utilize to help children reach their maximum potential.

Article   Prepared by: Chris J. Boyatzis, *Bucknell University*

The Touch-Screen Generation

Young children—even toddlers—are spending more and more time with digital technology. What will it mean for their development?

HANNA ROSIN

Learning Outcomes

After reading this article, you will be able to:

- Judge if the article presents compelling evidence of a positive or negative effect on children of using touch-screen technology.

- Describe different kinds of restrictions that parents place on their children's screen time.

- Understand some of the pros and cons in parents' thinking about technology in their children's lives.

On a chilly day last spring, a few dozen developers of children's apps for phones and tablets gathered at an old beach resort in Monterey, California, to show off their games. One developer, a self-described "visionary for puzzles" who looked like a skateboarder-recently-turned-dad, displayed a jacked-up, interactive game called Puzzingo, intended for toddlers and inspired by his own son's desire to build and smash. Two 30-something women were eagerly seeking feedback for an app called Knock Knock Family, aimed at 1- to 4 year-olds. "We want to make sure it's easy enough for babies to understand," one explained.

The gathering was organized by Warren Buckleitner, a long-time reviewer of interactive children's media who likes to bring together developers, researchers, and interest groups—and often plenty of kids, some still in diapers. It went by the Harry Potter–ish name Dust or Magic and was held in a drafty old stone-and-wood hall barely a mile from the sea, the kind of place where Bathilda Bagshot might retire after packing up her wand. Buckleitner spent the breaks testing whether his own

remote-control helicopter could reach the hall's second story, while various children who had come with their parents looked up in awe and delight. But mostly they looked down, at the iPads and other tablets displayed around the hall like so many open boxes of candy. I walked around and talked with developers, and several paraphrased a famous saying of Maria Montessori's, a quote imported to ennoble a touch-screen age when very young kids, who once could be counted on only to chew on a square of aluminum, are now engaging with it in increasingly sophisticated ways: "The hands are the instruments of man's intelligence."

What, really, would Maria Montessori have made of this scene? The 30 or so children here were not down at the shore poking their fingers in the sand or running them along mossy stones or digging for hermit crabs. Instead they were all inside, alone or in groups of two or three, their faces a few inches from a screen, their hands doing things Montessori surely did not imagine. A couple of 3-year-old girls were leaning against a pair of French doors, reading an interactive story called *Ten Giggly Gorillas* and fighting over which ape to tickle next. A boy in a nearby corner had turned his fingertip into a red marker to draw an ugly picture of his older brother. On an old oak table at the front of the room, a giant stuffed Angry Bird beckoned the children to come and test out tablets loaded with dozens of new apps. Some of the chairs had pillows strapped to them, since an 18-month-old might not otherwise be able to reach the table, though she'd know how to swipe once she did.

Not that long ago, there was only the television, which theoretically could be kept in the parents' bedroom or locked behind a cabinet. Now there are smartphones and iPads, which wash up in the domestic clutter alongside keys and gum and stray hair ties. "Mom, everyone has technology but me!" my

4-year-old son sometimes wails. And why shouldn't he feel entitled? In the same span of time it took him to learn how to say that sentence, thousands of kids' apps have been developed—the majority aimed at preschoolers like him. To us (his parents, I mean), American childhood has undergone a somewhat alarming transformation in a very short time. But to him, it has always been possible to do so many things with the swipe of a finger, to have hundreds of games packed into a gadget the same size as *Goodnight Moon*.

In 2011, the American Academy of Pediatrics updated its policy on very young children and media. In 1999, the group had discouraged television viewing for children younger than 2, citing research on brain development that showed this age group's critical need for "direct interactions with parents and other significant care givers." The updated report began by acknowledging that things had changed significantly since then. In 2006, 90 percent of parents said that their children younger than 2 consumed some form of electronic media. Nonetheless, the group took largely the same approach it did in 1999, uniformly discouraging passive media use, on any type of screen, for these kids. (For older children, the academy noted, "high-quality programs" could have "educational benefits.") The 2011 report mentioned "smart cell phone" and "new screen" technologies, but did not address interactive apps. Nor did it broach the possibility that has likely occurred to those 90 percent of American parents, queasy though they might be: that some good might come from those little swiping fingers.

I had come to the developers' conference partly because I hoped that this particular set of parents, enthusiastic as they were about interactive media, might help me out of this conundrum, that they might offer some guiding principle for American parents who are clearly never going to meet the academy's ideals, and at some level do not want to. Perhaps this group would be able to articulate some benefits of the new technology that the more cautious pediatricians weren't ready to address. I nurtured this hope until about lunchtime, when the developers gathering in the dining hall ceased being visionaries and reverted to being ordinary parents, trying to settle their toddlers in high chairs and get them to eat something besides bread.

I fell into conversation with a woman who had helped develop Montessori Letter Sounds, an app that teaches preschoolers the Montessori methods of spelling.

She was a former Montessori teacher and a mother of four. I myself have three children who are all fans of the touch screen. What games did her kids like to play?, I asked, hoping for suggestions I could take home.

"They don't play all that much."

Really? Why not?

"Because I don't allow it. We have a rule of no screen time during the week," unless it's clearly educational.

No screen time? None at all? That seems at the outer edge of restrictive, even by the standards of my overcontrolling parenting set.

"On the weekends, they can play. I give them a limit of half an hour and then stop. Enough. It can be too addictive, too stimulating for the brain."

Her answer so surprised me that I decided to ask some of the other developers who were also parents what their domestic ground rules for screen time were. One said only on airplanes and long car rides. Another said Wednesdays and weekends, for half an hour. The most permissive said half an hour a day, which was about my rule at home. At one point I sat with one of the biggest developers of e-book apps for kids, and his family. The toddler was starting to fuss in her high chair, so the mom did what many of us have done at that moment—stuck an iPad in front of her and played a short movie so everyone else could enjoy their lunch. When she saw me watching, she gave me the universal tense look of mothers who feel they are being judged. "At home," she assured me, "I only let her watch movies in Spanish."

By their pinched reactions, these parents illuminated for me the neurosis of our age: as technology becomes ubiquitous in our lives, American parents are becoming more, not less, wary of what it might be doing to their children. Technological competence and sophistication have not, for parents, translated into comfort and ease. They have merely created yet another sphere that parents feel they have to navigate in exactly the right way. On the one hand, parents want their children to swim expertly in the digital stream that they will have to navigate all their lives; on the other hand, they fear that too much digital media, too early, will sink them. Parents end up treating tablets like precision surgical instruments, gadgets that might perform miracles for their child's IQ and help him win some nifty robotics competition—but only if they are used just so. Otherwise, their child could end up one of those sad, pale creatures who can't make eye contact and has an avatar for a girlfriend.

Norman Rockwell never painted *Boy Swiping Finger on Screen,* and our own vision of a perfect childhood has never adjusted to accommodate that now-common tableau. Add to that our modern fear that every parenting decision may have lasting consequences—that every minute of enrichment lost or mindless entertainment indulged will add up to some permanent handicap in the future—and you have deep guilt and confusion. To date, no body of research has definitively proved that the iPad will make your preschooler smarter or teach her to speak Chinese, or alternatively that it will rust her neural circuitry—the device has been out for only three years, not much more than the time it takes some academics to find funding and gather research subjects. So what's a parent to do?

In 2001, the education and technology writer Marc Prensky popularized the term *digital natives* to describe the first generations of children growing up fluent in the language of computers, video games, and other technologies. (The rest of us are *digital immigrants,* struggling to understand.) This term took on a whole new significance in April 2010, when the iPad was released. iPhones had already been tempting young children, but the screens were a little small for pudgy toddler hands to navigate with ease and accuracy. Plus, parents tended to be more possessive of their phones, hiding them in pockets or purses. The iPad was big and bright, and a case could be made that it belonged to the family. Researchers who study children's media immediately recognized it as a game changer.

Previously, young children had to be shown by their parents how to use a mouse or a remote, and the connection between what they were doing with their hand and what was happening on the screen took some time to grasp. But with the iPad, the connection is obvious, even to toddlers. Touch technology follows the same logic as shaking a rattle or knocking down a pile of blocks: the child swipes, and something immediately happens. A "rattle on steroids," is what Buckleitner calls it. "All of a sudden a finger could move a bus or smush an insect or turn into a big wet gloopy paintbrush." To a toddler, this is less magic than intuition. At a very young age, children become capable of what the psychologist Jerome Bruner called "enactive representation"; they classify objects in the world not by using words or symbols but by making gestures—say, holding an imaginary cup to their lips to signify that they want a drink. Their hands are a natural extension of their thoughts.

Norman Rockwell never painted Boy Swiping Finger on Screen, and our own vision of a perfect childhood has never adjusted to fit that now-common tableau.

I have two older children who fit the early idea of a digital native—they learned how to use a mouse or a keyboard with some help from their parents and were well into school before they felt comfortable with a device in their lap. (Now, of course, at ages 9 and 12, they can create a Web site in the time it takes me to slice an onion.) My youngest child is a whole different story. He was not yet 2 when the iPad was released. As soon as he got his hands on it, he located the Talking Baby Hippo app that one of my older children had downloaded. The little purple hippo repeats whatever you say in his own squeaky voice, and responds to other cues. My son said his name ("Giddy!"); Baby Hippo repeated it back. Gideon poked Baby Hippo; Baby Hippo laughed. Over and over, it was funny every time. Pretty soon he discovered other apps. Old MacDonald, by Duck Duck Moose, was a favorite. At first he would get frustrated trying

to zoom between screens, or not knowing what to do when a message popped up. But after about two weeks, he figured all that out. I must admit, it was eerie to see a child still in diapers so competent and intent, as if he were forecasting his own adulthood. Technically I was the owner of the iPad, but in some ontological way it felt much more his than mine.

Without seeming to think much about it or resolve how they felt, parents began giving their devices over to their children to mollify, pacify, or otherwise entertain them. By 2010, two-thirds of children ages 4 to 7 had used an iPhone, according to the Joan Ganz Cooney Center, which studies children's media. The vast majority of those phones had been lent by a family member; the center's researchers labeled this the "pass-back effect," a name that captures well the reluctant zone between denying and giving.

The market immediately picked up on the pass-back effect, and the opportunities it presented. In 2008, when Apple opened up its App Store, the games started arriving at the rate of dozens a day, thousands a year. For the first 23 years of his career, Buckleitner had tried to be comprehensive and cover every children's game in his publication, *Children's Technology Review.* Now, by Buckleitner's loose count, more than 40,000 kids' games are available on iTunes, plus thousands more on Google Play. In the iTunes "Education" category, the majority of the top-selling apps target preschool or elementary-age children. By age 3, Gideon would go to preschool and tune in to what was cool in toddler world, then come home, locate the iPad, drop it in my lap, and ask for certain games by their approximate description: "Tea? Spill?" (That's Toca Tea Party.)

As these delights and diversions for young children have proliferated, the pass-back has become more uncomfortable, even unsustainable, for many parents:

> He'd gone to this state where you'd call his name and he wouldn't respond to it, or you could snap your fingers in front of his face . . .

> But, you know, we ended up actually taking the iPad away for—from him largely because, you know, this example, this thing we were talking about, about zoning out. Now, he would do that, and my wife and I would stare at him and think, *Oh my God, his brain is going to turn to mush and come oozing out of his ears.* And it concerned us a bit.

This is Ben Worthen, a *Wall Street Journal* reporter, explaining recently to NPR's Diane Rehm why he took the iPad away from his son, even though it was the only thing that could hold the boy's attention for long periods, and it seemed to be sparking an interest in numbers and letters. Most parents can sympathize with the disturbing sight of a toddler, who five minutes earlier had been jumping off the couch, now subdued and staring at a screen, seemingly hypnotized. In the somewhat alarmist *Endangered Minds: Why Children Don't Think—and What We Can Do About It,* author Jane Healy even gives the phenomenon a name, the "'zombie' effect," and raises the possibility that television might "suppress mental activity by putting viewers in a trance."

Ever since viewing screens entered the home, many observers have worried that they put our brains into a stupor. An early strain of research claimed that when we watch television, our brains mostly exhibit slow alpha waves—indicating a low level of arousal, similar to when we are daydreaming. These findings have been largely discarded by the scientific community, but the myth persists that watching television is the mental equivalent of, as one Web site put it, "staring at a blank wall." These common metaphors are misleading, argues Heather Kirkorian, who studies media and attention at the University of Wisconsin at Madison. A more accurate point of comparison for a TV viewer's physiological state would be that of someone deep in a book, says Kirkorian, because during both activities we are still, undistracted, and mentally active.

Because interactive media are so new, most of the existing research looks at children and television. By now, "there is universal agreement that by at least age 2 and a half, children are very cognitively active when they are watching TV," says Dan Anderson, a children's-media expert at the University of Massachusetts at Amherst. In the 1980s, Anderson put the zombie theory to the test, by subjecting roughly 100 children to a form of TV hell. He showed a group of children aged 2 to 5 a scrambled version of *Sesame Street:* he pieced together scenes in random order and had the characters speak backwards or in Greek. Then he spliced the doctored segments with unedited ones and noted how well the kids paid attention. The children looked away much more frequently during the scrambled parts of the show, and some complained that the TV was broken. Anderson later repeated the experiment with babies aged 6 months to 24 months, using *Teletubbies.* Once again he had the characters speak backwards and chopped the action sequences into a nonsensical order—showing, say, one of the Teletubbies catching a ball and then, after that, another one throwing it. The 6- and 12-month-olds seemed unable to tell the difference, but by 18 months, the babies started looking away, and by 24 months, they were turned off by programming that did not make sense.

Anderson's series of experiments provided the first clue that even very young children can be discriminating viewers—that they are not in fact brain-dead, but rather work hard to make sense of what they see and turn it into a coherent narrative that reflects what they already know of the world. Now, 30 years later, we understand that children "can make a lot of inferences and process the information," says Anderson. "And they can learn a lot, both positive and negative." Researchers never

abandoned the idea that parental interaction is critical for the development of very young children. But they started to see TV watching in shades of gray. If a child never interacts with adults and always watches TV, well, that is a problem. But if a child is watching TV instead of, say, playing with toys, then that is a tougher comparison, because TV, in the right circumstances, has something to offer.

How do small children actually experience electronic media, and what does that experience do to their development? Since the '80s, researchers have spent more and more time consulting with television programmers to study and shape TV content. By tracking children's reactions, they have identified certain rules that promote engagement: stories have to be linear and easy to follow, cuts and time lapses have to be used very sparingly, and language has to be pared down and repeated. A perfect example of a well-engineered show is Nick Jr.'s *Blue's Clues,* which aired from 1996 to 2006. Each episode features Steve (or Joe, in later seasons) and Blue, a cartoon puppy, solving a mystery. Steve talks slowly and simply; he repeats words and then writes them down in his handy-dandy notebook. There are almost no cuts or unexplained gaps in time. The great innovation of *Blue's Clues* is something called the "pause." Steve asks a question and then pauses for about five seconds to let the viewer shout out an answer. Small children feel much more engaged and invested when they think they have a role to play, when they believe they are actually helping Steve and Blue piece together the clues. A longitudinal study of children older than 2 and a half showed that the ones who watched *Blue's Clues* made measurably larger gains in flexible thinking and problem solving over two years of watching the show.

For toddlers, however, the situation seems slightly different. Children younger than 2 and a half exhibit what researchers call a "video deficit." This means that they have a much easier time processing information delivered by a real person than by a person on videotape. In one series of studies, conducted by Georgene Troseth, a developmental psychologist at Vanderbilt University, children watched on a live video monitor as a person in the next room hid a stuffed dog. Others watched the exact same scene unfold directly, through a window between the rooms. The children were then unleashed into the room to find the toy. Almost all the kids who viewed the hiding through the window found the toy, but the ones who watched on the monitor had a much harder time.

A natural assumption is that toddlers are not yet cognitively equipped to handle symbolic representation. (I remember my older son, when he was 3, asking me if he could go into the TV and pet Blue.) But there is another way to interpret this particular phase of development. Toddlers are skilled at seeking out what researchers call "socially relevant information." They tune in to people and situations that help them make a coherent narrative of the world around them. In the real world, fresh grass smells and popcorn tumbles and grown-ups smile at you or say something back when you ask them a question. On TV, nothing like that happens. A TV is static and lacks one of the most important things to toddlers, which is a "two-way exchange of information," argues Troseth.

A few years after the original puppy-hiding experiment, in 2004, Troseth reran it, only she changed a few things. She turned the puppy into a stuffed Piglet (from the Winnie the Pooh stories). More important, she made the video demonstration explicitly interactive. Toddlers and their parents came into a room where they could see a person—the researcher—on a monitor. The researcher was in the room where Piglet would be hidden and could in turn see the children on a monitor. Before hiding Piglet, the researcher effectively engaged the children in a form of media training. She asked them questions about their siblings, pets, and toys. She played Simon Says with them and invited them to sing popular songs with her. She told them to look for a sticker under a chair in their room. She gave them the distinct impression that she—this person on the screen—could interact with them and that what she had to say was relevant to the world they lived in. Then the researcher told the children she was going to hide the toy and, after she did so, came back on the screen to instruct them where to find it. That exchange was enough to nearly erase the video deficit. The majority of the toddlers who participated in the live video demonstration found the toy.

Blue's Clues was on the right track. The pause could trick children into thinking that Steve was responsive to them. But the holy grail would be creating a scenario in which the guy on the screen did actually respond—in which the toddler did something and the character reliably jumped or laughed or started to dance or talk back.

Like, for example, when Gideon said "Giddy" and Talking Baby Hippo said "Giddy" back, without fail, every time. That kind of contingent interaction (I do something, you respond) is what captivates a toddler and can be a significant source of learning for even very young children—learning that researchers hope the children can carry into the real world. It's not exactly the ideal social partner the American Academy of Pediatrics craves. It's certainly not a parent or caregiver. But it's as good an approximation as we've ever come up with on a screen, and it's why children's-media researchers are so excited about the iPad's potential.

A couple of researchers from the Children's Media Center at Georgetown University show up at my house, carrying an iPad wrapped in a bright-orange case, the better to tempt Gideon with. They are here at the behest of Sandra Calvert, the center's director, to conduct one of several ongoing studies on toddlers and iPads. Gideon is one of their research subjects. This study is designed to test whether a child is more likely to learn when the information he hears comes from a beloved and trusted source. The researchers put the iPad on a kitchen chair; Gideon immediately notices it, turns it on, and looks for his favorite app. They point him to the one they have invented for the experiment, and he dutifully opens it with his finger.

Onto the screen comes a floppy kangaroo-like puppet, introduced as "DoDo." He is a nobody in the child universe, the puppet equivalent of some random guy on late-night public-access TV. Gideon barely acknowledges him. Then the narrator introduces Elmo. "Hi," says Elmo, waving. Gideon says hi and waves back.

An image pops up on the screen, and the narrator asks, "What is this?" (It's a banana.)

"This is a banana," says DoDo.

"This is a grape," says Elmo.

I smile with the inner glow of a mother who knows her child is about to impress a couple strangers. My little darling knows what a banana is. Of course he does! Gideon presses on Elmo. (The narrator says, "No, not Elmo. Try again.") As far as I know, he's never watched *Sesame Street,* never loved an Elmo doll or even coveted one at the toy store. Nonetheless, he is tuned in to the signals of toddler world and, apparently, has somehow figured out that Elmo is a supreme moral authority. His relationship with Elmo is more important to him than what he knows to be the truth. On and on the game goes, and sometimes Gideon picks Elmo even when Elmo says an orange is a pear. Later, when the characters both give made-up names for exotic fruits that few children would know by their real name, Gideon keeps doubling down on Elmo, even though DoDo has been more reliable.

By age 3, Gideon would tune in to what was cool in toddler world, then drop the iPad in my lap and ask for certain games by their approximate description.

As it happens, Gideon was not in the majority. This summer, Calvert and her team will release the results of their study, which show that most of the time, children around age 32 months go with the character who is telling the truth, whether it's Elmo or DoDo—and quickly come to trust the one who's been more accurate when the children don't already know the answer. But Calvert says this merely suggests that toddlers have become even more savvy users of technology than we had imagined. She had been working off attachment theory and thought toddlers might value an emotional bond over the correct answer. But her guess is that something about tapping the screen, about getting feedback and being corrected in real time, is itself instructive and enables the toddlers to absorb information accurately, regardless of its source.

Calvert takes a balanced view of technology: she works in an office surrounded by hardcover books, and she sometimes edits her drafts with pen and paper. But she is very interested in how the iPad can reach children even before they're old enough to access these traditional media.

"People say we are experimenting with our children," she told me. "But from my perspective, it's already happened, and there's no way to turn it back. Children's lives are filled with media at younger and younger ages, and we need to take advantage of what these technologies have to offer. I'm not a Pollyanna. I'm pretty much a realist. I look at what kids are doing and try to figure out how to make the best of it."

Despite the participation of Elmo, Calvert's research is designed to answer a series of very responsible, high-minded questions: Can toddlers learn from iPads? Can they transfer what they learn to the real world? What effect does interactivity have on learning? What role do familiar characters play in children's learning from iPads? All worthy questions, and important, but also all considered entirely from an adult's point of view. The reason many kids' apps are grouped under "Education" in the iTunes store, I suspect, is to assuage parents' guilt (though I also suspect that in the long run, all those "educational" apps merely perpetuate our neurotic relationship with technology, by reinforcing the idea that they must be sorted vigilantly into "good" or "bad"). If small children had more input, many "Education" apps would logically fall under a category called "Kids" or "Kids' Games." And many more of the games would probably look something like the apps designed by a Swedish game studio named Toca Boca.

The founders, Emil Ovemar and Björn Jeffery, work for Bonnier, a Swedish media company. Ovemar, an interactive-design expert, describes himself as someone who never grew up. He is still interested in superheroes, Legos, and animated movies and says he would rather play stuck-on-an-island with his two kids and their cousins than talk to almost any adult. Jeffery is the company's strategist and front man; I first met him at the conference in California, where he was handing out little temporary tattoos of the Toca Boca logo, a mouth open and grinning, showing off rainbow-colored teeth.

In late 2010, Ovemar and Jeffery began working on a new digital project for Bonnier, and they came up with the idea of entering the app market for kids. Ovemar began by looking into the apps available at the time. Most of them were disappointingly "instructive," he found—"drag the butterfly into the net, that sort of thing. They were missing creativity and imagination." Hunting for inspiration, he came upon Frank and Theresa Caplan's 1973 book *The Power of Play,* a quote from which he later e-mailed to me:

What is it that often puts the B student ahead of the A student in adult life, especially in business and creative

professions? Certainly it is more than verbal skill. To create, one must have a sense of adventure and playfulness. One needs toughness to experiment and hazard the risk of failure. One has to be strong enough to start all over again if need be and alert enough to learn from whatever happens. One needs a strong ego to be propelled forward in one's drive toward an untried goal. Above all, one has to possess the ability to play!

Ovemar and Jeffery hunted down toy catalogs from as early as the 1950s, before the age of exploding brand tie-ins. They made a list of the blockbusters over the decades—the first Tonka trucks, the Frisbee, the Hula-Hoop, the Rubik's Cube. Then they made a list of what these toys had in common: None really involved winning or losing against an opponent. None were part of an effort to create a separate child world that adults were excluded from, and probably hostile toward; they were designed more for family fun. Also, they were not really meant to teach you something specific—they existed mostly in the service of having fun.

In 2011, the two developers launched Toca Tea Party. The game is not all that different from a real tea party. The iPad functions almost like a tea table without legs, and the kids have to invent the rest by, for example, seating their own plushies or dolls, one on each side, and then setting the theater in motion. First, choose one of three tablecloths. Then choose plates, cups, and treats. The treats are not what your mom would feed you. They are chocolate cakes, frosted doughnuts, cookies. It's very easy to spill the tea when you pour or take a sip, a feature added based on kids' suggestions during a test play (kids love spills, but spilling is something you can't do all that often at a real tea party, or you'll get yelled at). At the end, a sink filled with soapy suds appears, and you wash the dishes, which is also part of the fun, and then start again. That's it. The game is either very boring or terrifically exciting, depending on what you make of it. Ovemar and Jeffery knew that some parents wouldn't get it, but for kids, the game would be fun every time, because it's dependent entirely on imagination. Maybe today the stuffed bear will be naughty and do the spilling, while naked Barbie will pile her plate high with sweets. The child can take on the voice of a character or a scolding parent, or both. There's no winning, and there's no reward. Like a game of stuck-on-an-island, it can go on for five minutes or forever.

Soon after the release of Toca Tea Party, the pair introduced Toca Hair Salon, which is still to my mind the most fun game out there. The salon is no Fifth Avenue spa. It's a rundown-looking place with cracks in the wall. The aim is not beauty but subversion. Cutting off hair, like spilling, is on the list of things kids are not supposed to do. You choose one of the odd-looking people or creatures and have your way with its hair, trimming it or dyeing it or growing it out. The blow-dryer is genius; it achieves the same effect as Tadao Cern's Blow Job portraits, which depict people's faces getting wildly distorted by high winds. In August 2011, Toca Boca gave away Hair Salon for free for nearly two weeks. It was downloaded more than 1 million times in the first week, and the company took off. Today, many Toca Boca games show up on lists of the most popular education apps.

Are they educational? "That's the perspective of the parents," Jeffery told me at the back of the grand hall in Monterey. "Is running around on the lawn educational? Every part of a child's life can't be held up to that standard." As we talked, two girls were playing Toca Tea Party on the floor nearby. One had her stuffed dragon at a plate, and he was being especially naughty, grabbing all the chocolate cake and spilling everything. Her friend had taken a little Lego construction man and made him the good guy who ate neatly and helped do the dishes. Should they have been outside at the beach? Maybe, but the day would be long, and they could go outside later.

The more I talked with the developers, the more elusive and unhelpful the "Education" category seemed. (Is *Where the Wild Things Are* educational? Would you make your child read a textbook at bedtime? Do you watch only educational television? And why don't children deserve high-quality fun?) Buckleitner calls his conference Dust or Magic to teach app developers a more subtle concept than pedagogy. By *magic,* Buckleitner has in mind an app that makes children's fingers move and their eyes light up. By *dust,* he means something that was obviously (and ploddingly) designed by an adult. Some educational apps, I wouldn't wish on the naughtiest toddler. Take, for example, Counting With the Very Hungry Caterpillar, which turns a perfectly cute book into a tedious app that asks you to "please eat 1 piece of chocolate cake" so you can count to one.

Before the conference, Buckleitner had turned me on to Noodle Words, an app created by the California designer and children's-book writer Mark Schlichting. The app is explicitly educational. It teaches you about active verbs— *spin, sparkle, stretch.* It also happens to be fabulous. You tap a box, and a verb pops up and gets acted out by two insect friends who have the slapstick sensibility of the Three Stooges. If the word is *shake,* they shake until their eyeballs rattle. I tracked down Schlichting at the conference, and he turned out to be a little like Maurice Sendak—like many good children's writers, that is: ruled by id and not quite tamed into adulthood. The app, he told me, was inspired by a dream he'd had in which he saw the word *and* floating in the air and sticking to other words like a magnet. He woke up and thought, *What if words were toys?*

During the course of reporting this story, I downloaded dozens of apps and let my children test them out. They didn't much care whether the apps were marketed as educational or not, as long as they were fun. Without my prompting, Gideon fixated

on a game called LetterSchool, which teaches you how to write letters more effectively and with more imagination than any penmanship textbooks I've ever encountered. He loves the Toca Boca games, the Duck Duck Moose games, and random games like Bugs and Buttons. My older kids love The Numberlys, a dark fantasy creation of illustrators who have worked with Pixar that happens to teach the alphabet. And all my kids, including Gideon, play Cut the Rope a lot, which is not exclusively marketed as a kids' game. I could convince myself that the game is teaching them certain principles of physics—it's not easy to know the exact right place to slice the rope. But do I really need that extra convincing? I like playing the game; why shouldn't they?

Every new medium has, within a short time of its introduction, been condemned as a threat to young people. Pulp novels would destroy their morals, TV would wreck their eyesight, video games would make them violent. Each one has been accused of seducing kids into wasting time that would otherwise be spent learning about the presidents, playing with friends, or digging their toes into the sand. In our generation, the worries focus on kids' brainpower, about unused synapses withering as children stare at the screen. People fret about television and ADHD, although that concern is largely based on a single study that has been roundly criticized and doesn't jibe with anything we know about the disorder.

There are legitimate broader questions about how American children spend their time, but all you can do is keep them in mind as you decide what rules to set down for your own child. The statement from the American Academy of Pediatrics assumes a zero-sum game: an hour spent watching TV is an hour not spent with a parent. But parents know this is not how life works. There are enough hours in a day to go to school, play a game, and spend time with a parent, and generally these are different hours. Some people can get so drawn into screens that they want to do nothing else but play games. Experts say excessive video gaming is a real problem, but they debate whether it can be called an addiction and, if so, whether the term can be used for anything but a small portion of the population. If your child shows signs of having an addictive personality, you will probably know it. One of my kids is like that; I set stricter limits for him than for the others, and he seems to understand why.

In her excellent book *Screen Time,* the journalist Lisa Guernsey lays out a useful framework—what she calls the three C's—for thinking about media consumption: content, context, and your child. She poses a series of questions—Do you think the content is appropriate? Is screen time a "relatively small part of your child's interaction with you and the real world"?—and suggests tailoring your rules to the answers, child by child. One of the most interesting points Guernsey makes is about the importance of parents' attitudes toward media. If they treat screen time like junk food, or "like a magazine at the hair salon"—good for passing the time in a frivolous way but nothing more—then the child will fully absorb that attitude, and the neurosis will be passed to the next generation.

"The war is over. The natives won." So says Marc Prensky, the education and technology writer, who has the most extreme parenting philosophy of anyone I encountered in my reporting. Prensky's 7-year-old son has access to books, TV, Legos, Wii—and Prensky treats them all the same. He does not limit access to any of them. Sometimes his son plays with a new app for hours, but then, Prensky told me, he gets tired of it. He lets his son watch TV even when he personally thinks it's a "stupid waste." *SpongeBob SquarePants,* for example, seems like an annoying, pointless show, but Prensky says he used the relationship between SpongeBob and Patrick, his starfish sidekick, to teach his son a lesson about friendship. "We live in a screen age, and to say to a kid, 'I'd love for you to look at a book but I hate it when you look at the screen' is just bizarre. It reflects our own prejudices and comfort zone. It's nothing but fear of change, of being left out."

Prensky's worldview really stuck with me. Are books always, in every situation, inherently better than screens? My daughter, after all, often uses books as a way to avoid social interaction, while my son uses the Wii to bond with friends. I have to admit, I had the exact same experience with *SpongeBob.* For a long time I couldn't stand the show, until one day I got past the fact that the show was so loud and frenetic and paid more attention to the story line, and realized I too could use it to talk with my son about friendship. After I first interviewed Prensky, I decided to conduct an experiment. For six months, I would let my toddler live by the Prensky rules. I would put the iPad in the toy basket, along with the remote-control car and the Legos. Whenever he wanted to play with it, I would let him.

Gideon tested me the very first day. He saw the iPad in his space and asked if he could play. It was 8 a.m. and we had to get ready for school. I said yes. For 45 minutes he sat on a chair and played as I got him dressed, got his backpack ready, and failed to feed him breakfast. This was extremely annoying and obviously untenable. The week went on like this—Gideon grabbing the iPad for two-hour stretches, in the morning, after school, at bedtime. Then, after about 10 days, the iPad fell out of his rotation, just like every other toy does. He dropped it under the bed and never looked for it. It was completely forgotten for about six weeks.

Now he picks it up every once in a while, but not all that often. He has just started learning letters in school, so he's back to playing LetterSchool. A few weeks ago his older brother played with him, helping him get all the way through the uppercase and then lowercase letters. It did not seem beyond the range of possibility that if Norman Rockwell were alive, he would paint the two curly-haired boys bent over the screen, one small finger guiding a smaller one across, down, and across again to make, in their triumphant finale, the small *z.*

Critical Thinking

1. Does this article persuade you one way or the other about the value of touch screens in young children's lives? Why or why not?

2. What are some benefits for children from using touch screens? What are possible detrimental effects of too much technology time?

3. If children spend too much time with technology, what is lost from the rest of children's lives and experiences? As a future or current parent, teacher, or adult who may have some role in children's lives, how do your own memories of childhood affect your views of how children "should" spend their time?

Create Central

www.mhhe.com/createcentral

Internet References

American College of Pediatricians
http://www.acpeds.org

Study Finds Touch Screens Don't Help Toddlers Learn
http://www.clickondetroit.com/lifestyle/health/study-finds-touch-screens-dont-help-toddlers-learn/25882550

Touchscreens and Toddlers: The Research is Mostly Good News
http://national.deseretnews.com/article/341/Touchscreens-and-toddlers-The-research-is-mostly-good-news.html#O7DLLYieMMhJS5Cz.

http://national.deseretnews.com/article/341/Touchscreens-and-toddlers-The-research-is-mostly-good-news.html?pg=all

What You Need to Know about Babies, Toddlers, and Screen Time
http://www.npr.org/blogs/alltechconsidered/2013/10/29/228125739/what-to-know-about-babies-and-screen-time-kids-screens-electronics

HANNA ROSIN is a national correspondent for *The Atlantic.*

Article   Prepared by: Ellen N. Junn, *California State University, Dominguez Hills*

ADHD among Preschoolers

Identifying and treating attention-deficit hyperactivity disorder in very young children requires a different approach.

BRENDAN L. SMITH

Learning Outcomes

After reading this article, you will be able to:

- Prepare a presentation for parents and teachers on ADHD and controversies surrounding its incidence and treatment.

- Critique the different kinds of therapies for ADHD from medical to behavioral.

Preschoolers can be inattentive or hyperactive even on the best of days, so it can be difficult to accurately diagnose attention-deficit hyperactivity disorder. But a growing body of research has shown that early treatment can help struggling children and frazzled parents.

The diagnosis of young children with ADHD is "very contentious" since there is a blurry line between common developmental changes and symptoms of the mental disorder, says ADHD researcher Stephen Hinshaw, PhD, chair of the psychology department at the University of California at Berkeley. "The symptoms for ADHD are very ubiquitous and very age-relevant," he says. "It's hard to know if you're seeing the signs of a disorder or just the signs of a young kid."

Hinshaw and some other researchers believe ADHD can be reliably diagnosed in children as young as 3 after thorough evaluations. In one study of school-age children, mothers reported that symptoms of ADHD appeared at or before age 4 in two-thirds of the children (*Journal of Developmental & Behavioral Pediatrics,* Vol. 23, No. 1).

Researchers disagree about whether ADHD is overdiagnosed, which may lead to unnecessary medication of healthy children. There is a tendency to overdiagnose young children with ADHD because of a lack of understanding about normative development in toddlerhood and the early preschool years, says Susan Campbell, PhD, a psychology professor at the University of Pittsburgh who has researched ADHD for more than three decades. "The only reason to diagnose a young child is to access appropriate services to help the child and family," she says. "Sometimes the earlier the better."

Overall, more children of all ages are being diagnosed with ADHD since there is greater awareness of the disorder and improvements in treatment, says Russell Barkley, PhD, a psychologist and professor at the Medical University of South Carolina who studies ADHD. Some inaccurate media reports have fueled a public misperception that ADHD is overdiagnosed, Barkley says. But only 20 percent of children with ADHD received any treatment in the 1960s and '70s, compared with roughly 70 percent to 80 percent today, he says.

"The rise in diagnosis is not bad news. It's good news," Barkley says. "Frankly, we were doing an awful job 20 or 30 years ago."

Medication Issues

Often the first line of treatment for ADHD in school-age children is medication with stimulants, which have been found to be generally safe and effective. But drugs have less positive results for preschoolers. "I'm very opposed to the use of medication with young children because we don't really know the implications for brain development," Campbell says.

Approximately 4 million children—or 8 percent of all minors in the United States—have been diagnosed with ADHD, and more than half of them take prescription drugs. Methylphenidate hydrochloride (Ritalin) is the most commonly prescribed medication, but its use in children under 6 years old hasn't been approved by the Food and Drug

Administration, which cites a lack of research for this age group. As a result, doctors are prescribing methylphenidate off label for preschoolers with ADHD.

The most comprehensive study on medication of preschoolers with ADHD showed mixed results for 3- to 5-year-old children. Funded by the National Institute of Mental Health, the multisite Preschool ADHD Treatment Study enrolled 303 preschoolers and their parents in a 10-week behavioral therapy course. Children with severe symptoms who didn't respond to therapy were given low doses of methylphenidate or a placebo. The medicated children showed a marked reduction in symptoms compared with the placebo group, according to the study results published in 2006.

"It's crazy to me that we use the same criteria for a 3-year-old as we do for a 35-year-old."

—George Dupaul, Lehigh University

More troublesome, though, was the fact that almost a third of parents reported that their medicated children experienced moderate to severe side effects, including weight loss, insomnia, loss of appetite, emotional outbursts, and anxiety. Eleven percent of the preschoolers dropped out of the study because of their reactions to methylphenidate. During the study, the medicated children also grew about half an inch less in height and weighed about three pounds less than expected based on average growth rates (*Journal of the American Academy of Child & Adolescent Psychiatry,* Vol. 45, No. 11).

"The bottom line to me is for this age group, I don't believe stimulant medication is a first-line treatment," says George DuPaul, PhD, a professor of school psychology at Lehigh University who studies ADHD.

Embracing Other Methods

Parental training and school-based interventions can be effective in treating preschoolers with ADHD, DuPaul says. His book, "Young Children With ADHD: Early Identification and Intervention" (APA, 2011), co-written with Lehigh University colleague Lee Kern, PhD, describes one of their studies of nondrug interventions with 135 preschoolers with ADHD.

Parents were given 20 training sessions on behavior problems, basic math and language skills, and child safety since children with ADHD often suffer accidental injuries because of their hyperactivity and impulsivity. One group of children also received individual assessments in the home and at preschool

or day care. Both groups of children showed marked improvements in ADHD symptoms, although there was no significant advantage for the children with individual assessments (*School Psychology Review,* Vol. 36, No. 2). One limitation of the study was the lack of a control group because of ethical considerations about providing no treatment.

While older children can sometimes be taught to manage their ADHD symptoms, the training of preschool children has been more difficult, in part because cognitive-behavioral therapy doesn't work, Barkley says. Preschoolers with ADHD are delayed in communication skills, and language hasn't been internalized yet, so they can't use mental instructions or self-monitoring to change their behavior.

"It failed so we abandoned that after multiple studies found it had little or no influence," Barkley says.

But some behavioral management techniques are effective, including a token reward system and praise to provide extra motivation for preschoolers with ADHD, Barkley says. Teachers can seat children with ADHD near the teacher's desk and provide detailed explanations of class rules and disciplinary procedures, such as time-out or loss of tokens. Frequent class breaks and shorter work assignments also can help maintain children's attention and reduce outbursts.

Symptoms of ADHD can be exacerbated in children by impulsive parents who also have ADHD, Campbell says. Parents who are quick to anger and who frequently use physical punishment also can be detrimental. "There is going to be an interaction between the genetic risk and the support or lack of parental support the child has," she says.

Looking Ahead

As the diagnosis of preschoolers with ADHD has increased, so have questions about the lack of age-specific symptoms in the Diagnostic and Statistical Manual of Mental Disorders, Fourth Edition. "It's crazy to me that we use the same criteria for a 3-year-old as we do for a 35-year-old," DuPaul says.

Scheduled for publication in 2013, the fifth DSM edition should require a greater number of symptoms for diagnosing young children with ADHD and more age-specific symptoms instead of generic descriptions such as fidgeting or running around and climbing, DuPaul says. "How do we apply that to a 17-year-old kid in a high school classroom?" he says. "They don't run about and climb on things."

Despite the risks, early identification and treatment of ADHD can provide substantial benefits for children and their families, Campbell says. "It can help so that when the child gets to the first grade, he isn't the only child no one else wants to play with and no teachers want in their class," she says.

Critical Thinking

1. How can you tell if a child has ADHD or is just being a normal preschooler?

2. Do you think ADHD is overdiagnosed? If so, why, and if not, why not?

3. Are there ways to treat ADHD other than medicine? What might be better versus poorer choices?

Create Central

www.mhhe.com/createcentral

Internet References

Children and Adults with ADHD.org
http://www.chadd.org/understanding-adhd.aspx

National Institute of Mental Health.org
http://www.nimh.nih.gov/health/topics/attention-deficit-hyperactivity-disorder-adhd/index.shtml

WebMD.org
http://www.webmd.com/add-adhd

Article   Prepared by: Chris J. Boyatzis, *Bucknell University*

1 in 68 Children Now Has a Diagnosis of Autism Spectrum Disorder. Why?

With rates of the disorder yet again rising according to new CDC numbers, a look at how doctors are diagnosing autism spectrum disorder in children, and what might be done better.

ENRICO GNAULATI

Learning Outcomes

After reading this article, you will be able to:

- Understand what it means for a child to receive a false-positive diagnosis and how this diagnosis will influence the child throughout his or her lifetime.

- Create a list of possible reasons for why children are being diagnosed with false-positives. Understand how a slow-to-mature toddler and a would-be-mildly-autistic toddler share many things in common.

- Develop an understanding of what it means to have a "theory of mind" and what it would be like to work with someone who may not have one.

Rates of autism spectrum disorder (ASD) are not creeping up so much as leaping up. New numbers just released by the Centers for Disease Control and Prevention reveal that one in 68 children now has a diagnosis of ASD—a 30 percent increase in just two years. In 2002, about one in 150 children was considered autistic, and in 1991, the figure was one in 500.

The staggering increase in cases of ASD should raise more suspicion in the medical community about its misdiagnosis and overdiagnosis than it does. Promoting early screening for autism is imperative. But, is it possible that the younger in age a child is when professionals screen for ASD—especially its milder cases—the greater the risk that a slow-to-mature child will be misperceived as autistic, thus driving the numbers up?

The science stacks up in favor of catching and treating ASD earlier because it leads to better outcomes. Dr. Laura Schreibman, who directs the Autism Intervention Research Program at the University of California, San Diego, embodies the perspective of most experts when she says, "Psychologists need to advise parents that the 'wait-and-see' approach is not appropriate when ASD is expected. Delaying a diagnosis can mean giving up significant gains of intervention that have been demonstrated before age six."

The younger in age we assess for problems, the greater the potential a slow-to-mature kid will be given a false diagnosis.

There is a universal push to screen for ASD at as young an age as possible and growing confidence that the early signs are clear and convincing. Dr. Jose Cordero, the founding director of the National Center on Birth Defects and Developmental Disabilities conveys this fervor.

"For healthcare providers, we have a message that's pretty direct about ASD. And the message is: The 4-year-old with autism was once a 3-year-old with autism, which was once a 2-year-old with autism."

Many researchers are now on the hunt for atypical behaviors cropping up in infancy that could be telltale signs of ASD. For instance, a team of experts led by Dr. Karen Pierce at the Autism Center of Excellence at the University of California, San Diego, has used eye-tracking technology to determine that infants as young as 14 months who later were diagnosed as autistic showed a preference for looking at movies of geometric shapes over movies of children dancing and doing yoga. This predilection for being engaged by objects rather than "social" images is thought to be a marker for autism.

Even the quality of infants' crying has come under scientific scrutiny as a possible sign of the disorder. Dr. Stephen Sheinkopf and some colleagues at Brown University compared the cries of a group of babies at risk for autism (due to having an autistic sibling) to typically developing babies using cutting-edge acoustic technology. They discovered that the at-risk babies emit higher-pitched cries that are "low in voicing," which is a term for cries that are sharper and reflect tense vocal chords. Dr. Sheinkopf, however, cautioned parents against over-scrutinizing their babies' cries since the distinctions were picked up by sophisticated acoustic technology, not by careful human listening.

"We definitely don't want parents to be anxiously listening to their babies' cries. It's unclear if the human ear is sensitive enough to detect this."

What gets lost in the debate is an awareness of how the younger in age we assess for problems, the greater the potential a slow-to-mature kid will be given a false diagnosis. In fact, as we venture into more tender years to screen for autism, we need to be reminded that the period of greatest diagnostic uncertainty is probably toddlerhood. A 2007 study out of the University of North Carolina at Chapel Hill found that over 30 percent of children diagnosed as autistic at age two no longer fit the diagnosis at age four. Since ASD is still generally considered to be a life-long neuropsychiatric condition that is not shed as childhood unfolds, we have to wonder if a large percentage of toddlers get a diagnosis that is of questionable applicability in the first place.

Expanding autistic phenomena to include picky eating and tantrums can create more befuddlement when applied to small children.

The parallels between a slow-to-mature toddler and a would-be-mildly autistic one are so striking that the prospect of a false diagnosis is great. Let's start with late talkers. Almost one in five 2-year-olds are late talkers. They fall below the expected 50-word expressive vocabulary threshold and appear incapable of stringing together two- and three-word phrases.

Data out of the famed Yale Study Center have demonstrated that toddlers with delayed language development are almost identical to their autistic spectrum disordered counterparts in their use of eye contact to gauge social interactions, the range of sounds and words they produce, and the emotional give-and-take they are capable of. Many tots are in an ASD red-zone who simply don't meet standard benchmarks for how quickly language should be acquired and social interactions mastered.

Expanding autistic phenomena to include picky eating and tantrums can create more befuddlement when applied to small children. Several years ago, a study published in the *Journal of the American Dietetic Association* tracking over 3,000 families found that 50 percent of toddlers are considered picky eaters

by their caregivers. The percentage of young children in the U.S. who are picky eaters and have poor appetites is so high that experts writing in the journal *Pediatrics* in 2007 remarked, ". . . it could reasonably be said that eating-behavior problems are a normal feature of toddler life."

Tantrums also are surprisingly frequent and intense during the toddler years. Dr. Gina Mireault, a behavioral scientist at Johnson State College in Vermont, studied kids from three separate local preschools. She discerned that toddlers tantrumed, on average, once every few days. Almost a third of the parents surveyed experienced their offsprings' tantrums as distressing or disturbing.

Too much isolated play, manipulating objects in concrete ways, can also elicit autism concerns. But, relative to young girls, young boys are slower to gravitate toward pretend play that is socially oriented. In a French study of preschoolers' outdoor nursery play published in *PLoS One* in 2011, the lead investigator Stéphanie Barbu concluded, ". . . preschool boys played alone more frequently than preschool girls. This difference was especially marked at 3–4 years."

This is significant, since there is a strong movement to detect autistic spectrum disorder earlier, with the median age of diagnosis now falling between ages 3 and 4. Boys' more solitary style of play during these tender years, without gender-informed observation, can make them appear disordered, rather than different.

Parents and educators shouldn't assume the worst when male toddlers play alone. Many little boys are satisfied engaging in solitary play, or playing quietly alongside someone else, lining up toy trains, stacking blocks, or pursuing any range of sensorimotor activities, more mesmerized by objects than fellow flesh-and-blood kids. According to Dr. Barbu, it's not until about age four or five that boys are involved in associative play to the same extent as girls. That's the kind of play where there's verbal interaction, and give-and-take exchanges of toys and ideas—or, non-autistic-like play.

One in 42 boys is now affected by autism, a ratio that calls into question whether boys' differences get abnormalized.

It is commonly believed that autism spectrum kids lack a "theory of mind." I'll provide a layman's definition of this term first, by a layman. Josh Clark, a senior writer at HowStuffWorks.com, provides a fine, no-frills definition: "It refers to a person's ability to create theories about others' minds—what they may be thinking, how they may be feeling, what they may do next. We are able to make these assumptions easily, without even recognizing that we are doing something fundamentally amazing."

It's this very ability to "mind read," or understand that others have thoughts, feelings, and intentions different from our own, and use this feedback to be socially tuned in, that is considered a hallmark sign of autism. However, between the ages of three and four the average girl is roughly twice as capable as the average boy at reading minds, and the gap doesn't markedly close until they reach about age five or older.

That was the conclusion arrived at by Sue Walker, a professor at Queensland University of Technology, Brisbane, Australia, in her 2005 *Journal of Genetic Psychology* study looking at gender differences in "theory of mind" development in groups of preschoolers. Being mindful of boys' less mindfulness during the early toddler years needs to be considered to prevent an inappropriate diagnosis of mild ASD.

Faulty fine-motor skills are often seen as part of an autistic profile. Yet, preschool aged boys have been shown to lag behind their female classmates in this domain. A classic study of preschoolers by Drs. Allen Burton and Michael Dancisak out of the University of Minnesota discovered that females in the 3- to 5-year-old range significantly outperform boys at this age in their acquisition of the "tripod" pencil grip. The so-called "tripod" pencil grip, where the thumb is used to stabilize a pencil pressed firmly against the third and forth digits, with the wrist slightly extended, is generally considered by teachers and occupational therapists as the most effective display of fine-motor dexterity when it comes to writing and drawing.

Finger pointing is one of the fundamental ways that young children express and share their interests, as well as manifest curiosity in the outside world. It's scant use is seen as a warning sign of autism. However, researchers at the University of Sussex in England conducted tests at monthly intervals on 8-month-old infants as they emerged into toddlerhood and found that girls learn to point earlier than boys.

Which is all to say that young boys' social-communication approaches, play styles, and pace of fine-motor development leave them living closer to the autistic spectrum than girls. This confound may explain why boys are five times more likely than girls to be ascribed the diagnosis. One in 42 boys are now affected by autism, a ratio that calls into question whether boys' different pace at acquiring social, emotional, and fine-motor skills gets abnormalized.

It's important to not overstate the case. The possibility that a slow-to-mature toddler will be confused as a moderately or severely autistic is slim. On the extreme end, autism is, more often than not, a conspicuous, lifelong, disabling neurological condition.

Roy Richard Grinker, in his acclaimed book *Unstrange Minds,* masterfully documents the challenges he faced raising Isabel, his daughter with pronounced autism. At age two, she only made passing eye contact, rarely initiated interactions, and had trouble responding to her name in a consistent fashion.

Her play often took the form of rote activities such as drawing the same picture repeatedly or rewinding a DVD to watch identical film clips over and over. Unless awakened each morning with the same greeting, "Get up! Get up!," Isabel became quite agitated. She also tended to be very literal and concrete in her language comprehension: expressions like "I'm so tired I could die" left her apprehensive about actual death. By age five, Isabel remained almost completely nonverbal.

When the signs of autism spectrum disorder are indisputable, as in Isabel's case, early detection and intervention are crucial to bolster verbal communication and social skills. The brain is simply more malleable when children are young. Isabel's story in *Unstrange Minds* is a heroic testament to the strides a child can make when afforded the right interventions at the right time.

Diagnostic conundrums enter the picture when we frame autism as a spectrum disorder (as it is now officially designated in the newly minted *Diagnostic and Statistical Manual 5th Edition,* the psychiatric handbook used to diagnose it) and try to draw a bold line between a slow-to-mature toddler and one on the mild end of the spectrum. What is a doctor to make of a chatty, intellectually advanced, three-year-old patient presenting with a hodgepodge of issues, such as poor eye contact, clumsiness, difficulties transitioning, overactivity or underactivity, tantruming, picky eating, quirky interests, and social awkwardness? Does this presentation indicate mild ASD? Or, does it speak to a combination of off-beat developmental events that result in a toddler experiencing transitory stress, who is otherwise normal, in the broad sense?

We entrust our children to professionals like psychiatrists and psychologists to tease apart the delicate distinctions between mild ASD and a slower pace of development. The trained professionals are supposed to know best. But, do they? A pediatrician is the professional who is most likely to be consulted when a child is suspected of having ASD. While most pediatricians are adequately educated and trained to assess for ASD, a good many of them aren't. How many pediatricians who actually call themselves pediatricians have specialized training in pediatric medicine and/or pediatric mental health?

Several years ago, Gary L. Freed, MD, chief of the Division of General Pediatrics at the University of Michigan, initiated a survey of physicians listed as pediatricians on state licensure files in eight states across the United States: Ohio, Wisconsin, Texas, Mississippi, Massachusetts, Maryland, Oregon, and Arizona. According to the survey, 39 percent of state-identified pediatricians hadn't completed a residency in pediatrics. And even for those who had, their training in pediatric mental health was minimal.

Currently, the American Academy of Pediatrics estimates that less than a quarter of pediatricians around the country have specialized training in child mental health beyond what they receive in a general pediatric residency. The latest data

1 in 68 Children Now Has a Diagnosis of Autism Spectrum Disorder. Why? by Enrico Gnaulati

179

examining pediatricians who have launched themselves into practice reveals that 62 percent of them feel that mental health issues were not adequately covered in medical school. These figures hardly inspire widespread confidence as regards relying on pediatricians to accurately diagnose ASD.

In a 2010 study, 45 percent of graduate students in child psychology had little exposure to coursework in child/adolescent lifespan development.

This brings me to my own cherished profession: child psychology. What does survey data tell us about the current training of child psychologists that speaks directly to their ability to separate out abnormalcy from normalcy?

Poring over the numbers of a 2010 study out of the University of Hartford in Connecticut, I discovered that 45 percent of graduate students in child psychology had either no exposure to or had just an introductory-level exposure to coursework in child/adolescent lifespan development. It is in these classes that emerging child psychologists learn about what is developmentally normal to expect in children.

It would appear that the education and training of a sizable percentage of pediatricians and child psychologists leaves them ill-equipped to tease apart the fine distinction between mild ASD and behaviors that fall within the broad swath of normal childhood development.

When the uptick in ASD numbers was made public by the Centers for Disease Control and Prevention the week before last, Dr. Marshalyn Yeargin-Allsopp, chief of their Developmental Disabilities Branch, said in a press release, "The most important thing for parents to do is to act early when there is a concern about a child's development. If you have a concern about how your child plays, learns, speaks, acts, or moves, take action. Don't wait."

On the one hand, a clarion call of this nature is the push the parents of a child with an unmistakable case of moderate-to-severe ASD (like Isabel above) absolutely need. On the other hand, Dr. Yeagin-Alsopp's remark seems to stoke the very anxiety that haunts the average parent of a slow-to-mature, but otherwise normal kid, edging that parent to transport the kid to a doctor, where there's a good chance that doctor will lack a solid knowledge-template as to what constitutes normal.

Early screening and treatment for ASD must remain a top public health priority, but the numbers make it clear that professionals would benefit from familiarizing and re-familiarizing themselves with the broad range of what is considered normal early childhood development, and with how young boys and girls differ in behaviors that resemble autistic phenomena. Otherwise, the ASD numbers will rise, yet again, with a pool of slow-to-mature children being falsely diagnosed.

Critical Thinking

1. What are some of the serious benefits and drawbacks of early screening for autism in children? Do you think that one of the options outweighs the other?

2. What do you think should be done with the information that "over 30 percent of children diagnosed as autistic at age two no longer fit the diagnosis at age four"? What do you believe is happening to these children?

3. How does gender play a role in the diagnosing of autism? Do you believe that gender differences should be accounted for when conducting early screenings?

Create Central

www.mhhe.com/createcentral

Internet References

American Speech-Language-Hearing Association
http://www.asha.org/public/speech/disorders/autism

AutismSpeaks.org
http://www.autismspeaks.org/family-services/tool-kits/100-day-kit/ten-things-every-child-autism-wishes-you-knew

HelpGuide.org
http://www.helpguide.org/mental/autism_help.htm

KidsHealth.org
http://kidshealth.org/kid/health_problems/brain/autism.html

National Autistic Society.uk
http://www.autism.org.uk/about-autism/all-about-diagnosis/diagnosis-the-process-for-children.aspx

Article   Prepared by: Chris J. Boyatzis, *Bucknell University*

Caring for Chronically Ill Kids

Many parents are struggling to manage their children's care. Here's why.

ELIZABETH LEIS-NEWMAN

Learning Outcomes

After reading this article, you will be able to:

- Based on the research, advise pediatricians on how to increase chronically ill children's adherence to treatment.

- Design an educational program to help children and parents stick to their treatment programs.

- Understand the ways in which the entire family is impacted by the child's chronic illness.

It's the news no parent wants to hear: Your child has been diagnosed with a chronic, potentially life-threatening illness.

Luckily, treatments for diseases like asthma, diabetes and cystic fibrosis have made these diseases manageable. But the latest research on parents' involvement in children's chronic illnesses indicates that parents may be struggling to find a balance between letting their children take responsibility and letting go too soon, which puts their children at risk for medical complications that can lead to hospitalization.

When this under-supervision occurs, it can be for a number of reasons, psychologists say: a lack of understanding about a disease, the potential for the primary caretaker to become depressed and ill-equipped and, in later years, a parent who is simply worn out by teenage rebellion. Parents, it seems, may be giving over the child's care to the child too early, says Suzanne Bennett Johnson, PhD, a Florida State University School of Medicine professor and APA's 2012 president.

"We do have some parents who stymie the child by exerting too much control, but there's a clinician's fallacy about the over-involved parent," she says.

What parents and health-care providers need, she and others say, are more realistic expectations of children's abilities to manage such illnesses.

Lack of Understanding

Psychologists and physicians can begin to address this problem by making sure the parent and child understand the severity of the illness and the potentially fatal impact of not treating it thoroughly, says Johnson.

That can be difficult when the child's symptoms are not consistently present, says Kristin A. Riekert, PhD, who co-directs the Johns Hopkins Adherence Research Center. In a 2003 study in *Pediatrics* (Vol. 111, No. 3), Riekert and other researchers at Johns Hopkins University looked at asthmatic children in Baltimore elementary schools to see which parents were giving the physician-prescribed asthma medication. They found that poor communication between a physician and the primary caregiver led to the child's underuse of asthma medicines. In addition, they found that caregiver beliefs about asthma management were the most significant factor in whether the child's medication protocol was followed. In addition, a lack of time during a meeting with a physician was often cited as the main reason for poor communication— indicating physicians need to spend more time explaining the disease and the treatment.

Health-care providers also need to remember that with diseases like asthma, the parent wants to see a difference when a child uses a medication, Riekert says. A child may skip using his inhaler for a few days and appear fine, for example, and the parent may believe that he or she doesn't really need it. "It's not uncommon to see a reaction of 'no symptoms, no asthma,' among inner-city families," Riekert says.

This dynamic also can be true of epilepsy. Avani Modi, PhD, assistant professor of pediatrics at Cincinnati Children's Hospital Medical Center, is conducting a five-year study funded by the National Institutes of Health that examines adherence to anti-epileptic medications for children with new-onset epilepsy. She says some parents may fail to give the child his or her medications on a day-to-day basis, but then administer the medication each day right before seeing the child's physician—the phenomenon known as white-coat compliance.

"This can be dangerous with epilepsy as the physician measures the drug levels every time the child goes in [for a clinic visit]," says Modi. "If the parent has just started giving the medication, it may not be indicative of what is going on most of the time and clinical decisions may be made on this false level."

So far, her data indicate that roughly 40 percent of children newly diagnosed with epilepsy adhere almost religiously to the medication protocol, with 13 percent completely dropping off and the other 47 percent taking medications only some of the time. The only medical/sociodemographic factor that correlates with adherence is higher socioeconomic status—nothing else, including the epilepsy type or medication, matters.

Adolescent Turmoil

No matter which chronic illness a child has, adherence falls off around adolescence, researchers say. Teenagers yearn for privacy, and resent their parents asking them to keep their bedroom or bathroom doors open in case of a medical emergency. "There is growing evidence that the patient, family and healthcare team need to anticipate, in a collaborative manner, how care will be handled during adolescence," says Anne E. Kazak, PhD, a professor of pediatrics in the University of Pennsylvania School of Medicine. "At the end of adolescence, after all, most teens will be more autonomous in general as they enter early adulthood."

Plus, after what can be as long as a decade of dealing with a child's chronic illness, parents may be tempted to turn over the medical management once the child hits 13.

"That may not be developmentally appropriate," Modi says. While adolescents are old enough to understand a disease, she says, often they do not see the consequences of ignoring the treatments.

"With a disease like CF, an hour a day of medication and therapy takes them away from their social activities, from their friends, from their clubs. It's not malicious, but they forget to keep up and the consequences can be serious," she says.

Parents may think they need to lay off nagging their teens to take along their insulin to a friend's house or packing their inhaler before a day out. Riekert remembers a teenage CF patient who went on at length about how much he hated his parents nagging him. When she asked what would help him manage his CF, he grumbled, and said, "for them to bug me."

"It can be accepted as a necessary evil," Riekert says.

A parent simply being in the same room as their child during CF treatment raises compliance, says Alexandra Quittner, PhD, a psychology professor at the University of Miami.

"Parents and medical teams don't understand that the parent doesn't have to set up the treatment," she says. "We need to remind the parent how important their presence is. It's like a child sitting at the kitchen table doing his homework—he is more likely to do it if the parent is there."

What else improves adherence among teens? More time with mom and dad, according to a 2006 study by Modi and Quittner published in the *Journal of Pediatric Psychology* (Vol. 31, No. 8). In the study, they asked adolescents about barriers to adherence and what would motivate them to be more compliant.

"We have been very surprised—often when a child is asked what he or she would like to receive as a reward, it's a special outing with his or her mother or father," Quittner says. "It's important to spend that time together."

Modi encourages parents to think of their child managing his illness as a process akin to learning how to drive.

"There needs to be a learner's permit," she says. "At some point, you let go, but there needs to be a bridge to the child managing his or her medication. We work with parents on that so by the time the child is 17 or 18, they can relinquish control."

Depression and Anxiety

One of the more common challenges parents face when managing the care of their chronically ill children is that they simply may not have the ability to cope. "Generally, the research shows that when moms are depressed, adherence will go down," Johnson says.

New insight on that problem is coming from the first large-scale international study to evaluate levels of depression and anxiety among children with cystic fibrosis and their parents.

The study evaluated nearly 1,000 mothers and 182 fathers.

"What we are seeing is that 30 percent of [mothers] meet the clinical criteria for depression . . . double the rate of a regular sample," says Quittner, principal investigator for the study, known as the TIDES International Depression/Anxiety Epidemiological Study.

The study also found that more than 55 percent of the children's primary caregivers were anxious. These parents feel isolated and stressed by such challenges as obtaining insurance when a child has a pre-existing condition and the financial strain of co-payments for doctors' visits and medications.

In particular, says Quittner, "mothers often don't get enough support from their spouse and they end up handling the load."

The preliminary results of her study indicate that health-care providers need to spend more time evaluating depression and anxiety. "We are going to recommend annual screenings of both children with CF and their parental caregivers for anxiety and depression, and recommend paths for intervention," Quittner says.

Guiding these parents toward treatment will likely improve their child's health.

The other good news for struggling parents is that the difficult years of a child's illness can make the family stronger, Johnson says. A 2006 study in the *Journal of Pediatric Psychology* (Vol. 31, No. 4) by researchers Lamia P. Barakat, PhD, Melissa A. Alderfer, PhD, and Kazak indicated that adolescent cancer survivors and their mothers reported at least one positive outcome stemming from the illness, with 86 percent of mothers saying that cancer "had a positive impact on how they think about their lives."

"There's a tendency to assume that a chronic illness will be a negative experience for the family," Johnson says. "While it is stressful, families are quite resilient, and psychologists should emphasize that."

It's also important for health-care providers to be sympathetic to parents. Even when efforts fall short, parents are dedicating a major chunk of their lives to managing their child's illness, says Kazak. "Most families are doing the best they can," she says.

Critical Thinking

1. Do most children with chronic illness take their medicines? In what ways do parents contribute for better or worse to helping their children's to their treatment programs?

2. How does a child's age and developmental stage influence their adherence to a treatment program for a chronic illness?

Create Central

www.mhhe.com/createcentral

Internet References

American Psychological Association.org
http://www.apa.org/monitor/2011/03/ill-children.aspx

Kids Health.org
http://kidshealth.org/parent/system/ill/seriously_ill.html

National Association of School Psychologists.org
http://www.nasponline.org/publications/cq/36/1/families.aspx

Psych Central.com
http://psychcentral.com/news/2013/09/20/parenting-chronically-ill-kids-can-stress-entire-family/59730.html

Article   Prepared by: Ellen Junn, *California State University, Dominguez Hills*

The Human Child's Nature Orientation

PATRICK C. LEE

Learning Outcomes

After reading this article, you will be able to:

- Advocate for the implementation of programs and practices that give children first-hand experience with nature.

- Explain how children may have a fundamentally and developmentally important connection with nature.

- Reflect on the different psychological benefits for children that come from owning a pet in childhood.

The purpose of this article is to explore the hypothesis that the human child has a basic and developmentally significant orientation toward nature. To frame the discussion, two points should be made clear at the outset. First, the child's nature orientation is not proposed as a competitive alternative to what might be called a "human orientation." Quite the contrary, it is understood, on both evolutionary and developmental grounds, to be fundamental to the child's *humanization* process. Second, the term *nature* is used here in an inclusive and intuitively recognizable sense, referring to animals, pets, plant life, parks, streams, woodlots, irrigation ditches, mud, sand, overgrown and abandoned city lots, and so on.

Unfortunately for the position taken here, the models and/or theories that have most deeply characterized child studies over the years share a strongly anthropocentric worldview. These include, among others, traditional behaviorism and learning theory, social learning theory, various psychoanalytic approaches, formal structuralist (e.g., Chomsky) and/or constructivist approaches (e.g., Piaget, Kohlberg), Vygotsky's social constructivism, Bronfenbrenner's misleadingly labeled "ecological" model, and—in its chosen emphasis—attachment theory. What these accounts share in common is a view of child development as overwhelmingly determined by the forces of human society, culture, and history. Explicit attention to the child's experience of nature is much more the exception than the rule.

But this imbalance is correctible. In fact, one of the conventional approaches, constructivism, has recently been modified by Peter Kahn to explore the child's nature orientation (Kahn, 1997, 1999, 2002, 2006). There are also a small number of studies grounded in attachment theory that examine the attachment value of children's pets (e.g., Rost & Hartmann, 1994; Triebenbacher, 1998). Analogously, Bronfenbrenner's "ecological" approach could easily be extended to nonhuman settings such as those listed above: parkland, nature trails, neighborhood woodlots, and the like.

This article is not the first to point out the field's self-limiting anthropocentric bias. Others who have explicitly expressed a need for a complementary ecological and/or evolutionary orientation include Kaplan and Kaplan (1989, pp. 198, 203), Melson (2000, p. 376; 2001, pp. 4–5, 7–21, 188 ff.), Heerwagen and Orians (2002, pp. 29, 33, 57), Bjorklund (1997), Simpson and Belsky (2008, p. 150), Kahn (1997, p. 54; 1999, p. 87), Mithen (1996, pp. 61–71), and Serpell (1999).

Why the recent stirring of interest in the child and nature? The field's concern is probably a subset of the larger society's concern about environmental issues. Since 1960, the human population of Earth has more than doubled, and in approximately the same time frame, our footprint on the planet—that is, our use of water, arable land, and fossil fuel—has more than *tripled* (Harrison & Pearce, 2000, pp. 12–14; Hunter, 2000, pp. 12–13, 37). An important part of reducing our footprint is raising and educating children who themselves will have the awareness, knowledge, and will to reduce it further. For the field, this is arguably one of the most critical issues of the 21st century.

This article pursues three interwoven objectives: (a) to make a case for the developmental significance of the child's nature orientation; (b) to show that this orientation does not threaten, but rather complements, enriches, extends, and interacts with the standard anthropocentric view of the child; and (c) to briefly review empirical findings that have a good fit with the nature-orientation hypothesis. I start by laying out an evolutionary framework for the adaptive significance of the human child's nature orientation, then proceed to the developmental case.

Evolutionary Background of the Child's Nature Orientation

There are two major hypotheses that posit humanity's interaction with animals as a central driving force in human evolution: sociobiologist E. O. Wilson's "biophilia" (1984) and paleoanthropologist Pat Shipman's "animal connection" (2010). Wilson argues that the tendency to orient toward other life forms—observing their behavior, figuring out when and how to approach or avoid them, and so on—would have made such a contribution to our species' fitness during evolution that it would have spread throughout the human gene pool. In fact, the plausibility of Wilson's hypothesis has encouraged several child developmentalists to adopt a modified version of biophilia—one that incorporates both innate and learned features—as a heuristic starting point to their research on the child–nature relationship (cf. Kahn, 1999, p. 34; Melson, 2000, p. 375; Kellert, 2002, p. 129).

As far as it goes, Wilson's position is compatible with Shipman's, but Shipman takes the matter a lot further. She argues that humanity's connection to animals is the "underlying link" (2010, p. 519) among the three well-known adaptive strategies that, taken together, distinguish humanity from all other species: complex use and production of tools, symbolic behavior (language, art, ritual, etc.), and domestication of plants and animals. In her view, the "animal connection" is so fundamental to the human type that it at least qualifies as a fourth diagnostic indicator of our species and may even be our foundational adaptive strategy. In this scenario, the other three strategies (tools, symbols, and domestication) would serve as particular expressions of, and vehicles for, the animal connection.

Put briefly and concretely, Shipman's position is that throughout our evolution, the human line has been preoccupied with animals. We obsessively observe them; use tools to scavenge them, hunt them, and process their carcasses; symbolically merge with them in myth and ritual; compile and communicate information about them; draw, carve, and sculpt representations of them; and domesticate them into "living tools." We also reciprocally exchange adaptations with them—we select them for human-friendly features (e.g., domesticability), even as they select us for animal-friendly features, such as the ability to tolerate animal-transmitted diseases (e.g., mumps, measles, the common cold). Finally, we bring them as companions into our families and homes.

In other words, over evolutionary time, the *humanization* of our species has involved sustained, close, and progressive interaction with animals and their habitats. Our children have been right at the center of all this, spontaneously, routinely, and unavoidably participating in the animal connection. By Shipman's account, this connection would be as typical and defining of human childhood as is acquiring language and drawing pictures (symbolic behavior), playing rule-bound games (ritual), digging holes with sticks and pulling wagons (tool use), and keeping pets (domestication).

Wilson's and Shipman's hypotheses about humanity's *evolutionary* background generate several questions regarding the human child's *developmental* foreground. For example, is there good evidence for the child's having a special orientation toward animals and other features of nature (e.g., pets, mud play, etc.)? If so, does this orientation undergo qualitative change with age? Does the child's nature orientation potentiate or interact with other aspects of the developmental process, such as linguistic, cognitive, moral, or affective development? Does the child's human support system facilitate or obstruct the child's nature orientation? Do children with disabilities benefit from interaction with animals? And so on.

Is There Evidence of a Special Child–Nature Relationship?

Despite its understandably anthropocentric bias, the large literature on early language and affect offers an occasional study indicating that the young child is precociously oriented toward nature. Nelson (1973, pp. 32–33), for example, found that seven animal names (e.g., *cow, duck, horse,* etc.) are commonly included in toddlers' first 50 words and that toddlers use the terms *dog* and *cat* more than any other words except *mommy* and *daddy*. Related to this point, Serpell (1999, pp. 87–88) rightly notes the high frequency of animal characters in children's stories and animal decorations and toys in children's environments. There is also evidence that living animals—that is, family pets—can, like stuffed teddy bears, serve as Winnicott's (1953) "transitional objects" (cf. Triebenbacher, 1998) or even as attachment figures in their own right when human caregivers are absent or ineffective (cf. Rost & Hartmann, 1994).

Somewhat related to pets' attachment value are the benefits that companion animals bring to children with disabilities. For example, an observational study by Mader, Hart, and Bergin (1989) showed how trained companion dogs enhance the social acceptability of wheelchair-bound children in shopping malls. These children received more than twice as many friendly greetings from strangers than did a matched sample without companion dogs. Perhaps the most systematic research in this area stems from A. H. Katcher's work with 9- to 15-year-old boys diagnosed with severe conduct and oppositional defiant disorders in a residential treatment facility (Beck & Katcher, 1996, pp. 143–147; Katcher, 2002; Katcher & Wilkins, 2000). These boys spent 5 hr a week at the facility's "Companion Zoo," where they cared for a variety of indoor and outdoor animals, such as rabbits, tropical fish, frogs, chickens, sheep, and so on. Carefully conducted observations showed a marked decrease in antisocial behaviors alongside improvements on all measures of symptomatology and social aptitude, as contrasted to a matched sample of boys who had Outward Bound experience. Interestingly, these results were achieved not because the animals "cared" for the boys but because of the boys' taking care of the animals.

It is also relevant to ask what research such as the foregoing tells us about the child's human support system. If caregivers participate in the child's acquisition and use of animal names, tell animal stories to the child, decorate the child's environments with animal representations, and incorporate pets as members of the family, then the child's human surround would seem to actively *support* his or her propensity to affiliate with nature. If biophilia and the animal connection have contributed in an important way to human fitness, then it would be adaptive for caregivers and child therapists to convey biophilic (nature-approaching) and—when safety is at risk—biophobic (nature-avoiding) messages to the child. It would be maladaptive for them to shut out nature. Viewed this way, the child's human support system does not see the child's nature orientation as competing with the ongoing process of human socialization. Rather, caregivers spontaneously interpret the orientation as compatible with, perhaps even contributing to, the humanization process—just as Shipman (2010) would predict.

Does the Child–Nature Relationship Change With Age?

I briefly consider four promising approaches to the developmental question of whether the child–nature relationship changes with age: (a) Stephen Kellert's child survey research, (b) Peter Kahn's child interview studies, (c) the relatively large body of research on the child's animate–inanimate distinction, and (d) observational studies of children's behavior in natural settings.

Kellert's Survey Research

Kellert and Kahn both pursue a double agenda: to identify developmental levels in children's ideas about nature and to discover whether children's understanding of nature–human interaction includes a clear moral–ethical dimension.

Kellert (1996, pp. 37–51; 2002, pp. 129–138) began his investigation by positing several "values," some antagonistic to human–nature relations and some friendly. Using survey methodology, he studied the prevalence of these values in the thinking of 3- to 17-year-olds and identified four age-related periods (later reduced to three). Without going into the particulars of

each period, it is fair to say that Kellert's research yielded several straightforward age-related trends. In general, he found that, with age, three negative values *decreased* and three positive attitudes *increased*. The survey responses of the youngest children were characterized by fear and avoidance of unfamiliar animals (not family pets), attitudes of control and dominion, and a utilitarian, self-serving perspective on nature. During the middle-childhood and preadolescent period, this pattern of negative attitudes was progressively replaced by more positive values, which in turn achieved strong expression by adolescence. The older participants reported an ecological appreciation of the complex relations between organisms and their habitats; a naturalistic orientation toward conservation, wild animals, and wild nature; and moral concern for nature's well-being, backed up by a strong sense of stewardship.

Kahn's Interview Studies

In contrast to Kellert's use of survey methodology, Kahn (1997, 1999, 2002, 2006) has employed the semistructured interview technique associated with Piaget and Kohlberg. He has conducted four studies with youngsters from first grade to college level to classify the reasoning, most particularly the moral–ethical reasoning, that underlies their relation to nature. His probing interviews yielded three age-related moral orientations: anthropocentric, biocentric, and "compositional." The anthropocentric type assigns value to nature because of the benefits it provides to humanity. In contrast, biocentric reasoning sees nature as having inherent value, that is, moral standing in its own right. Compositional reasoning coordinates the other two types into a more comprehensive and integrated framework (Kahn, 2002, pp. 98–100).

One study of elementary school children showed anthropocentric reasoning occurring at each grade level, whereas the biocentric type jumped from use by only 7% of first graders to 56% of fifth graders. In another study that added eighth graders, Kahn found that both types of reasoning increased with age (1997, pp. 44–45). A third study, which included older high school and college students, showed even further increases in biocentric thinking. Moreover, there were step-by-step increments of higher order compositional reasoning from only 3% of fifth graders to 71% of college-age participants (Kahn, 2002, pp. 97–101).

In addition, by fifth grade, some of Kahn's participants began to show awareness that environmental pollution harmed not only animals and plants but abiotic nature as well (e.g., water and air). This finding suggests that the child's orientation toward nature goes beyond a simple focus on animals to incorporate other dimensions of natural ecology, including the impact of human activity on ecosystems (Kahn, 2006, pp. 463–464).

The Child's Animate–Inanimate Distinction

Although research on the development of the animate–inanimate distinction is not usually understood as addressed to the child's nature orientation, it can be fruitfully reframed as such. Doing so shows, first, the precocious development of this subset of the child's nature orientation; second, the functional relation between the distinction and Shipman's animal connection; and, third, the potentially rich contribution the animal connection makes to cognitive, perceptual, and behavioral development (cf. recent reviews by Gelman & Opfer, 2002; Rakison & Poulin-Dubois, 2001).

By 2–3 months of age, infants clearly distinguish a living person from a doll, a musical mobile, or a toy monkey (Gelman & Opfer, 2002, p. 153). By 9 months, babies differentiate birds from airplanes and animals from vehicles, and they attribute behaviors like drinking and sleeping to novel animals but not to novel vehicles (Mandler & McDonough, 1993, 1996). They are also more attracted to real animals than to their fake counterparts (Ricard & Allard, 1993).

Three- to 4-year-old children typically interpret self-generated or goal-directed movement as diagnostic of life and recognize life as a precondition to these kinds of movement. They identify even unfamiliar animals (photos of a praying mantis, an echidna, etc.) as animate and judge them capable of self-generated movement (Gelman & Opfer, 2002, p. 161; Massey & Gelman, 1988). Four-year-olds understand that artifacts do not die but that animals and plants have to die and that they "stay dead after they die" (Gelman & Opfer, 2002, p. 160). By age 4½ years, children define plants as animate because, like animals, plants grow, change shape, and heal themselves when scratched; they also recognize that the opposite applies to inanimate objects (e.g., tables don't grow and, when scratched, don't heal on their own).

By age 4½ years, then, children seem to have consolidated a robust and elaborate animate–inanimate distinction, which serves as the foundation for a naïve theory of biology and for a number of other broadly applicable conceptual distinctions—for example, between different kinds of causality (such as physical contact vs. action at a distance) and between different categories of change and movement (such as internally generated vs. externally imposed, linear vs. nonlinear, goal-directed vs. random). On these grounds, the animate–inanimate distinction seems to be more fundamental and broadly adaptive than most other categorical distinctions, such as those based on shape, color, size, and so on.

Moreover, for the animal connection to have been as adaptive as Shipman (2010) claims, it must have incorporated an all-but-foolproof version of the animate–inanimate distinction. Viewed this way, the distinction would seem to be both a developmental instantiation of, and an evolutionary precondition to, the animal connection.

In summary, the animate–inanimate distinction in early child development may play a role roughly analogous to the animal connection in human evolution. Both processes are viewed as "fundamental . . . foundational . . . central . . . deeply rooted" in their respective disciplines (Gelman & Opfer, 2002, pp. 151, 163, 166; Shipman, 2010, pp. 522, 525). The adaptive advantage conferred by the animal connection over evolutionary time would seem to innately predispose the human child to an early and fundamental sensitivity to life and its properties: growth and reproduction; contingent, goal-directed, and self-generated movement; and so on. Moreover, the connection's adaptive payoff would likely have encouraged the child's caregivers to nurture this predisposition. Interestingly, the best evidence for or against the caregiver-nurturance hypothesis would probably be generated by developmental (not evolutionary) investigations. The earlier point made about contemporary caregiver support of the child's nature orientation would seem to speak to the nurturance hypothesis.

The Need for Systematic Observational Studies

Although Kahn's and Kellert's developmental accounts may differ on some details, they generally agree on the overall direction of children's understanding of nature. Even so, the current state of developmental research calls for at least one caveat. Both Kahn and Kellert relied exclusively on children's *verbal reports* for their findings. But so far, there have been no comparably systematic investigations of age-related changes in children's *behavior* vis-à-vis animals or natural settings.

Of course, there have been more than a few observational reports on children's play and behavior in countryside, parks, zoos, playgrounds, vacant urban lots, and so forth (e.g., Nabhan & Trimble, 1994; Pyle, 2002; Sobel, 1993; Wood, 1993). Wood's observational study (1993), for example, shows that toddlers and preschoolers enthusiastically play with mud, sand, and water in natural settings—an attitude not revealed in the negative verbal reports of Kellert's youngest participants (2002). But such accounts, however rich and insightful, are typically not cast in a full and systematic developmental framework. The problem with this mix is that it leaves us ignorant of the correspondence between what children say about nature and what they actually do in natural settings.

Closing Considerations

The goal of this article has been to explore the hypothesis that the human child has a basic and developmentally significant orientation toward nature. In the process, I have drawn upon research and informed commentary from two disciplines, trying to integrate them into a coherent account of the child's relationship with nature. At present, however, this line of inquiry is still relatively underdeveloped, leaving several major questions unresolved.

First, is the child's nature orientation innate, learned, or both? Unsurprisingly, the evolutionary approach tends to emphasize the genetic tracking of strongly adaptive human behaviors, such as those described by Wilson (1984) and Shipman (2010). The human infant's precocious ability to make fairly sophisticated animate–inanimate distinctions in the 1st year of life also suggests a genetic component. On the other hand, the evident support of the child's caregiving system argues for a strong nurturing role in the acquisition of a nature orientation. Moreover, a small but growing body of evidence and commentary indicates that *non*facilitative experiential inputs—for example, the incremental urbanization and computerization-virtualization of childhood experience—may permute the child's nature connection into a disconnection (Kareiva, 2008; Louv, 2008; Pergams & Zaradic, 2008; Pyle, 2002; Rideout, Foehr, & Roberts, 2010). At this point, the available evidence suggests that the child's nature orientation is a function of interaction among hereditary, experiential, and developmental factors.

Second, where do we go from here? Again, in an area as underdeveloped as this, it would be premature to advance a confident list of testable, falsifiable hypotheses. At present, we need the kind of research that identifies *patterns of correspondence* among relevant variables: for example, as already noted, between children's verbal reports (e.g., the Kahn and Kellert studies) and their actual behavior in natural settings (e.g., Wood, 1993), between parental attitudes toward nature and the child's access to nature (e.g., visits to national parks, unsupervised play in natural settings), between school-based programs that promote the acquisition of "ecological intelligence" (Goleman, 2009) and the development of Kahn's biocentric and compositional levels of reasoning about nature, between pet ownership and Kahn's levels of reasoning, and so on. Once an adequate baseline of correspondence patterns is in place, this area can begin to formulate testable cause-and-effect hypotheses: for example, that pet ownership would partially mitigate the nature-blunting effects of the child's computer time; that the closer the child–pet relationship, the greater the mitigation effect; and so on.

Finally, are there other topics that might fall under the general rubric of the child's nature orientation? Due to space limitations, several related lines of inquiry have gone unmentioned. These include, for example, the developmental precursors and consequences of animal abuse in childhood (cf. Ascione, 2005; Ascione & Arkow, 1999; Melson, 2001, pp. 159–187); how children's oral and written nature stories might shape their attitudes toward nature (cf. Serpell, 1999), and adults' retrospective reports of their childhood experience of nature (cf. Chawla, 1986, 1990; Cobb, 1977).

In conclusion, the child-and-nature focus proposed here shows promise on both scientific and policy grounds. First, it calls attention to features of childhood that are overlooked by the field's dominant emphasis on the child's sociocultural context. Second, it has already generated a modest body of empirical findings. Finally, it would better position the field to address 21st-century environmental issues and policy as they affect the child.

References

Ascione, F. R. (2005). *Children and animals: Exploring the roots of kindness and cruelty.* West Lafayette, IN: Purdue University Press.

Ascione, F. R., & Arkow, P. (Eds.). (1999). *Child abuse, domestic violence, and animal abuse: Linking the circles of compassion for prevention and intervention.* West Lafayette, IN: Purdue University Press.

Beck, A., & Katcher, A. (1996). *Between pets and people: The importance of animal companionship.* West Lafayette, IN: Purdue University Press.

Bjorklund, D. F. (1997). The role of immaturity in human development. *Psychological Bulletin, 122,* 153–169.

Chawla, L. (1986). The ecology of environmental memory. *Children's Environments Quarterly, 3,* 34–42.

Chawla, L. (1990). Ecstatic places. *Children's Environments Quarterly, 7*(4), 18–23.

Cobb, E. (1977). *The ecology of imagination in childhood.* New York: Columbia University Press.

Gelman, S. A., & Opfer, J. E. (2002). Development of the animate-inanimate distinction. In U. Goswami (Ed.), *Blackwell handbook of child cognitive development* (pp. 151–166). Malden, MA: Blackwell.

Goleman, D. (2009). *Ecological intelligence.* New York: Broadway Books.

Harrison, P., & Pearce, F. (2000). *AAAS atlas of population and environment.* Berkeley: University of California Press.

Heerwagen, J. H., & Orians, G. H. (2002). The ecological world of children. In P. H Kahn Jr. & S. R. Kellert (Eds.), *Children and nature: Psychological, sociocultural, and evolutionary investigations* (pp. 29–63). Cambridge, MA: MIT Press.

Hunter, L. M. (2000). *The environmental implications of population dynamics.* Santa Monica, CA: Rand.

Kahn, P. H., Jr. (1997). Developmental psychology and the biophilia hypothesis: Children's affiliation with nature. *Developmental Review, 17,* 1–61.

Kahn, P. H., Jr. (1999). *The human relationship with nature: Development and culture.* Cambridge, MA: MIT Press.

Kahn, P. H., Jr. (2002). Children's affiliations with nature: Structure, development, and the problem of environmental generational amnesia. In P. H. Kahn Jr. & S. R. Kellert (Eds.), *Children and nature: Psychological, sociocultural, and evolutionary investigations* (pp. 93–116). Cambridge, MA: MIT Press.

Kahn, P. H., Jr. (2006). Nature and moral development. In M. Killen & J. G. Smetana (Eds.), *Handbook of moral development* (pp. 461–480). Mahwah, NJ: Erlbaum.

Kaplan, R., & Kaplan, S. (1989). *The experience of nature: A psychological perspective.* Cambridge, UK: Cambridge University Press.

Kareiva, P. (2008). Ominous trends in nature recreation. *Proceedings of the National Academy of Sciences, 105,* 2757–2758.

Katcher, A. (2002). Animals in therapeutic education: Guides into the liminal state. In P. H. Kahn Jr. & S. R. Kellert (Eds.), *Children and nature: Psychological, sociocultural, and evolutionary investigations* (pp. 179–198). Cambridge, MA: MIT Press.

Katcher, A. H., & Wilkins, G. G. (2000). The centaur's lessons: Therapeutic education through care of animals and nature study. In A. H. Fine (Ed.), *Handbook on animal assisted therapy: Theoretical foundations and guidelines for practice* (pp. 153–177). San Diego, CA: Academic Press.

Kellert, S. R. (1996). *The value of life: Biological diversity and human society.* Washington, DC: Island Press.

Kellert, S. R. (2002). Experiencing nature: Affective, cognitive, and evaluative development in children. In P. H. Kahn Jr. & S. R. Kellert (Eds.), *Children and nature: Psychological, sociocultural, and evolutionary investigations* (pp. 117–151). Cambridge, MA: MIT Press.

Louv, R. (2008). *Last child in the woods: Saving our children from nature-deficit disorder.* Chapel Hill, NC: Algonquin Books of Chapel Hill.

Mader, B., Hart, L., & Bergin, B. (1989). Social acknowledgements for children with disabilities: Effects of service dogs. *Child Development, 60,* 1529–1534.

Mandler, J. M., & McDonough, L. (1993). Concept formation in infancy. *Cognitive Development, 8,* 291–318.

Mandler, J. M., & McDonough, L. (1996). Drinking and driving don't mix: Inductive generalization in infancy. *Cognition, 59,* 307–335.

Massey, C., & Gelman, R. (1988). Preschoolers decide whether pictured unfamiliar objects can move themselves. *Developmental Psychology, 24,* 307–317.

Melson, G. F. (2000). Companion animals and the development of children: Implications of the biophilia hypothesis. In A. H. Fine (Ed.), *Handbook on animal assisted therapy: Theoretical foundations and guidelines for practice* (pp. 375–383). San Diego, CA: Academic Press.

Melson, G. F. (2001). *Why the wild things are: Animals in the lives of children.* Cambridge, MA: Harvard University Press.

Mithen, S. (1996). *The prehistory of the mind: A search for the origins of art, religions and science.* London: Thames and Hudson.

Nabhan, G. P., & Trimble, S. (1994). *The geography of childhood: Why children need wild places.* Boston: Beacon Press.

Nelson, K. (1973). Structure and strategy in learning to talk. *Monographs of the Society for Research in Child Development, 38* (Serial No. 149).

Pergams, O. R. W., & Zaradic, P.A. (2008). Evidence for a fundamental and pervasive shift away from nature-based recreation. *Proceedings of the National Academy of Sciences, 105,* 2295–2300.

Pyle, R. M. (2002). Eden in a vacant lot: Special places, species, and kids in the neighborhood of life. In P. H. Kahn Jr. & S. R. Kellert (Eds.), *Children and nature: Psychological, sociocultural, and evolutionary investigations* (pp. 305–327). Cambridge, MA: MIT Press.

Rakison, D. H., & Poulin-Dubois, D. (2001). Developmental origin of the animate-inanimate distinction. *Psychological Bulletin, 127,* 209–228.

Ricard, M., & Allard, L. (1993). The reaction of 9- to 10-month-old infants to an unfamiliar animal. *Journal of Genetic Psychology, 154,* 5–16.

Rideout, V. J., Foehr, U. G., & Roberts, D. F. (2010). *Generation M²: Media in the lives of 8- to 18-year-olds.* Menlo Park, CA: Henry J. Kaiser Family Foundation.

Rost, D. H., & Hartmann, A. (1994). Children and their pets. *Anthrozoös, 7,* 242–254.

Serpell, J. (1999). Guest editor's introduction: Animals in children's lives. *Society and Animals, 7,* 87–94.

Shipman, P. (2010). The animal connection and human evolution. *Current Anthropology, 51,* 519–538.

Simpson, J. A., & Belsky, J. (2008). Attachment theory within a modern evolutionary framework. In J. Cassidy & P. R. Shaver (Eds.), *Handbook of attachment: Theory, research, and clinical applications* (pp. 131–157). New York: Guilford.

Sobel, D. (1993). *Children's special places. Exploring the role of forts, dens, and bush houses in middle childhood.* Tucson, AZ: Zephyr Press.

Triebenbacher, S. L. (1998). Pets as transitional objects: Their role in children's emotional development. *Psychological Reports, 82,* 191–200.

Wilson, E. O. (1984). *Biophilia: The human bond with other species.* Cambridge, MA: Harvard University Press.

Winnicott, D. W. (1953). Transitional objects and transitional phenomena. *International Journal of Psychoanalysis, 34,* 89–97.

Wood, D. (1993). Ground to stand on: Some notes on kids' dirt play. *Children's Environments, 10*(1), 3–18.

Critical Thinking

1. What evidence does the article provide for a child having a developmentally significant orientation toward nature?

2. How does the child's nature orientation hypothesis enhance or complement anthropocentric models of child development?

3. Identify some of the age-related trends in a child's nature orientation. What might these trends suggest about cognitive, moral, and emotional development?

4. How can we use biophilia and animal connection to educate children about environmental conservation? What can children teach us?

Create Central

www.mhhe.com/createcentral

Internet References

Children and Nature Network
http://www.childrenandnature.org

National Environmental Education Foundation
http://www.neefusa.org/health/children_nature.htm
National Wildlife Federation.org
http://www.nwf.org/What-We-Do/Kids-and-Nature.aspx
Nature Conservancy
http://www.nature.org/newsfeatures/kids-in-nature

Article   Prepared by: Chris J. Boyatzis, *Bucknell University*

The Problem with Rich Kids

In a surprising switch, the offspring of the affluent today are more distressed than other youth. They show disturbingly high rates of substance use, depression, anxiety, eating disorders, cheating, and stealing. It gives a whole new meaning to having it all.

Suniya S. Luthar

Learning Outcomes

After reading this article, you will be able to:

- Describe the ways in which affluent youth suffer more psychological problems than less affluent youth.

- Understand what has been described as a relentless pressure for "high-octane achievement" in youth.

- Explain why affluent youth may not show problems associated with their social class until adolescence.

It is widely accepted in America that youth in poverty are a population at risk for being troubled. Research has repeatedly demonstrated that low family income is a major determinant of protracted stress and social, emotional, and behavioral problems. Experiencing poverty before age 5 is especially associated with negative outcomes.

But increasingly, significant problems are occurring at the other end of the socioeconomic spectrum, among youth en route to the most prestigious universities and well-paying, high-status careers in America. These are young people from communities dominated by white-collar, well-educated parents. They attend schools distinguished by rich academic curricula, high standardized test scores, and diverse extracurricular opportunities. The parents' annual income, at $150,000 and more, is well over twice the national average. And yet they show serious levels of maladjustment as teens, displaying problems that tend to get worse as they approach college.

My first glimpse of this phenomenon was entirely serendipitous. In the mid-1990s, I was recruiting youth in a prosperous suburban community in the Northeast as a comparison sample for a study of inner-city teens. Much to my surprise, the affluent teens turned out to fare significantly more poorly than their counterparts of low socioeconomic status on all indicators of substance use, including hard drugs. I later replicated those findings among 10th-graders in a different Northeast suburb. And other researchers have since corroborated the findings of high alcohol use, binge-drinking, and marijuana use among offspring of well-educated, white, high-income, two-parent families.

But substance use is not the only errant behavior among the children of privilege. Crime is also widely assumed to be a problem of youth in poverty, but I have found comparable levels of wrongdoing among well-off suburban students and inner-city youth. What does differ are the types of rule-breaking—widespread cheating and random acts of delinquency, such as stealing from parents or peers, are more common among the rich, while inner-city teens are apt to commit crimes related to self-defense, such as carrying a weapon.

The children of wealth have serious internalizing problems as well. In 1999, I reported significant depression in one in five girls. Since then, studies I have conducted show that, on average, serious levels of depression, anxiety, or somatic symptoms occur twice as often or more among these boys and girls, compared to national rates.

Such problems are not confined to the East Coast or to schools in suburbs. We have studied private schools in large cities and affluent communities in the Northwest. Students in the Northwest did not show the extremes of substance abuse we observed on the East Coast (where rates of being drunk in the past month were about twice those of national norms), but they did display high levels of depressive and anxiety symptoms, self-injurious behavior such as cutting and burning, and rule-breaking behaviors. The bottom line: Across geographical areas and public and private schools, upper-middle-class youngsters show alarmingly high rates of serious disturbance.

The high rate of maladjustment among affluent adolescents is strikingly counterintuitive. There is a tacit assumption—even among those most affected—that education and money procure well-being, and that if children falter, they will swiftly get the appropriate services. Education and money may once have served as buffers against distress, but that is no longer the case. Something fundamental has changed: The evidence suggests that the privileged young are much more vulnerable today than in previous generations.

"Please Give Me a Break"

I have spent the last decade researching why this is the case. The evidence all points to one cause underlying the different disturbances documented: pressure for high-octane achievement. The children of affluent parents expect to excel at school and in multiple extracurriculars and also in their social lives. They feel a relentless sense of pressure that plays out in excessive substance use; as the kids stoutly proclaim, "We work hard—and we play hard!" It plays out in crippling anxiety and depression about anticipated or perceived achievement "failures." It plays out in random acts of delinquency—stealing from a friend, shoplifting, defacing property.

It isn't as if these youngsters need the money. For many, it may well be a plea: "Please give me a break, I can't handle this all." It's as if the pressure cooker is about to explode.

It's true, the pressure to do well in school and get into a prestigious college is shared by many teens. But maintaining the mantle of success is a special imperative for the well-off, for whom expectations are especially high. Adolescents of affluence want to meet the standard of living they are used to.

What's more, achievement of their extremely lofty goals is tantalizingly within reach, which renders it all the more obligatory. There are few accomplishments that privilege can't bolster, whether it's improved test scores or squash skills, and affluent parents acquire whatever coaching is necessary to achieve the very best. The life credo of these youths becomes, "I can, therefore, I must." As one high school junior said, "I can get the best SAT tutoring, so I must get my scores to 2300. I can take five AP courses so, of course, I will. I can be first chair in the orchestra so I work hard with my private teacher."

Interestingly, affluent youths are not more troubled than others prior to adolescence. The first signs of problems emerge around seventh grade, when they are almost 13. By this age, 7 percent of these boys are using marijuana and getting drunk at least once a month. And symptoms of depression and anxiety begin to rise, especially among girls.

Why do problems emerge in the seventh grade? Some experimentation with alcohol and drugs is normal for teens. But moneyed adolescents generally have easier access to substances, ample money to purchase them, good entree to providers, and the best fake IDs.

Then there are peer norms: "Getting wasted" is often entirely expected at social gatherings. And, of course, there is collusion by some parents, who are all too willing to actively bail out their teens if discovered by authorities. Not surprisingly, high schoolers who anticipate meager consequences from their parents are among the heaviest substance users.

The seventh grade is also a developmental marker for when children begin to think seriously about their long-term life goals. With the capacity for abstract thinking, youths around 13 begin identity exploration, grappling with the critical question of "Who am I?" In hypercompetitive, upper-middle-class communities, this broad question narrowly morphs into, "What will I amount to? Will I get into a top-ranked college? How do I get there?"

By middle school, these youths come to believe there is one path to ultimate happiness—having money—which in turn requires attending a prestigious college. They grow preoccupied with becoming highly marketable commodities, pursuing activities chiefly if they will look good on resumes. There is scant time for exploration of who they are as individuals or for nurturing unique interests.

Perceptions of Criticism

Whence the unrelenting pressure? Some comes from families. There are certain high-pressure traps that white-collar parents, more than others, can fall into.

The first is excessive emphasis on children's accomplishments. Most parents fervently wish for their children to enjoy the same gratifications that they have been fortunate enough to receive from their own rich educational experiences and professional careers.

Wanting children to do the best they are capable of is certainly appropriate. But too often, what parents want is over the top. My graduate students and I have observed such expectations in action while studying children's perceptions of their parents' values. When children feel that their parents disproportionately value personal successes (in today's grades or tomorrow's careers), far more than they value their personal decency and kindness, the children show elevated symptoms of depression and anxiety.

For children, perceived parental pride in them, and thus their own self-worth, rests largely—perilously—on achieving and maintaining "star" status. The message they hear from the parents is not, "Sweetheart, do the best you're capable of." Instead, it is, "You had better score while the scout's at today's game," or "You've got to ace the AP test today; you fell behind last semester." Such critical messages do not even need words; they can be conveyed by a raised eyebrow or a turned back in response to a judged failure.

The high pressure for achievement is thus experienced as parental criticism. Children come to feel that any failure to accomplish will seriously diminish the acceptance and esteem with which their parents regard them.

The perception of parental criticism is so consistently related to young people's attitudes about themselves that we measure it in every sample we study: "I am punished for doing things less than perfectly." "My parents never try to understand my mistakes." Perceived parental criticism is linked with a variety of adjustment problems: depressive and anxiety symptoms as well as acting-out behaviors.

It's important to note that adult criticism is not annulled by attention or even affection. Parents might think it's okay to keep the pressure on because they eat dinner together and attend all their children's athletic events and performances. But such positive gestures do not cancel out criticism. Psychologists have firmly established that disparaging words or attitudes have a much stronger impact than words of praise—by at least a factor of three.

Parents, however, are but one part of the equation. It is not family wealth per se but living in the cultural context of affluence that confers risk. Impossibly high expectations are transmitted not only by parents but by the entire community—teachers, schools, coaches, and peers. Athletic coaches can be fiercely invested in a team's star status; as one captain said, "Our coach tells me all the time that the whole team depends on me to win the championship. Before every game, he tells me that I am the backbone of the entire team and if I don't play well, the team will give up." Teachers and guidance counselors push for the highest possible SAT scores. Indeed, real estate prices depend on standardized test scores maintained in suburban schools.

Cheers from Peers

In upper-middle-class settings, kids who have the gumption to defy certain rules achieve high status among their schoolmates. The freshman who can chug down a six-pack after a baseball game, the sophomore who has made it with many of the hottest girls—they command wide respect in the peer group.

But there are double standards based on gender. Particularly distressing are the double standards about physical appearance: Peers place an enormous emphasis on attractiveness among affluent girls. Across the board, the more attractive kids—boys or girls, rich or poor—are more likely to be most popular with their peers. But for girls of high socioeconomic status, the onus on being attractive is incredibly high. In our research, we have found that links between peer admiration and beauty were almost twice as strong among affluent girls as compared with affluent boys, and also compared with inner-city girls and boys. Looking "like a scrub" is simply not acceptable for well-off young women.

The enormous pressures that girls face from the peer group are matched by the impossibly high demands from adults to succeed in domains that are traditionally male, such as academics and sports, and also in the "feminine" domains of caring and kindness. They must not only be highly accomplished but also polite and likable, and they are expected to master the competing demands without any display of visible effort. Daughters of the rich, therefore, strive for effortless perfection—which is not merely challenging to their well-being but ultimately soul-draining.

It is not surprising, therefore, that the girls are more troubled than the boys. They show greater problems across multiple domains. In general, girls and women show their upset in internalizing problems, such as depression and anxiety. Affluent girls, however, show serious symptoms also in the most typically male forms, by acting out—rule-breaking, delinquency, and alcohol and drug use. Today's girls are involved in cheating scandals. They drink and do drugs. They have eating disorders. They steal from parents and friends. They are overrepresented across all domains of maladjustment. They have it all.

By no means are boys immune; they too face gender-specific challenges as they negotiate the culture of affluence. Rich boys can be disturbingly preoccupied with gaining high power in the peer group, which becomes tied, by late adolescence, to grandstanding via money and sex. Through high school, social dominance is related to good looks, athletics, and the "cool" factor of substance use. In college, it becomes more about wealth. Moneyed young men ("guys who drop a cool thousand on any given Friday") are most likely to achieve the ultimate alpha male stamp—being desired by many girls.

Striving ever harder to be at the top—or, in their vernacular, a "baller," one whose status in society has been earned by his possession of "game"—puts such boys at risk for limited compassion and kindness. They can have low capacity for tenderness in close relationships, high capacity for chauvinism and narcissism. In a recent study, we found that narcissistic exhibitionism scores among affluent boys at elite private schools were almost twice the average scores of a more diverse sample.

Now More Than Ever

Why is it that high socioeconomic status brings more risk for young people today than it once did? There have been major shifts in aspirations and cultural values toward materialism that can be especially pronounced among the affluent. In 1967, for example, 86 percent of college freshmen rated "developing a meaningful philosophy of life" as an essential life goal. In 2004, only 42 percent of freshmen agreed with them. Over that time, values such as "being well-off financially" and "attaining prestigious jobs" rose equivalently in importance. Again, aspiring for status is likely highest among youth in upper-middle-class communities.

Also, the ultimate goal of getting into a good college is decidedly more competitive today than it used to be. Among top-tier colleges, the number of applicants has doubled or tripled over the last five years.

Privileged adolescents tend to define being well-off relative to what they see in their own parents. But in today's economy, it is much more difficult to maintain one's parents' standard of living. As one high school student said, "I want to make what my dad does, so I must get into Wharton. By 30 or 35, I should be making at least a quarter of a million a year."

One of the most established facts of psychology is that people evaluate themselves by comparing themselves with others. Wealth is relative in that we adopt the standards of our own immediate contexts, comparing ourselves with those we see doing better than us. The phenomenon of relative deprivation thus becomes a psychological cost of life in the fast lane, surrounded by the extremely successful.

Among youth in high-achieving schools, students are constantly gauging where they stand relative to others in the intense competition for distinction. "We compare ourselves with each other all the time. We know who made the AP classes and who dropped out because they couldn't keep up," says a student. "And we know everyone's top choices of colleges. In my grade, two other athlete-scholars want to go to Duke; we never talk about it openly, but we're constantly weighing our own chances of beating them in getting in."

Enter envy. My colleagues and I recently found that, compared to inner-city counterparts, students at elite, upper-middle-class schools, especially girls, experienced significantly more envy of peers who they felt surpassed them in popularity, attractiveness, academics, and sports.

At the same time, the intense push for superachievement deprives affluent adolescents of one of the critical safety valves of life—the deep social connectedness of friendship. The very path they take for success inhibits the development of intimacy. The durability, sustainability, and strength of relationships are constantly threatened by competition for highly sought-after goals. There's only one valedictorian. How can two people be friends if the self-worth of both depends on being the one chosen for a sought-after goal? One's gain is the other's loss.

Friendships are threatened also by the lack of leisure activities engaged in simply for fun and without a scrutinizing adult audience. Children today play sports watched by parents who are often much more invested in team wins than are the children themselves. Individual players' slip-ups are very public, bringing chagrin if not outright shame.

The pursuit of distinction leaves affluent adolescents with days that are heavily scheduled with academic and extracurricular activities. And while my studies show that extensive time in extracurricular activities is not a risk factor in itself—a sense of pressure, criticism, and overly high expectations from adults matter far more—participation restricts socializing to students in the same activities. Further, the constant competition, along with the necessity to display effortless perfection, demands that students show no vulnerabilities. Secrecy about weaknesses inhibits intimacy and further isolates them in their suffering.

Yet another contribution to vulnerability may be an inflated sense of control over one's life. As my colleague Barry Schwartz has shown, affluence leads people to believe they are wholly responsible for their own success. The wealthier people become, the more they believe that they can control many aspects of their life and design exactly the kind of life they want. They come to expect perfection.

Parents' overestimation of what they can actually control is reflected in the illusions harbored by their accomplished children—that one more point on the GPA, one more achievement, will push them over the edge to success, acceptance to a top-ranked college. The fallout? Any "failure" on any of these fronts can bring a rush of self-blame, shame, and depression.

Tomorrow's Leaders

Why should we care about the problems of rich kids? Most important, because no child should be left behind, regardless of parental education or income. Any young person who remains in anguish deserves and needs adult intervention. Minimizing the problems of rich kids is as ill-founded as accepting death by guns as just what happens to inner-city youth.

Further, today's highly educated youths will disproportionately hold positions of power in the next generation. Their values will disproportionately shape norms in education, politics, and business.

The distress and substance use children are experiencing can have considerable long-term costs. At a personal level, depressive episodes during adolescence bring elevated risk for recurrent episodes later in life. Prolonged feelings of stress can affect not just psychological well-being but also physical health and productivity at work. At a societal level, people who are unhappy, with a fragile sense of self, can be more acquisitive than philanthropic, more focused on gaining more for themselves than on improving the lot of others.

The high levels of substance use can affect the developing brain, impair coping ability, and impede everyday functioning.

How many will not mature out of adolescent alcohol and marijuana abuse? If students must have Adderall to maintain 4.0 GPAs, how will they manage when they have real jobs in high-pressure settings?

What Can We Do?

Putting a brake on the development of symptoms among ambitious youth is not easy; it will require changes at multiple levels, from systems of secondary and higher education to individual families. At high-achieving schools, the leadership needs to understand that the relentless pursuit of star status can powerfully thwart the well-being of students.

Parents can, and must, play a central role in mitigating pressures on children. They are, after all, the immediate buffers of the culture, with great power to help children remain grounded in a value system that emphasizes decency and kindness as much as getting ahead. The importance of this task is paralleled by its difficulty: It takes an enormous amount of strength to be a lone parental voice amidst a community crescendo of "Do More!"

For some highly educated adults, a sense of success as parents rests on the splendor of their children's accomplishments. That is not a healthy burden for them. Or for parents. In shaping the next generation, parents would do well to ponder: Prestige, power, privilege—at what price?

Critical Thinking

1. Is it difficult to understand or empathize with the idea that rich kids are at risk for a variety of psychological problems than other youth?

2. Based on the information in this article, what changes—from family life to college and career pressures—would you change to reduce the problems suffered by affluent youth?

3. What are some reasons why affluent girls are at higher jeopardy than boys for these problems?

Create Central

www.mhhe.com/createcentral

Internet References

Children of the Affluent: Challenges to Well-Being
http://www.ncbi.nlm.nih.gov/pmc/articles/PMC1948879

How Does Affluence Affect Child Development?
http://everydaylife.globalpost.com/affluence-affect-child-development-2750.html

The Price of Affluence: New Research Shows that Privileged Teens May be More Self-Centered—and Depressed—Than Ever Before.
https://www.apa.org/monitor/2009/01/teens.aspx

Luthar, Suniya S. "The Problem with Rich Kids", Psychology Today, Nov/Dec 2013. Reprinted with permission from Psychology Today Magazine, (Copyright © 2013 Sussex Publishers, LLC.).